EXPLORING
THE SPANISH LANGUAGE

EXPLORING
THE SPANISH LANGUAGE

CHRISTOPHER J. POUNTAIN
Senior Lecturer in Romance Philology,
University of Cambridge and Director of Studies in
Modern Languages, Queens' College

A member of the Hodder Headline Group
LONDON
Distributed in the United States of America by
Oxford University Press Inc., New York

First published in Great Britain in 2003 by
Hodder Arnold, a member of the Hodder Headline Group
338 Euston Road, London NW1 3BH

http://www.arnoldpublishers.com

Distributed in the United States of America by
Oxford University Press Inc.,
198 Madison Avenue, New York, NY10016

British Library Cataloguing in Publication Data
A catalogue record for this book is available from the British Library

Library of Congress Cataloging-in-Publication Data
A catalog record for this book is available from the Library of Congress

ISBN 0 340 71946 X

1 2 3 4 5 6 7 8 9 10

Cover image: © Owen Franken/Corbis

Typeset in 11 on 14 Adobe Garamond by Phoenix Photosetting, Chatham, Kent
Printed and bound in Malta

What do you think about this book? Or any other Arnold title?
Please send your comments to feedback.arnold@hodder.co.uk

*For all young explorers of the Spanish
language, and especially Frances*

Sea, pues, la conclusión de mi plática, señor hidalgo, que vuesa merced deje
caminar a su hijo por donde su estrella le llama; que, siendo él tan buen
estudiante como debe de ser, y habiendo ya subido felicemente el primer
escalón de las esencias, que es el de las lenguas, con ellas por sí mesmo
subirá a la cumbre de las letras humanas, las cuales tan bien parecen en un
caballero de capa y espada, y así le adornan, honran y engrandecen, como
las mitras a los obispos, o como las garnachas a los peritos jurisconsultos.

Miguel de Cervantes Saavedra, *El ingenioso hidalgo
Don Quijote de La Mancha*, II, ch. 16)

Contents

Foreword

My aim in writing this book is twofold. First of all, it is designed to introduce readers to some basic notions of descriptive linguistics, illustrated with Spanish data. However, the focus is firmly on the data rather than on linguistic theory: my priority has always been to achieve a better awareness of specific linguistic features of Spanish than to introduce different theoretical approaches for their own sake. I think it is very important that beginners in linguistics are not at first limited to one particular theoretical approach, since if they do eventually go on to work within one theoretical model they will then be better able to maintain some critical detachment from it. I have tried to give the reader a broad appreciation of the structures and varieties of modern Spanish, but that is not to say that my own preferences and preoccupations have not come to the surface, and these are particularly reflected in Chapters 5 and 10 – though they are more controversial in nature, I hope they will make the book more interesting. My second aim has been to try and get readers thinking and exploring for themselves: seeing what data still needs to be discovered and described, and appreciating areas in which there is debate and controversy. It is for that reason that this book also contains exercises, which are emphatically not intended to test understanding of the material covered, so much as to invite readers to carry the subject-matter of each chapter further for themselves. These will be best approached in consultation with a tutor, and I should stress that the notes to the exercises offered for those who do not have the benefit of a tutor's help are not necessarily the 'right' answer – indeed, I shall look forward to receiving both students' and tutors' views and reactions.

Christopher J. Pountain
Cambridge, May 2003

Acknowledgements

The chief source of inspiration for this book has been the many generations of lively students to whom I have had the privilege and pleasure of teaching a course entitled 'Introduction to the structures and varieties of modern Spanish', and it is to them I wish to express my chief thanks. Over the years I have explored with them most of the topics covered here; they have asked the big questions and repeatedly forced me to clarify my thinking, as no doubt their successors will continue to do. Several of them have gone on to be true explorers of the Spanish language, undertaking interesting undergraduate and graduate projects in Spanish-speaking countries in a whole range of areas, and have generously shared their results with me. There are too many to record individually by name, but one or two are specifically acknowledged in the text.

This is also the first writing project I have undertaken which has made substantial use of the Internet, and I hope I have stressed sufficiently in the course of the book the richness and usefulness of the World Wide Web as a linguistic resource. All sources are duly acknowledged, so far as I am aware, but inevitably web addresses are volatile.

My family, as ever, have suffered abandonment while writing is in progress, and I must thank them as always for their forbearance and understanding, which I fear I have often taken for granted. At least on this occasion I hope that my labours may prove of direct use to my eldest daughter, as she prepares to become an explorer of the language of Cervantes, Maradona and the street children of a hundred cities.

Abbreviations

Br.Eng.	British English
Cast.	Castilian
Cat.	Catalan
Cha.	Chabacano
Du.	Dutch
Eng.	English
Fr.	French
Gal.	Galician
GASp.	Golden-Age Spanish
Gk.	Greek
IPA	International Phonetic Association
JSp.	Judeo-Spanish
l.	line
Lat.	Latin
ll.	lines
MSp.	Modern Spanish
OCast.	Old Castilian
p.	person; page
Pal.	Palenquero
Pap.	Papiamentu
Pg.	Portuguese
pl.	plural
pp.	pages
RAE	Real Academia Española
sg.	singular
Sp.	Spanish

1 | Introduction

This book is about describing the Spanish language. Take some time to think about what the word 'description' actually means. It means standing back from language and looking at it objectively. In doing this, we have no preconceptions about what might be 'better' or 'worse' or what might be deemed 'correct' or 'incorrect'. If you are not a native speaker of Spanish, you are at something of an advantage in this respect, because you will not have been brought up to have value judgements about the way in which people use the language, and you will not be defensive about a particular variety of it. But you will probably have encountered reactions from native speakers about the way in which you use Spanish as a foreigner. Sometimes a native-speaking friend will simply point out that a particular form does not exist in the language, and that you have made a foreigner's 'mistake', as, for example, if you use *devolvido* as the past participle of *devolver* instead of *devuelto*.[1] You may also, however, be taken to task for having adopted a local usage. In Chile, verb forms such as *hablái(s)* rather than standard *hablas* for the second person singular are used, though no one (except authors trying to give an impression of local colour) would write them (see **6.2.4.2.3**). This is a different kind of phenomenon, since some native speakers use such forms all the time, and they are an integral part of their language. This kind of 'mistake' consists of using forms that are not part of the 'standard' language even though they are a part of many native speakers' usage. This is an important distinction from the descriptive point of view, for while it would be inappropriate to include *devolvido* in a description of Spanish, it would be arbitrary, or prescriptive, to exclude *hablái(s)*. Descriptively, we simply observe that there are a number of variant ways of speaking, some of which are associated with the standard language, and some of which are considered non-standard.

1.1 Prescription and description

Much popular writing about language (letters to newspapers, press articles) and most course books and manuals that you are likely to have met are prescriptive rather than descriptive in their approach: that is to say, they express personal or official views on what is 'correct' and give instructions on how 'correctness' in language is to be achieved. Another typical concern of the prescriptive approach to language is cultivating use of 'good' language: the first sentence in many traditional grammars runs along the lines of that in Chapter 1 of the first *Gramática* of the Real Academia Española (RAE), published in 1771: '*La Gramática* es arte de hablar bien'. Descriptive linguists are, at their most

---

[1] As is usual in writing about language, an asterisk (*) indicates that a form is unacceptable to a native speaker.

extreme, not interested in such prescriptive concerns; their object of interest is what native speakers know intuitively about their language, irrespective of how 'correct' or 'good' their actual usage may be judged to be. For them, the only valid notion of 'correctness' is conformity to the intuitions of a native speaker, and rather than speak of forms and constructions being 'correct', they usually adopt the term 'acceptable'. For such a descriptive linguist, then, a **grammar** is simply a description of what is acceptable to a native speaker, not a codification of what some arbitrary authority deems 'correct', and 'rules' are observed regularities, not principles which must be applied (the term 'law' is often used in much the same way in science).

Let us look at a particular case of this difference in approach. In the manual of house style for the Spanish newspaper *El País*, the following prescriptive rule appears:

> Los adverbios modifican a los verbos, los adjetivos o a otros adverbios, y
> sólo así deben utilizarse. Es correcto escribir 'va deprisa', puesto que
> *deprisa* es adverbio y modifica al verbo. Pero no 'trabaja duro', porque
> *duro* es adjetivo y, junto al verbo, ocupa el lugar del adverbio. Lo correcto
> sería 'trabaja duramente'. (*El País*, 1990: 119)

From the descriptive point of view, this is an arbitrary rule which does not correspond to actual native speaker usage. *Duro* is one of a number of adjectives which also appear to function as adverbs in modern Spanish, especially in common collocations such as *trabajar duro* (similarly, *hablar claro*,[2] *respirar hondo, jugar limpio*; for other examples, see De Bruyne 1995: 120–3). The decision that *duro* is an 'adjective' and not an 'adverb' is also arbitrary: there is no reason why one word cannot have two functions, and furthermore there are many languages (for example, German) in which there is no formal difference between adjectives and manner adverbs anyway. The use of adjectives as adverbs is actually a tendency which is on the increase in modern Spanish, especially in informal colloquial usage (see **7.1**), and there is every sign that it will migrate into more formal kinds of usage, following the model of such words as *barato* and *caro*, which already have a double function:

(1.1)   **a.**   *un piso barato*
            'a cheap apartment' (adjective)

        b.   *lo vendieron barato*
            'they sold it cheaply' (adverb: there is no form **baratamente*, in
            fact)

(1.2)   **a.**   *unos pendientes muy caros*
            'very expensive earrings' (adjective)

        b.   *estos pendientes me costaron caro(s)*
            'these earrings cost me a lot' (adverb: *caramente* would sound
            very strange in this context; although *caro* may still agree with a
            noun to which it relates as if it were an adjective, it is
            increasingly used invariably)

---

[2] Ironically, *Hablando claro* was the title of a Spanish TV programme devoted to questions of usage.

1.2 Pedagogical rules

If you are learning Spanish as a non-native speaker, you will have also come across rules of a pedagogical kind. While reference books written for foreign learners naturally present the prescriptive rules of the standard language, they also usually give some account of non-standard variants, sometimes in a fairly objective way. But they may also offer a 'rule of thumb', a more easily memorable, though simplified, recommendation which will ensure that the learner is always 'right'. For example, Butt & Benjamin (2000) give a very complete description of the variation observable in the use of the third person object pronouns *lo*, *la* and *le* in the Spanish-speaking world, as well as an account of what is considered prescriptively correct, but they also suggest (pp. 149–50) that beginners should adopt the simple scheme of using *lo* and *la* for direct objects and *le* for indirect objects, which 'will produce correct sentences in over 90 per cent of cases'; the learner is thus offered a straightforward principle pending a deeper knowledge of the language.

Such rules often make good sense in a pedagogical context (provided that it is made quite clear that they are only an approximation) but are inadequate descriptively because they are not exhaustive. Perhaps because human beings like to reduce complex phenomena to simple principles, learners of languages often find such simplifications curiously attractive and hold on to them tenaciously; the task of the descriptive linguist however, is to make sure that all cases are accounted for in a descriptive rule. The following is a first pedagogical rule given for the use of the 'personal' *a* in Spanish:

> The Personal **a**. This is placed before the direct object, if the direct object is a person or proper name. The personal **a** is not translated. **a quién** and **a quiénes** equal *whom* (Jackson & Rubio, 1969 [1955], p.49).

However, we shall see later (**5.2**) that this rule is very far from being a complete account of this complex phenomenon, and so is descriptively inadequate.

1.3 Standard language and prestige norms

Many descriptive linguists are also interested in giving an account of attitudes towards different linguistic variants, and in the evolution of **standard languages** or **prestige norms**. Objectively speaking, a standard language is based on a linguistic variant which (mainly for political and economic reasons) has come to be regarded as the variant which it is desirable to emulate. Historically, the linguistic variety which achieved greatest prestige in medieval Castile was that of the upper classes of Toledo, though in the 16th century the speech of the new capital, Madrid, gained more prestige. Today the speech of Old Castile, especially that of educated speakers in such cities as Valladolid and Burgos, is most highly regarded in Spain (we shall examine this question in more detail in **6.2.3.1.3.**) Castilian underwent much diversification as it came to be used over a wider area of the Iberian Peninsula as a result of the southerly expansion of Castile. This diversification has continued with the progressive adoption of Castilian in non-

Castilian-speaking areas of the Peninsula, and with the Spanish colonisation of the Americas. Today a number of regional prestige norms can be identified in addition to that of Old Castile, most notably in Spain itself that of the educated speech of Seville, with, amongst other features, its characteristic *seseo* (see **6.2.3.2.1**). In Latin America the educated speech of national capitals usually constitutes the prestige norms (see **6.2.4.2.5**).

The written norm for the whole of the Spanish-speaking world is, effectively, provided by the Real Academia Española (RAE), founded in 1713, although the Spanish Academy has more recently worked progressively more closely with the parallel Academies in the other 21 Spanish-speaking countries of the world (including those of the USA and the Philippines) within the Asociación de Academias de la Lengua Española. The RAE has sought approval for its latest dictionary (the 22nd edition, published in 2001) with the Comisión Permanente of the Asociación de Academias, and has itself paid much more attention to American usage and the use of Spanish worldwide (see **10.3.3**). Traditionally, the RAE has maintained three ongoing publications: the *Ortografía* (the last revisions to which, also agreed by the Asociación de Academias, were made in 1999), the *Diccionario* (*DRAE*) and the *Gramática* (the latest official normative grammar is the *Esbozo* of 1973, although two important works have recently been published under the Academia's authority: the late Emilio Alarcos Llorach's 1994 grammar and the much larger project of Ignacio Bosque and Violeta Demonte, begun in 1999). An important popularisation of the RAE's views has been Manuel Seco's *Diccionario de dudas*. A former Director, Fernando Lázaro Carreter, writes regular press articles on contemporary usage, some of which have been collected in Lázaro Carreter (1998).

The RAE has often been derided as being behind the times and ultra-conservative in its attitude to usage, and it has to be said that this attitude is quite widespread in the English-speaking world, perhaps because English speakers, not having an Academy of their own, are not sympathetic to such regulatory bodies (we shall return to this question in Chapter 10): see, for example, Stewart (1999: 19–21). It has also suffered from comparison with the Académie Française, in imitation of which it was originally founded. It has become something of a sport, for instance, for rival dictionaries to point out which of their entries do not yet have a parallel in the *DRAE* (see, for example, *Clave*). However, it is inevitable that the Academy should exercise caution with regard to lexicography, since many textually attested words, especially anglicisms, are in fact ephemeral (see Smith 1975) and would be out of date almost as soon as the dictionary was published. It is therefore more prudent to wait and see what happens, and only to record a word in the *DRAE* when it is undeniably in common usage, which will inevitably be some years after its first appearance. The latest edition of the *DRAE* has been created on the basis of a lexical database of some 270 million words (*CREA*, see below), and is as a result quite permissive in this respect: its entry for *light*, for example, runs as follows:

> *light.* (Voz ingl.). adj. Dicho de una bebida o de un alimento elaborado: Con menos calorías de las habituales. || **2.** Dicho de un cigarrillo: Que se presenta como portador de menos elementos nocivos. || **3.** irón. Que ha perdido gran parte de sus caracteres esenciales. *Un comunista light.*

This is descriptively appropriate, unlike *Clave*'s entry, which cannot resist the prescriptive remark 'Su uso es innecesario y puede sustituirse por expresiones como *bajo en calorías*, *ligero o suave*', and does not record the last meaning (though it gives an example of it in *Lleva una vida "light" y aburrida, sin el más mínimo espíritu de aventura*). It is in fact this meaning that is really the most telling in terms of acceptance into Spanish, since whereas the first two meanings have been popularised directly as a result of advertising, the third shows a **semantic** development (i.e. development in meaning) in Spanish which is quite independent of English; *light* now means 'insipid', 'decadent', 'without health risk' (and is actually not at all the same thing as *ligero* or *suave* in this sense – see Pountain 1999: 38).

The reference works of the RAE could obviously be more up-to-date if new editions were published more frequently, and a combination of commercial sponsorship and modern technology is giving the RAE the means of doing this (in fact, amendments to the *Diccionario* are regularly published in the *Boletín de la Real Academia Española*). Currently, the RAE's website (http://www.rae.es/) gives on-line access to its dictionary and amendments to the dictionary, as well as to two major linguistic databases, the *Corpus de referencia del español actual* (*CREA*) and the *Corpus diacrónico del español* (*CORDE*). Another section of the website deals with questions of usage. It seems very likely that the provision of this facility, with its powerful global possibilities, will be the preferred means of delivery of the Academia's publications in the future (the current *Diccionario* is already available as a browser button).

1.4 Variation

All natural languages vary in a number of ways. Even languages spoken over relatively small geographical areas show **diatopic** variation, or variation according to geographical location; such diatopic variants are often informally referred to as dialects. Spanish, which is a **diasporic** language (a language whose spread is the consequence of the expansion of a political empire), is spoken over a huge geographical area. There are significant differences between Peninsular Spanish and the Spanish of Latin America: for example, to Peninsular *Te dejo sólo por un minuto* corresponds Mexican *Por un minuto nomás te dejo*. But there is also variation on a smaller scale: within Spain, different diminutive suffixes characterise some regions, so that in Asturias one will hear *un momentín* instead of the more widespread *un momentito*. Languages also vary according to the social group of speakers (**diastratic** variation) or the context in which language is used. In popular speech, such constructions as *Si tuviera dinero, lo compraba* may be heard instead of the usual written form *Si tuviera dinero, lo compraría*, or *Tiene más dinero que no yo* instead of *Tiene más dinero que yo*. These kinds of variation will be the subject of Chapters 6 and 7. Another dimension of variation is **diachronic** (variation over time; see also **10.1**): in the 13th century, a polite way of asking where someone was might have been *¿O sodes?*, corresponding to modern *¿Dónde está usted?*, and to modern *Hace muchísimo tiempo* corresponded *Muy gran tiempo ha*.

These factors are not necessarily mutually exclusive: features of popular speech are sometimes also associated with particular regions or with innovations or archaisms. For example, in the rural speech of the northwest of the Peninsula it is common to hear **clitic pronouns** (that is, pronouns which cannot stand on their own but which always occur with a verb, such as *me, lo, os,* etc.) placed after a finite verb rather than before (i.e. *Fuese* rather than *Se fue*); this is also a feature of older Castilian. In parts of Latin America, the verb *ver* has the preterite forms *vide* and *vido* (as opposed to standard *vi, vio*): these too are in the medieval language.

1.5 The organisation of this book

Chapters 2–5 of this book are an introduction to the ways in which linguists describe the various aspects, or **levels**, of linguistic structure. Chapters 6–9 deal with some of the many different varieties of Spanish, and Chapter 10 offers some thoughts on the position of Spanish in the world and its future prospects. At the end of each of Chapters 2–10 there are exercises which it is hoped will encourage readers to explore some of the issues raised in the chapter further; notes on the exercises are given on pp. 276–89 for those who are working on their own.

Special linguistic terms are generally explained on first mention, where they are highlighted in bold type, as in this chapter. The Index also shows in bold the section or sections in which a particular term is defined or explained, so you should refer to the Index in case of difficulty. The traditional grammatical terms are defined in the Glossary on p. 290.

2 | The sounds of Spanish

2.1 How to describe and represent sounds

A very important distinction, which must be borne in mind continually by the reader, is the difference between sounds and letters. Sounds are units of speech (pronunciation), while letters are units of **orthography** (writing or spelling). It is also important in writing about language to make a distinction between letters and sounds, letters being written as italics (e.g. *a*, *b*, *c*) and sounds as special symbols enclosed in square brackets (e.g. [a], [b], [β]). The series of special symbols used to represent sounds in this book is the International Phonetic Alphabet (IPA), which is the system most commonly used in European publications. However, in the early 20th century, the *Revista de filología española* (*RFE*) developed its own system which has been tenaciously adopted in Spanish linguistic atlases and dialect studies (though with some idiosyncratic modification by individual researchers, usually with the aim of reflecting greater phonetic detail), and we shall indeed see (Chapter 6) that for the description of Spanish varieties, the *RFE* system does have advantages. In Tables 2.1–2.3, the principal symbols in both these systems are given (*RFE* equivalents for some of the sounds which are specific to English are given in brackets). The terminology used in describing these sounds will be explained in 2.1.1–2.1.4.

The IPA system tends to suit the English vowels, in which opening is associated with centralisation and shortening (e.g. *beat* [biːt], *bit* [bɪt]). In Spanish, however, phonetic differences in vowels are much more clearly dependent on aperture alone. Opening is shown in the *RFE* system by the use of one or more subscript reverse commas: thus [ȩ] and [ḙ] are progressively more open. Closure is shown by the use of one or more points: thus [ẹ] and [ẹ] are progressively more close. Centralisation in the *RFE* system is shown by a superscript diaeresis: Fr. *yeux* is [jø] in the IPA system and [jö] in the *RFE* system. In both systems, nasalisation is indicated by a superscript tilde, e.g. [õ], and length by a colon [oː].

Because all languages which have alphabetical writing systems show some correspondences between a particular letter and a particular sound (some more systematically than others, as we shall see), it is tempting to think that a letter 'has' a sound. In Spanish, for example, there is a very regular correspondence between the letter *t* and the sound [t]. But such a regular correspondence is not inevitable: in English, where the relation between letters and sounds is much less regular, the letter *g* can represent the sounds [g], as in *gun*, and [dʒ], as in *Roger*, and does not correspond to any sound at all in *right*. Spelling is therefore not a very reliable basis for describing pronunciation.

Table 2.1 The principal phonetic symbols used in this book (vowels)

IPA symbol	*RFE* symbol	Description	Example	Notes
a	a	central open vowel	Sp. *asa* ['asa]	
ɑ	(à)	central-back open vowel	Standard Br.Eng. *ask* [ɑːsk], *art* [ɑːt]	The sound is normally lengthened in standard Br.Eng.
æ	(ä)	central-front open vowel	Standard Br.Eng. *hat* [hæt]	
e	e	half close front vowel	Sp. *beno* ['eno]	In standard Br.Eng., the sound exists only as the first element of a diphthong: *play* [pleɪ]
ɛ	ę	half open front vowel	Eng. *yet* [jɛt]	
i	i	close front vowel	Sp. *fino* ['fino], Eng. *meet* [miːt]	The sound is normally lengthened in standard Br.Eng.
ɪ	ː	close front-central vowel	Eng. *bit* [bɪt]	The sound is normally short in standard Br.Eng.
o	o	half close back vowel		In standard Br.Eng., the sound exists only as the first element of a diphthong: *stone* [stoʊn]

Symbol	Description	Examples	Comments
ɔ	half open back vowel	Eng. *hot* [hɔt]	
u	close back vowel	Sp. *mula* ['mula], Br.Eng. *fool* [fuːl]	
ʊ (ʉ)	close back-central vowel	Br.Eng. *took* [tʊk]	The sound is normally short in standard Br.Eng.
ʌ (no distinct *RFE* symbol)	half open central vowel	Br.Eng. *bud* [bʌd], *bird* [bʌˌd]	
ə (no distinct *RFE* symbol)	the 'neutral' vowel (mid central)	Br. Eng. *the* [ðə]	
ː	length mark		
˜	nasalisation		
¨	centralisation		
no separate symbol			

Table 2.2 The principal phonetic symbols used in this book (semivowels)

IPA symbol	*RFE* symbol	Description	Example	Notes
j	y or j	front semivowel (onglide)	Sp. *bien* [bjen], Eng. *yes* [jɛs]	
w	w	back semivowel (onglide)		
i̯	i̯	front semivowel (offglide)	Sp. *peine* ['pei̯ne]	In Eng. diphthongs the vowels [ɪ] and [ʊ] are usually used in IPA to denote the offglide.
u̯	u̯	back semivowel (offglide)	Sp. *Europa* [eu̯'ropa]	

Table 2.3 The principal phonetic symbols used in this book (consonants, etc.)

IPA symbol	RFE symbol	Description	Example	Notes
b	b	voiced bilabial plosive	Sp. _bueno_ [ˈbweno], Eng. _bell_ [beɫ]	
β	ƀ	voiced bilabial fricative	Sp. _labio_ [ˈlaβjo]	
d	d	voiced alveolar(-dental) plosive	Sp. _día_ [ˈdia], Eng. _day_ [deɪ]	The alveolar-dental Spanish sound is more accurately symbolised as [d̪]
ð	đ	voiced dental fricative	Sp. _miedo_ [ˈmjeðo], Eng. _this_ [ðɪs]	The Spanish sound is usually much more weakly articulated
dz	ẑ	voiced alveolar affricate	See 6.2.3.1.1.	
dʒ	ŷ	voiced palatal affricate	Eng. _just_ [dʒʌst]	Also some varieties of Sp. _llama_ [ˈdʒama]: see 2.2.2
f	f	voiceless labiodental fricative	Sp. _fiel_ [fjel], Eng. _feast_ [fiːst]	
ɸ	ɸ	voiceless bilabial fricative	See 6.2.3.1.1.	
g	g	voiced velar plosive	Sp. _gana_ [ˈgana], Eng. _get_ [get]	
ɣ	ǥ	voiced velar fricative	Sp. _lago_ [ˈlaɣo]	
h	h	voiceless (glottal) aspirate	Eng. _hat_ [hæt]	

continued

Table 2.3 continued

IPA symbol	RFE symbol	Description	Example	Notes
k	k	voiceless velar plosive	Sp. _como_ ['komo], Eng. _count_ ['kaʊnt]	
l	l	voiced alveolar lateral	Sp. _leo_ ['leo], Eng. _lie_ ['laɪ]	
l̥	l̥	voiceless alveolar lateral	Welsh _llan_ [l̥an]	
ɬ	ɬ	voiced velarised lateral ('dark' _l_)	Br.Eng. _full_ [fʊɬ]	
ʎ	ʎ	voiced palatalised alveolar lateral	Standard Sp. _llamo_ ['ʎamo]	
m	m	(voiced) bilabial nasal	Sp. _mero_ ['mero], Eng. _mint_ [mɪnt]	
ɱ	ɱ	(voiced) labiodental nasal	Sp. _énfasis_ ['eɱfasis], Eng. _emphasis_ ['eɱfəsɪs]	
n	n	(voiced) alveolar nasal	Sp. _antes_ ['antes], Eng. _any_ ['ɛnɪ]	
ɲ	ɲ	(voiced) palatalised alveolar nasal	Sp. _año_ ['aɲo]	
ŋ	ŋ	(voiced) velar nasal	Sp. _angosto_ [aŋ'gosto], Eng. _sing_ [sɪŋ]	

Symbol	Description	Example	Notes
p	voiceless bilabial plosive	Sp. p̪an [pan], Eng. pain [peɪn]	
r̃	voiced alveolar trill or vibrant	Sp. rayo ['rajo]	
ɾ	voiced alveolar flap	Sp. caɾa ['kaɾa]	
ɹ	voiced alveolar approximant	Br.Eng. right [ɹɑɪt]	
(no obvious distinct symbol: [ɹ] is the nearest approximation)	assibilated voiced alveolar approximant[1]	See 6.2.4.2.2.	
s̠	voiceless coronal sibilant	Eng. say [sɛɪ]	No distinction is generally made in this book between [s] and [s̠].
s̱	voiceless apico-alveolar sibilant	Standard Pen.Sp. s̱ol [s̱ol]	
ʃ̌	voiceless palatal sibilant	Eng. shake [ʃeɪk]	
t	voiceless alveolar-dental plosive	Sp. t̪é [te], Eng. t̪oy [tɔɪ]	The alveolar-dental Spanish sound is more accurately symbolised in IPA as [t̪].

continued

[1] Oroz (1966: 54) uses [r̃] for the 'short' voiced assibilated r, [ř] for the trilled r, [r̃̆] for the 'long' voiced assibilated r and [ř̥] for the 'long' voiceless assibilated r.

Table 2.3 *continued*

IPA symbol	*RFE* symbol	Description	Example	Notes
ts	ŝ	voiceless alveolar affricate	See 6.2.3.1.1.	
tʃ	ĉ or ŝ̂	voiceless palatal affricate	Sp. *ocho* [ˈotʃo], Eng. *church* [tʃʌ˞tʃ]	
v	v	voiced labiodental fricative	Eng. *ever* [ˈɛvə]	
x	x	voiceless velar fricative	Sp. *ajo* [ˈaxo]	[x] and [χ] are not generally discriminated in this book.
χ	χ	voiceless uvular fricative	Sp. *crujo* [ˈkruχo]	
z	z	voiced coronal alveolar sibilant	Eng. *easy* [ˈiːzɪ]	
ż	ż	voiced apico-alveolar sibilant	See 5.2.2.2.1.	
ʒ	ž	voiced palatal fricative	Eng. *pleasure* [ˈplɛʒə]	Also some varieties of Sp. *calle* [ˈkaʒe]: see 2.2.2.
ʔ		glottal stop	See 2.2.1.	
ˌ		dental mark		
̥		devoicing mark		

ˈa	primary stress mark (precedes the syllable; shown with the vowel [a])	
ˌa	secondary stress mark (precedes the syllable; shown with the vowel [a])	

2.1.1 Vowels, consonants, semivowels and liquids

The sounds of language fall into two major categories, **vowels** and **consonants**, and though these are terms which are current in everyday speech, they need rigorous definition if they are to be used satisfactorily in linguistic analysis. Vowels and consonants are characterised by the manner of their articulation and by their function. A vowel is typically a **voiced** sound, that is, one in which the vocal cords vibrate, and the vocal tract (through which air passes to make the sound) is relatively unrestricted; a vowel functions as the **nucleus** (centre) of a **syllable** (see **2.5** below). A consonant can be voiced or **unvoiced**; the vocal tract may be constricted (as in the case of [f], for example, in which there is a tight constriction between the top teeth and bottom lip) or even temporarily occluded altogether (as in [p], in which the lips are held firmly together); consonants function as the beginning (**onset**) or the end (**coda**) of a syllable. Although these distinctions may seem quite straightforward, there are in fact some interesting 'twilight' categories of sounds which are neither clearly vowels nor consonants according to these definitions.

A class of sounds we shall discuss further below (**2.1.4**, **2.3**) are the **semivowels**, which, while they are vowel-like as regards the manner of their articulation, never function as the nucleus (centre) of a syllable; Spanish has two such sounds, occurring in such words as *ya* [ja] and *huella* ['weʎa], in which they are the onsets (beginning the syllable), and *hay* [ai̯] and *aula* ['au̯la], in which they are codas (ending the syllable). Different phonetic symbols are sometimes used, as here, for the onset and coda occurrences, [j] and [w] being reserved for onsets and [i̯] and [u̯] for codas. This reflects the fact that the onsets are more consonant-like than the codas: indeed, in some varieties of Spanish, *ya* and *huella* would be pronounced with true consonantal onsets such as [dʒ] and [gw] (for the latter, see **6.2.3.1.3**). Some linguists (e.g. Quilis & Fernández 1969: 70) make a distinction between [j] and [w] as 'semiconsonants' and [i̯] and [u̯] as 'semivowels'. (For further discussion of the structure of syllables, see **2.5.1**.)

Liquid consonants (the main ones are [l], [r], [m] and [n]) are, like vowels, usually voiced (though unvoiced liquids do occur in many languages, for example the [l̥] of Welsh *llan* [l̥an] 'enclosure (of a church)'), and in some languages they can function as syllable nuclei (in standard English, [l] constitutes a syllabic nucleus in the pronunciation of *little* as ['lɪtl̩], and [n] is syllabic in the rapid pronunciation of *indulgence* as [n'dʌldʒns]).

2.1.2 Describing consonants

Consonants can be successfully described according to their place and manner of articulation. The usual strategy is to begin by saying whether the sound is voiced or unvoiced, since many consonants can potentially be either, then to describe its place of articulation and lastly its manner of articulation. For example, the sound [k] can be described as a voiceless velar plosive:

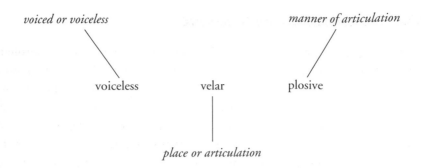

Figure 2.1 Description of the consonant sound [k]

The possible places of articulation are shown in the cross-section of the vocal tract below:

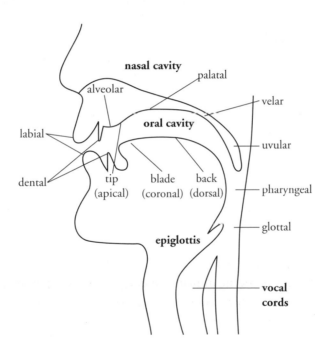

Figure 2.2 Areas of the vocal tract

Spanish has consonants in all these categories apart from the pharyngeal and glottal areas:

Articulations involving the lips as the primary articulator:

● **(Bi)labial** (articulated with the lips in contact): [p], [b], [β], [m]. Examples: *pan* [pan], *venir* [beˈniɾ], *estaba* [esˈtaβa], *muro* [ˈmuɾo].

● **Labiodental** (the bottom lip contacts the upper teeth): [f], [ɱ]. Examples: *fe* [fe], *énfasis* [ˈeɱfas̩is̩].

Articulations involving the tongue as the primary articulator:

- **Dental** (the tongue contacts the upper front teeth): [θ], [ð]. Example: *cero* ['θeɾo], *sentido* [ṣen'tiðo].
- **Alveolar** (the tongue contacts or approximates to the alveolar ridge): [t], [d], [ṣ], [l], [n], [ɾ], [r]. Examples: *tener* [te'neɾ], *doy* [doi̯], *siete* ['ṣjete], *ala* ['ala], *nariz* [na'ɾiθ], *caro* ['kaɾo], *perro* ['pero].
- **Palatal** (the tongue contacts or approximates to the hard palate): [tʃ]. Example: *ocho* ['otʃo].
- **Palatalised** (the tongue moves towards the hard palate in the course of articulation): [ʎ], [ɲ]. Examples: *hallar* [a'ʎaɾ], *año* ['aɲo].
- **Velar** (the back of the tongue contacts or approximates to the velum, or soft palate): [k], [g], [x], [ɣ]. Examples: *como* ['komo], *goma* ['goma], *ojo* ['oxo], *lago* ['laɣo].
- **Uvular** (the very back of the tongue approximates to the uvula): the articulation of *j* before a *u* is often in this area, so *jugo* is pronounced ['χuɣo].

English has the **glottal stop**, symbolised by [ʔ], which appears in the usual rapid pronunciation of *rotten* as ['ɹɔʔn], and also very distinctively in the Cockney pronunciation of *butter* ['bʌʔə].

A large number of consonants fall into the alveolar area in Spanish, as in many languages, and further distinctions can be made among them. The area between the back of the upper teeth and the hard palate is actually a continuum with no firm boundaries, and the precise placing of of the tongue varies very considerably. Spanish [t] and [d] are **dental-alveolar** sounds, in which the tip of the tongue lies across the teeth and the very front of the alveolar ridge; [l] is more properly an alveolar pure and simple, since the tip of the tongue contacts only that point; [tʃ], though often described as a palatal, in fact begins its articulation in the alveolar area and so is perhaps better described as an **alveolar-palatal**.

The area of the tongue used in the **sibilant**, or [s]-like sounds, of Spanish (see also below), is also important. In what may be taken as standard Castilian pronunciation (the north and centre of Spain), the [s] is an **apico-alveolar** sound, articulated with the very tip of the tongue raised towards the alveolar ridge, which is represented in IPA notation by the symbol [ṣ], while in much of Andalusia and very generally in Latin America, the sound is **coronal**, i.e. articulated with the blade of the tongue raised towards the alveolar ridge, as in standard English (represented by IPA [s]). In some areas of Andalusia, the [s] is **predorsal**, the tip of the tongue actually contacting the lower teeth and the tongue consequently brought very far forward in its contact with the alveolar ridge; a convenient IPA symbol for this is [ṣ]. (From now on in this book, however, the simple symbol [s] will be used unless such phonetic detail is being specifically discussed.) These tongue positions are illustrated in Figure 2.3.

There are a number of different manners of articulation:

- **Plosive:** There is a complete closure of the vocal tract, as a result of which pressure builds up behind the closure, and articulation consists in releasing the closure. The plosive consonants found in Spanish are [p], [b], [t], [d], [k] and [g].

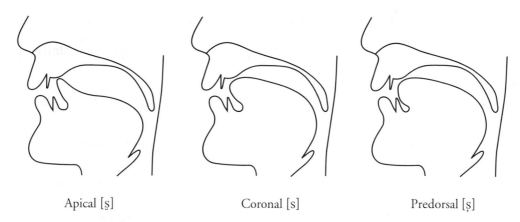

Apical [ş]   Coronal [s]   Predorsal [s̺]

Figure 2.3 The [s] sounds of Spanish

- **Fricative**: Here there is no closure of the vocal tract, but a constriction through which air passes. [β], [ð], [ɣ], [f], [s] and [x] are fricatives.
- **Affricate**: The sound begins like a plosive but continues as a fricative. Spanish only has one such sound: [tʃ]. In IPA, for historical reasons, affricates are represented by two separate symbols, sometimes connected by a ligature (though the ligature is not used in this book): [tʃ].
- **Nasal**: The mouth is completely occluded and air passes through the nasal cavity. Nasals are naturally voiced sounds. [m], [ɱ], [n], [ɲ] and [ŋ] are nasals.
- **Lateral**: The air passes down the sides of the tongue, which makes complete central contact with another organ of speech. [l] is a lateral.
- **Trill** (or **roll**): One organ of speech (normally the tongue) vibrates against another. [r] is a trill in which the tongue vibrates against the alveolar ridge.
- **Flap**: A single, or very short, vibration of a trill. [ɾ] is a flap.

In addition to these basic manners of articulation, it is usual to distinguish two major classes of consonantal sounds. Sibilants are a subcategory of fricatives which give an acoustic impression of hissing, such as [s] (and in English [z], [ʃ] and [ʒ]). **Liquids** give an acoustic impression of smoothness; as we saw in **2.1.1**, they are capable of being syllabic in some languages. They include consonants which are neither plosives, fricatives nor affricates: [l], [r] and [ɾ].

2.1.3 Describing vowels

Rather different parameters of description are used for vowels. Vowels all broadly share the same manner of articulation, though **nasal** vowels, in which air passes through the nasal as well as the oral cavity, are distinctive in some languages (e.g. Portuguese and French), and even in Spanish, vowels are often nasalised before a following nasal consonant: thus *bien* may be pronounced [bjẽŋ] in some areas, and even in standard [bjen], the [e] is slightly nasalised. Otherwise, vowels are usually described according to their position of articulation, taking into account two parameters, the position and height of the tongue; they may be represented diagrammatically in what has come to be known as the **vowel triangle**. Spanish has a very simple five-term vowel system, as can be seen in Figure 2.4.

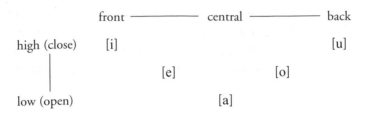

Figure 2.4 The vowels of Spanish in the 'vowel triangle'

It is possible to observe finer distinctions in Spanish vowels, especially in some regional varieties. In those areas where syllable-final [s] is subject to **aspiration** (pronunciation as [h]) or loss (see **6.2.3.2.1**), the preceding vowel is usually lowered (opened); this phenomenon is especially noticeable with a preceding [e] or [o]:

	standard	parts of Andalusia
costa	[ˈkosta]	[ˈkɔhta]
vestir	[besˈtiɾ]	[bɛhˈtiɾ]

Even in standard pronunciation, [e] and [o] are lowered slightly before [l] and [r], so that *papel* and *perro* tend towards [paˈpɛl] and [ˈpɛro]. Some phoneticians give more importance to this phenomenon than others; but in standard Spanish pronunciation the observable differences are nowhere near as great as between the [e] and [ɛ] of French *fée* [fe] and *fait* [fɛ]or the [o] and [ɔ] of *côte* [kot] and *cotte* [kɔt].[2]

2.1.4 Diphthongs and triphthongs

Before leaving our discussion of the description of vowels we must introduce the notion of the **diphthong**. A diphthong consists of a sequence of a semivowel ([j] or [w]) and a full vowel (e.g. *bien* [bjen], *bueno* [ˈbweno]), in which case it is called a **rising** diphthong, or of a full vowel followed by a semivowel (e.g. *hay* [ai̯], *deuda* [ˈdeu̯ða]), in which case it is known as a **falling** diphthong. All combinations of vowels and semivowels are attested, though some combinations, especially [wo] and [ou̯], are relatively infrequent. A **triphthong** is a combination of semivowel+vowel+semivowel, e.g. [wai̯] in *averiguáis* [aβeriˈɣwai̯s], [jei̯] in *limpiéis* [limˈpjei̯s].

[2] See, for example, the distinctions discussed by Navarro Tomás (1970: 35–64). Navarro uses different symbols for close, open and 'relaxed' (unstressed) vowels, e.g. [e] [ẹ] and [ə] (the latter in his symbolisation is a 'relaxed' *e* and not the neutral vowel represented by IPA [ə]).

2.2 A comparison of features of English and Spanish pronunciation

2.2.1 Vowels

Spanish vowels, as we have seen, are relatively few in number but well discriminated within the vowel triangle. English, on the other hand, has many different vowels, though the vowels tend not to occupy the extremes of the vowel triangle; the British English system, which in type if not in detail is typical of the English-speaking world as a whole, is as follows:

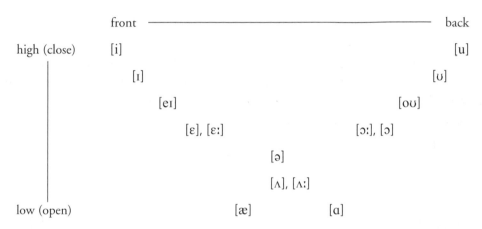

Figure 2.5 The vowels of English

Spanish does not use length to make such primary distinctions in vowels; no vowels in Spanish are inherently long or short, unlike English *hard* [hɑd] (long) as opposed to *had* [hæd] (short), *Luke* [luk] (long) as opposed to *look* [lʊk] (short). In English there are also important contrasts based on vocalic length between words such as *bud* [bʌd] / *bird* [bʌːd], *fled* [flɛd] / *flared* [flɛːd] and *nod* [nɔd] / *gnawed* [nɔːd]. Spanish does have some such contrasts, but they are always the result of two identical vowels coming together in sequence (e.g. in fast speech, *azar* [aˈθaɾ] / *azahar* [aˈθaːr], *lores* [ˈloɾes] / *loores* [ˈloːɾes], *pasé* [paˈse] / *paseé* [paˈseː]). There are also regional and stylistic varations in Spanish: a feature of Argentine Spanish is the lengthening of its stressed vowels, so that pronunciations like *bueno* [ˈbweːno] are heard, and in emphatic speech generally it is not uncommon to hear pronunications like *¡síiiii!* [siː] or *¡qué bien!* [keˈβjɛːn].

Spanish vowels are **monophthongal** in nature, that is to say, they do not change their position during the articulation of the vowel's sound (although, as we saw in **2.1.4**, groups of semivowels and vowels can constitute diphthongs), whereas some English vowels are in many varieties, including the standard, inherently diphthongal: *play* [pleɪ], *show* [ʃoʊ]; and for many speakers *fair* [fɛː(ə)], *moor* [mɔː(ə)].

Turning to some finer phonetic details, initial vowels in English are preceded by a glottal stop or closure, while Spanish vowels are not; conversely, final vowels in Spanish end with a glottal closure, while English vowels do not. Thus Spanish *entra* ['entra] contrasts with English *enter* ['(ʔ)ɛntə] and Spanish *sé* [se(ʔ)] with English *say* [seɪ]. Vowels in Spanish separated by a word-boundary form a continuous group known technically as synaloepha (Sp. *sinalefa*); in English, such sequences of vowels are often separated by a glottal stop or even a consonant. The English phrase *law or injustice* is often articulated as [lɔːʔɔːʔɪn'dʒʌstɪs] or [lɔːɹɔːɹɪn'dʒʌstɪs] whereas Spanish *cinco u ocho* is ['θiŋko‿u‿'otʃo]. (We shall discuss the phenomenon of *sinalefa* further in **2.5**.)

In Spanish, all vowels occur both in unstressed and stressed syllables. In English, the '**neutral**' vowel /ə/ is only used in unstressed position, and there are many vocalic alternations (see **3**) in English which are determined by stress, for example, *present* [pɹɪ'zɛnt], *present* ['pɹɛz(ə)nt]. Contrast with such relations the three Spanish words *término* ['termino], *termino* [ter'mino], *terminó* [termi'no], which, while they differ in the position of stress, have vowels in each syllable which are very similar.

2.2.2 Consonants

Some consonants found in Spanish are not present in standard English: these are the fricatives [β], [x] and [ɣ] (though [x] is familiar to British speakers from Scots English in words such as *loch* [lɔx]). Conversely, consonants existing in English but not in Spanish are the voiced affricate [dʒ] and the fricatives [z], [v], [ʃ] and [ʒ] (again, some of these sounds are familiar from regional variants: [dʒ] and [ʒ] are a feature of River Plate *rehilamiento* (see **6.2.4.2.2**); [ʃ] is a variant pronunciation of [tʃ] in Chile and [z] can often be heard in fast speech in words such as *mismo* [mizmo] (Navarro Tomás 1970: 108). Some other consonants, though roughly equatable, are not strictly identical in phonetic terms. Voiceless plosives in word-initial position preceding a vowel are aspirated in English but not in Spanish.

English	Spanish
tea [tʰi]	*ti* [ti]
Spain [speɪn]	*España* [es'paɲa]

[t] and [d] are dental-alveolar in Spanish (and so most accurately represented in IPA as [t̪] and [d̪]), but they are alveolar in English. [s], as we have seen in **2.1.2**, is apico-alveolar in standard (north and central) Peninsular Spanish (and so most accurately represented in IPA as [s̺]) but coronal in English. [ɾ] and [r] are vibrants in Spanish while standard British and American English [ɹ] is more appropriately described as an **approximant** (because there is no actual contact between tongue and alveolar ridge).

In addition, there are also some positional, or **phonotactic**, differences, between the two languages. English [s] may appear in an initial sequence of [s] + plosive (+ liquid), e.g. *spray* [spɹeɪ], while in Spanish such a sequence is always preceded by a vowel (see also **2.5**), e.g. *espliego* [es'pljeɣo], and in borrowed words of this kind Spanish always adds a **prothetic** [e] even though this is sometimes not represented in the spelling, e.g. *stárter* [es'tarter]. Spanish [ŋ] only appears before a velar consonant (as is also the case in English), but additionally in English, it may also appear intervocalically and finally: *singing* ['sɪŋɪŋ]. In English, the plosives may appear word-finally (e.g. *hop* [hɔp], *cub* [kʌb], *dog* [dɔg]), but in Spanish they rarely do so (indeed, words ending in plosives are neologisms or borrowings of one sort or another, e.g. *BUP* [bup], *Jacob* [xaˈkob], *boicot* [boiˈkot], *tic* [tik]; in the course of time, the pronunciation of many such words has been adapted to the more normal patterns of Spanish, e.g. *zinc* [θin] from *zinc* [zɪŋk], *yate* [ˈjate] from *yacht* [jɔt]). In Spanish, [ð] does not appear in initial position, unlike English *there* [ðɛːə]. English has a 'dark' (**velarised**) [l] (symbolised [ɫ]) in syllable-final position (*fulfil* [fʊɫˈfɪɫ])whereas the [l] of Spanish is always 'light' (alveolar), e.g. *alfil* [alˈfil].

2.3 Sounds and phonemes

2.3.1 Phonemes and allophones

Every speaker of a language speaks slightly differently; in fact, there is now good evidence for supposing that a 'voiceprint' is as reliable an indicator of an individual's identity as a fingerprint. When sounds appear in different contexts, they are often grossly different: the [x] that we hear in Spanish *eje*, while still a velar sound, is articulated very much further forward in the mouth than the [x] of *jugo*, which, as we saw in **2.1.2**, is almost uvular in nature. The proximity of one sound to another can result in quite striking assimilations in which one sound takes on the features of its neighbour: see **6.2.3.2.1**. How is it, then, that we perceive some sounds as being the same, and others as being different, when objectively every utterance of every sound is potentially slightly different? The answer is that we perceive some sounds as being functionally the same as others, even if they are physically different. Despite the difference between the two instances of [x] we have just identified, native speakers of Spanish do not generally notice that there is any difference at all between them.

Whether two sounds are considered as functionally 'the same' or not by native speakers varies from language to language. In Spanish, for instance, native speakers perceive the sound represented by the letter *d* in *día* and *ida* as being the same, though it is obvious to an English speaker that they are phonetically different: the *d* of *día* represents a sound rather like that represented by the *d* of English *dear* (in fact, as we have seen, it is an alveolar-dental sound [d̪], but for convenience we will use the straightforward phonetic symbol [d] to represent it), whereas the *d* of *ida* is more like [ð], the sound represented by *th* in English *either*. The reason this difference is so clear to English speakers is that for them the difference between [d] and [ð] is functional as well as phonetic: we can find pairs of words in English (**minimal pairs**) which are different in meaning and are distinguished by a contrast, or **opposition**, between [d] and [ð], such as *dare* ([dɛːə] or [dɛːɹ]) and *there* [ðɛːə] or [ðɛːɹ]. But no such minimal pairs exist in Spanish. In fact, what we soon notice about Spanish is that the occurrence of [d] or [ð] is determined by the phonetic context, and we can devise a descriptive rule to specify exactly when each will be used, as follows:

Use [ð]:

between vowels	*tenido* [te'niðo]
at the beginning of a word after a vowel	*la dama* [la 'ðama]
at the end of a word	*virtud* [biɾ'tuð]
after [ɾ]	*verde* ['beɾðe]

Use [d]:

at the beginning of a word after a pause	*doy* [doi̯]
after [n] or [l]	*donde* ['donde],
	sueldo ['sweldo]

We say that [d] and [ð] are in complementary distribution, since they never occur in exactly the same phonetic context.

Speakers may not all conform exactly this rule, or they may conform to it in some styles of their speech and not in others. For example, the majority of Spanish speakers today miss out [ð] altogether or articulate it very lightly indeed between the vowels [a] and [o], and their pronunciation of *comprado* is [kom'prao] or [kom'pra°o]; at the end of a word, *d* is variously pronounced as [ð], [θ], [t] or nothing at all. But, whatever the variation observable, one thing remains constant: no Spanish speaker makes a functional distinction between [d] and [ð].

To label this notion of sounds which are objectively different but functionally the same, many linguists use the term **phoneme**. It is a very convenient and intuitively satisfactory notion, though, as we shall see even in this introductory discussion of the sound-system of Spanish, it is not without problems. In English, then, there is a phonemic opposition between [d] and [ð], while in Spanish there is not: we say that in Spanish [d] and [ð] are **allophones** (i.e. variant forms) of the same phoneme. We now introduce another notational device: we will represent the functional notion of the phoneme by using a suitable phonetic symbol between obliques, e.g. /d/. (The choice of phonetic symbol in representing a phoneme is actually arbitrary, because we are not thinking of the exact phonetic value of a single sound but rather of a functional class constituted by a number of sounds.)

2.3.2 Phonemic status of the semivowels

Now let us look at one or two knotty problems for this notion of the phoneme which occur in Spanish. The first has to do with the phonemic status of the semivowels [j]~[i̯] and [w]~[u̯]. As we saw in **2.1.1**, they are phonetically very similar to the vowels [i] and [u], but different in function, since they never constitute the nucleus of a syllable. Some examples of how semivowels are used in this way are:

mayor [ma'joɾ]: [j] is the onset of the syllable whose nucleus is [o]
peine ['pei̯ne]: [i̯] is the coda of the syllable whose nucleus is [e]
agua ['aɣwa]: [w] is the onset of the syllable whose nucleus is [a]
áureo ['au̯reo]: [u̯] is the coda of the syllable whose nucleus is [a]
buey [bwei̯]: [w] is the onset and [i̯] the coda of the only syllable, whose
   nucleus is [e]

Because semivowels and vowels appear in different contexts, then, they can never be the basis for a truly minimal contrast. This would suggest that they are allophones of the same phoneme and that the phonemic structures of the above words are /maˈioɾ/, /ˈpeine/, /ˈagua/, /ˈaureo/ and /buei/ respectively. But the contexts which determine allophonic choice are not definable simply in terms of linear sequences of sounds, since vowels can appear together without forming a diphthong; there are such contrasting pairs as the following, where [i] and [j]~[i̯] and [u] and [w]~[u̯] respectively occur with exactly the same sounds preceding and following them.

> *hay* [ai̯] / *ahí* [aˈi]
> *sabia* [ˈsaβja] / *sabía* [saˈβia]
> *aun* [au̯n] / *aún* [aˈun]
> *continua* [konˈtinwa] / *continúa* [kontiˈnua]

This would seem to suggest that we need to maintain distinctive phonemic representations using semivowels. We do not need to distinguish phonemically [j]~[i̯] and [w]~[u̯], since their occurrence is governed entirely by their position before or after a vowel, so we will use the single phonemic symbols /j/ and /w/ for the semivowels, and suggest that the phonemic structures of the above words are /aj/ vs. /ai/, /sabja/ vs. /sabia/, /awn/ vs. /aun/ and /kontinwa/ vs. /kontinua/. However, this is a somewhat counterintuitive solution. The difference between these pairs actually lies not so much in the linear phonetic environment as in syllable division. A semivowel must always come before or after a vowel, and within the same syllable: thus in the examples above we have [ai̯] (one syllable), [ˈsa-βja] (two syllables), [au̯n] (one syllable) and [kon-ˈti-nwa] (three syllables). This allows us to formulate a rather more satisfactory rule for the distribution of the allophones of our proposed /i/ and /u/ phonemes. Assuming once more that [i], [j] and [i̯] are allophones of /i/, and that [u], [w] and [u̯] are allophones of /u/, we can give the following rules:

/i/	/u/	
Use [i]	Use [u]	when there is no other vowel in the same syllable
Use [j]	Use [w]	before a vowel in the same syllable
Use [i̯]	Use [u̯]	after a vowel in the same syllable

But the price of regarding [i], [j] and [i̯] as allophones of /i/ and of regarding [u], [w] and [u̯] as allophones of /u/ is that we must give syllable division a phonemic role, and so the phonemic structure of the words in question must be /ai/ vs. /a-i/, /sa-bia/ vs. /sa-bi-a/, /aun/ vs. /a-un/ and /kon-ti-nua/ vs. /kon-ti-nu-a/.[3] (In fact, Spanish orthography has devised ways of representing syllable boundaries: see the comments on the use of the written accent and on *h* in **2.6**.)

---

[3] A summary of some of the positions which have been taken on this issue is to be found in Macpherson (1975: 51–2).

2.3.3 Contextual neutralisations

A second kind of problem can be illustrated by looking at the distribution of [r] and [r]. It is clear that these form a phonemic opposition **intervocalically** (i.e. when they occur between vowels), so *caro* ['kaɾo] contrasts with *carro* ['karo]. But in fact, this is the only context in which this happens. [ɾ] and [r] are otherwise in complementary distribution: [ɾ] never occurs initially in a word, and (except in very deliberate and exaggerated pronunciation styles) [r] never occurs before or after a consonant, or at the end of a word. Thus we have:

> *rojo* ['roxo]
> *abrir* [a'bɾiɾ] (the final [ɾ] is actually very often voiceless: [ɾ̥])
> *verde* ['berðe]

We noticed above that some phonemic oppositions have been neutralised in some Spanish-speaking areas. In the case of the opposition between /ɾ/ and /r/, we can make use of the same concept of neutralisation and say that the opposition is neutralised in the contexts we have just identified. (It is not a historical process in this case, incidentally; it is just part of the phonemic structure of modern Spanish.) Alternatively, we might simply say, as we said to start with, that /r/ or /ɾ/ do not occur in certain contexts.

However, the situation with neutralisations is sometimes not so clearcut. The opposition between /m/ and /n/ at first appears to be a similar case: they are clearly in contrast in initial and intervocalic position (*mueve* /muebe/ versus *nueve* /nuebe/, *llama* /ʎama/ versus *llana* /ʎana/), but before a consonant they never contrast, except in extremely slow, careful speech. The following examples show the nasal sounds that actually occur in a number of such contexts:

> *inmediato* [imme'djato] (careful speakers may succeed in saying [inme'djato]
> if they try hard enough; many people *think* they say [inme'djato], but
> actually they don't!)
> *enfático* [eɱ'fatiko]
> *hincha* ['intʃa]
> *angosto* [aŋ'gosto]

There is obviously a neutralisation of the opposition between /m/ and /n/ here; but would it also be possible, as it was in the case of the contrast between /r/ and /ɾ/, to say that one or the other phoneme simply does not occur in a preconsonantal context? The answer to this is not so straightforward, since it is not clear to which phoneme, /m/ or /n/, such a variety of sounds as [m], [ɱ], [n] and [ŋ] would belong. Looking back at /r/ and /ɾ/, we can now see that we applied a phonetic criterion in assigning occurrences of [r] to the /r/ phoneme and occurrences of [ɾ] to the /ɾ/ phoneme, but if we try to do the same with the assigning of [m], [ɱ], [n] and [ŋ] to the /m/ and /n/ phonemes we run into difficulties with [ɱ], which is somewhere between [m] and [n]; moreover, [ŋ] as a velar consonant is not on phonetic grounds an obvious candidate for membership of the /n/ phoneme. Here, then, it would seem that neutralisation is the only way of describing the situation: preconsonantal /m/ and /n/ are sometimes said to constitute an archiphoneme, or point at which allophones of these two phonemes intersect.

2.3.4 Phonetic and phonemic changes in progress in varieties of modern Spanish

We saw in **2.3.1** that there could be a great deal of allophonic variation between speakers of Spanish, but even the number of phonemes is not necessarily constant from speaker to speaker. In much of Andalusia and in Latin American Spanish, for instance, the phonemic opposition between /s/ and /θ/ of standard Peninsular Spanish and the Spanish of most of the northern and central Peninsular has been neutralised to /s/ (see **6.2.3.2.1**). Such speakers pronounce *cima* (standard: ['θima]) and *sima* (standard: ['sima]) in the same way, as ['sima] (with a coronal rather than an apical [s]), and perceive no difference between them. (This phenomenon is known as *seseo*.) Another neutralisation that is very widespread, even within the Peninsula, is that between /ʎ/ and /j/: for such speakers *halla* (standard: ['aʎa]) and *haya* (standard: ['aja]) are identically pronounced (see **6.2.3.1.3**), most frequently as [j], a phenomenon known as *yeísmo*. Does such neutralisation cause problems for Spanish, given that phonemic differences distinguish minimal pairs which are often quite different in meaning? This is an interesting question. Sometimes it seems that when, as a result of phonemic neutralisation, inconvenient **homonyms** (words which sound the same but which are different in meaning – sometimes also called **homophones**) are created, speakers adopt strategies to compensate. It has been suggested, for example, that the homonymy of *cocer* 'to cook' and *coser* 'to sew' for many speakers of Spanish has encouraged the use of *cocinar* for 'to cook' rather than *cocer* (Kany 1960: 235). But looking at the question the other way round, it may be that neutralisations occur only when the risk of creating large numbers of homonyms is not great; using the same example, we might say that the availability of *cocinar* as an alternative to *coser* means that the homonymy of *cocer* and *coser* will not cause problems for conveying one's meaning.

Seseo and *yeísmo* are both instances of historical **phoneme merger**, the last stages of which, we might hypothesise (but see Chapter 10), are being played out in modern Spanish. Phoneme merger takes place when the allophones of two phonemes evolve to a point at which they become phonetically indistinguishable. In *yeísmo*, for example, what seems to be happening is that the lateral palatal [ʎ] loses its lateral quality to become identical with the semivowel [j], whose phonemic status we discussed in **2.3.2**. (*Seseo* cannot be explained quite as simply: it is the product of the merger of two affricate phonemes of Old Castilian, /ts/ and /dz/ and involves the **deaffrication** of both [ts] and [dz] and the **devoicing** of [dz]; but we can imagine the crucial stage at which [s] became an allophone common to both phonemes, so precluding any contrast between them; this change is discussed further in **6.2.3.2.1**) We can also observe processes of **phoneme split**, which typically occurs when the determining context for different allophonic variants is lost; an example of this in modern Spanish is the incipient opposition between open and close vowels, especially [e] / [ɛ] and

[o] / [ɔ] in Andalusian Spanish, consequential upon the loss of the syllable-final /s/ which determines the occurrence of [ɛ] and [ɔ] (see **6.2.3.2.2**).

2.4 The relation between pronunciation and spelling

Spanish is often popularly said to be a 'phonetically' spelt language, by which it is meant that there is a regular correspondence between letters and sounds. In this section we shall consider to what extent this is true.

2.4.1 Spelling systems

Spanish, like all modern Western European languages, is spelt alphabetically. (Alphabetical spelling is not the only possible system for representing a language graphically: other well-known systems of spelling are syllabic, in which written symbols correspond to syllables, and pictographic, in which written symbols correspond to words or morphemes. Even in alphabetic spelling systems, occasional pictograms, such as $ and &, are occasionally used.) In an alphabetic system of spelling, it is in theory possible to have each letter corresponding to a single phoneme of the language, so that the orthography is really nothing more than a phonemic transcription. In such a case, it would be appropriate to say that the language is spelt 'phonemically', not phonetically, since the orthography would not reflect allophonic variation; none the less, phonetic values for each phoneme could be predicted by allophonic rules such as the one we gave in **2.3.1** for /d/. However, in practice, strictly phonemic alphabetical spelling is disturbed by a number of factors. First, if the alphabet in question was designed for use with another language, it may not be appropriate for languages to which it is subsequently applied. This is the case with Spanish and other languages which use the Roman alphabet, which was used to write Latin, for which it seems to have been broadly appropriate (though, interestingly enough, the Roman alphabet does not represent the Latin phonemic distinction between long and short vowels, often indicated in modern spellings of Latin by the use of a superscript macron and breve, e.g. ā / ă). Secondly, since the sound systems of languages change in the course of time, an alphabetical spelling system which suits one stage of the language may not be appropriate for a subsequent stage, and yet the force of tradition and the authority of the written word conspire to provoke antipathy towards changes to the spelling; so many languages with a long history of written texts have a spelling system today which is **etymological** (based on the historical origins of words) rather than phonemic (English is a prime example of this phenomenon, many spellings of modern English words actually being phonemic representations of Middle English pronunciations, e.g. *knight* [kniːçt], *calf* [kalf]). Thirdly, spelling may be subject to fashion or to the whim of prestigious individuals.

We can see all these forces at work in the history of Spanish spelling. The Roman alphabet maps oddly on to the phonemic system of modern Spanish, there being no convenient letter to represent the phonemes /tʃ/, /ʎ/, /ɲ/, /θ/ and /x/, which did not exist in Latin, and so new letters or combinations of two letters (**digraphs**) have sometimes been pressed into service (*ch*, *ll*, *ñ* – the *ñ* is in origin an abbreviation for *nn* – are essentially the late 15th-century proposals of Antonio de Nebrija),[4] one letter is made to do double duty (*c* for /k/ and /θ/, *g* for /g/ and /x/), or one phoneme is represented by more than one letter (*c* and *z* for /θ/, *g* and *j* for /x/). There are also some etymological features of Spanish spelling which are due to Latin. The initial *h* in such words as *haber* < Lat. HĂBĒRE , *hoy* < Lat. HŎDĬĒ and *hora* < Lat. HŌRA is totally without phonemic (or phonetic) value and is sometimes due to imitation of Latin spelling which was confirmed by the Real Academia Española (RAE) in the 18th century (the most frequent medieval spellings of these words were *aver*, *oy* and *ora*). Other instances of initial *h* in Spanish are those corresponding to the [h] of Golden Age Spanish, which derived from certain Latin words beginning with F- (see also **6.2.3.2.1**), e.g. *hablar* /ablaɾ/ < GASp. /hablaɾ/ < Lat. FĀBŬLĀRE, *harina* /aɾina/ < GASp. /haɾina/ < Lat. FĀRĪNA; the *h* was regularly used in Golden Age spellings, where it had the phonemic value /h/, and was preserved by the RAE even after the phoneme /h/ had disappeared. The varying values of *c* and *g* are also due to the maintenance of Latinate spellings (*cebo* ['θeβo] < Lat. CĬBU(S) versus *caballo* [ka'βaʎo] < Lat. CĂBALLU(S); *general* [xene'ɾal] < GĔNĔRĀLE(M) (by **learned** borrowing – see **3.1**) versus *goma* ['goma] < Lat. GUMMA): in Latin, C corresponded to /k/ and G to /g/, but in the evolution to Spanish /k/ and /g/ palatalised before a front vowel (/i/ or /e/) first to [ts] and then to [θ]. Modern Spanish spelling would in fact achieve a better correspondence between letter and phoneme if /k/ were consistently represented by *k* and /x/ by *j*.

Despite such apparent inefficiencies, it is nevertheless the case that standard Spanish pronunciation is broadly deducible from the official spelling. Even though, as we have seen, *c* and *g* each have two phonemic values, it is always possible to decide which value they will have, since this is entirely dependent on the context, /k/ and /g/ being their respective values before *a*, *o* or *u* and /θ/ and /x/ being their values before *e* and *i*. The redundant *h* can simply be ignored. The digraphs do not occur as combinations of separate letters, and so *ch* and *ll* will always correspond to /tʃ/ and /ʎ/, never to */kh/ and */ll/.

In areas of *seseo* and *yeísmo* (see **2.3.4**) the orthographic distinctions between *s* and *c* or *z*, and between *ll* and *i* or *y*, are redundant. The learning of the official spelling is therefore difficult for such speakers (who constitute, incidentally, the vast majority of the world's Spanish speakers – see Chapter 10), since for them differences such as *casa/caza*, *ralla/raya* are purely etymological. However, looked at the other way round, the use of such redundant distinctions does not compromise the prediction of the pronunciation of these speakers on the basis of spelling. We can now appreciate a rather interesting paradox with regard to phonemic spelling. If the spelling system of Spanish is to remain strictly phonemic, different regional variants with different phonemic systems must have different spellings; but if a common spelling system for the whole Spanish-speaking world is to be preserved, the spelling system must contain redundancies for some, if not the majority of, speakers. The

---

[4] The decision in 1994 by the Asociación de Academias de la Lengua Española no longer to consider *ch* and *ll* as separate letters does not mean that they are no longer digraphs, nor that the existing relation between letters and phonemes is not maintained. The only practical consequence of this decision was for the setting of alphabetical order, so that, for example, *ch* henceforward was considered as coming after *ce* and before *ci*, whereas previously *ch* followed *cu*.

latter is the solution which has been adopted, and it is in some ways convenient that standard Spanish pronunciation, to which the modern orthographic system corresponds, is the most 'conservative' variety of Spanish in possessing the greatest number of phonemic oppositions, since while any system worked out for this variety will be capable of representing the phoneme systems of other varieties, the reverse would not hold.

The RAE has on the whole successfully implemented the policy of phonemically-based spelling. Successive *Ortografías* from 1741 to 1815 progressively abandoned the orthographical distinctions which continued to be made on the basis of the medieval phonemic system (*ç/z* corresponding to OCast. /ts/ and /dz/, *x/j* corresponding to OCast. /ʃ/ and /(d)ʒ/, *ss/s* corresponding to OCast. /s/ and /z/). It simplified the spelling of complex etymological groups to reflect their actual pronunciation (e.g. *suntuoso* rather than *sumptuoso*, *pronto* for *prompto*), and it is striking that where there is major ongoing variation (*septiembre* or *setiembre*, *obscuro* or *oscuro*) variant spellings are also admitted. In the second *Ortografía* of 1763 the digraphs associated with Greek borrowings (*th, ch* and *ph* corresponding to Greek θ, φ and χ) were simplified to *t, f* and *c*; initial *ps-* corresponding to Greek ψ was also simplified to *s-*, although conformity with international practice has encouraged its restitution and nowadays both *sicología* and *psicología* are admitted, with a preference, on practical grounds, for the latter. The spelling of foreign borrowings has also reflected their eventual pronunciation in Spanish: *espray* [es'prai̯] (< Eng. *spray* [spɹeɪ]), *suéter* ['sweteɾ] (< Eng. *sweater* ['swɛtə]).

However, foreign borrowings represent by far the most severe challenge to the spelling system of modern Spanish. An increasing number of words which apparently have been fully assimilated into Spanish retain features of the spelling of their lending languages which are not paralleled in their phonemic form, and dictionaries of Spanish have to indicate their pronunciation, which is otherwise unpredictable from the spelling. Some examples are: *sándwich* ['saŋgwitʃ], *stripteasera* [estripti'seɾa], *soufflé* [su'fle], *soutien* [su'tjen]. It will be interesting to see how this problem is eventually resolved (see also **10.4.3.2**).

2.4.2 Text messaging

The advent of text messaging on mobile phones has led to some interesting experiments in spelling. Text messaging is driven by economy, but a (phonemic) alphabetical spelling system is perhaps the least economical system from this point of view. At the simplest level, digraphs are avoided, so that *ch* replaced by *x, ll* by *y* and *qu* by *k*. *Ñ* is retained, since it is only one letter and represents an important linear phonemic unit, but accented vowels, despite their availability, are replaced by the plain letter. Etymological redundancy is pruned, so that *hablar* becomes *ablr*. Further economies are effected by standard abbreviations such as *tb* (*también*), *1* (*un(o)/a*) and *sbdo* (*sábado*) and by the omission of easily predictable vowels, e.g. *k qrs* (*¿qué quieres?*), *kdms* (*¿quedamos?*), which leads to an almost syllabic spelling. Pictograms are extensively exploited: not only the conventional + (= *más*), *x* (= *por*), but also emoticons (*emoticonos*) such as :-((sadness), :-O (surprise).

2.5 Spanish syllable structure and the phenomenon of *sinalefa*

2.5.1 Syllables

The **nucleus** of a Spanish **syllable** is always a vowel (**V**), and indeed a syllable may consist of nothing more than a vowel. The **onset** (beginning) of the syllable may consist of a semi-vowel (**S**), one or two consonants (**C** or **CC**), or a combination of up to two consonants and a semivowel (**CS** or **CCS**); the **coda** (end) of the syllable may consist of a semivowel (**S**), one or two consonants (**C** or **CC**), or a combination of a semivowel and a consonant (**SC**). The various possibilities are illustrated in Table 2.4:

Table 2.4 Spanish syllable types

		Codas				
		(zero)	S	C	CC	SC
Onsets	(zero)	*a*-mo	*oi*-ga	*ac*-to	*abs*-trac-to	*aun*-que
	S	*hue*-co		*yun*-que		
	C	*la*-na	*pei*-ne	*tan*-to	*cons*-ti-pa-do	*vein*-te
	CC	*pla*-za	*grey*	*tran*-ví-a	*trans*-por-tar	*trein*-ta
	CS	*lue*-go	*buey*	*tuer*-ce		en-*viáis*
	CCS	*true*-no		mu-*grien*-to		am-*pliáis*

Some of these sequences are more frequent than others, and subject to a number of constraints. The commonest syllable type in Spanish is **CV**, and a sequence of **VCV** is always syllabified **V-CV**, never *VC-V: thus *a-la*, *pa-ta*. Syllables with two consonants as their coda occur relatively rarely; the second coda consonant is always /s/. Syllables ending in a semivowel and two consonants (**SCC**) are unknown within words, although they are possible across word-boundaries, e.g. *hombre instruido* [om-breins-trui-ðo] (see Canellada & Madsden 1987: 44–46). In an onset consisting of two consonants C_1 and C_2, C_1 is always a plosive consonant or /f/ and C_2 is always a liquid consonant. This is an important contrast with English, where C_1 can be /s/ (e.g. *spit*); another feature of English is that a syllable can have an onset consisting of three consonants C_1, C_2 and C_3, of which C_1 must be /s/, e.g. *split*, and C2 and C3 are subject to the same constraints as C_1 and C_2 in Spanish. These principles also determine where the syllable boundary falls between consonants in sequence within a word. A sequence of a plosive or /f/ and a liquid is never split by a syllable boundary, while for all other combinations of two consonants the boundary falls between them; thus:

> a-*gri*o, de-*pri*-mir, a-*fli*-gir (plosive or /f/ + liquid)
> *ap*-to (plosive + plosive)

en-te (nasal + plosive)
ha-blar-le (liquid + liquid)
a-bier-to (liquid + plosive)

/s/ is never the initial consonant of an onset consisting of more than one consonant:

ais-lar, *es-tre-nar*

Despite the foregoing, **morphological** considerations (see Chapter 3) can sometimes override purely phonemic criteria in the assignment of syllable boundaries. The sequence of /bɾ/ (plosive + liquid) in *subrepticiamente*, for example, is divided *b-r* (*sub-rep-ti-cia-men-te*) because the initial *sub-* is considered a morphological unit; *transacción* is syllabified *trans-ac-ción* rather than *tran-sac-ción* because *trans-* is similarly thought of as a unit.

2.5.2 Hiatus

The behaviour of vowels with respect to syllable boundaries is an extremely interesting area of Spanish **phonotactics**. A sequence of two or more phonemic vowels may belong to the same syllable or be separated by a syllable-boundary. If the former, then they form a **diphthong** or **triphthong** (e.g. *pei-ne* ['pei̯-ne], *hie-rro* ['je-ro], *cam-biéis* [kam-'bjei̯s]); if the latter, then the vowels are said to be in **hiatus** (*re-ír* [re-'iɾ], *ba-úl* [ba-'ul]).

2.5.3 *Sinalefa*

We have so far considered only word-internal sequences of vowels. In the phenomenon of *sinalefa*, vowels form diphthongs, triphthongs and even longer syllabic sequences across word-boundaries. It is convenient to show *sinalefa* by using a ligature (‿).

esto‿es, no‿así, me‿alegro
hasta‿hoy, no‿hay, victoria‿insigne, sabia‿autoridad
odio‿a‿Europa

(For a comprehensive list of examples see Navarro Tomás 1970: 71–2.)

Sinalefa is of particular importance in the scansion of Spanish poetry and the underlaying of words in Spanish music. It is a curious phenomenon in that in *sinalefa* a larger range of diphthongs, triphthongs, etc. is permitted than word-internally. Thus in *me‿alegro* the sequence /e/ + /a/ is counted as belonging to one syllable, even though word-internally the same sequence would constitute a group in hiatus, e.g. *fe-a*.

There are constraints on *sinalefa*, however. While any two vowels (including the same vowels) can constitute *sinalefa*, groups of more than two vowels must conform to one of the following patterns:

A movement from open to close	Example: /a e u/	*culta_Europa*
A movement from close to open	Example: /i o a/	*genio_astuto*
A movement from close to open to close	Example: /e a i/	*muerte_airada*

But any grouping involving movement from open through close to open (e.g. /a i e/) will not constitute complete *sinalefa*: the group /a/ + /i/ + /e/ in *apaga y enciende* cannot form *sinalefa* in its entirety, but must have a syllable boundary, most normally between /a/ and /i/: *apaga y_enciende*.

2.6 Stress: the issue of 'predictability' of word stress in Spanish

So far we have been looking at sounds which are produced by the organs of speech and occur in a chain or sequence; such phenomena are sometimes known as **linear**. However, other phenomena, such as stress and pitch, are also involved in speech production and can also be responsible for meaningful contrasts; these are sometimes referred to as **suprasegmental** or prosodic features. In this section we shall examine the stress pattern of individual words in Spanish.

Spanish words may have a primary, or main, stress on the final, the penultimate or the antepenultimate syllable, e.g. *español*, *negro*, *hablábamos*. Technically, such words are referred to as **oxytones** (*agudas*), **paroxytones** (*llanas* or *graves*) and **proparoxytones** (*esdrújulas*) respectively. To these possibilities we might add words which are stressed on syllables before the antepenultimate, though such words are always verbs to which clitic pronouns (see 4.4.2) have been added, e.g. *¡escríbemelo!*, *¡cómetemelo!*, and it could be argued that it is only the rather idiosyncratic conventions of Spanish orthography that represent these as single words in the first place. However, there are no single words that are stressed in this way, and, significantly, the plural of the word *régimen*, which if morphologically regular might have yielded the form **régimenes*, actually forms its plural as a proparoxytone (*regímenes*), suggesting a fundamental resistance to such a 'superproparoxytonic' stress pattern. It is generally considered that Spanish word stress is, in absolute terms, unpredictable. That may seem a strange remark in view of the fact that the position of the stress in a Spanish word is infallibly deducible from the written form of the word; but of course it is precisely the irregularity of stress which makes it necessary to represent it by the use of the acute accent in Spanish spelling – if we were able to predict where the stress in any given word would fall, the use of the written stress accent would be totally redundant. The same linear sequence of phonemes can be stressed in different ways according to the meaning of the word, for example *practicó* ('he/she practised') / *practico* ('I practise') / *práctico* ('practical').

Having said that, Spanish stress is actually more regular than might at first be suspected. The very fact that it has not been found necessary to use an orthographic stress accent for all Spanish words of more than one syllable suggests that some assumptions have been made by the language planners about the normal position of stress, so examination of the orthographic stress rule may be a good starting-point. The assumption behind this rule is that all Spanish words ending in a vowel, *n* or *s* are stressed paroxytonically (on the penultimate syllable) and words ending in any other consonant are stressed oxytonically (on the final syllable), exceptions to this 'rule' being signalled by the use of the written accent. Let us see how well-motivated this rule is linguistically. Indeed, it is the case that the vast majority of Spanish words ending in a vowel are paroxytonically stressed and the vast majority of Spanish words ending in a consonant are oxytonically stressed. Even singular nouns and adjectives ending in *s* and *n* are usually oxytonically stressed: *francés, cortés, azafrán, común*. However, *-s* (or *-es*) and *-n* have a special morphological status because they are very regular markers of plurality in nouns and the third person of verbs respectively; this is an important consideration in the assigning of stress, because the addition of a plural marker does not change the position of the stress:

Nouns
sg.   pl.
bueno   *buenos*
papel   *papel+es*
francés   *frances+es*

Verbs
3sg.   3pl.
canta   *canta+n*
comía   *comía+n*
saldrá   *saldrá+n*

Since nearly all singular nouns and third person singular verbs have plurals, it follows that plurals ending in *s* and *n* account for a very large proportion of the Spanish vocabulary, and the orthographic stress rule has therefore sought to minimise the number of cases in which a written accent will be needed. However, this very sensible practical solution obscures the true linguistic regularity, which is that the addition of these plural morphemes does not affect the position of the word stress (except in a handful of cases: *régimen-regímenes* (see above), *espécimen-especímenes* and *carácter-caracteres*).

Once morphological considerations are taken into account, other instances of seemingly irregular stress can be seen as predictable. The form *tamizó* looks irregular because it is a word ending in a vowel which is stressed oxytonically, but once it is known that it is a third person singular preterite form, that is exactly where the stress would be expected to fall. The same applies to many verb forms: the proparoxytonic stress of first person plurals of imperfects and conditionals (*-ábamos, -íamos*), the oxytonic future tense endings (*-é, -ás, -á, -éis, -án*), and so on. Similarly, the addition of a clitic pronoun sequence to a verb form does not result in a change of the position of stress in the verb form itself.

A less obvious case of the relevance of morphology in predicting stress has to do with proparoxytonically stressed nouns. Spanish has a number of such nouns which correspond in a regular way to verbs, e.g.:

Verb	1st pers. sg. present	3rd pers. sg. pret.	Noun
animar	*animo*	*animó*	*ánimo*
criticar	*critico*	*criticó*	*crítico*
terminar	*termino*	*terminó*	*término*
etc.			

What the verbs have in common is that their infinitives consist of three syllables; the nouns formed from them also have three syllables and end in *-o*. Once this relation is perceived, the placing of stress in the noun is more predictable.

Another category of words which are regularly stressed according to the simple descriptive rule we have given above and yet carry a written stress accent are those which end in a group of two vowels in hiatus, e.g. *encía*, *confío*, *sonríe*. In fact, the written stress accent is being used with a slightly different purpose in such cases, to distinguish between sequences of vowels which are in hiatus from those which form a diphthong: contrast *varia* and *varía*, *continuo* and *continúo*. From the descriptive linguistic point of view, the written accent is effectively serving as a syllable boundary marker rather than as a marker of stress (all the words discussed here conform to the regular Spanish stress pattern, since they end in a vowel and are stressed paroxytonically), although of course it is placed on the syllable that is actually stressed; thus *va-ria* is disyllabic while *va-rí-a* is trisyllabic (see the discussion on the phonemic importance of the syllable boundary in **2.3.2**). Once more, this is an economical language-planning solution. The written accent is needed in any case as a marker of unpredictable stress, and so it can be exploited to distinguish diphthongs from vowels in hiatus.

The last use of the written stress accent is in the discrimination of homonyms. Spanish has relatively few homonymic pairs compared with, say, French or English (where it is often argued that the discrimination of homonyms is a powerful justification for the maintenance of etymological spellings, cf. Eng. *bow/bough*, Fr. *chêne/chaîne*). Some examples are *sí* 'yes' / *si* 'if', *de* 'of' / *dé* 'give!'; a number of homonyms are closely related semantically, e.g. *este* (adjective) / *éste* (pronoun), *solo* (adjective) / *sólo* (adverb). The accent also discriminates interrogative and exclamatory usages:, e.g. *¿Qué?* and *¡Qué bien!* as opposed to other uses of *que*. In all these cases, the written accent is used on the word which is most likely to receive stress within a sentence: contrast *ésta* and *esta* in *Ésta es la pregunta que quería hacer / Quería hacer esta pregunta*.

As with spelling, the RAE's use of the written accent has changed over the years, and in fact such changes have been the main thrust of the spelling reforms of the last hundred years. The treatment of hiatus in particular has varied: in the *Nuevas normas* of 1959 it was decided to ignore the presence of an orthographic *h* for accentuation purposes: thus *búho* and *vahído* are written with accents as if they were spelt *búo* and *vaído* (the accent is used to show that the vowel sequences /uo/ and /ai/ are in hiatus: /bu-o/, /ba-i-do/). Ironically, this was the one use of *h* which might have been claimed to serve some useful purpose, since in the old spellings *buho* and *vahido* the *h*, like the stress accent which is now used, effectively marked the syllable boundary between the vowels in hiatus. In 1974 it was decided that oxytonic words ending in a diphthong should not carry an accent, but the latest norms have restored the accent, e.g. *marramáu* ('cat's miaow') – this only affects very few words.

The latest reforms also reflect an interesting change in the language. They decree that any combination which constitutes a diphthong for some speakers but not others will be written without an accent as if it were a diphthong, e.g. *jesuita* (whether syllabified /je-sui-ta/ or /je-su-i-ta/), which is evidence that a number of hiatus groups are increasingly being pronounced as diphthongs.

The written stress mark on monosyllables has also varied. Verb forms such as *fue, fui, dio*, took an accent until 1959, though they are not homonymic with other words in Spanish. The latest norms suppress the written accent on such words as *guion, fie, hui, riais, truhan* also, again, because they are increasingly being realised as monosyllables (e.g. [fje] rather than [fi-'e], [rjai̯s] rather than [ri-'ai̯s]).

2.7 Some intonation patterns in Spanish

2.7.1 Stress

We saw in **2.6** that stress is crucial to the semantic discrimination of some pairs of words in Spanish, e.g. *hablo / habló, este / esté, abre / habré*. In this respect Spanish is very like English, which has such contrasts as *conquer / concur, defect* (noun) / *defect* (verb) (although there is considerable variation in stress placement in the English-speaking world, and it could further be argued that such contrasts rely equally, if not more, on the sometimes quite considerable differences in the quality of vowels in stressed and unstressed syllables, e.g. *conquer* /'kɔnkə(ɹ)/ vs. *concur* /kən'kʌː(ɹ)/. Closely related to this feature is the fact that, in English, stressed syllables are on the whole much longer than unstressed syllables – in British English the pronunciations *concur* [kᵊŋ'kʌː] and *defect* ['diːfɛkt] are common – while in Spanish the length of stressed and unstressed syllables is much more similar (English is characterised by phoneticians as having a **stress-timed rhythm** while Spanish has a **syllable-timed** rhythm.)

However, English makes use of stress in other ways which on the whole are not paralleled in Spanish. Within a noun phrase, stress in English is utilised to discriminate a number of different relations between nouns and their modifiers, e.g.:

(2.1)	**a.**	the <u>White</u> House	**b.**	the white <u>house</u>
	c.	a <u>French</u> teacher	**d.**	a French <u>teacher</u>
	e.	a <u>green</u>fly	**f.**	a green <u>fly</u>

As can be seen from the Spanish equivalents, Spanish has no similar resource. (2.1a) and (2.1b) cannot be discriminated: both *la Casa Blanca* and *la casa blanca* have the main stress on the syllable *blan-*. The difference between (2.1c) and (2.1d) is rendered syntactically: *un(a) profesor(a) de francés / un(a) profesor(a) frances(a)*. And it is perhaps hardly surprising that (2.1e) and (2.1f) are distinguished lexically as *pulgón* and *mosca verde*.

2.7.1.1 CONTRASTIVE STRESS

English also employs very extensively the phenomenon of **contrastive stress**. In an English sentence, contrastive stress can fall in a wide variety of places, generally corresponding to the word, or even, as in (2.5), to the morpheme that is being contrasted, or brought into focus (see **2.7.2.1**):

(2.2)   **a.**   *John writes poetry in the <u>garden</u>* (not, for example, in the kitchen)
        b.   *<u>John</u> writes poetry in the garden* (not his sister Margaret)
        c.   *John writes <u>poetry</u> in the garden* (not bodice-ripping novels)

(2.3)   *Is she a <u>first</u>-year student or a <u>second</u>-year student?*

(2.4)   *Do you want a room <u>with</u> a bath or <u>without</u> a bath?*

(2.5)   *Are you tying it or <u>un</u>tying it?*

Spanish, on the other hand, signals contrast very differently. The main stress in a Spanish sentence usually falls at the end, so while (2.6a), which corresponds to this pattern, is quite natural, (2.6b) and (2.6c) do not, and are rather odd:

(2.6)   **a.**   *Juan escribe poesías en el <u>jardín</u>*
        b.   *ʾ<u>Juan</u> escribe poesías en el jardín*[5]
        c.   *ʾJuan escribe <u>poesías</u> en el jardín*

Moreover, since the stress in (2.6a) is in the normal position, it is not necessarily contrastive. To make the contrasts expressed by (2.6a–c), Spanish speakers would use the cleft sentence construction, which has the effect of bringing the clefted element into focus or contrast (see **4.4.3**).

(2.7)   **a.**   *Donde Juan escribe poesías es en el <u>jardín</u> / Es en el <u>jardín</u> donde Juan escribe poesías*
        b.   *Quien escribe poesías en el jardín es <u>Juan</u> / Es <u>Juan</u> quien escribe poesías en el jardín*
        c.   *Lo que escribe Juan en el jardín son <u>poesías</u> / Son <u>poesías</u> lo que escribe Juan en el jardín*

The cleft sentence construction has the effect of placing the stressed element either immediately after the clefting verb or at the end of the sentence. The association between phrase-final position in particular and stress is very strong in Spanish, and appears to override any association of contrastive stress with the semantically corresponding element. Thus the Spanish equivalents for (2.3), (2.4) and (2.5) are:

(2.8)   *¿Es alumna de primer <u>año</u> o de segundo <u>año</u>?*
        not
        ʾʾ¿Es alumna de <u>primer</u> año o de <u>segundo</u> año?

(2.9)   *¿Quiere una habitación con <u>baño</u> o una habitación sin <u>baño</u>?*
        not
        ʾʾ¿Quiere una habitación <u>con</u> baño o una habitación <u>sin</u> baño?

---

[5] Raised question marks before a sentence or word indicate that a native speaker is doubtful about their acceptability.

(2.10) *¿Lo atas o lo des<u>atas</u>?*
not
??¿Lo atas o lo <u>des</u>atas?

2.7.1.2 ENGLISH STRESS AND SPANISH ADJECTIVE POSITION

Another very interesting difference between English and Spanish which involves the use of stress in English as against syntactic structure in Spanish has to do with adjectives. In English, adjectives normally precede the noun, while in Spanish they may follow or precede. One of the factors determining adjective position in Spanish (there are several others) is that when an adjective denotes a distinctive property of the noun, it follows the noun, whereas when it denotes an expected or inherent property of the noun, it precedes. It is according to this principle that adjectives denoting such distinctive properties as nationality, colour or other class-membership usually follow the noun; we can think of the properties of the nouns in (2.11) as weakly contrastive or brought into focus, in fact:

(2.11) a. *mi amigo belga*
(as opposed to *mi amigo ruso*)
b. *una nube gris*
(as opposed to *una nube blanca*)
c. *una asociación atea*
(as opposed to *una asociación católica*)

In (2.12), however, the properties denoted by the adjectives are the expected ones, and contrast is actually difficult to envisage:

(2.12) a. *los feroces tigres*
b. *la blanca nieve*
c. *la Santa Iglesia*

One of the reasons that adjective position in Spanish is so complex to describe systematically is that expectations about 'inherentness' can be deliberately modified by speakers. The following are therefore perfectly possible with the meanings described:

(2.13) a. *la madrileña Calle Serrano*
'the Calle Serrano, which (as everyone knows) is in Madrid'
b. *la verde campiña holandesa*
'the (typical) green Dutch countryside'
c. *los tigres feroces*
'the fierce tigers (as opposed to the docile ones)'
d. *la nieve blanca*
'the white snow (as opposed to the dirty snow)'

In English, such discrimination can only be carried out by the use of stress, a stressed adjective indicating a distinctive property and an unstressed adjective an inherent property:

(2.14) **a.** *the fierce <u>tigers</u>*
(simply describes the tigers, or implies that tigers are normally fierce)
b. *the <u>fierce</u> tigers*
(as opposed to the docile ones)
c. *the grey <u>clouds</u>*
(simply describes the clouds)
d. *the <u>grey</u> clouds*
(as opposed to the white ones)

In extreme cases, if normal **pragmatic** expectations (expectations about the nature of the world as we know it) are broken, we get similar oddities in Spanish and English:

(2.15) **a.** *los mansos corderos / ''los corderos mansos⁶*
b. *the gentle <u>lambs</u> / ''the <u>gentle</u> lambs*
(Lambs are assumed to be gentle, so the implied contrast with any other kind of lamb is strange.)

Taking each noun phrase individually, it can be seen that, once again, the main stress in Spanish falls at the end of the phrase, which is where the contrastive element stands:

(2.16) **a.** *mi amigo <u>belga</u>*
b. *una nube <u>gris</u>*
c. *una asociación <u>atea</u>*

(For further discussion of this complex question, see Pountain 1995.)

2.7.1.3 STRESSED AND UNSTRESSED PRONOUNS IN SPANISH AND ENGLISH

In the following pair of sentences, the use of stress in English expresses two different references for the pronoun *him*:

(2.17) **a.** *Charlie hit Peter and then <u>John</u> hit him (= Peter)*
b. *Charlie hit Peter and then John hit <u>him</u> (= Charlie)*

In the Spanish equivalents of these sentences, the stressed element stands as usual in rightmost position, and word order is manipulated accordingly. Notice also how Spanish has two sets of personal pronouns: *le, lo, me, te,* etc. are the atonic (or unstressed) forms, which always stand next to a verb, and always in front of a finite verb; *él, ella, mí, ti,* etc. are the **tonic** (or stressed) forms which are used with prepositions, and can hence occupy a position at the end of the sentence.

(2.18) **a.** Carlitos le dio un golpe a Pedro y luego le (= Pedro) dio un golpe <u>Juan</u>
b. Carlitos le dio un golpe a Pedro y luego Juan le dio un golpe a <u>él</u>
(= Carlitos)

2.7.2 Pitch contours

In this section we shall look at some of the **pitch** patterns, or **tunes**, that are associated with Spanish sentences.

Most phoneticians who have investigated Spanish intonation have come to the conclusion that in Spanish three distinctive pitches are distinguished; in the notation used in this book, these are numbered 1–3 from lowest to highest. To describe the intonation of a phrase, each stressed syllable is marked with one of these pitches; additionally, it is necessary to mark the direction in which the pitch is going at the end of the phrase (the **terminal juncture**), and the three encountered in Spanish (rising, falling and level) are symbolised by ↓, ↑, and | respectively. Thus we can represent the intonation of the sentence *Tiene muchos amigos, ¿verdad?* as:

> **(2.19)**   2   2   1 | 1   2↑
> Tiene muchos amigos, ¿verdad?

In Spanish, intonation is of crucial importance in distinguishing statements from **polar** ('yes-no') **questions**, since syntactically there is often no difference between the two:

> **(2.20)**   1 2   1   1↓
> Salimos esta noche
>
>   1 2   2   2 ↑
> ¿Salimos esta noche?

Different intonation patterns can also signal different attitudes. The following patterns (Matluck 1965: 19–20) are associated with a question involving an interrogative element (***wh-question***):

> **(2.21) a.**   1   2   1   1↓
> ¿Por qué no me lo dices?
> (neutral)
>
> **b.**   1   2   2   2 ↑
> ¿Por qué no me lo dices?
> (showing impatience)
>
> **c.**   1   2   3   1 ↓
> ¿Por qué no me lo dices?
> (more emphatic, stressing *dices*)

2.7.2.1 INTONATION AND WORD ORDER

The intonation pattern of a Spanish **declarative sentence** (that is, a sentence which makes a statement) is very closely related to the thematic functions of sentence elements, which we

---

[6] Raised exclamation marks before a sentence denote pragmatic oddity.

shall also be considering in relation to word order (see **4.4.3**). As a simple example, let us consider a sentence which has as its constituents a subject and a verb. From the syntactic point of view, these may occur in either order (2.22a–d). The difference between (2.22a) and (2.22b) lies in what the speaker represents as the 'new' information (the **comment**, **rheme** or **focus**) as opposed to the 'old' information (the **topic** or **theme**); most clearly, (2.22a) would be the likely answer to the question *¿Qué hizo Juan?* (so *Juan* is the topic and *cayó* is the comment) while (2.22b) would answer *¿Quién cayó?* (where *cayó* is the topic and *Juan* is the comment). In each case the main stress and summit of the pitch contour falls on the comment or rheme. It is, however, also possible to signal the thematic status of the sentence's constituents through intonation and stress even if this normal word order is varied, as in (2.22c–d).

(2.22)   2   2↓
   a.   Juan <u>cayó</u>

          2   2 ↓
   b.   Cayó <u>Juan</u>

          2   1↓
   c.   <u>Juan</u> cayó

          2   1   ↓
   d.   <u>Cayó</u> Juan

For further discussion of this phenomenon, see Contreras (1976: 103).

2.7.2.2 SOME DIFFERENCES BETWEEN SPANISH AND ENGLISH

English is normally reckoned to distinguish four rather than three levels of pitch. This contrast between the two languages no doubt has to do with the greater importance of contrastive stress in English noted in **2.7.1.1**, since the fourth level is usually found on a contrastively stressed element:

(2.23)   2   31↑ 2   3   2 4 ↓
         Charlie hit Peter   and then John hit <u>him</u>

However, the range of pitches used in English tends to be rather wider than in Spanish generally, with the third level being regularly employed where it would sound over-emphatic in Spanish. A typical greeting in Spanish would be:

(2.24) 2 1| 1 1↓
         Hola, ¿qué tal?

whereas in English a similar utterance might be:

(2.25) 3↓ 2   3   2 |
         Hi, how are you?

The tunes associated with lists have different terminal junctures in Spanish and English. Compare:

(2.26) Spanish:
```
 2 1↓    2  1↓   2 2↑    2  1↓
```
Los lunes, los miércoles, los jueves y los viernes

English:
```
 2  2↑ 2    2↑  2  2↑     2 1↓
```
Mondays, Wednesdays, Thursdays and Fridays

and a similar pattern obtains in the intonation of relative clauses or adverbial phrases, e.g.:

(2.27) Spanish:
```
  2       2 ↓ 2       2↑    2     21↓
```
Detrás de la puerta, donde no se veía, se escondió el niño

English:
```
  2       2↑   2              2↑   2  1↓
```
Behind the door, where he couldn't be seen, the child hid

2.7.2.3 REGIONAL VARIATION

A great deal of research still needs to be done on the variation in intonation patterns in the Spanish-speaking world, the more so since impressionistically native speakers often regard intonation as the most characteristic aspect of a regional accent, especially in Latin America, where a common word for 'accent' is *tonada* or *tonillo*. Matluck (1965: 30–2) briefly describes the distinctive 'circumflex' intonation of the Valle de México, which involves a slightly higher pitch on the stressed syllable of every word, a lengthening of the vowel of the final syllable and a level terminal juncture in situations where a falling terminal juncture would be expected in more educated speech; thus:

(2.28) Standard:
```
1  2                         2 1↓
```
Aquí en esta casa no sucede nada

'Circumflex'
```
1    2 1.8   2.2  1.8  2.2 1.8  2.2  1.8 2.2 1.8  2.2  1.8:|
```
A q u í en esta casa no sucede nada

Fontanella de Weinberg (1980) describes the differences between the intonation of Córdoba, Tucumán and Buenos Aires. Córdoba Spanish has four, rather than three, pitch levels, and its most striking feature is that an unstressed syllable which precedes a main stressed syllable within the same word is lengthened and has a pitch rise or fall, e.g.:

(2.29)
```
 1       24 2   1↓
```
No la conozco

Tucumán speech appears to have a syllable-timed rhythm, with considerable lengthening of vowels in stressed syllables and shortening of vowels in unstressed; it is also reported as not having falling terminal junctures.

EXERCISES

1. Describe as accurately as you can the difference between the pronunciation of the *ns* in Spanish *enfático* and *ente*, and the *ps* in English *pot*, *spot* and *shop*.

2. How many homonyms created by the neutralisation of /θ/ and /s/ can you find? Is such homonymy likely to create difficulties of understanding?

3. Identify the number of syllables in the following phrases:
   Fresco y claro arroyuelo
   Porque de esa parte está

4. Can you think of any other way in which Spanish orthography might distinguish between diphthongs and sequences of vowels in hiatus?

Spanish words and their structure

The languages of the world are often characterised by their position on a scale the extremes of which are described as **isolating** and **agglutinating**. In isolating languages, words are themselves the smallest units which carry meaning or grammatical information, while in agglutinating languages words have a high degree of internal structure, individual parts of the word having discrete functions with different combinations of the same elements being used to create different words. Spanish lies somewhere between these extremes, and is often described as being an **inflecting** language. Although it does have some words which are neither subdivisible into smaller functional units nor usable in combination with other elements, e.g. the adverb *hoy*, the vast majority of words have agglutinating characteristics.

Spanish verbs, nouns and adjectives have a highly structured series of endings or **inflections** indicating such fundamental functions as number, gender and tense:

(3.1)		masc.	fem.
	sg.	*buen+o*	*buen+a*
	pl.	*buen+o+s*	*buen+a+s*

(3.2)		present	imperfect
	2 p.sg.	*trabaj+as*	*trabaj+ab+as*
	1 p.pl.	*trabaj+amos*	*trabaj+áb+amos*

Such constituent parts of words are known as **morphemes**. The notion of the morpheme was developed in parallel to that of the phoneme (see **2.3.1**), though, as we shall see below, it is in fact a much more problematic concept. But the parallel between morphemes and phonemes can be exploited to a certain extent. In particular, it can be seen that just as phonemes are considered to have allophones which vary according to the phonetic context in which they appear, so some morphemes may be considered to have **allomorphs**. A very simple example of such variation or **alternation** is afforded by the plural morpheme of Spanish, which in the vast majority of cases is /s/ for a noun or adjective ending in a vowel and /es/ for a noun or adjective ending in a consonant: *libro+s*, *pared+es*. Verbal morphology in Spanish provides many examples of such alternation: look at the form of what may be taken to be the stem morpheme of the verb *sentir* in the following words:

(3.3)	**a.**	*sient+o*
	b.	*sent+imos*
	c.	*sint+ió*
	d.	*sent+í*

Here, we can see that /sent/ has three allomorphs: /sient/, /sent/ and /sint/. Superficially, we might envisage that the form of the stem morpheme depends simply on the tense, person and number of the verb form; learning about allomorphic variation in this way is essentially what foreign learners of Spanish are encouraged to do. However, allomorphic variation is often not haphazard, but is the result of interaction with other structural features of the language. In the present tense of *sentir* and of many other Spanish verbs, there is an alternation beween stem morphemes which relates regularly to stress, a diphthong appearing when the stem is stressed; these are the verbs generally known as radical-changing verbs:

> **(3.4)** unstressed   stressed
>   sent+*i*mos   s*ie*nt+o
>   quer+*e*mos   qu*ie*r+o
>   pod+*e*mos   p*ue*d+o
>   esforz+*a*mos   esf*ue*rz+o

In the above examples, all the morphemes are **bound**, that is, they cannot stand alone, but must be attached to other morphemes to form words. Other morphemes are **free** in the sense that they may form words in their own right: clear examples of free morphemes in Spanish are *bien, sol, voz*. Free morphemes may combine with other morphemes to form compound words, e.g. *bienestar, tornasol, altavoz*.

3.1 Criteria for morphological analysis

The identification of morphemes can be approached in two different ways. So far, it has been suggested that a morpheme is the minimum element within a word which carries an identifiable meaning or function; but because words in agglutinating languages are highly structured morphologically it is in fact often possible to carry out morphological analysis without any regard to the actual semantic content of such units. In Spanish, for example, we do not need to know that -*mos* has the meaning of first person plural to see that it is a recurring element in a number of words. Indeed, some such elements which are identifiable on this basis as morphemes have no obvious meaning, and some do not have a single meaning. Once again, we will look at some features of Spanish verbs to demonstrate this. Spanish verbs fall into three principal formal categories (usually called **conjugations**) which are characterised by different vowels in their person-number inflections (this vowel is sometimes known as a **theme** or **root vowel**):

> **(3.5)** *hablAr*   *comEr*   *escribIr*
>   *hablAmos*   *comEmos*   *escribImos*

Although the theme vowel is readily analysable as a distinct morpheme, it bears no distinctive meaning; conjugation types in Spanish are purely formal categories of the language and their members have nothing obviously in common from the semantic point of view. Another regularly recurring verbal morpheme is the marker of what is traditionally called the subjunctive:

(3.6)

indicative	subjunctive
habla	hablE
come	comA
hablaba	hablaRA
comía	comieRA

Yet, as we shall see in **5.3**, the subjunctive does not have a single meaning, and sometimes it seems not to have any meaning at all: in (3.7) the subjunctive form *tenga* of the verb *tener* is required by the verb *dudar*, and since the indicative *tiene* is simply not acceptable, it is impossible to establish any meaningful contrast between the two forms.

(3.7) *Dudo que tenga / *tiene tanto dinero como dices*

There is an interesting tension between formal and semantic criteria for morphological analysis. Applying a purely semantic criterion may lead us to suppose that there is allomorphic alternation between elements which are not formally related. Spanish, like English, has a large number of adjectives which are obviously derived from nouns; noun and adjective are related in form as well as in meaning:

(3.8)

noun		adjective	
ángulo 'angle'	ángul+o	angular 'angular'	angul+ar
casa 'house'	cas+a	casero 'domestic; home-loving; homemade'	cas+ero
masa 'mass'	mas+a	masivo 'massive'	mas+ivo
música 'music'	músic+a	musical 'musical'	music+al
nube 'cloud'	nub+e	nuboso 'cloudy'	nub+oso
Roma 'Rome'	Rom+a	romano 'Roman'	rom+ano

In each of the above cases, it is possible to analyse the adjective as a stem morpheme and an adjectival suffix; the corresponding noun is the same stem morpheme, sometimes with a (meaningless) gender inflection. Sometimes, however, the formal relation between a noun and its semantically corresponding adjective is highly irregular, even to the point of being almost unrecognisable:

(3.9)

corazón 'heart'	corazón	cardíaco 'cardiac'	cardíac+o
hierro 'iron'	hierr+o	férreo 'made of iron'	férr+eo
lado 'side'	lad+o	lateral 'lateral'	later+al
leche 'milk'	lech+e	lácteo 'dairy'	láct+eo
Londres 'London'	Londres	londinense 'from London'	londin+ense
muerte 'death'	muert+e	mortal 'mortal'	mort+al
obispo 'bishop'	obisp+o	episcopal 'episcopal'	episcop+al

In still further semantically related noun/adjective pairs, there is no formal relation at all between the two:

(3.10) *caballo* 'horse'   *equino* 'equine'
        carta 'letter'   *epistolar* 'epistolary'
        perro 'dog'   *canino* 'canine'

It would clearly be totally inappropriate to claim that the stem morphemes of the pairs in (3.10) are in any sense the 'same' morpheme, despite their semantic relatedness. But the pairs of (3.9) pose a thornier question, since their stem morphemes do have some formal similarity. It would not be unreasonable to view *muert-* ~ *mort-* as an allomorphic variation, the more so because the two forms *muerte* and *mortal* vary in exactly the same way as we have seen that the stem morphemes of radical-changing verbs vary, i.e. having a diphthong when stressed and a monophthong when unstressed (compare *muerte* and *mortal* with *muer+o* and *mor+imos*). The pair *hierr-* ~ *férr-* pose more problems. Although here we apparently see alternation between a diphthong and a corresponding monophthong, the contextual basis we have previously identified for this alternation is absent, since both *hierr-* and *férr-* are stressed. The different initial consonants (an orthographic *h* in *hierro*, which has no phonetic value, as against the /f/ of *férreo*) would at first seem to be quite unrelated. But if we look at the historical development of Spanish, such an alternation will call to mind the very striking sound change whereby an initial Latin /f/ becomes first /h/ and then disappears altogether in a number of phonetic contexts (the Latin origin of Sp. *hierro* was FĔRRUM). In fact, history explains the *hierro~férreo* alternation: *hierro* is a 'popular' word which has come down directly from Latin and undergone all the expected phonetic changes along the way whereas *férreo* is a 'learned' word, that is, a word borrowed directly from Latin FĔRRĔUS in the late Middle Ages and preserving most of the latter's characteristics. Because of this, *hierro* and *férreo* are sufficiently similar to be recognisable in some sense as having the 'same' stem morpheme, yet too different for the stem morpheme alteration to be described by any systematic **synchronic** rule (that is to say, a rule which applies to the language as it exists at one particular time, in this case, the present day: see **10.1**). The apparent alternation between *cor-* and *car-* in *corazón* and *cardíaco* is even more remote and is again due to the etymologies of these words: *corazón* derives from an augmented form of Latin CŎR (?CORATIONE[1]) while *cardíaco* is a 'learned' borrowing from the Latin form CARDĬĂCUS which in turn is a borrowing from Greek *kardiakós*. The similarity of the first syllable of the Latin and Greek words (which may have encouraged the borrowing of *kardiakós* into Latin) is due to a much deeper common Indo-European etymology (shared also, incidentally, by Eng. *heart*), but is essentially coincidental. The last pair of words in (3.9), *obispo* and *episcopal*, are similarly 'popular' and 'learned' respectively, both deriving from the Latin stem ĔPĪSCŎP-, though such has been the complexity of the phonetic evolution of *obispo* from ĔPĪSCŎPUS that in this case the formal relation between the two words is relatively opaque.[2]

Learned borrowings have undeniably produced great complication in the morphological structure of Spanish (and, indeed, of other European languages). However, the basic point being made here is that, since many popular and learned forms are clearly semantically related,

---

[1] A question mark before a Latin word denotes that the word is not textually attested in the Classical language: see Pountain (2001: 11–13).
[2] For discussion, see Corominas & Pascual (1980–91: IV, 258).

the insistence on an exclusively semantic criterion for the identification of morphemes might lead us to regard forms which are impossible to relate formally as being morphemic alternants.

On the other hand, it is also clear that the application of an exclusively formal criterion for the identification of morphemes is also unsatisfactory. As a simple example of this, we might notice that there are some pairs of words in Spanish which apparently differ in the presence or absence of the prefix morpheme *dis-*, which has a 'negative' meaning:

> **(3.11)** *continuo* 'continuous'   *dis+continuo* 'discontinuous' (='NEG
>   continuous')
>   *función* 'function'   *dis+función* 'dysfunction' (= 'NEG function')
>   *gusto* 'pleasure'   *dis+gusto* 'disgust' (= 'NEG pleasure')
>   *tender* 'to stretch'   *dis+tender* 'to slacken' (= 'NEG to stretch'

There are more words which might on formal grounds be analysed as containing an initial morpheme *dis-*, but it is difficult to see that *dis-* is associated with any regular meaning, and certainly not the 'negative' meaning referred to above:

> **(3.12)** *curso* 'course'   *dis+curso* 'speech' (≠ 'NEG course')
>   *parar* 'to stop'   *dis+parar* 'to fire' (≠ 'NEG to fire')
>   *poner* 'to put'   *dis+poner* 'to place' (≠ 'NEG to put')
>   *traer* 'to bring'   *dis+traer* 'to distract' (≠ 'NEG to bring')

Once again, historical developments have sometimes brought about this situation. In origin, *disparar* was indeed the opposite of *parar* in its original Latin meaning of 'to prepare', since a weapon which was fired was no longer prepared, or loaded. However, the Latin prefix DIS- also had the meaning 'apart, in pieces', and it is that meaning that we see historically in *dis-traer* (from Latin DIS+TRĂHĔRE 'to pull apart'), *disponer* (from Latin DIS+PŌNĔRE 'to place here and there', hence 'to arrange') and *discurso*, which derives from the verb DIS+CURRĔRE 'to run to and fro', hence 'to speak at length'). In still other cases of apparent formal parallelism, there is no relation, synchronic or diachronic, to be found: *disputa* 'argument' has nothing to do with *puta* 'prostitute'!

The above considerations make rigorous morphological analysis extremely difficult, since they militate against **transparency**, or a clear one-to-one relation between morphological unit and meaning. Thus although Spanish makes extensive use of inflectional morphology, as we noted at the outset of this chapter, patterns of alternation are often highly irregular.

3.2 Some patterns in derivational morphology

To illustrate both the richness and complexity of **derivational morphology** in Spanish, we shall look at the many forms which are associated with *pelo* 'hair'. Spanish inherits a number of these forms directly from Latin: *pelo* itself, from Lat. PĬLU[S], the verb *pelar* from Lat. PĬLĀRE [PĬLO] in its meaning of 'to deprive of hair' (the Latin verb also meant 'to grow hair') and the adjective *peloso* from Lat. PĬLŌSU[S] 'hairy'. The adjective and noun are in a regular formal and semantic relation, both in Latin and Spanish, since the inflection *-oso* attached to a noun stem usually denotes the notion of having (a lot of) the noun in question:

> **(3.13)** *dicha* 'luck' → *dichoso* 'lucky'
> *fango* 'mud' → *fangoso* 'muddy'
> *jugo* 'juice' → *jugoso* 'juicy'
> *miedo* 'fear' → *miedoso* 'fearful'
> *pringue* 'grease' → *pringoso* 'greasy'
> *sospecha* 'suspicion' → *sospechoso* 'suspicious'

Another adjective formed from *pelo* is *peludo* 'hairy, furry'; the *-udo* suffix often has the meaning of having the noun in question in abundance:

> **(3.14)** *barba* 'beard' → *barbudo* 'bearded'
> *cachaza* 'slowness in acting' → *cachazudo* 'sluggish'
> *carrillo* 'cheek' → *carrilludo* 'having puffy cheeks'
> *melena* 'long hair, bob' → *melenudo* 'long-haired'
> *nariz* 'nose' → *narizudo* 'big-nosed'

Although there are many noun-verb relations of the *pelo-pelar* type which suggest a regular relation between an infinitive and a corresponding noun ending in *-o*, there are also a number of other formal possibilities which prevent viewing this as a regular relationship; the best we can say is that it is **semi-regular**:

> **(3.15)** noun ending in *-o* (like *pelo*):
> *acechar* → *acecho*
> *atisbar* → *atisbo*
> *atracar* → *atraco*
> *escarbar* → *escarbo*
> *estorbar* → *estorbo*
> *robar* → *robo*
> *surcar* → *surco*
>
> noun ending in *-a*:
> *buscar* → *busca*
> *escuchar* → *escucha*
> *luchar* → *lucha*
> *pizcar* → *pizca*
> *sospechar* → *sospecha*
> *trabar* → *traba*
> *trancar* → *tranca*
>
> noun ending in *-e*:
> *atacar* → *ataque*
> *chocar* → *choque*
> *desembocar* → *desemboque*
> *enfocar* → *enfoque*
> *picar* → *pique*
> *tocar* → *toque*

noun ending in -*ción*:
> *comprobar* → *comprobación*
> *complicar* → *complicación*
> *evocar* → *evocación*
> *explicar* → *explicación*
> *modificar* → *modificación*
> *multiplicar* → *multiplicación*

noun ending in -*io*:
> *edificar* → *edificio*
> *indicar* → *indicio*

As we move away from this basic relation between noun, adjective and verb, the situation becomes even more unpredictable and yet the patterns observed are often paralleled elsewhere in the language.

The noun *pelambre* 'tuft of hair' shows the suffix -*ambre* used with the noun stem; this suffix, the modern derivative of Latin -ĀMĬNE[M], seems to have a collective meaning in a handful of other words (enough to warrant an entry in the *DRAE*, p. 91, describing it as a suffix which 'forma sustantivos colectivos o que indican abundancia'), though the allomorphic variation observable in the stem of these words is irregular:

(3.16) *cuero* 'leather' → *corambre* 'collection of skins'
> *raíz* 'root' → *raigambre* 'root system'

The collective notion is also no doubt reinforced by *enjambre* 'swarm', although this word has no transparent stem morpheme in modern Spanish (it derives from Lat. EXĀMĬNE [EXĀMEN], which is associated with EXĪRE 'to go out').

Another nominal derivative is *pelaje* 'animal's coat, fur', in which a suffix -*aje* is added to the stem morpheme. However, while there are other examples of the -*aje* suffix being used with a collective meaning (*cuerda* 'rope' → *cordaje* 'rigging', *andamio* 'scaffolding' → *andamiaje* 'scaffolding, framework'), its more usual meaning with noun stems is that of 'rate' (*almacén* 'warehouse' → *almacenaje* 'storage', *puerto* 'port' → *portaje* 'portage', *amarre* 'mooring' → *amarraje* 'mooring fee'). In some cases the transparency of the relation has been completely lost (if, indeed, it was ever present, since many words ending in -*aje* are in fact borrowings from Occitan or French, e.g. *viaje*, *lenguaje*, *ultraje*).

The adjective *pelón* 'bald' has the suffix -*ón* attached to the noun stem, which may be taken as indicating the notion of privation: another common example is *rabón* 'tailless, short-tailed' from *rabo* 'tail'. However, when attached to a noun stem, -*ón* is more frequently an augmentative suffix, often lexicalising (*camisa* 'shirt' → *camisón* 'nightdress', *mosca* 'fly (in general)' → *moscón* 'bot-fly') and otherwise with a pejorative meaning (*soltero* 'bachelor' → *solterón* 'confirmed bachelor', *crítico* 'critic' → *criticón* 'faultfinder, gossip').

Pelo, as the allomorphic variant *peli*-, participates in a number of compound words: *peliblanco* 'white-haired', *pelicano* 'grey-haired', *pelicorto* 'short-haired', *pelilargo* 'long-haired', *pelinegro* 'black-haired', *pelirrojo* 'red/ginger-haired', *pelirrubio* 'fair-haired'. This has been a particularly **productive** area in more recent Spanish, perhaps because such compounds have a more transparent relation between form and meaning than such adjectives as *canoso* 'white-/grey-haired', *moreno* 'dark-haired, dark in complexion', *rubio* 'fair-haired, fair in complexion'.[3] It may also be that these compounds are more discriminating in their meaning, since they can only refer to hair rather than to complexion in general, and *pelirrubio* and *pelirrojo* make a distinction that the simple word *rubio* does not make. An example of a compound verb is *pelechar* 'to moult'.

Sometimes the morphological derivation has lost any obvious semantic association with the stem morpheme. This is the case of the verb *pelear* 'to quarrel, argue', which in origin may have had to do with fighting by tearing the opponent's hair. The same is true of the verbs *espeluznar* and *despeluzar*, which in origin were no doubt associated with the notion of causing a person's hair to stand on end with fear, and now have the meaning of 'to horrify'.

The above discussion has only covered a small number of the derivatives of *pelo* which figure in modern Spanish. The following list will give some idea of the rich possibilities of derivational morphology, many of which appear to be idiosyncratic to this particular stem, however. The verb *pelar* yields the adjectival past participle *pelado* 'shaven, peeled' and the agentive noun *pelador* 'peeler'; from *pelado* we have *peladura* 'peeling(s)' (the results of the action of *pelar*), and *peladero* 'place where animals are shorn or plucked'. The feminine of *pelado*, *pelada*, means 'shorn skin of a sheep'. From *pelambre* (see above) we have *(a)pelambrar* 'to remove hair from a hide', *pelambrero*, the person who carries out the activity of *(a)pelambrar*, *pelambrera* 'mop of hair' or 'baldness' (an interesting example of two apparently opposing meanings, brought about perhaps as a result of ironical usage: *¡qué pelambrera lleva!* 'he's as bald as a coot'). The rather rare word *pelete* has the meaning of someone who is poor (*pelado* 'shorn (of money)', but its apparent derivatives *peletería* 'furrier's (shop)' and *peletero* 'furrier' are common. Other more unusual derivatives of *pelo* are *pelote* 'goat's hair', *pelusa* 'down', *peluche* 'felt', *repelo* 'protruding splinter'.

The rather bewildering array of data described above shows not only the enormous possibilities for derivational morphological inheritance and creation in Spanish, but also the difficulties of identifying a systematic relation between form and meaning on a large scale. Why, for example, does *pelón* mean 'bald' rather than 'large hair'? How do we predict when the *-aje* suffix has its collective meaning and when it has its meaning of rate? We could simply say that morphology is an inherently irregular area of linguistic structure and leave things there, but for these particular questions a rather more interesting and significant answer is available. Morphological creation is not simply a matter of exploiting the formal possibilities of a language but is more likely to respond to pragmatic need. Thus the notion of a 'large hair' is pragmatically a rather unusual one, almost a contradiction in terms, since a hair is typically regarded as a small object (indeed, that is the basic value of Spanish *pelo* in a number of idiomatic expressions, such as *por un pelo* 'by the skin of my teeth', *un pelo* 'a bit', *ni un pelo* 'not an inch'). Thus *pelón* is not likely to mean 'large hair' and the morphological combination can be used for another purpose. Similarly, the *-aje* suffix in its meaning of 'rate' will only be used with stems for which a rate is relevant, typically with regard to

---

[3] The term 'productive' is used in a technical sense in linguistics to denote a form-class which is continuing to add to its membership through the development of new words.

charging; while *pelaje* theoretically could have been used for the meaning of 'rate per hair', it is an extremely unusual concept, and so once again the suffix is exploited differently.

Other 'irregularities' in morphology may have a more structural explanation. There is nothing inherently impossible about the concept 'brown-haired', and so we might envisage that the 'possible' word **pelicastaño* is an **accidental gap** in the Spanish lexicon (vocabulary) that may in due course be filled (and would certainly be understood even now); perhaps it has not been filled so far because the distinction between shades of dark hair is not as important as that between fair and dark, or between white/grey and other shades.

Finally, we have repeatedly observed how language change brings about lack of transparency in morphological structure as words extend their original meanings and eventually move away from those meanings completely. However, sometimes the force of **analogy** (development of one form in parallel with another) can bring about unexpectedly greater transparency. The word *peluca* 'wig' (and its principal derivatives *peluquero, peluquería*) is in fact a borrowing from Fr. *perruque* and has nothing to do with *pelo*; however, it is likely that the phonetic change of /r/ to /l/ is made by a process often known as **popular etymology**, in order to achieve a formal similarity with *pelo*.

3.3 Spanish affective suffixes

An exceptionally complex area of Spanish from the point of view of the relation between morphological form and meaning is that of **affective** suffixes. Spanish has a considerable range of suffixes which with often denote size, thus:

(3.17)	*mes+ita*	'small table'
	puebl+ecito	'small village'
	chiqu+illo	'small child'
	hombre+cillo	'little man'
	arroy+uelo	'small stream'
	plaz+uela	'small square'
	narig+ón	'having a big nose'
	choque+tazo	'big shock'

So far, the only complexities are purely formal ones. In the first place, it is not always possible to predict what the exact form of the suffix will be. For example, the *-ito/a* suffix is normally added without modification to stem morphemes which end in *-o* or *-a* (where the final vowel is effectively transferred to the suffix, as seen in *casa* → *cas+ita*) or in a consonant other than *n* or *r* (e.g. *animal* → *animal+ito*), while *-cito/a* is used with stems ending in *-e*, *-n* or *-r* (e.g. *madre* → *madre+cita*, *cajón* → *cajón+cito*, *mayor* → *mayor+cito*). Monosyllabic stems usually take *-ecito/a*: *sol* → *solecito*, *pan* → *panecito*. However, many exceptions to such 'rules', and much variation in usage, is found, e.g. *pie+cecito* rather than *?pie+(e)cito* (a rare example of a monosyllable ending in *e*) and *señor+ito* rather than *?señor+cito*. *Café* has two forms, perhaps in this case to achieve semantic discrimination: *cafetito* 'small coffee' and *cafecito* 'small café'. The stem morpheme usually undergoes no change, though in a relatively small number of cases we can observe the same kind of diphthong–monophthong alternation as that encountered in radical-changing verbs (see 3.3): *viejo* → *vej+ete, cuerpo* → *corp+ecito* or *cuerp+ecito*. Another formal difficulty is that in (3.17) the basis for the choice of diminutive suffix is not entirely clear: although it is more usual to use the *-ito* suffix with the majority of nouns, *-(ec)illo* is very commonly used with *chico* and *hombre*, while *-uelo/a* is always used with *arroyo* and *plaza*. Why such forms as *hombrecito, arroyito* and *placita* have not been adopted is an interesting question, and we shall return to it below. There is quite a lot of variation in the form of diminutive suffixes within the Spanish-speaking world, especially within the Iberian Peninsula. While the *-ito* suffix is most frequent generally and especially in Latin America, Aragon is particularly associated with *-ico*, Asturias with *-ín* and Galicia with *-iño*.

It is much more problematic, however, to establish semantic values for the affective suffixes. In the first place, it has sometimes happened over the course of time that a suffix has become so firmly associated with a stem in a particular meaning that stem and suffix cannot appropriately be analysed as discrete morphological units from the semantic point of view; this is in principle the same kind of phenomenon as we observed in 3.1 above. A number of words, though apparently consisting of a stem plus a diminutive suffix, and sometimes being loosely or vestigially related in meaning to the stem morpheme, must from the semantic point of view none the less be considered as single morphological units in themselves; they have **lexicalised**, or become independent words, as is reflected in the fact that they usually have separate entries in dictionaries. The word *bonito* 'pretty' is clearly related to the meaning of its stem morpheme *bueno* 'good', though it now has a specific meaning which cannot be construed as the sum of *buen-* 'good' + *-ito* 'small'; it is possible that *bonito* 'tuna' is also associated originally with *bueno*, although that association is now completely lost).[4] Similarly *carretilla* 'wheelbarrow', like its stem morpheme *carro*, is a wheeled vehicle of sorts, though of a very individual kind. *Barquillo* 'wafer' has lost all association with *barco* 'boat', although originally the word indeed referred to a boat-shaped pastry. Conversely, these suffixes, which were originally associated with nouns, have developed such an independent meaning that they can be attached to other parts of speech as well (in this case, obviously, only with affective meaning), with the exception of verbs. (The suffixes, are, however, sometimes exploited to create adjectival and nominal derivatives of verbs, e.g. *tragar* 'to swallow' → *tragón* 'greedy, glutton(ous); a glutton', and are even used as the basis for new verbal creations, e.g. *dormir* 'to sleep' → *dormitar* 'to doze'.) Some examples of affective suffixes in use with other parts of speech are:

(3.18) a. Gerund:
Delante iba Santiago, con la cruz, silbandillo y dando patadas a los guijarros (C.J. Cela, *La familia de Pascual Duarte*, 19th ed., Barcelona: Destino, p. 55)
'Santiago went in front with the cross, whistling gently and kicking at the pebbles'

b. Adverb:
Nunca, nunquita he visto ojos más espantados (Ciro Alegría, quoted in Walsh 1944: 19).

---

[4] Corominas & Pascual, 1980–91, I: 621.

The main problem with the description of the meaning of affective suffixes is that the meaning of the suffix itself is not constant. The reason why these suffixes are called 'affective' is that, while they sometimes denote purely notions of size (**diminutive** 'small' or **augmentative** 'large'), they also denote attitudes (pejorative or affectionate). Indeed, all the suffixes in this category have affective meanings, and some appear to be used exclusively in an affective way (e.g. *-acho/a*, *-ucho/a* and *-uzo/a*), while others have meanings of both size and affective attitude. The meaning of a particular combination of stem and suffix seems often to be idiosyncratic. Gooch (1970: 12) cites the following examples of both pejorative and favourable use of *-azo/a* with the same noun stem:

> **(3.19) a.** *un filosofazo magnífico* 'a superb philosopher'
> **b.** *un filosofazo de tres al cuarto* 'a tin-pot philosopher'
> **c.** *una barbaza imponente* 'a magnificent beard'
> **d.** *una barbaza feísima* 'a hideous great beard'

Although a great deal of data on affective suffix use has been collected, there is no extensive study of this particular problem. What we know about the noun pragmatically is clearly important. If someone speaks of a *fiestón*, for example, the augmentative *-ón* suffix is likely to be favourable in affective meaning, since most people think that the bigger, longer or better-attended a party, the better it is. On the other hand, a *novelón* is more likely to be a pejorative notion, since length is not commonly seen as a virtue in a novel (despite the fact that some of the classic novels of world literature have been long!). But pragmatic knowledge is not always so easy to catalogue. The nouns on which the examples in (3.19) are based are in themselves less predictable in their pragmatic associations: philosophers are of variable quality, and beards are of variable attractiveness. More than anything else, it seems to be the adjectives which accompany them which determine the interpretation of the affective suffix. Alonso (1951 [1935]) suggests that the value of diminutives is often related to the whole sentence, to the attitude of the speaker towards an object or towards another person. Here are three of the examples he discusses:

> **(3.20)** Teacher to recently graduated students:
> *–¿Y cuándo esperan ustedes conseguir una cátedra?*
> *–Ya tendremos que aguardar unos añitos.* (p. 205)
> 'When do you hope to get a professorship?'
> 'We'll have to wait a few years.'

> **(3.21)** *A mediodía, cuando el sol quema más, el pueblo entero empieza a*
> *humear y oler a pino y a pan calentito. A todo el pueblo se le abre*
> *la boca.* (p. 220, quoted from J.R. Jiménez, *Platero y yo*)
> 'At midday, when the sun is hottest, the whole village begins to
> smoke and smell of pine and nice hot bread. It opens everyone's
> mouth.'

> **(3.22)** *Yo quisiera hablarle a usted de un asuntillo* (p. 226)
> 'I wanted to talk to you about something.'

For (3.20), Alonso comments that *añitos* denotes the 'resignado humorismo' associated with the whole sentence, not simply a subjective view of 'years'. In (3.21), the diminutive suffix in *calentito* signifies the pleasurable expectation the bread awakens, the attitude of the villagers towards the bread, and in (3.22), *asuntillo* denotes a respectful attitude on the part of the speaker towards the addressee.

3.4 Word meaning

We have already seen in this chapter how the meaning of a word cannot always necessarily be construed as the sum of the meaning of its constituent morphemes, and we shall see later in this book how similarly the overall meaning of a sentence depends on much more than simply the sum of the meanings of its constituent words. Yet the meaning of words has traditionally occupied a privileged place in linguistic analysis. Monolingual dictionaries, which are perhaps the most familiar form of linguistic description for most people, are essentially lists of words with some representation of their meanings. Dictionaries use a variety of strategies for describing the meaning of words. Larger dictionaries make extensive use of **periphrastic** definitions: consider the following entries taken from *DRAE*:

> **(3.23) alerón**: Aleta giratoria que se monta en la parte posterior de las alas de un avión y que tiene por objeto hacer variar la inclinación del aparato y facilitar otras maniobras. (p. 69)
>
> **pardo**: Del color de la tierra, o de la piel del oso común, intermedio entre blanco y negro, con tinte rojo amarillento, y más oscuro que el gris. (p. 1141)

Let us look more closely at what is happening linguistically in such paraphrases. The definition of *alerón* begins by giving a word which means roughly the same thing, a near **synonym**, *aleta*, which, however, is much broader in its meaning than *alerón*, which has the specific meaning described here. To narrow down the precise meaning of *alerón*, it is related to a number of other notions with which it is closely associated and hence in terms of which it can be described (*ala, avión*) its nature (*giratoria*) and function (*hacer variar …*) are also explained. The definition of the colour adjective *pardo* tells us some things which are typically of this colour (*tierra, oso común*), as well as making use of the technique of plotting the colour on a scale with other colours (*blanco, negro, rojo, amarillo, gris*). More economical strategies are the simple use of near synonyms, as in (3.24a), or of **antonyms** (opposites), as in (3.24b); another kind of relation often exploited is that of **hyponymy,** or set-membership, as in (3.24c), where *laúd* is initially defined as a member of the set of musical instruments:

> **(3.24) a.** **confuso**: mezclado, revuelto (*VOX*, p.283)
> **b.** **liso**: sin labrar o adornar (*ib.*, p.664)
> **c.** **laúd**: instrumento músico de cuerda, de caja cóncava en su parte inferior, que se toca pulsando las cuerdas (*ib.*, p. 650)

In all these cases we can see that one word is being defined in terms of others, and so, taking the dictionary overall, a whole network of semantic relations is implicitly being laid down for the language in question. Normally, we never see this network as such in dictionaries because each word is dealt with individually, though it could be inferred. Table 3.1 shows information about Spanish verbs generally meaning 'to shine', drawn from the individual word entries in *Clave*:

Table 3.1 Spanish verbs for 'to shine'

word	network information	paraphrase	example
brillar		despedir rayos de luz, propia o reflejada	*El sol brilla en el firmamento*
centellear	… de intensidad cambiante	despedir rayos de luz …	*Los brillantes del anillo centelleaban a la luz del sol*
destellar	… generalmente intensos y de breve duración	despedir … rayos de luz …	*Las estrellas "destellan" en la noche*
lucir	brillar suavemente		*Las estrellas … lucen en el cielo*
refulgir	resplandecer o brillar		*Las estrellas refulgen en el cielo nocturno*
relampaguear	brillar de manera intensa e intermitente		*La luz del faro relampagueaba en la oscuridad de la noche*
relucir	brillar	despedir rayos de luz	*Las estrellas relucen en el cielo*
relumbrar	resplandecer	despedir intensos rayos de luz	*Las armaduras de los caballeros relumbraban bajo el sol*
resplandecer	brillar intensamente	despedir rayos de luz	*Ha dejado tan limpia la plata que resplandece*
titilar	centellear … con un ligero temblor	despedir rayos de luz …	*Las estrellas titilan en el cielo*

On the basis of this information, we might draw the following structural conclusions. All the verbs are near synonyms, or at least fall within the same **semantic field** or area, since they share the periphrastic definition 'despedir rayos de luz'. Other information given serves to discriminate them according to two principal parameters. *Centellear, destellar, relampaguear* and *titilar* involve intermittent or non-constant light by contrast with the other verbs in the list. Plotting on a scale of intensity is also possible: *lucir* and *titilar* come towards the bottom of this scale while *destellar, refulgir, relampaguear* and *resplandecer* are towards the top. Another possible parameter concerns whether the light emanates from the subject itself, or is reflected; this is not explicitly referred to except in the case of *brillar*, which is indifferent to this parameter, but it may be inferred from some of the examples given. *Brillar* occupies a special status, since it is the verb in terms of which many of the others are defined, and so it is likely that it is the broadest, that is to say, least specific, in meaning, and that the other verbs are in a hyponymic relation with it. This information could be summarised schematically by using a series of semantic features (Table 3.2):

Table 3.2 A featural characterisation of Spanish verbs for 'to shine'

	strong (+)/weak (−)	constant (+)/ intermittent (−)	own light (+)/ reflected light (−)
brillar			
centellear		−	−?
destellar	+	−	+?
lucir	−		+?
refulgir	+		+?
relampaguear	+	−	+
relucir			+?
relumbrar	+		−?
resplandecer	+		
titilar	−	−	+?

Interestingly, this is enough information to give the majority of words in this list a unique featural specification, even though many blanks have been left. Even the two verbs which are identically specified, *destellar* and *relampaguear*, could presumably be discriminated if further contexts were examined, since *relampaguear* is strongly associated with large-scale sources of light, such as lightning flashes and lighthouse beams, whereas *destellar* is more typical of smaller-scale objects such as jewellery or eyes.

The relations of near synyonymy, antonymy, hyponymy and position on a semantic scale hold between words which have the same syntactic function or fill the same 'slots' in a sentence, e.g.:

(3.25) near synonymy:

Rusia es un país { *enorme* / *gigantesco* / *colosal* }

antonymy:

Es un chico muy { *hermoso* / *feo* }

hyponymy:

En mi jardín hay muchas { *flores* / *rosas* / *margaritas* / *violetas* } positions on semantic scale:

Me { incomoda / enfada / cabrea } su falta de respeto (weakest ... strongest)

Such relations are known as **paradigmatic** relations, and it is fair to say that they have until relatively recently been the paramount consideration of dictionary-makers. However, paradigmatic relations may not in themselves be enough to chart the meaning of a word, and most learners of a foreign language will have had the experience of sometimes not being left much the wiser when a hitherto unknown word is described in this way. Equally important in establishing the meaning of words, especially when it comes to discriminating the meanings of near synonyms, are the contexts in which they can appropriately be used, and modern dictionaries are usually at pains to give contextualised examples of the usage of words. The relations a word contracts with its surrounding context are called **syntagmatic** relations. In (3.26), the verb *leer* is in syntagmatic relationship with its subject, *mi padre*, and its object, *el periódico*. Although it may seem at first sight that such a relationship is of purely syntactic importance, the links between these three elements have a semantic side too: the subject of *leer* must be a human (someone who is capable of reading) and the object must be something that contains the written word and thus susceptible of being read.

(3.26) *Mi padre* ⟵————————— *leía* —————————⟶ *el periódico*

(It may be helpful to think of these two dimensions of structural relationships, paradigmatic and syntagmatic, as being respectively 'vertical' and 'horizontal'.)

We have just seen how important syntagmatic relations were in discriminating *destellar* and *relampaguear*. Another example of a semantic area where context is crucial to an elucidation of meaning is in the Spanish words for the English notion of 'slice'. Spanish has a number of words, some of which are very specific as regards the contexts in which they are used:

(3.27) **a.** *Una rebanada de pan*

    b. *Una rodaja de* { *merluza / chorizo / pepino / limón / piña / ...* }

    c. *Una loncha de jamón*
    d. *Una raja de melón*
    e. *Una tajada de carne*

This does not mean that the establishing of paradigmatic relations, or the various strategies we have so far identified for defining words, are superfluous; on the contrary, it is helpful to know that *rodaja* is characterised by the idea of roundness, and that *raja* can be used of most things that are usually cut in several directions (thus *raja* tends not to be used of bread or ham, which are cut in specific ways) while *tajada*, while used especially of meat, also has the general idea of 'something cut'. All these words are in hyponymic relation with the general words for 'piece', *pedazo* and *trozo*.

Idioms are a very special case of the importance of syntagmatic relations. An **idiom** is precisely a syntagmatic sequence whose meaning does not equal the sum of the meanings of its individual constituents, or necessarily have anything to do even with any one of them. (It may also be that idioms are syntactically odd too, e.g. *a pie juntillas* 'to the letter, literally'.) Some examples are:

(3.28) idiom	literal meaning	actual meaning
hacer buenas migas con alguien	to make good crumbs with	to get on with
charlar por los codos	to chat through one's elbows	to talk incessantly
ser harina de otro costal	to be flour from another sack	to be a different matter

Miga, *codo* and *costal* do not have their normal meanings in these contexts; moreover, the contexts are fixed, and even slight modification will destroy their idiomatic value. Thus the following expressions would be semantically odd (they would be interpreted humorously, since the assumption would be that the speaker or writer had deliberately modified the idiom for stylistic effect):

(3.29) ¡*hacer migas enormes con alguien*[5]
        ¡*dibujar por los codos*
        ¡*ser harina del mismo costal*

Word meaning also has to do with much more elusive factors. Even setting aside the specialised context of idioms, words are not always used in their normal, or **literal**, meanings. They are sometimes used **figuratively**, in a 'transferred' or **metonymic** sense: this is especially common in poetry and other creative writing, and we shall examine some cases of such meanings in **8.2** when we consider figures of speech. But as we shall also see in **8.2**, the figurative use of words is all around us in everyday speech: the word *enlace*, for instance, not only means a literal link or tie (the notion that is still predominantly present in the corresponding verb *enlazar*) but also a connection in a very general figurative sense, such as a transport or communications link, or the relationship of marriage (in fact, it is often difficult to draw a clear dividing line between literal and figurative meaning in such commonly used words). Another kind of distinction we can make is between **denotative** meaning and

---

[5] An exclamation mark indicates that the sentence in question is semantically odd, even though syntactically acceptable, to a native speaker.

connotative meaning. Words which denote or refer to what is objectively the same notion may none the less differ because they are associated with different syntagmatic associations, or different registers (see Chapter 7). *Gordo* and *rollizo* both denote the notion of fatness; but while *gordo* has fairly neutral connotations, *rollizo* is particularly associated with babies, and would have a moderately insulting connotation if applied to adults.

3.5 Semantic fields and their structure

In **3.2** we looked at some formal relations between words and saw that formal relatedness does not necessarily imply close semantic relatedness. In this section we perform the converse operation of looking at the semantic relations which a word may contract with other words. We shall also examine more critically the notion of 'semantic field' which we introduced in **3.4**.[6]

The structure of a semantic field may be reflected in the form of its constituent words. Terms for some family relations in Spanish and English are an interesting example of this (see Table 3.3). In Spanish, male/female counterparts within each relationship category are often represented by distinctions of gender inflection; in English, on the other hand, such distinctions are made by discrete lexical items. But in English there is a consistent representation of the notion of 'next-but-one' generation (*grand-*), 'parent of' (*father / mother*) and 'child of' (*son / daughter*). English has a different lexical item again for the notion 'male + female counterparts' (*parents, siblings, children*) which in Spanish is expressed by a masculine plural (*padres, hermanos, hijos*). These English terms in the singular are unspecified as regards reference to sex; while in Spanish the masculine term can be used in this way, it does not uniquely have such an unspecified reference.

More often than not, however, there is no observable formal marking of such semantic features, and a much less **isomorphic** relation (form-by-form correspondence) between Spanish and other languages. Even the features themselves can be difficult to establish. Spanish and English both have many words which fall into the semantic field of 'thief', that is to say, a person who steals something from someone else. The two languages correspond in having a general word for this notion, Eng. *thief* and Sp. *ladrón*, though English has two other very general terms, *robber* and *swindler* (Spanish, perhaps surprisingly, has no agentive noun corresponding to the two principal verbs which mean 'to steal', *robar* and *hurtar*). English has specific terms for a thief who breaks into a house (*burglar, housebreaker*) and for a thief who steals game (*poacher*), while Spanish has no single-word equivalents for these notions. A comparison of some of the main words involved is given in Table 3.4.

In looking at family relations and 'thief' we have been in little doubt that these general notions are reasonably identifiable as semantic fields. Yet the identification and labelling of semantic fields itself is not always so straightforward. To what extent is it possible to organize the vocabulary of a language in semantic fields? This is the kind of concern of a

---

[6] An accessible account of semantic field theory is Lehrer (1974).

Table 3.3 Basic family relations in Spanish and English

English	Spanish	sex	generation	relation
father	*padre*	male	next	parent of
mother	*madre*	female	next	parent of
son	*hijo*	male	next	child of
daughter	*hija*	female	next	child of
brother	*hermano*	male	same	sibling of
sister	*hermana*	female	same	sibling of
grandson	*nieto*	male	next but one	child of
granddaughter	*nieta*	female	next but one	child of
grandfather	*abuelo*	male	next but one	parent of
grandmother	*abuela*	female	next but one	parent of
parents	*padres*	male + female	next	parent of
siblings	*hermanos*	male + female	same	sibling of
children	*hijos*	male + female	next	child of
grandparents	*abuelos*	male + female	next but one	parent of
grandchildren	*nietos*	male + female	next but one	child of
parent	*(padre)*	unspecified	next	parent of
sibling	*(hermano)*	unspecified	same	sibling of
child	*(madre)*	unspecified	next	child of
grandparent	*(abuelo)*	unspecified	next but one	parent of
grandchild	*(nieto)*	unspecified	next but one	child of

thesaurus, or semantically organised dictionary. In a thesaurus, the main entries are headwords which have a wide range of meaning, under which are grouped semantically related words which are more restricted in meaning or which partially overlap with the headword in their meaning. María Moliner (1998: xvi–xvii) considered that the whole vocabulary of Spanish could be structured in this way, that is to say, as a series of hyponymic relationships, and that the definition of a word is essentially a 'triangular' relation between the word itself, the generic category under which it immediately falls and the differentiating term which limits it meaning. The meaning of the word *silla*, for example, can be characterised as follows:

Table 3.4 Words for 'thief' in Spanish and English

General		Specific manner of theft		Specific object of theft	
Spanish	English	Spanish	English	Spanish	English
		Involving violence: *atracador*		Money: *desfalcador* *estafador*	*embezzler* *swindler* *fiddler*
		By breaking into a property:	*burglar* *housebreaker*	Items of small value: *garduño* *randa*	*pilferer*
		In the countryside: *bandido* *bandolero*	*bandit* *brigand*	Livestock: *cuatrero*	*rustler*
		On the road: *salteador*	*highwayman*	Animals or birds on private land:	*poacher*
		From property left vulnerable through disaster or war: *saqueador*	*looter* *pillager*		

ladrón	thief		
	robber		
		Taking something from a shop without paying:	shoplifter
		mechero	
		Taking something from someone's clothes:	pickpocket
		carterista	
		ratero	
		Giving wrong change or weight	
		sisador	
		timador	
		As a result of picking a lock:	picklock
		ganzúa	
		Opportunism:	
		descuidero	
		As a result of breaking into a safe:	cracksman

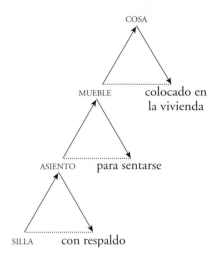

Figure 3.1 *Silla* as part of a series of hyponymic relations (after Moliner 1966, I: facing xvi)

It is an interesting question as to whether one could devise a list of headwords that would be universal to all languages.[7] The assumption behind many thesauruses is that this is the case. However, what may appear to be a suitable headword on the basis of one language does not necessarily hold for another. The English notion of 'feeling' may appear to label a discrete semantic 'field', but there is no exact equivalent for such an over-arching notion in Spanish. Spanish distinguishes a number of general notions in this area, which can be categorised roughly as follows:

Table 3.5 Spanish words corresponding to the English notion of 'feeling'

Physical	ability to feel	*sensibilidad*	*He perdido la sensibilidad en mis pies* 'I've lost the feeling in my feet'
	sense of feeling	*tacto*	*Por el tacto, supe que era un objeto redondo* 'By feeling, I knew that it was a round object'
	quality which is sensitive to the sense of feeling	*tacto*	*Los aguacates tienen un tacto rugoso* 'Avocados have a rough feel'
	result of external agency	*sensación*	*De repente me acometió una sensación de dolor muy agudo* 'Suddenly a feeling of acute pain assailed me'

---

[7] For a limited attempt at such an enterprise, see Wierzbicka (1996); also Lehrer (1974: 150–2).

Table 3.5 *continued*

Emotional	internal, natural emotion	*sentimiento*	*El amor es tal vez el más fuerte de los sentimientos* 'Love is perhaps the strongest of the feelings'
	demonstrated sensitivity	*sentimiento*	*Tocó la sonata con sentimiento* 'She played the sonata with feeling'
	result of external agency	*sensación*	*Me produjo una sensación de miedo* 'It caused me a feeling of fear'
	ability to feel	*sensibilidad*	*Carece casi totalmente de sensibilidad hacia la música* 'He is almost totally lacking in feeling for music'
Intellectual		*opinión*	*Mi opinión es que hay que buscar un patrocinador* 'My feeling is that we should seek a sponsor'

There are of course, as in English, many words which are in a hyponymic relation with the words in the table and which denote more specific kinds of feeling, such as *dolor* 'pain' (physical), 'grief' (emotional), *molestia* 'discomfort' (physical), *desasosiego* 'unease', *miedo* 'fear', *angustia* 'anguish, distress' (emotional), *convicción* 'conviction', *recelo* 'mistrust, suspicion', *impresión* 'impression' (intellectual), but we will limit our discussion here to the more general terms. It can be seen that these sometimes span more than one notional category, especially the physical and the emotional: *sensación* is characterised by more than anything else by the idea of the feeling produced by external agency and *sensibilidad* by the notion of the ability to feel. The words in the table themselves have other meanings: *sentimientos* often has the more specific meaning of 'good feelings', as in *no tienes sentimientos* 'you have no (good) feelings'; *tacto* means 'tact'; *sensibilidad* 'sensitivity' also applies to a scientific measuring instrument (a notion for which 'feeling' is not used in English), and *sensación* means 'sensation' in the sense of 'momentous news'.

EXERCISES

1. The alternation between /e/ and /i/ and, less frequently, between /o/ and /u/ in certain tenses of a number of *-ir* verbs has been the subject of much discussion among Spanish linguists. Are there any phonetic factors on which the appearance of /i/ might depend? Consider the following:

sentí	sintió	sintiera	dormí	durmió	durmiera
sentiste	sintieron	sintieras	dormiste	durmieron	durmieras
sentimos		sintiera	dormimos		durmiera
sentisteis		sintiéramos	dormisteis		durmiéramos
		sintiérais			durmiérais
		sintieran			durmieran

2. Spanish has a great many nouns ending in *-ión* which are sometimes said to be 'formed from' verbs. Looking at the following list, can you detect which might be thought of as being in a regular relationship with a verb, which might be thought of as being in a 'semi-regular' relationship (see **3.2**), and which might be thought of as being completely irregular? (Look for other examples of your own, and try and get an impression from a dictionary of the relative numbers involved. If you can find a 'reverse' dictionary, i.e. one that lists words in reverse alphabetical order, you will find this easier; electronic dictionaries usually have such a facility, or see Stahl & Scavnicky 1973.)

aceptar	acepción	optar	opción
corregir	corrección	percibir	percepción
corromper	corrupción	prohibir	prohibición
dirigir	dirección	reaccionar	reacción
imaginar	imaginación	suspender	suspensión
infectar	infección	transcribir	transcripción
introducir	introducción		

3. Here are some of the other words which Moliner includes as being in a hyponymic relation with *asiento*:

> banco, banqueta, butaca, diván, mecedora, puf, sillín, sillón, sofá, taburete, trono

How might they be distinguished?

4 | Spanish sentences and their structure

In this chapter we are going to look at some features of Spanish **syntax**, or sentence structure. Spanish syntax is on the whole very well described in the large reference grammars of Spanish, and it would be superfluous and inappropriate to try and condense such compendious material into a few pages in this book. The intention here is therefore to give a slightly different slant to the description of Spanish syntax by concentrating on a number of issues which may set you thinking further:

- What do we mean by a 'sentence'?
- How many different sentence types are there?
- Why do sentences contain different types of constituent?
- What is the relation between syntactic functions and meaning?
- Do different registers of Spanish (see Chapter 7) have different syntaxes?

4.1 What is a sentence?

The notion of a **sentence** (*frase* or, more formally, ***oración*** in Spanish), like that of a word, is notoriously elusive, and it is probably not possible to give any linguistically rigorous definition of the term. Within traditional grammar, however, we find two kinds of definition, both essentially arbitrary, which have won wide acceptance in normative and pedagogical circles. One is semantic in nature, and usually runs along the lines that a sentence expresses a 'complete thought'. A typical example is the following:

> La intención del hablante divide la locución en <u>unidades de sentido completo en sí mismas llamadas *oraciones*</u> (*Esbozo* 1973: 349; my underlining)

It is difficult to envisage any rigorous notion of what might constitute a 'complete thought'; in practice, it probably amounts to much the same thing as the usual syntactically-based definition, which characterises a sentence as a structure which has a 'subject' and a '**predicate**' (by 'predicate' is meant what is said about the subject, including the verb and its objects and adverbial elements which express such notions as time, place, manner, cause, etc.). Thus:

> Frase simple es la que consta de un sujeto y un predicado (Alonso 1968: 163).

The latter kind of definition has been particularly influential, leading to the insistence that all 'full' sentences must contain a verb as the minimum element of the predicate, with the result that indeed all sentences in the educated written language, in Spanish as well as English, satisfy this requirement. Such sentences as the following illustrate this pattern (the subject is underlined):

> (4.1)   a.   <u>Juan</u> estaba preparando su tesina.
>   b.   <u>Mi hermano</u> vive en Madrid.
>   c.   <u>Este libro</u> es difícil.

4.1.1 Spanish as a 'pro-drop' language

In Spanish, the subject need not be present, or overt; its number and person are sometimes said to be 'understood' from the verbal inflection. In sentences (4.2a–b) the 'understood' subject is given in brackets, but the identity of these pronouns is already deducible from the verb-forms *soy* and *vamos*:

> (4.2)   a.   (<u>Yo</u>) soy muy aficionado a la lectura.
>   b.   (<u>Nosotros</u>) vamos esta noche al cine.

Third person verb-forms are slightly different, however: their subject can be understood as a variety of pronouns (*él, ella, usted* in the singular), or as a full noun as in (4.1a–c). None the less, once the identity of a third person subject is known, its restatement is often unnecessary in Spanish, except to resolve ambiguity. In modern grammatical terminology, a language which has this property is sometimes known as a **pro-drop** language, because it can 'drop' the subject pronoun which is obligatory in a language like English or French. Personal pronoun subjects are for this reason often described as being 'optional' in Spanish; but while from a strictly syntactic point of view this is true, their presence usually produces a rather different meaning, and so from the functional point of view they are not optional if such a meaning is intended. One such function is that of contrastive stress (see 2.7.1.1): to omit *yo* as in (4.3a) would actually make the sentence odd (4.3b):[1]

> (4.3)   a.   Pedro no quiere salir, pero yo sí que quiero.
>   b.   ''Pedro no quiere salir, pero sí que quiero.

4.1.2 Impersonal verbs

Some verbs in Spanish never take a subject at all, however; one such group of verbs are the so-called **impersonal verbs**, which typically denote the weather:

> (4.4)   a.   Llueve a cántaros.
>   b.   Empieza a nevar.

---

[1] Some other discourse functions of the subject pronoun are described in Stewart (1999: 108–10).

Notice how in the English translations of these sentences a 'dummy' subject, *it*, is used: '<u>It</u>'s raining cats and dogs', '<u>It</u>'s beginning to snow'; this is entirely consistent with the fact that in English the expression of a syntactic subject is always obligatory. Another, more general, category of verbs in Spanish which apparently have no subject are 'indefinite subject' reflexives; the presence of an overt subject with such verbs, as in (4.5b), results in a quite different meaning:

> **(4.5)** **a.** *Se ha criticado mucho a los dirigentes de la lotería.*
> 'People have criticised the directors of the lottery a lot'
> **b.** *Uno / La gente se ha criticado.*
> 'People have criticised themselves'

In principle, any verb in Spanish, except for verbs which are inherently reflexive (such as *arrepentirse*: there is no non-reflexive verb **arrepentir*), can belong to this category; we shall look again at this interesting construction in 5.4.1.

4.2 'Sentences' in the spoken language

If we look at actual speech we find that many utterances which are perfectly intelligible within the discourse do not contain a verb. Here are some examples:

> **(4.6)** **a.** *Sí.*
> **b.** *En Madrid.* (in answer to *¿Dónde vives?*)
> **c.** *Porque está prohibido.* (in answer to *¿Por qué no nos podemos bañar?*)

This is because spoken language in particular exhibits a high degree of **ellipsis** (omission of words), or, put another way, tries to minimise redundancy. The answer to a question, for instance, usually consists only of an indication of whether a statement is true or false (in the case of a polar question, answered by *sí* or *no*) or of the information that is actually sought: a question beginning with *¿dónde?* will be answered, as in (4.6b), by the corresponding locative adverbial phrase, and the answer to a question beginning with *¿Por qué?* will consist simply of the reason, as in (4.6c).

The view that all sentences must contain a verb stems from the priority given in pedagogical grammar from Classical times to the cultured written language. The very notion of ellipsis on which we have called to describe sentences of the spoken language implies a shortfall with respect to the prescriptive norm; it is an interesting question as to whether utterances like (4.6a–c) really do have something 'missing'. However, in such utterances it is possible to reconstruct, or 'recover' material from the discourse context. (4.6a) implies the affirmation of whatever sentence has formed the basis of the question just asked; (4.6b) implies *[Vivo] en Madrid* and (4.6c) implies *[No nos podemos bañar] porque [el bañarse] está prohibido.*

4.3 The constituent elements of a sentence: the valency of verbs

In looking at relations between the constituent parts of sentences, it is desirable to maintain a rigorous distinction between semantic, or functional, relations and syntactic, or formal, relations, and I will as far as possible use different terminology to make this distinction clear. It is also important not to confuse these syntactic and semantic relations with the morphological categories ('parts of speech') to which constituent elements of the sentence belong.

For the reasons given in **4.1** and **4.2**, we will assume that Spanish sentences archetypically contain a verb. Indeed, the verb may be regarded as the pivotal element of the sentence, the element on which all other major elements depend and in terms of which they may be defined. Consider the following sentence:

(4.7) *Juan dio una caja de bonbones a mi hermana para su cumpleaños*

(This is not necessarily the most natural way of expressing this notion, but it will keep things as simple as possible for the time being.) The verb in (4.7) is *dio*, and it has four major **arguments**, or elements which relate to it. I will describe each of these arguments in turn, from both the semantic and functional point of view, as well as noting the parts of speech which are used:

Table 4.1 The arguments of *dar*

Argument	Semantic relation with verb (semantic labels will be shown in small capitals)	Syntactic relation with verb	Part(s) of speech (morphological categories) involved
Juan	Juan is the person who carries out the action of the verb: the AGENT.	*Juan* is the **subject** of the verb; this is shown in Spanish by the agreement of the verb, which is in the third person singular.	Noun.
una caja de bombones	The box of sweets undergoes the action of the verb: the PATIENT.	*Una caja de bonbones* is the **direct object** of the verb; in this case there is no formal marking of this function (but see **5.2**).	A noun phrase consisting of a noun (*caja*) preceded by an indefinite article and a prepositional phrase consisting of a preposition + noun.
mi hermana	My sister is the recipient of, or benefits from, the action of the verb: the BENEFICIARY	*Mi hermana* is the **indirect object** of the verb, indicated by the preposition *a*.	A noun phrase consisting of a noun preceded by a possessive adjective or determiner.
para su cumpleaños	This expresses the PURPOSE or motive of the gift.	*Para su cumpleaños* is an adverbial phrase; it qualifies, or gives more precise information about, the verbal activity. Adverbs may be single words (many of these end in *-mente*) or, as here, a prepositional phrase, consisting of a preposition + noun phrase.	A prepositional phrase consisting of a preposition + noun.

Verbs differ very greatly in the collocational possibilities they permit for their dependent elements, a property that is sometimes termed the **valency** of the verb. It is possible for a number of valency patterns to be associated with the same verb. *Cobrar*, for example, participates in the following valency patterns, reflected in the differing English translations:

> **(4.8)** **a.** *La empresa le cobró a Pedro 80 euros*
> 'The company charged Pedro 80 euros'
> **b.** *Pedro cobra 1.600 euros al mes*
> 'He earns 1.600 euros a month'

In (4.8a), *cobrar* takes three principal arguments: a subject, which is the AGENT of the charging; an object which is the AMOUNT CHARGED, and an object who PAYS THE AMOUNT CHARGED. In (4.8b), it has two principal arguments: an object which is the AMOUNT EARNED and a subject who is the BENEFICIARY. It can be seen that this verb has a very particular argument structure with regard to the type of noun that can fill the various argument slots.

Syntactic relations, semantic relations and syntactic category are all relevant to the definition of valencies, and I will deal with each of these briefly in turn.

4.3.1 Syntactic relations

The Spanish verb *gustar* takes a subject and an indirect object, though not a direct object. In

> **(4.9)** *A Juan le gustan las gambas*

las gambas is the subject, as can be seen from the fact that the verb, *gustan*, agrees with it in the third person plural, and *Juan* is the indirect object, indicated by the preposition *a*. The verb *saber*, on the other hand, usually takes a direct object (4.10a), but cannot take an indirect object, as shown by the strangeness of (4.10b):

> **(4.10) a.** *María sabía la respuesta*
> **b.** **María le sabía la respuesta a Juan*

A distinction is usually made in traditional grammar and in most modern dictionaries between two basic valency types: verbs which take direct objects (**transitive** verbs) and those which do not (**intransitive** verbs). A category of verbs which does not easily fit into this binary classification but which has been recognised in traditional grammar is that of the **copulas** (i.e. verbs like *be* and *become*, which will be the subject of further discussion in **5.5**. Copular verbs are often said to take '**complements**' rather than objects, and we shall maintain this traditional terminology, even though we will also use the term 'complement' to refer to embedded sentences (see **4.3.3**). Though very firmly entrenched and convenient to maintain for some purposes, the categories of transitive and intransitive are in fact far too general. For example, some dictionaries draw a distinction in their entry for the verb *pagar* between a 'transitive' and an 'intransitive' usage: the *Oxford Spanish Dictionary (OSD)*, p. 534, classifies (4.11a–c) as 'transitive' and (4.11d–f) as 'intransitive':

(4.11) **a.** *Sus abuelos le pagan los estudios*
      b. *¿Cuánto pagas de alquiler?*
      c. *¿Y pagaste $100 por esa porquería?*
      d. *Pagan bien*
      e. *Quiero pagar al contado*
      f. *¿Le has pagado a la limpiadora?*

The basis for this is actually rather arbitrary. *Pagar* takes a number of different kinds of object: one kind of object is what is paid for (PURCHASE) (*los estudios* in 4.11a, *alquiler* in 4.11b); another is the amount paid (PAYMENT) (*¿Cuánto?* in 4.11b and *$100* in 4.11c), and another is the person who receives payment (PAYEE) (*le* in 4.11a and *la limpiadora* in 4.11f). Sometimes more than one of these objects can be used simultaneously (PURCHASE and PAYEE in 4.11a, PURCHASE and PAYMENT in 4.11b–c). What test could we apply to see which of the (at least) three types of object of *pagar* is the 'direct' object? One assumption about direct objects which is sometimes made is that, unless they are 'personal', they are not introduced by a preposition. All three kinds of object could be considered to be 'direct' on this basis. PAYMENT is never introduced by a preposition. PAYEE is usually 'personal' and would therefore always be introduced by *a*. The use of prepositions with PURCHASE varies: PURCHASE is introduced by a preposition if there is also PAYMENT, as in (4.11b–c), but takes no preposition otherwise (4.11a). Another criterion for establishing which is the direct object concerns patterns of pronominalisation, a noun which can be substituted by *lo(s)* or *la(s)* being a direct object and a noun which can be substituted by *le(s)* an indirect object (this criterion would of course not apply to a *leísta* area – see **6.2.3.1.3**). On this ground, PAYEE might seem to be the least likely candidate as 'direct' object because it is pronominalised by *le(s)* (4.11a and f). PURCHASE is pronominalised by a direct object pronoun, so (4.11a) could become *sus abuelos se los pagan*; PAYMENT cannot be pronominalised, so (4.11c) cannot become *'¿Y los pagaste por esa porquería?*. A third criterion for direct objects is that they can form the subject of passive sentences, which indirect objects in Spanish usually cannot: thus (4.12b), the passive of (4.12a), is acceptable but (4.12b) is not:

(4.12) **a.** *Pedro dio el libro* ('direct' object) *a María* ('indirect' object)
      b. *El libro fue dado a María (por Pedro)*
      c. **María fue dada el libro (por Juan)*

In formal register, PURCHASE can be the subject of a corresponding passive sentence, e.g. *Sus estudios le fueron pagados por sus abuelos* (corresponding to 4.11a). Rather less usually, so can PAYEE:

(4.13) *Brown no volvió a los emparrillados y fue despedido por los Cafés en septiembre del 2000. Pero fue pagado por los tres primeros partidos de la temporada.* (Terra Lycos,
http://www.terra.com.mx//deportes/articulo/061686/)

PAYMENT is more resistant to passivisation: a sentence such as *'Quinientos dólares fueron pagados por el libro* is unusual to the point of unacceptability, although such nouns representing PAYMENT as *factura, importe, precio, dinero,* etc. can be the subject of a passive sentence:

(4.14) *El importe pendiente fue pagado en su totalidad a los proyectos SM/PO/7/91 y SM/ES/17/91* (EUR-Lex, http://europa.eu.int/ eur-lex/es/lif/dat/1998/es_398Y1216_02.html)

Thus none of these tests gives us a firm syntactic criterion for the identification of a 'direct' object, though *OSD* appears to have assumed that both PURCHASE and PAYMENT can constitute a direct object.[2] It might be thought that the *OSD*'s division rests on surer ground when *pagar* takes no object at all, as in (4.11d–e), but the use of *pagar* in (4.11d–e) is not 'intransitive' in the way that such verbs as *ir, salir, tiritar* and *morir* are 'intransitive'. The latter simply cannot have direct objects under any circumstances; but in (4.11b) *pagar* seems to maintain essentially the same meaning as it has in (4.11a), even though in this case it has no object overtly expressed. Many other common verbs behave like *pagar* in this respect: some examples are *comer, enseñar, escuchar, esperar, leer* and *saber,* e.g.:

(4.15) a. *Mi padre leía el periódico*
     b. *Mi padre leía*

(4.16) a. *Me gusta enseñar el francés*
     b. *Me gusta enseñar*

Another subclass of transitive verbs which it may be useful to distinguish is that of **causative**. In (4.17a) *la fragata* is traditionally considered the direct object of *hundir,* and hence *hundir* is classified as transitive; but *hundir* is different from other purely transitive verbs in that its AGENT is the perpetrator, or CAUSE, of something which happens to the object. (4.17a) can thus be paraphrased by (4.17b) in a way that (4.18a) cannot be paraphrased by (4.18b):

(4.17) a. *El crucero hundió la fragata*
     b. *= El crucero hizo que se hundiera la fragata*

(4.18) a. *El marinero vio la fragata*
     b. *≠ El marinero hizo que se viese la fragata*

4.3.2 Semantic relations

As examples of the importance of semantic relations in the description of the valency of a verb, we will consider the verbs *costar* and *subir.*

In the sentence

(4.19) *Este collar me costó veinte mil pesos*

---

[2] I discuss this issue in greater detail in Pountain (1993).

the noun subject of *costar*, *este collar*, can hardly be described as an AGENT, since it does not perform any activity; similarly, the object, *veinte mil pesos*, is not appropriately described as a PATIENT. The object of *costar* is in fact always a VALUE which is predicated of something.

In the sentence

(4.20) *María bajó la escalera*

la escalera, the apparent direct object of *bajar*, is not so much the PATIENT of the verb as the expression of a MEANS.

We can see, therefore, that syntactic subjects and objects do not always have the same semantic function vis-à-vis the verb: in particular, it should now be apparent that the subject is not always an AGENT and the direct object is not always a PATIENT.

4.3.3 Syntactic category

Syntactic functions other than subject and direct object are indicated by the use of prepositions in Spanish. One important difference to note between English and Spanish is that while in English an indirect object sometimes does not take the preposition *to*, in Spanish an indirect object formed from a full noun always takes the preposition *a*:

(4.21) *John lent <u>Mary</u> a biro*
　　　　 Juan le dejó un boli <u>a María</u>

Another, well-known, difference between Spanish and many other languages is that certain direct objects in Spanish take the preposition *a*, a phenomenon known as the 'personal' *a* (in Spanish *a* personal); this is discussed more extensively in **5.2**.

Prepositions have many other functions apart from signalling direct and indirect objects, and it is a matter of some debate as to which of these functions are involved in the valency of the verb and which are so loosely connected with individual verbs that they play no significant part in the specification of its valency (see Blake 1994: 32–4, who proposes a distinction between 'core' and 'peripheral' cases). One function which appears to be closely connected with the valency of the verb is that of INSTRUMENT, often signalled by the preposition *con* in Spanish:

(4.22) *Susana recortó el anuncio con <u>unas tijeras</u>*

It would seem that from a semantic point of view an instrument is an essential part of the structure of *recortar* and similar verbs, since they typically involve an agent who must use an instrument in order to carry out the action of the verb. On the other hand, the function of PRIVATION, which is indicated by the preposition *sin*, does not seem to be so closely tied to particular verbs, but is rather a piece of supplementary, non-integral information.

(4.23) *Nos vamos de vacaciones sin nuestra hija menor*

Subject and object functions can also sometimes be performed by other sentences, or **clauses**, which are then said to be **embedded** in the main sentence and are often referred to as **complements** of the verb. Embedded sentences are instantly recognisable because they, like the main sentence, have their own verb as the essential component; in Spanish, the verb may be a **finite** verb (in which the person and number of the subject are indicated by the verbal ending, e.g. *hablamos, creyesen, mantuvo,* etc.; this kind of complement is introduced by the complementiser *que*) or as an infinitive (e.g. *hablar, creer, haber mantenido*). For example, verbs of thinking and perception usually have an embedded sentence as their direct object: in the sentences of (4.24), the embedded sentences are single-underlined, their verbs are double-underlined and a schematic representation of what might be construed as the 'full' sentence follows.

> **(4.24) a.** *Creemos que ha habido irregularidades en las elecciones*
> *Creemos [ha habido irregularidades en las elecciones]*
> **b.** *Vi salir a los niños*
> *Vi [los niños salían]*

An example of a Spanish verb which takes a subject complement is *extrañar*; note that the subject complement may precede (4.25a) or follow (4.25b) the verb and has a slightly different form accordingly:

> **(4.25) a.** *El que decidiera marcharse me extrañó*
> **b.** *Me extrañó que decidiera marcharse*
> *[Decidió marcharse] me extrañó*

We shall return to a discussion of complement structures in **4.5.1**.

4.3.4 The interplay of syntax and semantics in the valencies of verbs

The various elements involved in the valency of the verb may relate to the verb in different structural ways. Consider the following sentences:

> **(4.26) a.** *Cargaron el camión con cien cajas de fusiles*
> **b.** *Cargaron cien cajas de fusiles en el camión*

The semantic relation between the verb *cargar,* the nouns *camión* and the noun phrase *cien cajas de fusiles* is the same in both instances: the boxes of rifles are the PATIENT, the element which directly undergoes the action of the verb and the lorry is what may be called the EXPERIENCER, the element that is affected by the verbal activity. From the point of view of syntactic relations, however, *camión* is the direct object of (4.26a) but part of a prepositional complement in (4.26b); conversely, *cien cajas de fusiles* is the direct object of (4.26b) but part of a prepositional complement in (4.26a). The specification of such various configurational possibilities is part of the valency structure of the verb *cargar*.

The pattern observable in (4.26) appears to be particular to *cargar*. Even semantically quite closely related verbs are unlike *cargar* in this respect: *llenar, colmar* and *abrumar*, for example, only take the EXPERIENCER as their direct object – hence the oddity of (4.27b):

(4.27) a. *Llenaron el vaso de agua*
b. *⁇Llenaron agua en el vaso*

Some valency patterns are much more general, however. One is the relation between what are traditionally known as **active** and **passive** sentences, which is typical of transitive verbs (see also **4.3.4.1**):

(4.28) a. *Picasso pintó este cuadro* (active)
b. *Este cuadro fue pintado por Picasso* (passive)

In sentence (4.28a), the noun *Picasso* is the subject of the verb *pintó*, and also its AGENT; *este cuadro* is the direct object and the PATIENT. In (4.28b) *este cuadro* becomes the syntactic subject of the verb and *Picasso* is part of a prepositional complement introduced by *por*; but the semantic functions of the two nouns remain the same (and indeed the meaning of the two sentences is basically the same). The verb also changes in form, and in the passive sentence consists of the verb *ser* followed by the past participle of *pintar*. This pattern is so general that the relation between active and passive sentences is often presented as being purely formal, or syntactic, in nature; but it can quickly be seen that the semantic function of the subject and the direct object of transitive verbs also has a role to play, even though such constraints are currently not yet fully understood. For instance, if the subject of the active sentence is not also the AGENT of the verb and the direct object not also the PATIENT, then passivisation seems to be prohibited. In

(4.29) a. *Marta espera el autobús*
b. **El autobús es esperado por Marta*

there is no true agent-patient relation between *Marta* and *el autobús*, since Marta is not actually doing anything to the bus; in some ways Marta is more of an EXPERIENCER and the bus is not so much a patient as a more neutral OBJECT. Another such case is (4.20), in which the direct object is a MEANS and the subject is not obviously an AGENT, since María is not doing anything to the stairs; (4.30) is impossible as an equivalent of (4.20):

(4.30) **La escalera fue bajada por María*

However, *bajar* does have another configurational possibility in its sense of 'to bring down'. Here, the subject is also the AGENT and the direct object the PATIENT, so (4.31a) does have the passive equivalent (4.31b):

(4.31) a. *Juan bajó las maletas*
b. *Las maletas fueron bajadas por Juan*

4.3.4.1 ACTIVE AND PASSIVE

The relation between active and passive sentences has been much discussed in descriptive syntax. It was one of the first structural syntactic relations to be described by Noam

Chomsky in his elaboration of 'transformational generative grammar' (Chomsky 1957). However, it is a much more fundamental and important relation in the syntactic structure of English than in that of Spanish. Passivisation is much less constrained in English: indirect objects and even prepositional objects can become the syntactic subjects of passive verbs in English in a way that is quite impossible in Spanish:

> **(4.32) a.** *Mary's boyfriend gave her a necklace → Mary was given a necklace by her boyfriend*
>
> **b.** *El novio de María le regaló un collar → *María fue regalada un collar por su novio*

> **(4.33) a.** *The candidate has already written on this paper → This paper has already been written on by the candidate*
>
> **b.** *El candidato ya ha escrito en este papel → *Este papel ya ha sido escrito en por el candidato*

Not only do the two languages differ in this systematic way, but in Spanish there appear also to be many more idiosyncratic constraints on the passivisation of individual verbs than in English. It has often been noted that sentences such as the following, which parallel passive constructions in English, as can be seen from the translations given, are unacceptable in Spanish, though all the verbs otherwise appear to be transitive: no systematic principle to account for their unacceptability has so far emerged.

> **(4.34) a.** **La calle fue limpiada por el empleado*
> *The street was cleaned by the workman*
>
> **b.** **La ventana fue rota por el muchacho*
> *The window was broken by the boy*
>
> **c.** **Los ancianos fueron cansados por el viaje*
> *The old people were tired by the journey*

Furthermore, the *ser* + past participle passive construction is extremely infrequent in spoken register and is often resisted as being 'unnatural' by Spanish native speakers. Having said that, it must be emphasised that the construction is not at all infrequent in formal written register, especially in journalism, and so is not in such circumstances necessarily to be avoided (Green 1975). On the other hand, it has incurred the wrath of prescriptivists who see in its frequent use even in these registers evidence of the influence of English, of which, as we have seen, it is a stereotypical characteristic (Lorenzo 1996: 622–30).

4.3.4.2 REFLEXIVE

In Spanish, we must consider another construction which is systematically related to the active and passive, and hence to verbal valency in general: the reflexive. The reflexive is often used in a way which resembles the *ser* + past participle construction, to the extent that it is now increasingly referred to as a 'passive'. In such reflexive constructions, the patient is in fact the syntactic subject of the verb, just as in the *ser* + past participle passive:

(4.35) a. *Vendían las naranjas a 20 pesos el kilo → Las naranjas se vendían a 20 pesos el kilo*

b. *No puedes escribir así una tesina de licenciatura → Una tesina de licenciatura no se escribe así*

However, this reflexive construction is not exactly the equivalent of the *ser* + past participle construction. Most obviously, it cannot freely have an agent expressed (4.36a–b) – though, as sentences (4.36c–d) show, not all configurations of verbs and apparent agents appear to be subject to this constraint:

(4.36) a. *Las señoras vendían las naranjas a 20 pesos el kilo → ?Las naranjas se vendían a 20 pesos el kilo por las señoras*

b. *Teresa ha escrito una tesina de licenciatura → ?Una tesina de licenciatura se ha escrito por Teresa*

c. *Espasa-Calpe publica las obras de referencia de la Real Academia Española → Las obras de referencia de la Real Academia Española se publican por Espasa-Calpe*

d. *Los dos ministros firmarán mañana el nuevo convenio → El nuevo convenio se firmará mañana por los dos ministros*

In fact, the meanings of the reflexive passive and the *ser* + past participle passive are not exactly the same. The reflexive passive does not have the same dynamic nature as the *ser* + past participle passive (this no doubt connected with the difficulty in the expression of an agent with the reflexive passive and with the need for there to be a true agent-patient relation in the *ser* + past participle passive). This is very clear, for example, in the case of (4.35a), where *las naranjas se vendían* has the stative meaning of 'the oranges were on sale' while *las naranjas eran vendidas* would have the dynamic (and pragmatically more unlikely) meaning of 'the oranges were being (actively) sold'. The reflexive passive has indeed sometimes been described as a '**middle**' voice, corresponding to the English notion of 'to get done' rather than 'to be done'. The reflexive is also, not surprisingly in the light of what we have just seen, used for activities in which no agent is involved:

(4.37) a. *La puerta se abrió* 'The door opened'

b. *Se me perdieron las llaves* 'My keys have got lost'

4.3.5 Differing valencies in English and Spanish

The discussion in **4.3.4** leads naturally on to the observation that many structural differences between Spanish and English can be described in terms of the differing valencies of what superficially may appear to be similar verbs (similar, that is, in the sense that in a dictionary, one is given as a lexical equivalent of the other). This approach to comparing the two languages has not been widely followed in the past, although modern dictionaries have begun to give attention in their lexical entries to much of the relevant data. This book can only scratch the surface of what is an enormous project, and I offer here one or two general observations and a case study; readers may like to undertake more themselves.

4.3.5.1 GENERAL

One very striking property of English verbs is that the same verb can have both a transitive and an intransitive valency without undergoing any morphological modification, whereas in Spanish the intransitive valency is often marked morphologically by a reflexive:

(4.38)		English	Spanish
	a.	Peter melted the ice	Pedro derritió el hielo
	b.	The ice melted	El hielo se derritió
	c.	The teacher shut the door	La profesora cerró la puerta
	d.	The door shut	La puerta se cerró
	e.	I tore the paper	Rasgué el papel
	f.	The paper tore	Se rasgó el papel

It is for this reason that the Spanish reflexive is often described as having an 'intransitive' function in some reference grammars (see, for example, Butt & Benjamin 2000: 355–7), though it is very close to, if not identical with, the 'middle' function we noted in **4.3.4.2**. Another characteristic of English is that verbs which are truly reflexive or reciprocal may sometimes maintain this reflexive or reciprocal valency (often characterised as intransitive) even when a reflexive or reciprocal pronoun object is not expressed; this never happens in Spanish:

(4.39)	a.	John didn't wash for a week (= John didn't wash himself...)	Juan no se lavó durante una semana
	b.	The friends met in Madrid (= The friends met each other / one another...)	Los amigos se conocieron
	c.	Eggs and butter mix easily (= Eggs and butter mix easily with one another)	Los huevos y la mantequilla se mezclan fácilmente

4.3.5.2 A CASE STUDY

The verb *fly* is multivalent in English, and it corresponds to Spanish *volar* only in a limited number of valencies. We will restrict our attention to those usages which clearly have something to do with literally travelling through the air. Consider the following translation equivalents:

(4.40)	a.	The plane flew to Singapore	El avión voló a Singapur
	b.	John flew to Singapore	Juan voló a Singapur
	c.	John flew the plane to Singapore	Juan pilotó el avión a Singapur
	d.	The company flew John to Singapore	La empresa le pagó a Juan el avión a Singapur

(4.40a) may perhaps be regarded as the basic usage of *fly*, denoting the manner in which the plane travelled. *The plane* is in itself a machine capable of flight; *John*, on the other hand, in

(4.40b), is in a slightly different relation to the verb, since he is not capable of flight; the sentence implies that he travelled on a vehicle which could fly. Both these intransitive patterns can be translated by Spanish *volar*, and so the precise differencies in valency relations are not important to a contrastive study of English and Spanish. In any case, pragmatic considerations discriminate the two valencies. (4.40c and d) are both causative usages of *fly* in which the agent, in different ways, causes flight to take place: in (4.40c) John causes the plane to fly, as in (4.40a), while in (4.40d) the company enables John to travel by air in the sense of (4.40b). Neither of these causative valencies is available to Spanish *volar*, and so the English meanings have to be rendered in Spanish much more explicitly.

4.4 Other simple sentence types

So far we have been looking for the most part at **declarative sentences**, that is, sentences which make a statement. Sentences may perform other functions; sometimes the function is reflected in a distinctive syntactic structure, but sometimes the match between form and function is not straightforward.

4.4.1 Interrogative sentences

The syntax of interrogative sentences, or questions, is often not significantly different from that of declarative sentences in Spanish. Polar questions (see **4.2**) are often signalled by nothing more than a rising terminal juncture in speech (see **2.7.2**) and by the use of question marks in writing.   Questions introduced by an interrogative element (sometimes known as a ***wh*-word** in English) are more distinctive superficially, but may similarly have a rising terminal juncture. A third kind of question is the **tag-question**. In English the syntax of such questions is complex: an inverted auxiliary verb construction is used, and the polarity of the tag can indicate an invitation to agree or disagree; in Spanish a much simpler tag, generally *¿verdad?* or *¿no?*, with a rising terminal juncture, is used:

(4.41) English

She doesn't know, does she?
She does know, doesn't she?
She knows, does she?

Spanish

No lo sabe, ¿verdad?
Lo sabe, ¿verdad?
Cannot be rendered by a tag-question in Spanish

4.4.2 Imperative sentences

Imperative sentences (sentences which express a command) are often characterised by the use of an imperative verb form, which usually stands first in the sentence and has no overt subject; in the positive imperative, clitic pronouns are placed after the verb, but in the negative imperative any clitic pronouns precede:

(4.42) a.   *¡Dale un beso a Papá!*
b.   *¡No me vengan con excusas!*

Both (4.42a and b) are second-person imperatives, in which the speaker (the first person) is ordering the interlocutor (the second person) to do or not to do something. Pragmatically speaking, this is the only situation in which true ordering can take place. However, because of the syntactic similarities to the second-person imperative, the term 'imperative' is often applied to situations such as the following:

(4.43) a.   *¡Vámonos en seguida!*
b.   *¡Que no digan nada de eso!*
c.   *Agítese bien*

In (4.43a), a suggestion is being made to a group of two or more people which includes the speaker. (4.43b), logically, is a more indirect kind of command or the expression of a wish; indeed, it might be seen as an ellipsis for a sentence such as *espero que no digan nada de eso*. (4.43c) is pragmatically a command, although it is an 'indefinite subject' reflexive (see **4.1.2**) which does not refer to a specific agent. In all these sentences the precise nature of the activity that is taking place depends crucially on, and is predictable on the basis of, the person or persons (first, second or third) involved.

Second-person commands can also be expressed in other ways apart from the use of an imperative form of the verb. Both declarative and interrogative sentence types are used in this way, as can be seen in the following examples:

(4.44) a.   *Me cobra, por favor*
'Could I have the bill, please?' (lit. 'You charge me, please')
b.   *¿Le importa cerrar la ventana?*
'Do you mind shutting the window?'

4.4.3 Word order in simple sentences

We have seen in **4.4.1** and **4.4.2** that interrogative and imperative sentences are often associated with distinctive word order patterns. It is less easy to make such general statements about declarative sentences, however; in fact, it is commonly asserted that Spanish has a relatively 'free' word order.

Gili Gaya (1955: 82) laid out the possibilities for the ordering of a simple sentence consisting of a subject, verb, direct object and prepositional object as follows:

(4.45) a.   *El criado trajo una carta para mí*
b.   *El criado trajo para mí una carta*
c.   **El criado una carta trajo para mí*
d.   **El criado una carta para mí trajo*
e.   **El criado para mí una carta trajo*
f.   **El criado para mí trajo una carta*

g. *Una carta el criado trajo para mí
h. *Una carta el criado para mí trajo
i. Una carta trajo el criado para mí
j. Una carta trajo para mí el criado
k. *Una carta para mí el criado trajo
l. *Una carta para mí trajo el criado

m. Trajo el criado una carta para mí
n. Trajo el criado para mí una carta
o. Trajo una carta el criado para mí
p. Trajo una carta para mí el criado
q. Trajo para mí el criado una carta
r. Trajo para mí una carta el criado

s. *Para mí el criado trajo una carta
t. *Para mí el criado una carta trajo
u. Para mí trajo el criado una carta
v. Para mí trajo una carta el criado
w. *Para mí una carta el criado trajo
x. *Para mí una carta trajo el criado

This series of examples, which looks dauntingly complex at first sight, can in fact be described by two very general principles: (i) the verb can stand as the first element in a simple declarative sentence followed by any combination of other elements; (ii) otherwise one element, and one element only, can undergo what is sometimes referred to as **left-dislocation**, i.e. stand at the front of the sentence before the verb. We see, therefore, that although there are many acceptable permutational possibilities for this simple Spanish sentence, word order is principled and by no means 'free'.

The list of possibilities given in (4.45) is far from the end of the story, however. First, not every syntactically acceptable order shown there is equally frequent; in fact, (4.45a) is far and away the one most likely to be encountered, and (4.45i, j, u and v) are very unlikely possibilities. Secondly, they do not all mean exactly the same thing. The use of varying word order in Spanish is able to achieve subtle differences of emphasis of the kind often communicated in English by contrastive stress (see **2.7.1.1**). From this point of view, Spanish word order is governed by two principles: the leftmost element is the **topic**, or element which is already established in the discourse, and the rest of the sentence is the **comment**, or new information about the topic, with the rightmost element being the one on which most stress falls.[3] This can best be illustrated by considering sentences not in isolation, but in their discourse context:

(4.46) a. *Sonó el timbre del teléfono. Llamaba tu padre, sin duda.*
(The first sentence has referred to a telephone ringing, so the verb *llamaba*, referring to this 'topic', goes first in the second sentence; the new information, *tu padre*, follows.)

---

[3] Green (1977) argues that Spanish has two basic word orders: Verb-Subject-Object and Subject-Verb-Object as a 'topicalized alternative' (p. 26). This is essentially also the conclusion of Contreras (1976), in whose terminology 'topic' is 'theme' and 'comment' is 'rheme'. Inversion of comment and topic will produce an emphatic word order, which is signalled by intonation. Contreras also provides for the possibility of 'topicalisation' (see below).

b. *Fue entonces cuando vi por primera vez a Adela. Mi prima
parecía tener menos años que yo.*
(In the second sentence, *mi prima* refers to the 'topic', *Adela*.)

A very famous example of the above phenomenon was the announcement, on 20 November 1975, by the then Prime Minister of Spain, Arias Navarro, of the death of Franco. Arias said, *Españoles: Franco ha muerto.* Franco had been critically ill for some time, and medical bulletins concerning him had been the top news item for a number of days. Hence *Franco* was the natural 'topic' of the sentence and *ha muerto* the new information about him.[4] This no doubt accounts for Arias's choice in word order. On the other hand, if one heard a church bell ringing for a funeral and asked *¿Quién ha muerto?*, the more likely order of the response would be (for example) *Ha muerto mi vecino*, since the 'topic' is the notion of dying and the new information is the identity of the deceased.

In the light of this, we must once again call into question the supposed freedom of Spanish word order. Once we realise that it is semantically determined in the way suggested above, we can see that the availability of various syntactic possibilities has been, erroneously, equated with freedom. Moreover, bringing semantic factors into play also enables us to say why some of the syntactic patterns in (4.45) are less likely than others. (4.45i and j) are unlikely because once a letter has been identified in the discourse, it is subsequently more likely to be referred to using the definite, rather than the indefinite, article:

(4.47) *A la mañana siguiente llegó una carta de mi tía. El criado me trajo la
carta.* Or, with left-dislocation, *La carta no la trajo el criado*, cf. (4.50).

There is therefore a contradiction between the use of an indefinite article with *carta* and the role as a topic that left-dislocation implies. The distinction between topic and comment is of great importance in understanding other aspects of word order in Spanish, too. It is usual, especially in the spoken language, to left-dislocate the topic even if this means some reorganisation of the rest of the sentence, and Spanish has a number of ways of achieving such **topicalisation**:

(a) The signalling of each topicalised or left-dislocated element by a terminal juncture (see 2.7.2). The following example, also taken from Gili Gaya (1955: 85), shows a series of no fewer than three left-dislocated elements (prepositional phrase, subject, prepositional phrase) which the intonational pattern renders acceptable:

(4.48)   2   1   ↓   2   1 ↓
Para los pobrecitos huérfanos, los generosos Reyes Magos de Oriente, en
        2   2 ↑   2   1 ↓
las alforjas de sus camellos han traído este año valiosos juguetes

(b) The use of what is sometimes termed a '**resumptive**' clitic pronoun, representing a left-dislocated object, which is the underlined element in the sentences of (4.49). As in the case

---

[4] Although this is a well-known example, I am grateful to Brian Mott for calling attention to it.

of simple left-dislocation, the movement of more than one element is not acceptable, as is shown by the unacceptable example (4.49e), in which both *este libro* and *a Juan* have been left-dislocated:

(4.49) a. *Esta casa la compré hace veinte años*
     b. *A mí no me gustan las gambas*
     c. *A tu madre no le vas a decir nada*
     d. *Esto no lo había notado yo*
     e. **Este libro a Juan se lo di*

Conversely, Spanish, in common with English and many other languages, has a syntactic device to achieve contrastive stress or focus (see **2.7.1.1**): the **cleft sentence** construction. Superficially, this construction is a complex sentence since it consists of two clauses. The contrastive or focused element becomes the complement of the verb *ser* and the rest of the sentence is then introduced by a relativiser (see **4.5.2.1**). In standard Peninsular Spanish the form of the relativiser is strictly determined by the function of the topicalised element, though there is a tendency in Latin-American Spanish to use *que* as an all-purpose relativiser.

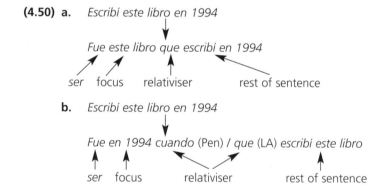

(4.50) a. *Escribí este libro en 1994*

Fue este libro que escribí en 1994

ser   focus   relativiser   rest of sentence

  b. *Escribí este libro en 1994*

Fue en 1994 cuando (Pen) / que (LA) escribí este libro

ser   focus   relativiser   rest of sentence

4.5 Complex sentence types

In our discussion of the valency of verbs in **4.3.3** we have seen that embedded sentences can act as the arguments, or complements, of verbs. In **complementation**, embedded sentences perform a nominal (i.e. noun-like) function. But embedded sentences can also function as adjectives and adverbs. We shall look at each of these three functions in the following sections.

4.5.1 Complementation

As we have seen in **4.3.3**, there are two principal complementation types in Spanish: full clause complementation and infinitive complementation. This is in contrast to English which in addition makes extensive use of the *-ing* forms of the verb. Compare the following English and Spanish complement structures (the complement is underlined):

(4.51)

	English	Spanish
a.	Cats hate <u>getting wet</u>	Los gatos odian <u>mojarse</u>
b.	<u>Riding a bicycle</u> is easy	Es fácil <u>montar en bicicleta</u>
c.	I began <u>playing the violin</u> last year	Empecé a <u>tocar el violín</u> el año pasado

Spanish does have a morphological form which is parallel to the *-ing* form of English: the *-ndo* form or gerund. But the *-ndo* form is used in the complements of only a very few verbs, the principal ones being *continuar* and *seguir*, verbs of perception (e.g. *ver, oír*), and with some common auxiliary verbs (*ir, andar, venir, llevar*) in special aspectual meanings (**aspect** is the way in which a state or activity is viewed: as in progress, beginning, completed, etc.):

(4.52)

a. *Seguimos haciéndolo*
'We carried on doing it'

b. *¡Vamos yendo!*
'Let's be going!'

c. *Vengo diciéndolo desde hace tiempo*
'I've been saying that for some time'

d. *Llevo estudiando tres meses*
'I've been studying for three months'

e. *Te vimos saliendo del cine*
(though *Te vimos salir* is also used and is in fact more usual, since its meaning is simply 'we saw you leave'; *saliendo* has the slightly different aspectual meaning of 'we saw you as you were coming out')

The resistance to gerund complementation in Spanish is no doubt connected with the fact that the *-ndo* form never functions as a verbal noun, unlike the *-ing* form of English. Most obviously, the gerund never participates in a subject complement in Spanish, cf. (4.51b). However, it is used in a wide variety of adverbial functions (see 4.5.3).

At first sight, the choice between full clause and infinitive complementation appears to be arbitrary and to depend simply on the verb of which the complement is an argument; another apparently arbitrary feature of infinitive complementation is that the infinitive is sometimes introduced by a complementising preposition such as *a, de* or *en*. On closer inspection, however, these choices are less unprincipled than might appear. Infinitive complementation usually implies that the subject of the infinitive complement is **coreferential** with (i.e. refers to the same notion as) the subject of the main clause verb:

(4.53)

a. *Quiero salir esta noche con mis amigos*
(The subject of both *quiero* and *salir* is *yo*)

b. *La secretaria empezó a archivar*
(The subject of both *empezó* and *archivar* is *la secretaria*)

c. *¡No dudes en contactarme!*
(The subject of both *dudes* and *contactar* is *tú*)

Although infinitive complementation is used in a number of other instances, most notably with verbs of perception and with some verbs of ordering, influence or encouragement, it is usually pragmatically quite obvious what the subject of the infinitive is where the two subjects are not coreferential:[5]

> **(4.54) a.** *Prohibimos salir al sospechoso*
> (It is pragmatically unlikely that the subject of *prohibimos* is also the subject of *salir*; the subject of *prohibimos* is *nosotros* and the subject of *salir* is *el sospechoso*)
> **b.** *Oyó cantar un villancico*
> (Here *un villancico* is pragmatically most likely to be the object both of *oir* and *cantar*)
> **c.** *Juan me ayudó a limpiar la habitación*
> (*Me* is pragmatically most likely to be the object of *ayudar* and the subject of *limpiar*)

However, in the majority of cases where there is no coreferentiality between the subject of the main verb and that of the complement verb, full clause complementation is used, and the presence of a finite verb in the complement makes its subject clear:

> **(4.55) a.** *Marta temía que nos enteráramos*
> (*Marta* is the subject of *temía* and *nosotros* the subject of *enteráramos*) contrasting with
> **b.** *Marta temía enterarse*
> (*Marta* is the subject of both *temía* and *enterarse*)
> **c.** *Sé que toca el contrabajo*
> (*Yo* is the subject of *sé* and a third person (*él* or *ella*?) is the subject of *toca*) contrasting with
> **d.** *Sé tocar el contrabajo*
> (*Yo* is the subject of both *sé* and *tocar*)

Even the bewildering array of prepositional usage with infinitive complements has a certain consistency. The preposition *a* tends to be used with the 'positive' complements of verbs of beginning, helping and motion, whereas the preposition *de* is more associated with 'negative' complements of verbs such as ceasing and causation:

> **(4.56)** With *a*:
> **a.** *María nos animó a seguir trabajando*
> **b.** *Echó a correr*
> **c.** *Fuimos a saludarle*
> With *de*:
> **d.** *¡Para de bromear!*
> **e.** *Pronto se cansó de escuchar*
> **f.** *Siempre se está quejando del precio de la vida*

---

[5] In Pountain (1998) I suggest that the evolution of infinitive complementation is in fact dependent on such pragmatic factors.

However, it cannot be denied that some usages are essentially idiosyncratic: the use of *con* with complements of *soñar* (4.57a) and of *a* with the apparently 'negative' verb *negarse* (4.57b), for example:

(4.57) **a.** *Soñé con ir a la Luna*
      b. *El ministro se negó a comentar*

It is possible for a verb to have alternative infinitive and full clause complementation types. In such cases, the infinitive construction is particularly associated with more informal registers:

(4.58) **a.** *Hace falta que venga / Le hace falta venir*
      b. *Le aconsejamos que lo hiciera cuanto antes / Le aconsejamos hacerlo cuanto antes*

4.5.2 Adjectival clause functions

4.5.2.1 FULL CLAUSES

Embedded sentences which qualify nouns and noun phrases and are realised as full clauses are traditionally referred to as relative clauses, and we shall examine these first. Relative clauses have a very characteristic syntax. The relative clause contains a **relativiser**, most usually a relative pronoun, which is coreferential with the noun or noun phrase being qualified, the latter being known as the **antecedent** of the relative clause. The relativiser stands first in the relative clause (unless it is part of a prepositional phrase, in which case it is preceded by its preposition), whatever its function:

(4.59) **a.** *Entonces conocimos al hombre que nos iba a ayudar*

(The constituent sentences are:
Main clause: *Entonces conocimos al <u>hombre</u>*
Relative clause: *<u>El hombre</u>* (subject) *nos iba a ayudar*
The coreferential elements are underlined.)

      b. *Esta es la habitación en la que murió Felipe II*

(The constituent sentences are:
Main clause: *Esta es <u>la habitación</u>*
Relative clause: *Felipe II murió en <u>la habitación</u>* (prepositional object)
The coreferential elements are underlined.)

Relative clauses can be **restrictive** or **non-restrictive**. Restrictive relative clauses define or limit their antecedent: both (4.59a and b) are restrictive relative clauses. Non-restrictive relative clauses, such as (4.60a), simply add information about the antecedent; they are characterised in speech by a falling **terminal juncture**, which is represented in writing by a comma. Restrictive relative clauses have no such terminal juncture.

(4.60) a.   ↓
    Fuimos a visitar el Prado, que es el museo más conocido de todo Madrid (non-restrictive)
    b.   *¿Conoces el restaurante que está en la Calle Argüelles?* (restrictive)

Relative pronouns in Spanish are interestingly complex in their use, which depends partly on syntactic and partly on semantic factors, not to mention considerations of register. The simplest form, *que*, can be used in subject (4.61a) or direct object (4.61b) function, and with reference to animate or inanimate nouns; it is also increasingly used with the prepositions *con* and *en*, especially in the spoken language (4.61c). Another feature of colloquial usage is that *que* can sometimes be used in place of a preposition + relativiser construction when the antecedent refers to a time or place (4.61d):

(4.61) a.   *El cirujano que me operó era un especialista de corazón muy conocido* (subject)
    b.   *La última novela que escribió Cervantes se llama* Persiles y Sigismunda (direct object)
    c.   *Los compañeros con que viajamos resultaban cansadísimos* (object of *con*)
    d.   *¿Te acuerdas de la noche que nos conocimos?* (*que = en (la) que*; it cannot represent a subject or object function)

In colloquial register, *que* has an even more extended function. In sentences like (4.63a), *que* is used to mark the beginning of a relative clause even though the pronoun function is represented separately within the clause. It is interesting that while such sentences are considered 'incorrect', there is sometimes no alternative way of expressing them if a relative clause is to be used at all: in the complex example (4.62b), the relativised element is in fact part of the complement of the verb *querer*, which in turn is the verb of the complement of *sé*; but (4.62b) cannot be otherwise structured as a relative (compare the unacceptable 4.62c):

(4.62) a.   ʹ*Es una manía que yo no la entiendo* (Carmen Martín Gaite, *El cuarto de atrás*, 6th ed., Barcelona: Deslino, p. 163)
    b.   ʹ*Este es el libro que no sé por qué lo quieres comprar*
    c.   **Este es el libro que no sé por qué quieres comprar*

The relative pronoun *quien* refers exclusively to animate antecedents, while the relative pronouns *el que*, *la que*, etc. and *el cual*, *la cual*, etc. refer to any antecedent; the latter series is relatively infrequent. They are used especially with prepositions, but also serve as more precise alternatives to *que* in any function except that of the subject of a restrictive relative clause. The choice of *quien*, etc., rather than *que* in such cases is thus motivated either by the need to disambiguate a potentially ambiguous function or to adopt a higher register. Seco

(1998: 316) gives the example (4.63a): the use of *que* rather than *quienes* (cf. 4.63b) could have the meaning of *ya que* 'because' in this context.

> **(4.63) a.** *Se comunicó la noticia a los padres, quienes no sabían nada*
> 'The parents, who knew nothing, were told the news'
> **b.** *Se comunicó la noticia a los padres, que no sabían nada*
> Could also mean 'The parents were told the news, for they knew nothing'

There are relativisers other than relative pronouns in Spanish. The adjective *cuyo* is used to express the notion of *de quien*, *del que* ('whose', 'of which'):

> **(4.64)** *Mercedes, cuyo libro era, no tenía la menor intención de prestarlo a nadie*

Cuyo is associated with more formal registers; in speech *de quien* is often used instead, or even a structure with the possessive adjective within a clause introduced by *que*, which resembles the colloquial use of *que* exemplified in (4.62a–c) above:

> **(4.65) a.** *Mi colega, cuyo piso acabamos de comprar, ...* (most formal)
> **b.** *Mi colega, de quien acabamos de comprar el piso, ...*
> **c.** *Mi colega, que acabamos de comprar su piso, ...* (least formal, 'incorrect')

Cuyo is also used as what is sometimes called a transition relative (see also **7.1**). Although this construction is limited to very formal registers, it is prescriptively castigated: Seco (1998: 143) gives the example

> **(4.66)** *Hay que asumir la defensa de la sociedad, cuya defensa ha de ser firme (= ... y esta defensa ha de ser firme)*
> 'We must take on the defence of society, and this defence must be firm'

commenting that it should be revised by simply omitting *cuya*; in fact, *cuya* has the **anaphoric** function of *esta* here (that is, the function of referring back to a noun or noun phrase, in this case is *defensa*, which has already been introduced).

Other elements which function as relativisers are what we might call relative adverbs such as *donde* and *como*:

> **(4.67) a.** *Todavía me acuerdo del hotel (en) donde pasamos nuestra luna de miel*
> **b.** *Me impresionó mucho la manera como te lo contó*

4.5.2.2 THE INFINITIVE

We now turn to the adjectival functions of embedded sentences which are realised by infinitive constructions. Such infinitive constructions have a limited number of semantic functions and are all linked to the nouns they qualify by a preposition. The preposition + infinitive constructions in the following three examples all have a precise aspectual meaning; they can be paraphrased by relative clauses which, however, are much more explicit:

> **(4.68) a.** *Una casa a medio construir = Una casa que está medio construida*
>
> **b.** *Un problema por resolver = Un problema que todavía no se ha resuelto*
>
> **c.** *Una pared sin pintar = Una pared que todavía no ha sido pintada*

Another element which here seems to act like a preposition in linking an infinitive to a noun is *que*; again, *que* + infinitive has a very precise meaning, though this time it is modal rather than aspectual:

> **(4.69)** *Muchos ejercicios que hacer = Muchos ejercicios que hay que hacer*

An interesting feature of such constructions is that the 'antecedent' noun is the object, not the subject, of the infinitive; as a result, it sometimes appears to English speakers that the infinitive has a passive meaning in such contexts, so that (4.68b), for example, may be rendered in English by 'a problem to be solved'.

4.5.2.3 THE GERUND

Some authorities would claim that the gerund is never used as an adjectival construction in Spanish, but it has to be said that this is a considerable overstatement (see Pountain 1998). There are substantial restrictions on its use, and it is more favoured in certain registers (notably journalistic); it is also nowhere near as frequent in such a function as the *-ing* form of English or the *-ant* form of French (contrast with which has persuaded a number of prescriptive Spanish grammarians to see the supposedly pernicious influence of English and French at work on their language and may be responsible for the venom with which its use is denounced). A gerund certainly cannot be used as an adjective pure and simple: the only examples of such a use in Spanish are in the relatively fixed expressions *agua hirviendo* 'boiling water' and *una casa ardiendo* 'a house on fire', but *hirviendo* and *ardiendo* are quite unlike other adjectives in that they can never be used contrastively (thus **El agua hirviendo es la del puchero pequeño* 'the *boiling* water is in the small pot')[6]. However, a gerund can in certain conditions be used as the realisation of the verb of a relative (i.e. adjectival) clause. Here are two examples: (4.70a) is typical of Spanish legal register, while (4.70b) might appear as a personal advert in a newspaper. In each case the gerund construction can be seen to be the equivalent of a relative clause:

> **(4.70) a.** *Decreto estableciendo nuevos impuestos = Decreto que establece nuevos impuestos*
>
> **b.** *Necesito señora sabiendo cocinar = Necesito una señora que sepa cocinar*

---

[6] Moliner (1982: 1394); see also Pountain (1994) and (1998).

Amongst the restrictions on the use of such 'adjectival' gerund constructions, even in such registers, is that they can only be used if they correspond to a restrictive relative clause that is used in a non-contrastive way. Thus (4.71a) is acceptable, but (4.71b) and (4.71c) are not:

(4.71) **a.** *Nos daban unos libretos explicando todas las cosas* (Esgueva & Cantarero 1981: 245) = *Nos daban unos libretos que explicaban todas las cosas*

b. **Nos daban sólo los libretos explicando todas las cosas* (contrastive)

c. **Nos daban los libretos azules, explicando todas las cosas* (non-restrictive; compare the acceptability of *Nos daban los libretos azules, que explicaban todas las cosas*)[7]

4.5.3 Adverbial clause functions

Full clauses and infinitive constructions have a wide range of adverbial functions. Once again, the full-clause realisation of the embedded sentence is more explicit and versatile than the infinitive. Some examples of adverbial clauses are:

(4.72) Temporal
a. *En cuanto vuelva a casa, te llamará*
(*En cuanto* does not normally take an infinitive)
b. *Después de descubrir el robo, llamó a la policía*
(The subjects of *descubrir* and *llamó* are coreferential.)

Causal
c. *Fuimos a pie por no tener dinero*
d. *Fuimos a pie porque no teníamos dinero*
(The infinitive is possible when the subjects of *fuimos* and *tener* are coreferential.)

Concessive
e. *No dudes en llamarme, aunque sea muy tarde* (*aunque* cannot take an infinitive)

Purpose (sometimes called **'final' clauses**)
f. *Pon la leche en la nevera para que no se estropee*
g. *Para mantenerte en buena forma, come más sano*
(The subjects of *mantenerte* and *come* are coreferential.)

Condition
h. *Si estás de acuerdo, levanta la mano*
i. *Caso de llegar después de medianoche, suene el timbre*
(The subjects of *llegar* and *suene* are coreferential.)

Consequence
j. *Juan se lo ha dicho a todo el mundo, de ahí que ya no sea un secreto*

---

[7] Pountain (1998: 289).

Miscellaneous
k. *Salimos <u>sin hacerles caso</u>*
(The subjects of *salimos* and *hacerles caso* are coreferential.)
l. *Salimos <u>sin que nos hicieran caso</u>*
m. *A pesar de no tener dinero, disfrutamos nuestro tiempo libre*
(The subjects of *tener* and *disfrutamos* are coreferential.)
n. *Estamos bastante cómodos aquí <u>a pesar de que no haya</u>*
<u>*electricidad*</u>

Some complex sentences in this category have very individual syntactic patternings which are well described in grammars of Spanish. Conditional sentences employing the conjunction *si* have very strict combinations of verb forms in their constituent clauses depending on their time-reference and whether or not they are **counterfactual** (i.e. envisaging a condition which was, or is not, or is not likely to be, fulfilled): for example, a past counterfactual conditional sentence has a pluperfect subjunctive verb form in its *si*-clause or **protasis** and a conditional or conditional perfect verb form in its main clause or **apodosis**:

(4.73) *Si no hubiera criticado al Primer Ministro, sería miembro del gobierno*

Concession is expressed in a very large number of ways, not only by conjunctions such as *aunque* exemplified in (4.72e) above, but also by constructions like the following:

(4.74) *Por mucho que protesten, no van a conseguir sus objetivos*

The sentences of (4.72) show that infinitives preceded by prepositions are formally very closely related to full-clause constructions, the infinitive construction generally being available and required when the subject of the main verb and that of the subordinate clause verb are coreferential, a phenomenon we have already observed in the case of complementation.

An interesting phenomenon in modern Spanish is the use, which is possibly on the increase, of such infinitive constructions where there is no coreferentiality between the two subjects. In such cases, the infinitive normally has its own overt subject which normally follows the verb (4.75a), although in some regional varieties of Spanish the subject may precede (4.75b – see also Lipski 1991):

(4.75) a. *Salieron sin saberlo yo*
b. *Salieron sin yo saberlo*

Two very versatile adverbial infinitive constructions are *al* + infinitive and *de* + infinitive. *Al* + infinitive most commonly (and prescriptively) has a temporal meaning (4.76a), but in Latin-American speech it can also serve as the equivalent of an adverbial clause of condition (4.76b) or cause (4.76c):

(4.76) a. <u>*Al verla,*</u> *sonrió*
'When he saw her, he smiled'
b. <u>*Al tener yo dinero,*</u> *me compraría una casa* (Kany 1951: 26)
'If I had money, I would buy myself a house' (This usage is prescriptively castigated.)

c. *Al no querer nadie hablarnos, tampoco teníamos nada que decir entre nosotros* (Kany 1951: 28)
'Since no one wanted to talk to us, we didn't have anything to say to one another either'

De and *a* + infinitive are used as the equivalent of a conditional clause:

(4.77) *De / a saberlo yo no habría ido*
'If I'd known, I would not have gone'

The adverbial function is the principal role of the gerund in Spanish. By default it has the function of an adverbial clause of manner or means and its subject is coreferential with the subject of the main clause verb (like the infinitive, the gerund is a non-finite verb form).

(4.78) a. *Juana entró sonriendo*
'Juana came in smiling'
(The subject of both *entró* and *sonriendo* is *Juana*)

b. *Aprendí el sánscrito leyendo las Vedas*
'I learned Sanskrit by reading the Vedas'
(The subject of both *aprendí* and *leyendo* is *yo*.)

In formal registers, the gerund may have an overt subject of its own which is not coreferential with that of the main verb; such constructions are often known as **absolute** constructions:

(4.79) a. *Habría bastado recorrer unos cientos de metros para que se calentara el neumático, produciéndose la explosión justo debajo del depósito de combustible* (Arturo Pérez-Reverte, *La tabla de Flandes*, p. 267)
(The subject of *calentara* is *neumático* and the subject of *produciéndose* is *la explosión*.)

b. *Siendo las cosas así, el Primer Ministro no vaciló en dimitir*
(The subject of *vaciló* is *el Primer Ministro* and the subject of *siendo* is *las cosas*.)

Finally, we should add that the past participle can, like the gerund, be used in an absolute construction with an adverbial value, usually temporal:

(4.80) a. *Terminada la guerra, hubo intentos de reconciliación por parte de ambos países*
'When the war had finished, there were attempts at reconciliation by both countries'

EXERCISES

1. Some linguists have suggested that the subject of 'indefinite subject' reflexive verbs (see **4.1.2**) might in fact be the pronoun *se*: what do you think are the arguments for and against such a position?

2. Look for other examples of ellipsis in spoken language. Here is another example:

   Mi hija, pues, nada = (depending on the discourse context, *nada* stands for a negative idea) *A mi hija no le gusta eso / Mi hija no hace nada / Mi hija no estudia*, etc.

3. In 4.3.5.2 we looked at the valencies of *fly* and *volar*. Make similar case-studies for *change / cambiar* and *sound / sonar*.

4. Examine the structure of the following sentence, which is taken from a real conversation in Spanish:

   Eso tenían que arreglarlo; porque yo, vamos, no creo que me pase a mí un caso así, pero vamos, hay muchas que las suele pasar y el marido, pues se queda con todo, y eso está muy mal.

5 | Themes in form and meaning: the 'genius' of Spanish

In this chapter, we will examine a number of well-known features of modern Spanish grammar. These have been chosen because they illustrate very clearly the tension which exists between form and meaning, and show the unsatisfactoriness of assuming that a one-to-one relation between form and meaning exists. In each topic, therefore, we will try to keep categories of form and meaning apart, using if necessary different terms, which may not be the traditional ones, to make the distinction. Each of the features we shall study represents what might be deemed a special characteristic of Spanish which has been exploited for a considerable period in the history of the language and which continues to be exploited today. This phenomenon, which is perhaps not recognised as extensively as it merits, was described by Sapir (1921:60) in the following terms:

> All languages evince a curious instinct for the development of one or
> more particular grammatical processes at the expense of others, tending
> always to lose sight of any explicit functional value that the process may
> have had in the first instance, delighting, it would seem, in the sheer play
> of its means of expression.

It is what I have referred to elsewhere, following an interesting French tradition, as the 'genius' (*génie*) of the language.[1]

5.1 Gender

'**Gender**' has come to be used in everyday speech in English, no doubt originally euphemistically, to refer to the sex of a human being, and we speak of 'gender studies', 'the gender gap', 'gender-bending', and so on. But it has long been used in grammatical terminology to refer to what, put most neutrally, are different formal classes of nouns on which agreements with adjectives (and in some languages with other parts of speech as well) depend. In traditional grammar, the genders have been named on the basis of a partial correlation between 'masculine' and 'feminine' gender and male and female sex, and this terminology has been in use since Classical times. Some European languages distinguish a third gender, the 'neuter' (originally a Latin word meaning 'neither'). It is not surprising, then, that 'gender' is so firmly associated with sex. But if we look a little further around the languages of the world we can see that gender categories do not necessarily correlate with sex. Swahili is a well-known example of a language which has seven 'genders' which partially correlate with five fairly arbitrary semantic categories (inanimate things, trees, people, animals

---

[1] For a further account of this phenomenon, particularly in relation to section **5.5** of this chapter, see Pountain (2000).

and family names, abstract entities), a sixth grammatical category (infinitives) and a seventh miscellaneous group; gender agreement in Swahili is marked not only in the noun phrase but also in the verb.

We will now examine the relation between gender and sex in Spanish a little further, rigorously using 'gender' as a category of form and 'sex' as a category of meaning (that is, we shall use 'gender' in a deliberately special way, not in the way it is currently used in everyday speech and writing). We must also distinguish the notion of gender morpheme or inflection, since a number of noun endings in Spanish serve as markers of one of the gender categories, the most common being the masculine ending *-o* and the feminine ending *-a*. The relations between these categories are illustrated in Figure 5.1 below:

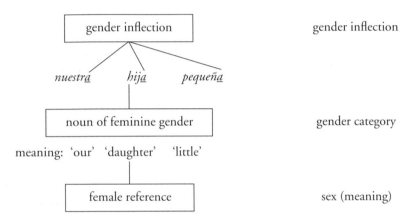

Figure 5.1 Relations between gender inflection, gender category and sex

We can see that the gender of a noun is revealed by other constituents of the noun phrase which agree with it. The noun *pared* has no obvious gender inflection, but in the phrase *una pared blanca*, the feminine forms *una* and *blanca* show that *pared* is feminine too. The noun *artista* appears to have a feminine gender inflection, *-a*, but agreements show that in fact it can be of either gender: *un artista muy conocido / una artista muy conocida*. (Notice that in establishing the gender of *pared* and *artista* we have paid no attention to the meaning of these words.)

It is trivial to show that gender does not always correlate with sex in Spanish, since while all nouns in the language are either masculine or feminine, not all their referents are capable of belonging to the male and female sexes. *Mesa* is a feminine noun, but there is nothing 'female' about a table, for instance. The best we can say is that gender seems to correlate with sex for nouns which refer to human beings. It is interesting that although animals fall into two sexes, names for animals can be either masculine or feminine (e.g. *rata* (feminine), *ratón* (masculine), *ardilla* (feminine), *conejo* (masculine)) and that these apply irrespective of sex; indeed, it is only with the most familiar animals (e.g. *zorro / zorra* or *raposa, perro / perra, caballo / yegua*) that any distinction between male and female is possible without resort being made to the invariable adjectives *macho* 'male' and *hembra* 'female' (e.g. *una ardilla macho* 'a male squirrel'). With human referents, however, the correlation between gender and sex is very strong, to the point that there are extremely few nouns in Spanish referring to males which are not masculine or nouns referring to females which are not feminine. The exceptions are nouns which have a very general reference indeed: *la persona* and *la víctima* are the principal cases, these nouns being feminine even when they refer to males exclusively. Otherwise, Spanish has adopted a number of strategies to bring about the gender-sex correlation. Most extremely, gender inflection is simply overridden by gender category. There are large numbers of nouns ending in *-a* which are masculine when referring to males, e.g. *el poeta, el cura, el atleta*, a whole host of 'occupation' nouns ending in *-ista* such as *el electricista, el periodista, el congresista*, and masculine forms of feminine nouns which denote a body of people, such as *el policía* 'policeman' (cf. *la policía* 'police force'), *el vigía* 'lookout' (cf. *la vigía* 'watchtower'). There are fewer example of nouns ending in *-o* referring to females which are feminine, although these have increased latterly: *la modelo, la miembro, la reo* and *la testigo* are well-established, while such creations as *la piloto* and *la soldado* are more recent. Another strategy is to bring the gender inflection into line with the gender category, a process sometimes known as the **hypercharacterisation of gender**. A number of feminine nouns originally ending in *-o* have undergone this process: *la ministra* is now preferred to *la ministro*, though we can still observe some variation between *la médico/a* and *la catedrático/a*. The 'feminising' of masculine nouns ending in a consonant has been an ongoing process in the history of Spanish: thus *el autor* → *la autora, el campeón* → *la campeona*; less regular is the replacement of the final *-e* of a masculine noun by *-a*, e.g. *el infante* → *la infanta, el sirviente* → *la sirvienta* (but not *el estudiante* → *la *estudianta, el anglohablante* → *la *anglohablanta, el creyente* → *la *creyenta*, etc.). The 'masculinising' of feminine nouns is much less frequent, since pragmatically, it has been much less needful. *El enfermero* has been formed from *la enfermera* and, very strikingly, *el modisto* from *la modista* (where the final *-a* is not even originally a marker of the feminine).

Providing feminine counterparts for masculine nouns has not always been straightforward in Spanish, for a number of reasons. First of all, the feminine form may exist already, but with a different meaning, so that the new feminine will cause potential **polysemy** (multiple meaning). It was customary until relatively recently to use the feminine form of many nouns indicating profession or rank to denote the notion 'wife of', so that *la alcaldesa* was not a female mayor, but the wife of the (male) mayor. These former meanings are rapidly becoming obsolete (though they are still listed in many dictionaries), and so the way is cleared for *alcaldesa* and similar words henceforward to mean only 'female mayor'. Sometimes the feminine had, and still has, an abstract meaning, e.g. *la física* 'physics', *la política* 'politics', *la crítica* 'criticism', and we have already noted the feminine forms of such nouns as *policía* and *guardia* in their meanings of 'police (force)' and 'guard (as a body)'. This is clearly more problematic, since the original meaning of the feminine is far from obsolete, but currently the resulting polysemy seems to be tolerated, and early circumlocutory experiments such as *la mujer policía* have largely been abandoned in favour of *la policía*. Interestingly, resistance to the coining of new feminine forms has sometimes come from the feeling that the new word has a pejorative meaning, or is somehow less respectful than the masculine. *La médica* has long been resisted, in Spain at least, as the word for 'female doctor', *la médico* being used instead. Margaret Thatcher was at first *la primer ministro*, though *la primera ministra* became much more usual during her period of office, and *la ministra* is now firmly established. *La catedrático* is still preferred by some speakers to *la catedrática*. The nouns mentioned earlier, *la miembro*, *la reo* and *la testigo*, show no signs of movement.

There seems little doubt, then, that with nouns referring to human beings, there is a strong association between gender category, gender inflection and sex, and that even though this relation is not always as straightforward as it might be, Spanish seems to manifest a certain internal dynamism in approximating to a regular relation. Is there anything more that can be said about gender as it relates to the meaning of inanimate nouns, or is that relationship a purely arbitrary one? Interestingly, it seems that in the course of the evolution of Spanish, gender distinctions have sometimes been exploited for semantic reasons, since the modern language has a a number of very partial, and essentially irregular, patternings. One such is the distinction between a tree and its fruit:

> **(5.1)** tree (masculine)   fruit (feminine)
> cerezo   cereza
> manzano   manzana
> naranjo   naranja
> canelo   canela

While by no means all trees and fruits are distinguished in this way (*el peral / la pera, la higuera / el higo, el limonero / el limón*), it is striking how this gender contrast has continually been exploited in Spanish with borrowings and neologisms such as *guindo* (*guindal* is also attested) / *guinda* 'morello cherry' (probably from Germanic), *granado / granada* 'pomegranate' (on the basis of *grana* 'vegetable seed' which came to denote a dye), *naranjo / naranja* 'orange' (from Persian), and *guayabo / guayaba, papayo / papaya* (from Amerindian languages). This seems to suggest that the semantic basis for this gender contrast is still productive in Spanish. Another relation sometimes signalled by gender is that of count and mass nouns (see **6.2.3.1.3**): *el leño* 'log' / *la leña* 'wood', *el fruto* 'piece of fruit' / *la fruta* 'fruit in general', *el huevo* 'egg' / *la hueva* '(frog)spawn'.[2] Finally, and perhaps most complex of all, gender sometimes seems to correlate with size:

> **(5.2)** small (masculine)   large (feminine)
> *río* 'river'   *ría* 'estuary'
> *cuenco* 'bowl'   *cuenca* 'basin (geographical feature)'
> *huerto* 'garden'   *huerta* 'market garden area'
> *ramo* 'branch (coming off a   *rama* 'large branch, bough'
>   larger branch)'
> *cubo* 'bucket'   *cuba* 'barrel'
> *charco* 'puddle'   *charca* 'pond'

Although it seems quite clear that in the course of the history of the language there has been a certain productivity in forming such gender pairs (for example, *río* and *huerto* derive

---

[2] In some Asturian and Castilian regional varieties (see **6.2.3.1.3**) the difference between count and mass nouns is overtly marked in third-person pronoun forms and sometimes in adjectival vocalic inflections (see especially Penny 2000: 90–3 and Fernández-Ordóñez 1994).

respectively from Lat. RĬVU(S) and HŎRTU(S), but *ría* and *huerta* have no origin in Latin and must be later creations), there does not seem to be any ongoing productivity. Moreover, there are several cases of semantically related gender pairs in which the basis of the relation is not obviously respective size:

(5.3)   <u>large (masculine)</u>   <u>small (feminine)</u>
barco 'boat (general)'   *barca* 'boat, typically a rowing boat or
                                 fishing boat'
cesto '(large) basket'   *cesta* 'basket'
manto 'cloak'   *manta* 'blanket, large shawl'

Sometimes it seems that empty gender 'slots' have been filled up in the course of the evolution of Spanish. The following pairs of words are certainly related in meaning, though no general principle for their relatedness is evident:

(5.4)   <u>masculine</u>   <u>feminine</u>
cometa 'comet'   *cometa* 'kite'
frente 'front'   *frente* 'forehead'
capital 'capital (money)'   *capital* 'capital (city)'
caza 'fighter plane'   *caza* 'hunting'
mañana 'future'   *mañana* 'morning'
orden 'order (arrangement)'   *orden* 'order (command)'
pendiente 'earring'   *pendiente* 'slope'

All these facts seem to suggest that in various ways Spanish has successfully exploited gender to extend its lexicon quite independently of any relation between gender and the sex of human beings. Indeed, on a purely formal level the exploitation goes even further, with the coincidental creation of gender pairs, usually through phonetic evolution towards homonymy or near homonymy. *Pez* can be either masculine or feminine in Spanish: in the masculine it means 'fish' and in the feminine 'pitch, tar'. The former is the derivative of Lat. PĬSCE(M) and the latter of Lat. PĬCE(M); these words retain their original Latin genders and so the homonymous result is in fact successfully discriminated. Further examples of a similar kind are *moral* (masculine) 'mulberry tree' derived from Lat. MŌRA 'berry' / *moral* (feminine) 'morals' < Lat. MORALE(M), and *coma* (masculine) 'coma' < Gk. *kôma* / *coma* (feminine) 'comma' < Lat. CŎMMA (in its turn from Gk. *kómma*).

A final question which it may occur to us to ask about gender in Spanish is whether each gender is equally important or whether one might be regarded as the **unmarked**, or 'default', gender (the implication being that the other gender would be **marked**, or more distinctive). There are in fact powerful reasons for thinking that the masculine is the unmarked gender. First, as we have seen, there are more masculine words with characteristic feminine inflections than feminine words with characteristic masculine inflections, although recently the latter have been increasing somewhat in number with such abbreviated forms as *la foto, la moto, la radio* (like *metro* 'underground, subway' in the Peninsula, *radio* is treated as masculine in Latin America). Most new borrowings are masculine, unless there is any powerful analogical reason for them to be feminine (so *fútbol, footing, CD, disquete, pub, software* are masculine, though *pizza* and *élite* are feminine following their Italian and French originals, as is *jet* 'jet-set', the latter perhaps by analogy with *gente* or *pandilla*). The gender of compound nouns follows a clear principle which similarly points to the unmarked nature of the masculine. In general, only compound nouns consisting of two feminine nouns are feminine overall (*bocacalle, maniobra, madreselva*); even if a feminine noun comprises one part of other compound patterns, the compound noun is usually masculine (*terremoto, abrelatas, paraguas, aguardiente, altavoz*), as are nominalized verbs and other phrases (*pésame, pormenor, porvenir* – the feminine *enhorabuena* and *sinrazón* are relatively rare exceptions). Lastly, while groups of males are referred to as masculine and groups of females as feminine, any mixed group, even if it is predominantly female, is referred to as masculine: a group of friends consisting of five girls and one boy, for example, must be *los amigos*. Pairs of male and female counterparts are also referred to with a masculine plural noun (*los tíos* 'uncle and aunt', *los padres* 'parents', *los reyes* 'the king and queen').

5.2 The 'personal *a*'

The preposition *a* has a very wide range of functions in Spanish. It is the marker of the indirect object of the verb (5.5a); it expresses the **allative** notion (motion towards) (5.5b) as well as being used in many semi-idiomatic expressions indicating a variety of adverbial functions (5.5c–d); it is used as a complementiser (see **4.5.1**) with a number of verbs (5.5e), and it also appears in certain circumstances with direct objects (5.5f). It is this last function which has come to be labelled the 'personal *a*', on the grounds that such direct objects generally denote human beings (5.5f), animals which are closely related with humans in some way (5.5g), or other objects which it is appropriate to think of as being in some way 'personified' (5.5h).

> **(5.5)** a. *Ofrecimos una cena a nuestros amigos*
> b. *El transatlántico zarpó con rumbo a Nueva York*
> c. *Asun está al teléfono*
> d. *Almorzamos al aire libre*
> e. *Juan se negó a contestar*
> f. *No vi a los compañeros por la Facultad*
> g. *Acarició al perro*
> h. *Amo a la justicia*

The traditional terminology again holds up the possibility of a one-to-one relation between form and meaning, the implication being that whenever a direct object objectively fulfils the semantic criteria set out above, the preposition *a* will be used. However, there are a number of problems with this. First, one condition for the appropriateness of the use of the 'personal *a*' seems to be that the direct object must be **particularised** – this special term is used to signify that there is an interest in the identity or individuality of the direct object, and that it does not, for example, represent a person considered as a category or as a hypothetical notion:

(5.6) **a.** *Vi a mis colegas en la calle*
but
b. *Vi los obreros salir de la fábrica*

(5.7) **a.** *Busco a un compañero llamado Alfonso*
but
b. *Busco un compañero para el viaje*

Particularisation is of great importance in accounting for the use of 'personal *a*' with direct objects denoting animals. *A* is appropriate only when the animal is considered as an individual (e.g. because it is a pet); non-mammals, wild animals and animals that are eaten are not generally thought of in this way, and so such sentences as the following would be unusual:

(5.8) **a.** *'Fotografiamos a muchos tigres en la reserva*
b. *'Maté a la avispa que me picó*
c. *'Ahora voy a preparar a la trucha*

Another factor on which the use of the 'personal *a*' seems to depend on what has been called **kinesis**.[3] Although many verbs take direct objects in a loose grammatical sense, there is considerable variation in the degree of effect that verbs have on their patient (see **4.3**). A verb like *traicionar* 'to betray', for example, has a very high kinesis in that it has a very definite effect on its patient, while a verb like *tener* is very low in kinesis, since it really only states a relation of possession between subject and object. Verbs of high kinesis are most likely to take the 'personal *a*' with their objects and verbs of low kinesis least likely. In fact, for these two extreme verbs cited, it is difficult to imagine any circumstance in which *traicionar* would not take *a* with its object (which, incidentally, normally refers to a person), or any case in which *tener* does take *a* if it simply expresses the notion of 'to have', even if its object is person-referring and particularised:

(5.9) **a.** **Ha traicionado su mujer*
b. **Tengo a tres sobrinos*

The object of the verb *tener* can take a 'personal *a*', but only when *tener* has the stronger kinetic value of 'to keep':

(5.10) *Tengo a mis dos hijos en casa porque están enfermos hoy*

A similar verb in this respect is *querer*, which has no 'personal *a*' in the low kinetic meaning of 'to want' but does have the *a* in the stronger kinetic meaning of 'to love':

(5.11) **a.** *Quiero un profesor*
'I want a teacher'
b. *Quiero a un profesor*
'I love a teacher'

---

[3] See Kliffer (1984), following Hopper & Thompson (1980)

In fact, as these examples show, kinesis and particularisation are often complementary, since the objects of verbs of high kinesis are usually particularised. The notion of kinesis also gives us a natural explanation of the use of the 'personal *a*' with so-called 'personified' nouns, since again certain verbs are more likely to be associated with this use of *a* than others; they are precisely those which are of high kinesis and typically take a particularised personal direct object. Some typical examples of the kind often cited in grammars are:

> **(5.12) a.** *Tú temes al éxito tanto como al fracaso* (Butt & Benjamin 2000: 323)
>
> **b.** *Yo bendigo a la técnica* (De Bruyne 1995: 305)

Now, it will be noticed that the 'rules' we have been establishing for the use of the 'personal *a*' are not hard-and-fast rules of the kind we could put forward for, say, the forms of verbs or gender agreements. They are relative principles which attribute a scale of values: the more particularised an object is and the higher in kinesis a verb is, the more likely it is that the 'personal *a*' will be used. It is also not the case that some of the sentences we have considered are 'right' or 'wrong' in the sense of being unequivocally acceptable or unacceptable to native speakers; rather, they are more or less likely. This is a very important point, since it is not the usual way in which such usages are described in pedagogical grammars, but we will see that such a principle is applied repeatedly in the remaining sections of this chapter.

However, 'personal *a*' is also complex for another reason, in that it appears also to be used for clarity, to mark the identity of the direct object of the verb, particularly in structures which might be prone to ambiguity of interpretation. There are four syntactic contexts in particular in Spanish in which there might be motivation for such a use of *a*: sentences in which the object appears first (5.13a), sentences in which the verb appears first, which are extremely frequent in Spanish (5.14), relative clauses (5.15) and the discrimination of the literal reflexive (5.16a) and indefinite subject reflexive (5.16b) constructions (see also **4.1.2, 5.4.1.3**):

> **(5.13) a.** *Al soldado le mató el general*
> 'The general killed the soldier'
> Compare:
>
> **b.** *El soldado (le) mató al general*
> 'The soldier killed the general'
>
> **(5.14) a.** *Mató el soldado al general*
> 'The soldier killed the general'
>
> **b.** *Mató al soldado el general*
> 'The general killed the soldier'
>
> **(5.15) a.** *El soldado que mató al general*
> 'The soldier who killed the general'
>
> **b.** *El soldado que mató el general*
> 'The soldier who(m) the general killed'
>
> **(5.16) a.** *Se mató el soldado*
> 'The soldier killed himself'
>
> **b.** *Se mató al soldado*
> 'The soldier was killed'

We must immediately make some fairly substantial qualifications about these areas of potential ambiguity, however. *Le* is optional in (5.13b);[4] but it is of course only if *le* appears in the sentence that it is potentially ambiguous with (5.13a), where *le* is obligatory in the object-first construction. And while sentences like those of (5.14) are possible, they are not usual, especially in speech.[5] Another obvious condition for ambiguity in (5.13)–(5.15) is that the subject and object nouns are both singular or both plural, since otherwise the verbal morphology will unambiguously make clear which is the subject. In (5.16) the noun will be ambiguously interpretable only if it is in the singular, since the indefinite subject reflexive construction is uniquely singular. The cases in which the 'personal *a*' provides crucial information are therefore limited. Nevertheless, there are other, and perhaps clearer, instances in which the *a* may have a disambiguating function. We find that the personal *a* is also used with the objects of verbs which express a relation of precedence and with verbs of certain other semantic classes, where, because subject and object belong to the same semantic category, there is a similar potential ambiguity, even with inanimate objects.

> **(5.17)** **a.** *Siguió la sequía a la lluvia*
> 'Drought followed the rain'
>
> **b.** *Afectó la guerra a la economía*
> 'The war affected the economy'[6]

(I have used a verb-first order in these examples in order to bring out more obviously the potential ambiguity if the personal *a* is omitted, although placing the subject first is usually preferred.) Another interesting case is that of sentences with verbs which typically have human direct objects and indirect objects. Here, *a* would seem to be required to mark both nouns, though in fact it is only used with the indirect object; hence it is the absence of the expected 'personal *a*' that provides an unequivocal marking of the direct object:

> **(5.18)** **a.** *Recomendó su amigo al jefe*
> **b.** *Presenté mis colegas al recién llegado*

The use of the 'personal *a*' in Spanish is thus a complex phenomenon. While sometimes its use appears to be very strictly determined, in many environments it seems to be 'optional' – though behind this syntactic 'optionality' in fact lies a series of rather subtle semantic distinctions (subtle, that is, in the sense that they cannot be succinctly rendered in English, or indeed in many other languages). We can also see how, through the use of the 'personal *a*',

---

[4] Silva-Corvalán (1984: 568) relates the presence of *le* to a number of pragmatic factors: 'recency of reference in the discourse, animacy and definiteness, related to the likelihood of a given noun phrase to qualify as the topic of a sentence or a discourse passage'.

[5] See Green (1988: 115), who goes so far as to mark *Compró Elena el coche* with a question mark for acceptability. Once again pragmatic factors intervene here: the verb-first order implies that the verb itself is the 'topic' while the rightmost noun carries most emphasis as the 'new' information. In a VSO order it is the O noun, rather than the S noun, that carries most stress; the order of V and S is not crucial from the semantic point of view, and so the more usual SVO order is adopted. It is really only in VS structures that Spanish regularly places S immediately after V, but SV is not a potentially ambiguous sequence.

[6] Green (1988: 107) cites *La rata cazó al gato* ('the rat chased the cat') and *la bicicleta dobló al camión* ('the bicycle overtook the lorry'). Here, however, the *a* may be used because of the pragmatic unlikelihood of the truth of these sentences.

certain verbs (I have discussed *tener* and *querer* above in this light) are able to have an extended semantic range by comparison with English. The use of *a* to achieve such discrimination is part of the 'genius' of Spanish.

The problems of describing the use of 'personal *a*' are compounded by the multiple use of *a* which in turn makes the distinction between direct and indirect object sometimes difficult to draw. In the sentences:

> **(5.19) a.** *La crisis petrolera afecta a todo el mundo*
> **b.** *La sequía no ha afectado a esta región*

it might seem at first sight that *todo el mundo* and *esta región* are direct objects and that therefore the *a* is somehow 'personal' (rather like the case of *temer* which we examined in (5.12a) above); after all, *afectar* seems to be entirely parallel in this sense to Eng. *affect*. Moreover, other criteria which are more specifically to do with Spanish suggest that *afectar* is indeed a verb with a direct object. Most convincingly, the sentence can be passivised to *Esta región no ha sido afectada por la sequía*, a fact which is very significant in Spanish, since, unlike in English, passivisation is not normally permitted with anything other than a direct object (see **4.3.4.1**). And the normal choice of pronoun corresponding to *esta región* is *la* rather than *le*, again suggesting its direct object status (see, however, **6.2.3.1.3**). Yet there is another way of looking at this usage. Consider the following sentences:

> **(5.20) a.** *Afectaba seriedad en su trato conmigo*
> 'He affected seriousness in his dealings with me'
> **b.** *A mi abuela la enfermedad le afectó los pulmones*
> 'The disease affected my grandmother's lungs'
> **c.** *La nueva legislación no afecta a la situación*
> 'The new legislation does not affect the situation'

We can see that the valency of *afectar* (see **4.3**) allows its participation in a number of constructions, in which the use of *a* varies considerably. *Seriedad* in (5.20a) is clearly a different kind of object from *la situación* in (5.20c): indeed, in dictionaries, these two usages are often given as different 'meanings' of *afectar*, *seriedad* being a kind of feature or behaviour which is assumed by the subject, while *la situación* is something on which the subject of *afectar* has an effect. In fact, it is possible to see the meaning of *afectar a* in (5.20c) as 'to have an effect on', in which case, it might be appropriate to think of *la situación* as being an indirect, or 'oblique', object of *afectar* (though, as we have seen, this does not square with the fact that it can form the subject of *afectar* in the passive: *la situación ha sido afectada por la nueva legislación*). What we may conclude is that *a* in (5.20c) and sentences like it is not really a 'personal *a*' in the senses we have established above, but simply a marker of this more indirect relationship, and that it is a means of distinguishing the different usages of *afectar*. (By the same token, we do not need to decide whether *la situación* is a direct object or not; it is simply one of the arguments *afectar* can take, part of the valency pattern of the verb.) In (5.20b) we see that the same kind of relationship as in (5.20c) is not marked by *a* when a clearly 'indirect' object is also present, presumably since *a* is reserved for use with the indirect object itself (cf. 5.18a–b). We may conclude, then, that *a* is part of the complex argument structure of *afectar* (see **4.3.4**), and not necessarily an instance of the 'personal *a*'. Spanish in fact has a number of verbs whose apparent direct objects take *a* in this way: *ayudar, obedecer, renunciar, suceder* and *sustituir* are some of them. It is part of the 'genius' of Spanish that *a* is available for this purpose.

5.3 Modality and the subjunctive

The subjunctive is traditionally considered to be a **mood**, a category of verb forms which from the semantic point of view express **modalities** such as possibility, command, etc. A great deal of scholarly effort has been expended on the question of how many meanings the Spanish subjunctive has: the record minimum appears to be two.[7] This quest has again been partially motivated by the laudable desire for maximum simplicity and generalisation in describing language, but partly once again because of a tacit assumption that to one form there ought to correspond one meaning. And once again we can see that Spanish has developed in such a way that what is important is not so much the semantic 'content' of the subjunctive so much as the presence of a contrast between subjunctive and indicative that can be exploited for meaningful purposes.

5.3.1 Subjunctive use determined by context

However, it is pertinent first of all to ask whether the subjunctive can be said to have a meaning at all in certain contexts. In many of its uses, it is required by a particular verb or construction, and an indicative is completely impossible. After the construction *para que*, for example, only the subjunctive can be used:

> **(5.21)** *Lea Vd. en voz alta para que oigan todos*

It would not be appropriate to claim here that the subjunctive form *oigan* in itself expresses purpose; the conjunction *para que* explicitly does that. Nor can we envisage what the meaning of the sentence might have been if the indicative mood of the verb had been used, since the indicative is simply not possible in this context. In this example, the subjunctive is automatically required; its use reminds us of gender and number agreements between nouns and adjectives, which are similarly completely automatic in Spanish and in themselves bear no meaning. A more complex, but even more revealing example, occurs in the syntactic relation sometimes known as negative-raising. The difference between sentences (5.22a and b) is that in (5.22a) the negative element *no* appears in the complement of *creo* while in (5.22b) it appears in the main clause with *creo* itself: it has been 'raised' from the subordinate to the main clause. The meaning of the sentence is essentially unchanged: both (5.22a) and

---

[7] See Bolinger (1974) and Lozano (1975).

(5.22b) mean 'What I think is that there is no possible solution' (the 'raised' construction certainly does not imply that there is no thinking on my part!). English, in fact, has a similar syntactic relation, as the suggested glosses show. However, negative-raising in Spanish brings about an automatic syntactic consequence: the mood of the complement verb changes from indicative to subjunctive. The fact that there is no significant change of meaning shows us that the choice between indicative and subjunctive is determined solely by the syntactic context.

>**(5.22) a.** *Creo que no hay ninguna solución posible*
>'I think there is no possible solution'
>**b.** *No creo que haya ninguna solución posible*
>'I don't think there is any possible solution'

However, it is not always such a straightforward matter to determine whether the subjunctive has meaning or not. It is often pointed out in pedagogical grammars that with the conjunctions *de modo que*, *de manera que* and *de forma que* the subjunctive / indicative contrast distinguishes between a consequence meaning and a purpose meaning, e.g.:

>**(5.23) a.** *Y entonces confesé mi culpa, de modo que todos supieron la verdad*
>'And then I confessed my guilt, so that (= as a result of which) everyone got to know the truth'
>**b.** *Y entonces confesé mi culpa, de modo que todos supieran la verdad*
>'And then I confessed my guilt, so that (= in order that) everyone should know the truth'

On the one hand, this seems a fairly clearcut example of a pair of sentences which contrast only in the use of the subjunctive or indicative, so we might plausibly conclude that it is indeed here that the contrast lies. On the other hand, it is clear that *de modo que*, etc., are ambiguous between consequence and purpose meanings. Conjunctions of purpose, as we have noted with *para que* (which has only this meaning), automatically require the subjunctive, so we could take the view that once it is known which meaning of *de modo que* is intended, there is effectively no choice of mood. A similar case arises with the complement of the verb *decir*, which can be used as either a **declarative** verb (a verb of saying) or an **imperative** verb (a verb of ordering):

>**(5.24) a.** *Le dije que cruzaba la frontera*
>'I told him that he was crossing the border'
>**b.** *Le dije que cruzara la frontera*
>'I told him to cross the border'

It so happens that *decir* can be used in both these senses; but there are many Spanish verbs which belong to either one class or the other, and for which the choice of complement mood is automatic. *Mandar*, *ordenar* and *pedir*, for example, can only be used as imperative verbs, while *comentar*, *declarar* and *observar* are normally used only as declarative verbs. Accordingly, in this case, it seems simplest to regard the indicative and subjunctive as being obligatorily used in the complements of declarative and imperative verbs respectively. In conclusion, the most we can say about the use of the subjunctive and indicative after *de modo que*, etc. and *decir* is that the choice of mood disambiguates these polysemous elements.

5.3.2 The subjunctive associated with particular contexts

For the contexts we have been looking at so far, it is therefore not really appropriate to claim that the subjunctive has meaning. What we can say, however, is that subjunctive use in Spanish is *associated with* a number of characteristic contexts; in other words, we can predict where the subjunctive will be used in terms of these contexts. They are the familiar headings of pedagogical grammars, and so will not be exhaustively exemplified here: complements of imperative verbs, complements of verbs of 'emotion', complements of verbs of denial, possibility and probability, future-referring temporal clauses and relative clauses whose antecedent (see **4.6.2**) is hypothetical or non-existent. This is quite a mixed bag about which it is difficult to make any generalisation that is not vacuous, though it can quickly be seen that the subjunctive is limited to subordinate clauses and that all these contexts seem to preclude the simple assertion of a fact. In some cases, the association with the subjunctive is a remarkably consistent one, as we have already noted for the complements of imperative verbs and conjunctions expressing finality or purpose. But in other cases the association is not consistent at all. I will look at two of these: constructions expressing hypotheses or conditions, and temporal clauses.

5.3.2.1 CONDITIONAL SENTENCES

The subjunctive is obligatory after a number of conditional conjunctions:

> (5.25) a. *Con tal que no llueva, hacemos una barbacoa*
> b. *Te dejo ir a condición de que me llames a medianoche*
> c. *Salgo mañana, siempre que no haya huelga*
> d. *Como suban los precios no podremos sobevivir*

Yet after *si*, which is the commonest and semantically most wide-ranging of the conditional conjunctions, the present subjunctive is impossible:

> (5.26) a. *Si no llueve, hacemos una barbacoa*
> b. *Te dejo ir si me llamas a medianoche*
> c. *Salgo mañana, si no hay huelga*
> d. *Si suben los precios no podremos sobevivir*

5.3.2.2 THE SUBJUNCTIVE IN TEMPORAL CLAUSES

As stated above, the subjunctive is used in all future-referring temporal clauses – this is an invariable rule of its use in Spanish. But it does not follow from this that the indicative is invariably used elsewhere: the conjunction *antes de que* always requires the subjunctive whatever the time-reference of its clause. An interesting development in the modern language is that conjunctions which primarily express posteriority (*después (de) que, luego que, desde que*, etc.) are increasingly used with the *-ra* form of the past subjunctive:

> **(5.27)** **a.** *Un portavoz de la compañía informó de la cancelación de quince vuelos de los 39 previstos entre las 13.00 y las 15.00 horas española, después de que hubiera suspendido otros siete anteriormente.* (http://www.espania.com/aspa/prensa.htm)
>
> **b.** *Asturnet es una empresa especializada en todo lo que tiene que ver con el mundo de las comunicaciones e Internet desde que iniciara su andadura en febrero de 1995* (http://www.asturnet.es/presentacion.htm)

It is perhaps not out of place to suggest some reasons for this usage, which disturbs the former clarity of subjunctive usage in temporal clauses. An obvious motivation is the obsolescence of the past anterior (*hubo hecho*) form, which is prescriptively required in a temporal subordinate clause when the main clause verb is in the preterite; thus corresponding to *después de que hubiera suspendido* in (5.27a) would be *después de que hubo suspendido*. The *-ra* form also has the advantage of being somewhat shorter than both the past anterior and the *había hecho* pluperfect, a property which may have commended it in journalistic register (see 7.2.1), where it is particularly common. Furthermore, the *-ra* form, which is etymologically descended from the Latin pluperfect (e.g. *amara* < AMĀVERAT) and was used as a pluperfect certainly until the Golden Age, has survived in Latin-American Spanish with this function (which has not affected its adoption as the past subjunctive of preference and which has not precluded its further extension in function as a general 'remote' past tense); indeed, it might be said to have an ambivalent modal status.[8] It may therefore be from this direction that the 'new' (in fact, coincidentally 'restored') usage in the Peninsula has sprung. Be all that as it may, the disturbance of the formerly rather clearcut rule concerning the use of the subjunctive in temporal clauses is likely to have been permitted just because in the end the distinction between the moods is not very clearly motivated.

5.3.2.3 OTHER IDIOSYNCRASIES OF SPANISH

Spanish subjunctive usage is full of such idiosyncrasies as the above. There are several words corresponding to the notion of English 'perhaps, maybe': *tal vez, quizá(s), acaso, a lo mejor*. The first three of these take either the indicative or subjunctive, a choice will be decribed further below, but *a lo mejor*, which is typical of the spoken language, takes only the indicative. We have already seen how conjunctions indicating consequence (*de modo que, de manera que, de forma que*) take the indicative; but *de ahí que*, which is a near synonym, takes only the subjunctive (it is no doubt significant that unlike the first three, *de ahí que* does not also function as a subordinating conjunction of purpose).

---

[8] See Kany (1951: 170–4) and the major study of Hermerén (1992).

5.3.3 Meaningful uses of the subjunctive

It was important to be rigorous about when the subjunctive cannot be said to have meaning in Spanish so that we can better appreciate those contexts in which it plausibly does have meaning. In **5.3.1** we examined the use of the indicative and subjunctive with the verb *decir* and concluded that *decir* belongs to two different meaning-classes of verbs, declarative and imperative, i.e. that it is lexically polysemous. Let us contrast that situation with the use of the indicative and subjunctive in the complement of the verb *temer*:

> **(5.28)** **a.** *Temía que lo supieran*
> 'I was afraid they would get to know'
> **b.** *Temía que no vendríais*
> 'I was afraid you wouldn't come'

The difference between the two is a subtle one, or at least appears subtle to English speakers because the English verbal expression *to be afraid* has similar semantic properties to Spanish *temer*. (5.28a) expresses a genuine fear while (5.28b) expresses a conventional, polite, fear. In English the difference is not signalled formally, but in Spanish it is only the meaning of genuine fear that requires the subjunctive. Should we, however, adopt the same solution as for *decir* (**5.3.1**), namely, that *temer* belongs to two quite different meaning-classes? This seems counterintuitive, since the two meanings of *temer* are much closer than the two meanings of *decir*; with *temer*, we are simply dealing with different degrees of fear, and it seems natural to conclude that it is these different degrees that the subjunctive / indicative contrast denotes.

5.3.3.1 POSSIBILITY

The situation with *temer* is not unlike another case in which it seems plausible to speak of a subjunctive / indicative contrast, this time based on degrees of likelihood with the adverbs *tal vez, quizá(s)* and *acaso* (already discussed in **5.3.2.3**). The contrast between

> **(5.29)** **a.** *Tal vez es demasiado corto*
> **b.** *Tal vez sea demasiado corto*

can be characterised as follows: (5.29a) is an open suggestion where if anything the speaker is asserting the view *es demasiado corto*; it is equatable with *Es demasiado corto, tal vez*. In (5.29b) the speaker's suggestion is much more tentative, or polite, because the degree of assertion is less and the dominant idea is the expression of possibility. Once again, it would be strange to suggest that *tal vez* has two different meanings, one requiring the indicative and the other the subjunctive, and so we conclude that the difference in meaning is a matter of degree and is signalled by the indicative/subjunctive contrast.

5.3.3.2 RELATIVE CLAUSES

A similar meaningful use of the subjunctive is in relative clauses. We have already noted in **5.3.2** that the subjunctive is required in relative clauses which have a negative or indefinite antecedent. Negative antecedents are lexically indicated: they include negative pronouns such as *nadie, nada* (5.30a), nouns preceded by *ningún* (5.30b) and, more generally, nouns which fall under the scope of negation (5.30c):

> **(5.30) a.** *No conozco a nadie que me pueda ayudar*
> **b.** *No hay ningún libro que explique este problema*
> **c.** *No hay razón que valga*

In such contexts the subjunctive is automatically required. But it is impossible to know whether a noun is definite or indefinite in its reference on the basis of its overt form; 'indefiniteness' is not so helpfully indicated. Sentences (5.31a) and (5.31b) are identical in all respects except for the indicative/subjunctive contrast:

> **(5.31) a.** *María quiere casarse con un hombre que tiene mucho dinero*
> **b.** *María quiere casarse con un hombre que tenga mucho dinero*

The meaning of (5.31a) is that the man who has a lot of money exists – he is the man María wants to marry. The relative clause is simply telling us something about this man. But the man in (5.31b) is only hypothetical, and María does not have anyone in particular in mind; here the relative clause is really setting the condition that must be met by the man she wants to marry. Here again, it would be strange to suppose that *un hombre* is in itself polysemous, and so we must conclude that the definite or indefinite nature of this antecedent noun is signalled entirely by the modal contrast in the relative clause.

5.3.3.3 EXTENDING THE RULES

Use of the indicative/subjunctive contrast to convey meaning is thus established as a feature of Spanish and is arguably one on which Spanish continues to build. However, the real 'genius' of Spanish comes with cases where in a sense the expected rules are broken; where contexts which appear automatically to require the indicative are used with the subjunctive, or vice versa. It is here that Spanish speakers can be seen to exploit the semantic contrast between indicative and subjunctive to the full.

We saw in **5.3.1** that the subjunctive is automatically required in negative-raised contexts. However, where the subject of the verb of thinking in the negative-raised main clause is not the speaker, there is room for the speaker to use an indicative rather than a subjunctive in the complement, and this has the semantic effect of dissociating himself or herself from the opinion given:

> **(5.32) a.** *Michael no cree que Panamá sea un país hispanohablante*
> **b.** *Michael no cree que Panamá es un país hispanohablante*

In (5.32a) the view given is simply represented as being Michael's, with no intervention by the speaker; in (5.32b), on the other hand, the speaker asserts that Panama is indeed a Spanish-speaking country, contrary to Michael's belief.

Verbs of thinking with no negative-raising do not normally take the subjunctive. But sometimes a subjunctive may be used by speakers to indicate a marked lack of certainty.

> **(5.33) a.** *Sospecho que es mentira*
> **b.** *Sospecho que sea mentira*

(5.33a) is the usual choice; (5.33b) has the meaning 'I suspect it may be untrue (but I'm not really sure)' (see Butt & Benjamin 2000: 258–9).

Finally, use of the subjunctive with a verb of thinking can turn the sentence into an invitation:

> **(5.34) a.** *Había pensado que os veníais a tomar una copa*
> 'I thought you were coming to have a drink' (implies 'but obviously not')
> **b.** *Había pensado que os vinierais a tomar una copa*
> 'I thought you might come and have a drink' (i.e. 'Please come and have a drink')

5.4 The reflexive

5.4.1 The versatility of the Spanish reflexive

In English, the reflexive pronouns (*-self*) are generally used with literal or what I shall call 'conventionalised' reflexive meaning:

> **(5.35) a.** Literal:
> *John saw himself in the mirror*
> (*Himself* is coreferential with the subject *John*)
> **b.** Conventionalised:
> *John found himself in trouble*
> (John did not literally 'find himself'; the expression means 'to be (in a situation)'

The Spanish reflexive, by contrast, has a remarkably wide range of functions, which are briefly characterised in Table 5.2.

For a number of these functions English uses quite different structures. The reciprocal is distinctively expressed in English by forms such as *each other*; the *be* passive renders the passive and middle functions; indefinite subjects are expressed by either an indefinite subject pronoun (e.g. *people, someone*) or by the *be* passive in the case of transitive verbs. The 'ergative' function often corresponds to the use of an English intransitive verb (see **4.3.5.1**):

> **(5.36)** Spanish:
> *La puerta se cerró con estrépito*
> English:
> *The door shut noisily*

Table 5.2 Functions of the Spanish reflexive

Example	Meaning-type	Relation of reflexive pronoun to subject	Syntactic function of reflexive pronoun
Juan **se afeitó** (a sí mismo)	literal	non-reciprocal	direct object
Juan **se vio** (*a sí mismo) en dificultades	conventionalised (see above): the meaning of *se vio* is not literally 'saw himself', but 'to be'. This is revealed in Spanish by incompatibility with the reinforcing phrase *a sí mismo*.	non-reciprocal	direct object
Los dos amigos **se abrazaron** (uno a otro)	literal	reciprocal: the diagnostic of this is compatibility with the reinforcing phrase *uno a otro*.	direct object
A veces yo **me preguntaba** por qué trabajaba tanto	literal	non-reciprocal	indirect object
Nos dimos la mano (uno a otro)	literal	reciprocal	indirect object
Me corté las uñas	literal	non-reciprocal	indirect object (benefactive)

Estos hongos no **se digieren** muy fácilmente	'**middle**': the middle voice may be thought of as a kind of passive, but one in which an action 'gets done', with no specific agent envisaged, though if an agent were involved, it would be distinct from the subject of the reflexive (here, mushrooms cannot digest themselves).
La ventana **se cerró** con estrépito	'**ergative**': the action is carried out of its own accord, without external agency.
El secreto **se reveló** mucho más tarde por un antiguo espía ruso	passive: this sentence is akin to the dynamic *ser* passive (see **5.5.1.4**) *el secreto fue revelado*.
Se despreciaba al dictador	indefinite subject: the meaning of this sentence is 'people despised the dictator / the dictator was despised'; no lexical subject is possible (cf. **la gente se despreciaba al dictador*). The verb in this example is transitive.
Aquí **se vive** bien	indefinite subject: as above; the verb here is intransitive.
Juan **se bebió** media botella de champán	'nuance': the reflexive is slightly different in meaning from the non-reflexive verb; in this particular example, *beberse* expresses **telic** aspect (implying the completeness of the action: 'drink up (completely)' rather than simply 'drink'). The verb here is transitive.
El techo **se** me **vino** encima	'nuance': similarly, *venirse* expresses the notion of 'come down, fall down' rather than simply 'come'. The verb here is intransitive.

As we saw in **4.3.6**, it is also interesting to note that English intransitive verbs sometimes express a reflexive notion too, e.g.:

(5.37) *John washed = Juan se lavó*

There is no regular equivalent of Spanish 'nuance' reflexives in English; however, we might note that many phrasal verbs in English perform very similar functions. The atelic/telic distinction pointed out for Spanish *beber/beberse* is paralleled in English *drink/drink up, write/write down, wash/wash up*, etc.

The Spanish reflexive thus has a remarkable versatility, and it might occur to us to ask why all its various functions do not clash and create ambiguity in the language. The answer is partly to do with general pragmatic considerations concerning the relation between the subject and the verb, and partly to do with the valency of verbs (see **4.3.5**).

5.4.1.1 PRAGMATIC CONSIDERATIONS

A verb which normally takes a personal subject and a non-personal object (e.g. *leer*) cannot be interpreted literally as a reflexive with a non-personal subject; in (5.37), we know pragmatically that newspapers are not capable of reading, only of being read, so there is no risk of this passive reflexive being interpreted as a literal reflexive:

(5.38) *Este periódico se lee en muchos países*

The same is true most of the time of reflexives and reciprocals, although the disambiguating devices *a sí mismo*, etc. (reflexive), and *uno a otro, mutuamente* (reciprocal) are available. In (5.39), it is hardly likely that the friends would be embracing themselves, and so the sentence has a reciprocal interpretation:

(5.39) *Los dos amigos se abrazaron*

Pragmatic considerations, usually involving a broader discourse context, are involved with the discrimination of literal and conventionalised meanings of reflexives. *Verse*, illustrated above in its conventionalised sense of 'to be', does of course have a literal meaning of 'see oneself' too:

(5.40) a. Conventionalised:
Juan se vio en dificultades
b. Literal:
Juan se vio en el espejo

But is is unlikely that Juan would literally be seeing himself in difficulty or that he would be situated in a mirror. (These readings are of course not totally impossible, but they go against our normal pragmatic expectations.)

Sometimes contextual factors of a much broader nature will be involved in the interpretation of reflexives. Consider the following sentences:

(5.41) a. *Me mojé con la lluvia* (middle)
'I got wet in the rain'
b. *¿Nos vamos a mojar?* (literal)
'Shall we go for a dip?'
c. *Carlitos se mojó* (conventionalised)
'Carlitos has wet himself'

Although the same verb is used in all three cases, there is no difficulty about deciding which is the appropriate interpretation. The mention of rain in (5.41a) indicates that getting wet was not deliberate, involving the subject as the agent, but was something that happened to the subject unintentionally. (5.41b), uttered in the context of a group on a beach, refers to going for a swim and so getting wet intentionally through one's own agency. The conventionalised interpretation of (5.41c) is perhaps likely only in the context that Carlitos is a little boy. (If you try switching these interpretations round you will see how unlikely they are!)

5.4.1.2 THE VALENCY OF VERBS

The valency of verbs is particularly important in the recognition of indefinite subject and nuance reflexives. For intransitives, which have no direct objects, the reflexive pronoun simply cannot be given a literal interpretation since there is no argument slot for it to fill (5.42a–b). For transitives, the presence of an object is incompatible with the interpretation of the reflexive pronoun as an object (5.42c–d), since the object slot is already filled.

(5.42) a. *Se está bien aquí* (indefinite subject intransitive)
(*Estar* can have no direct object, and so *se* cannot be given a
literally referring function)
b. *Se fue a la ciudad* (nuance intransitive)
(*Ir* can have no direct object)
c. *Se despreciaba al dictador* (indefinite subject transitive)
(*Se* cannot be interpreted as any other argument of *despreciar*
apart from the direct object, which is pre-empted by *el dictador*)
d. *Se comió la chuleta* (nuance transitive)
(It is difficult to envisage that *se* represents any argument of
comer)

5.4.1.3 OVERLAP OF FUNCTIONS

In some cases the semantic distinctions made in the table above are probably not very significant. We have distinguished the passive function of the reflexive from its indefinite subject function, largely on the grounds that in the example of the passive given there was an overt agent expressed. However, these two constructions often seem to be semantically very close. (5.43a) is apparently an example of a reflexive passive, and (5.43b) an example of an indefinite subject transitive; comparisons with more clearcut instances of these types, involving plural objects, are given:

(5.43) a. *Este libro se lee mucho* (passive)
Compare: *Estos libros se leen mucho*
b. *Se lee mucho este libro* (indefinite subject)
Compare: *Se critica mucho a los políticos*

The only formal difference between the two sentences is in the word order, and, even so, the order given appears to be obligatory only for the indefinite subject construction. Since a verb-first order is a perfectly admissible possibility in a Spanish declarative sentence, (5.43a) could in fact have been expressed in a way (*se lee mucho este libro*) which made it formally indistinguishable from (5.43b). Is there, then, any difference in meaning between the 'indefinite subject' reflexive and the 'passive' reflexive here? The different word order expresses a different choice of topic (cf. **4.4.3**), but apart from that there seems to be very little to choose between them.

5.4.2 Further exploitation of the reflexive in Spanish

The extensive use of the reflexive is undeniably part of the 'genius' of Spanish, where it has come to be used systematically as a means of expressing the passive notion (we may perhaps see the middle and ergative functions as aspects of this) and the notion of indefinite subject. The range of the reflexive does not there, however. One of the most interesting aspects of Spanish reflexive usage is what has here been labelled the 'nuance' usage. It is one of the most difficult phenomena of modern Spanish to describe, because it seems that each verb that participates in the nuance reflexive has an idiosyncratic behaviour, as a result of which no constant semantic value can be given to the reflexive (see Moreira Rodríguez & Butt 1996).

We will begin with an example that is relatively easy to describe. The reflexive use of *beber*, like *comer* (see **5.4.1**), contrasts with the non-reflexive to denote the completion of the action (telic aspect):

(5.44) a. *Hay que beber para vivir*
'One has to drink to live'
b. *Se lo bebió de un trago*
'He/she drank it down at one gulp'

Here, then, the reflexive seems to have an aspectual nuance; another pair of verbs which seems to behave in a similar way is *creer/creerse* 'to believe'/'to believe (fully)'. The same kind of distinction can perhaps also be seen in *volver/volverse* 'to turn'/'to turn (round)'. But there are several other bases for distinction. *Caer* has the general meaning of 'to fall': as a natural process (5.45a–b), a deliberate act (5.45c) or in a figurative sense (5.45d–e). *Caerse*, on the other hand, has the nuance of accidental (5.45f–g) or unexpected (5.45h) falling, corresponding roughly to English 'to fall over', 'to fall down'.

(5.45) a. *Cayó mucha nieve aquel año*
b. *La manzana cayó del árbol*

    c.   *Cayó de rodillas*
    d.   *La ciudad cayó en manos del enemigo*
    e.   *Este año Navidad cae en sábado*
    f.   *Se me cayó el jarrón*
    g.   *Mi hermanito se cayó al río*
    h.   *Se ha caído un árbol en el jardín*

Like *caer/caerse* is *parar/pararse* 'to stop'/'to stop (unexpectedly)'. The reflexive form of a number of verbs of motion seems to indicate movement away from a point of origin (5.46b) or towards a destination (5.47b), while the non-reflexive form simply denotes the action itself (5.46a and 5.47a):

    (5.46) a.   *¿Cómo marchan las cosas?*
              'How are things going?'
        b.   *Cuando me enteré de lo ocurrido, me marché de la casa*
              'When I found out what had happened, I left the house'

    (5.47) a.   *El tren llegó a las cinco*
              'The train arrived at five o'clock'
        b.   *Llégate al supermercado y compra algo para la cena*
              'Get down to the supermarket and buy something for supper'

Some verbs, however, seem quite idiosyncratic. As an example, we will examine the particularly problematic verb *quedar*, which has a 'nuance' reflexive *quedarse*. *Quedar* is often described as having the meaning 'to remain' in the sense of 'to be left' while *quedarse* has the meaning of 'to stay (for a time)':

    (5.48) a.   *No me quedan más*
              'I don't have any more left'
        b.   *Me quedé en casa todo el día*
              'I stayed at home all day'

But such is the range of usages of these verbs that this is only a very partial explanation of their meanings. Both verbs have **grammaticalised** (come to be used to indicate a grammatical function, and consequently semantically weakened) to the point at which they are little more than copulas (see **5.5**). *Quedar* is often the equivalent of *estar* (5.49a–b), and *quedarse* is one of the many ways of expressing the notion of 'becoming' ((5.49c), and see **5.5.2**):

    (5.49) a.   *El instituto queda en esa calle*
              'The institute is in that street'
        b.   *Queda claro que no va a admitirlo*
              'It's clear he/she is not going to admit it'
        c.   *Se está quedando sorda*
              'She's going deaf'

But the difference is not always so clearcut, and the two verbs appear to be almost interchangeable in some contexts (5.50a–b and c–d); the suggested glosses attempt to convey something of the subtleties of the meanings involved here:

(5.50) **a.** *Quedó huérfano a la edad de diez años*
'He was left an orphan at the age of ten'
b. *Se quedó huérfano a la edad de diez años*
'He became an orphan at the age of ten'
c. *Quedé en casa*
'I was left at home'
d. *Me quedé en casa*
'I stayed at home'

5.5 Being and becoming

English has two copular verbs (see **4.3.1**), *to be* and *to become*, which are extremely wide-ranging in their reference. They correspond almost exactly to similar verbs in a number of Western European languages: French *être* and *devenir*, German *sein* and *werden*, Latin ESSE and FIERĪ. As a result, the notions of 'being' and 'becoming' appear to speakers of these languages to be natural, well-defined concepts. However, if we look a little further around the languages of the world, we will see that this situation is very far from being universal, and it is, in fact, questionable whether these notions, which are often taken for granted in Western culture and philosophy, are as well-defined as they might appear: we have here a good example of **linguistic relativism**, which suggests that the thought of human beings is dictated by the language they speak.[9] One of the best-known features of Spanish is that it has two copular verbs, *ser* and *estar*, which both express, in English terms, the notion of 'being'.[10] What is less often pointed out, though it should perhaps come as no surprise given the relatedness of these concepts (since 'becoming' can be thought of as meaning 'beginning to be'), is that Spanish also has no single verb corresponding to English *become* but employs a range of verbal expressions and other devices to render this English notion.

5.5.1 *Ser* and *estar*

As has been the case with the other phenomena described in this chapter, the traditional pedagogical approach to describing the distribution of *ser* and *estar* has been to try to find an overarching semantic characterisation for each form. The most notorious of these, which still seems to be retailed in Spanish language teaching (although no currently respected reference work actually refers to it), is the idea that *ser* is somehow associated with permanence and *estar* with temporariness. This thoroughly misleading principle can instantly be disposed of by counter-examples such as the following:

(5.51) 'Permanence' with *estar*:
a. *El cuarto está permanentemente vacío*

---

[9] See, for example, Verhaar (1967–73).
[10] There is a vast bibliography on this subject; some references which are particular recommended are Luján (1980 and 1981), Molina Redondo (1987), Navas Ruiz & Jaén (1989) and Porroche Ballesteros (1988).

b. *María está siempre triste*

'Temporariness' with *ser*:

c. *El vicepresidente fue presidente en funciones durante dos meses*

5.5.1.1 *SER* AND *ESTAR* WITH ADJECTIVES

What is perhaps fruitful, however, is to look for a semantically-based principle to characterise the use of *ser* and *estar* with adjectives. Adjectives with *ser* denote inherent properties of nouns which relate to class-membership, physical characteristics, etc., while adjectives with *estar* denote non-inherent or 'accidental' properties. Thus:

> **(5.52)** Inherent properties:
> **a.** *Esta novela es muy triste*
> **b.** *Juana es muy guapa*
> Non-inherent properties:
> **c.** *Mi tía está enferma*
> **d.** *Estoy muy nervioso*

What is 'inherent' and what is 'non-inherent' is to a large extent clear pragmatically from what we know in general terms about the nature of the relation between noun and adjective. We know that being ill, or nervous, is not the natural, inherent, state of human beings, while a book can be inherently sad because of its theme or content, and a person can be inherently pretty. Spanish marks overtly semantic contrasts based on these meanings which remain covert in English: consider the following sentences:

> **(5.53) a.** *Aunque todavía no soy viejo, estoy viejo para bromas de este tipo*
> 'Although I'm not yet an old man, I'm too old for jokes of that sort'
> **b.** *Calzo el número 44, así que un 42 me está pequeño*
> 'I take size 44, so a 42 is small on me'

In (5.53a), *estoy viejo* does not imply that I am 'inherently' old, i.e. that I belong to the class of old people, and so there is no contradiction between the assertion of *estoy viejo* and the denial of *soy viejo*. In (5.53b), a size 42 is not a particularly small shoe inherently (one could say, quite consistently, for example, *los zapatos número 42 no son pequeños*), but it is small for someone who normally takes a size 44. The notion of non-inherentness also provides us with quite a powerful way of accounting for the effect of the use in Spanish of *estar* with an adjective where pragmatically *ser* might have been expected, and this is certainly another instance of the 'genius' of Spanish in exploiting a feature of the language in order to maximise its expressive power. Consider the following sentences:

> **(5.54) a.** *¡Qué blanca está la nieve!*
> **b.** *La ministra estuvo más flexible*
> **c.** *Antes cuando entré y te vi dormida estabas más guapa, parecías una niña* (Carmen Martín Gaite, *El cuarto de atrás*, 6th ed., Barcelona: Destino, p. 207)

In (5.54a) *¡qué blanca está!* has the meaning of 'how white it looks!'. Pragmatically, we know that snow is white (*la nieve es blanca*), but this sentence is suggesting that it is 'non-inherently', that is, extraordinarily, white, perhaps after a recent snowfall with the sun shining brightly. (5.54b) exploits the relation noted in the sentences of (5.53) that *estar* + adjective and *ser* + adjective are often incompatible: it implies that the minister was (unusually for her) behaving in a more flexible way, and so certainly does not imply the inherent property of *la ministra era flexible*. Similarly in (5.54c) there is no implication that the girl was in fact prettier (*eras más guapa*) but that she looked prettier as she slept.

However, even the notion of inherentness does not seem to explain all instances of the usage of *ser* and *estar* with adjectives. The following sentences, for example, do not seem to exemplify inherentness or non-inherentness in a very clearcut way:

    (5.55) a.   *Mi amigo es zoroástrico*
        b.   *La sala está limpia*
        c.   *Miguelito está contento*

What is 'inherent' about being a Zoroastrian? One might indeed have been born into the faith, but (5.55a) would be the only linguistic possibility for referring to even a recent convert. Similarly, it is not obvious that cleanliness cannot be an inherent property of a room or that a little boy cannot be inherently happy. It seems that notions of inherentness and non-inherentness will not completely account for the use of *ser* and *estar* with adjectives and we need to look more systematically at the behaviour of *ser* and *estar* in a wider range of contexts.

5.5.1.2 *SER* WITH NOUNS

Apart from their use with adjectives, *ser* and *estar* are used in several other contexts in Spanish, which are all much more straightforward to describe and which have nothing to do with the 'inherentness' / 'non-inherentness' distinction. With a noun or pronoun complement (equational sentences), *ser* is the only possibility; infinitives and clauses, because of their noun-like nature (see also **4.5.1**) are also used only with *ser*:

    (5.56) a.   *Pedro es profesor*
        b.   *El problema es ese*
        c.   *Lo importante es creer*
        d.   *El que el niño no quiera ir es lógico*

When an adjective is used predicatively as a noun, it follows that *ser* must be the copula:

    (5.57) a.   *Napoleón era un corso muy conocido*
        b.   *Mi amiga es una católica muy tradicional*

If *corso* and *católica* are not qualified by another adjective, as in (5.58a–b), these sentences become

    (5.58) a.   *Napoleón era corso*
           'Napoleon was a Corsican'

b. *Mi amiga es católica*
'My friend is a Catholic'

There is in fact a rather thin dividing line between adjectives and nouns in Spanish since, as in (5.58a–b), most adjectives can also be used as nouns. This is an important difference between Spanish and English: in English, although some forms denoting class-membership can indeed function as both adjectives and nouns (e.g. *(a) German*, *(a) Catholic*, but not *(*an) English*, *(*a) Spanish*), and still more adjectives are available as nouns in the plural (e.g. *the French*), most common descriptive adjectives seem to require a noun head in a singular or non-generic plural noun phrase (e.g. *the young* has only a generic (plural) meaning; it cannot have the meaning 'the young person' and cannot be pluralised as **the youngs*). The English translations of (5.58a–b) given above suggest that *corso* and *católica* are indeed essentially nouns, so sentences like these can be incorporated into our general principle that with noun complements only *ser* is used as a copula. So, we now have a grammatically-based explanation of why (5.55a) (*Mi amigo es zoroástrico*) involves *ser* which is much more satisfactory than the semantic principle of 'inherentness': *zoroástrico* may be construed as an adjective functioning as a noun in this sentence, and hence as forming part of an equational sentence with *ser*. With regard to sentences like (5.55a) and (5.58a–b) the question now arises, however, as to how we know when an adjective is functioning as a noun. Two kinds of answer can be given. In the first place, we can test the compatibility of sentences like those of (5.58) with the corresponding sentences of (5.57), where we see that indeed there is no essential difference in meaning as regards the relation between the subject and the adjective/noun complement: *Napoleón era un corso muy conocido* necessarily implies *Napoleón era corso*. Secondly, we may note that there is no relation between *Napoleón* and *corso* that can be expressed by using *estar*: **Napoleón estaba corso* simply has no plausible interpretation. This is rather unlike many instances of genuine predicative adjectives, where, as we have seen, important semantic contrasts are encoded by the choice between *ser* and *estar*. We might expect that the 'genius' of Spanish would come to extend the range of expressive possibilities in this area too, and, indeed, there are occasional examples of the type

(5.59) *Estás muy francesa*

which has the very marked meaning (see **5.1**) 'You're behaving in a very French way' and does not *necessarily* imply (though it may be the case) *eres francesa*.

The simple rule that *ser* is the equational copula is thus a very powerful one. Counter-examples of the following kind are sometimes proposed:

(5.60) *El mar está espejo*
'The sea is (like) a mirror'

but such sentences are always highly marked stylistically (see Chapter 8); (5.60) is a metaphor in which *espejo* is being used in an adjectival way, and is certainly not straightforwardly equational.

5.5.1.3 *SER* AND *ESTAR* WITH LOCATIVE COMPLEMENTS

Estar is the copula used to indicate position, whether physical, temporal or 'moral':

> **(5.61) a.** *Nuestra casa está en pleno centro de la ciudad* (physical location)
> **b.** *Estamos a 10 de mayo* (temporal location)
> **c.** *Estoy en dificultades* ('moral' location)

Ser is only used in this way with the adverbs *lejos* and *cerca* and to denote a geographical location, in which cases it is commutable with *estar*. The use of *ser* appears to be particularly favoured where no subject is expressed:

> **(5.62) a.** *No es/está lejos*
> **b.** *Es/está en Extremadura*

Otherwise, *ser* is used with locative complements to indicate where an event takes place:

> **(5.63)** *La conferencia es en esta aula*
> 'The lecture is (= is taking place) in this lecture-room'

The subject noun in such a case must denote an event. Contrast

> **(5.64) a.** *La clase es el tercer piso*
> **b.** *La clase está en el tercer piso*

(5.64a) means that the class (event) is taking place on the third floor while (5.64b) means that the class (the group of people comprising the class) is on the third floor.

Once again, this principle extends to include some kinds of adjective function. In the following sentence

> **(5.65)** *El señor Alvárez está muy alto en la organización*

alto indicates rank or position and so requires *estar* (we may contrast *es alto* which means 'he's tall').

5.5.1.4 *SER* AND *ESTAR* WITH PAST PARTICIPLES

Both *ser* and *estar* combine with past participles to form passives in Spanish (see 4.3.4.1). The distinction between the two is aspectual in nature: *ser* + past participle is what may be called the dynamic passive and *estar* + past participle the stative passive. The dynamic passive (4.3.4.2) is the exact equivalent of the corresponding active verb:

> **(5.66)** *La panadera vendió el pan = El pan fue vendido por la panadera*

The stative passive, by contrast, denotes a state which is the result of a dynamic action:

> **(5.67)** *El pan estaba vendido*

(5.67) does not denote the activity of selling, but the state of the bread's having been sold. This sentence would be appropriate if one was describing how one went into a baker's shop but found that all the bread on display was not in fact for sale but was reserved for customers who had already paid for it:

> **(5.68)** *En la panadería había mucho pan, pero estaba vendido todo*

These two passives have quite distinctive properties.[11] As we have seen (**4.3.4.1**), the *ser* passive is extremely restricted in spoken register. It is less frequently used in the 'imperfective' tenses (the present and the imperfect), though there is some evidence that in these tenses it is coming to have a progressive aspectual interpretation, e.g.:

> **(5.69) a.** *Los exámenes de ADN ya son permitidos como evidencia en casos de violación en el Reino Unido* (*El País*, 23.10.87)
> 'DNA tests are now being allowed as evidence in rape cases in the United Kingdom'
>
> **b.** *Las primas de Rolf Carlé eran requeridas en amores por un par de pretendientes* (Isabel Allende, *Eva Luna*, p. 89)
> 'Rolf Carlé's cousins were being wooed by a pair of suitors'

The *ser* passive can freely take an **agent** (see **4.3**), that is to say, the subject of the corresponding active sentence can participate in the *ser*-passive in a prepositional phrase introduced by *por*, as in (5.66) above. The *estar* passive can only have an agent in certain circumstances, namely, when the subject of the corresponding active verb is necessarily involved in the ongoing state represented by the past participle. Thus in (5.70a), where the resultant state of the window does not require the ongoing involvement of the agent who opened it, no agentive phrase is possible, whereas in (5.70b), where the presence of the rust is necessary for the window to remain blocked, an agentive phrase is acceptable:

> **(5.70) a.** *La ventana estaba abierta (*por la limpiadora)*
> **b.** *La ventana estaba bloqueada (por óxido)*

Not all superficial combinations of *ser* + past participle are passives, however, since past participles can also function as adjectives. In the following sentences we can tell that the past participles are adjectival because of (a) the presence of adjectival modifiers such as *muy* or the intensifying inflection *-ísimo* and (b) the lack of any exactly corresponding active sentence (I have suggested a possible agent, though in fact the expression of an agent in any of the sentences (5.71a–c) with the meanings given is impossible):

> **(5.71) a.** *Tu postura es muy exagerada*
> 'Your point of view is very exaggerated'
> Compare *Tu amigo exagera tu postura* 'Your friend exaggerates your point of view' = *Tu postura es exagerada por tu amigo* 'Your point of view is being exaggerated by your friend'

---

[11] For a detailed study of these constructions and the passive reflexive, see Pountain (1992).

b. *El alumno es muy aplicado*
'The pupil is very hard-working'
There is no plausible active equivalent: compare *"La maestra aplica mucho al alumno* '''The schoolteacher applies the pupil a lot'

c. *La película es aburridísima*
'The film is extremely boring'
Here there is no potential active equivalent since *aburrir* means 'to bore'

Past participles often have a different nuance when used as adjectives (compare *aplicado* in (5.72b)).

(5.72) a. *Esos días eran muy agitados*
'Those days were very hectic' (not 'agitated')
b. *Esta pintura es conocida de todos*
'This painting is well-known to everyone' (implies 'well-known', not just 'known')

All the above are examples of the adjective denoting an inherent property of the subject noun. With *estar* + past participle, however, the distinction between stative passive and copula + adjectival past participle is harder to draw. In (5.73a)

(5.73) a. *Estoy muy deprimido*
b. *Un joven muy deprimido*
c. *(Las noticias) me han deprimido mucho*

deprimido may well be an adjective (it can take the modifier *muy*), and can be used attributively as such (5.73b); but is also consistent with the active sentence (5.73c). We should also observe that *deprimido* is not an inherent property of *yo*, and this is also consistent with the semantics of the stative passive. There is an important overlap, then, between the past participles of stative passive constructions and adjectives which represent non-inherent properties of the subject noun. We can now see that a number of adjectives which occur with *estar*, though not morphological past participles, nevertheless are semantically very like past participles in nature:

(5.74) a. *La sala está llena de gente*
b. *Las peras no están maduras todavía*
c. *Estoy muy triste*

In (5.74a) the room has been filled as a result of people coming in; in (5.74b) natural processes, e.g. the sun, have not yet ripened the pears; in (5.74c) I have become sad perhaps as the result of something happening to me. (5.52c) and (5.52d) can be interpreted in the same light: in (5.52c) a virus or physical condition has made my aunt ill and in (5.52d) something has made me nervous. We may now also return to (5.51b); the fact that *vacío* is the opposite of *lleno* (cf. 5.74a) gives us a natural explanation as to why it too takes *estar*.

Contento (5.55c) may also be thought of as an adjective that is semantically very like a past participle.

The use of *ser* and *estar* with adjectives, then, appears to be the product of a number of different principles. Adjectives with *ser* represent inherent qualities, or they function as nouns. Adjectives with *estar* are stative, representing non-inherent properties, or they function as locative adverbs.

What we have seen in the course of all this discussion is how Spanish appears to exploit the *ser/estar* contrast in a number of ways. It is fairly clearcut with locative adverbs and past participles, but it is rather more complex with adjectives. Sometimes it seems that Spanish simply exploits a convenient gap: the use of *verde* with *estar* in the meaning of 'unripe' corresponds well with the use of its antonym, *maduro*, which was exemplified in (5.74b), and it provides a contrast with *ser verde* 'to be (= to have the inherent property) green'. It is part of the genius of Spanish to experiment with and build on these distinctions.

5.5.2 Becoming

Distinctions within the semantic field of 'becoming' may be seen as collateral to the distinctions made within the field of 'being'. The list of individual verbs of 'becoming' is more numerous, and all have slightly different nuances. The two most versatile verbs are *hacerse* and *volverse*, which can both be used with either nouns or adjectives. *Volverse* is perhaps the more neutral with adjective complements; in this context, *hacerse* is restricted to processes which can be thought of as in some way natural or expected. Thus (5.75b) is usual while (5.75d) is not:

> **(5.75) a.**   *Mi padre se vuelve viejo*
> **b.**   *Mi padre se hace viejo*
> **c.**   *Juan se volvió pálido*
> **d.**   *'Juan se hizo pálido*

With noun complements, on the other hand, *hacerse* is perhaps more neutral (5.76a), since *volverse* would here have the meaning of 'to turn into'; (5.76b) is thus natural, but (5.76c) is pragmatically odd:

> **(5.76) a.**   *Mi hijo se hizo abogado*
> **b.**   *La princesa se volvió rana*
> **c.**   *'Mi hijo se volvió abogado*

Having said that, *hacerse* implies evolution or progression rather than simple change. *Se hizo muchacho* means 'he grew up into a boy', not 'he became a boy again'. And although *hacerse* and *volverse* seem to be conventionalised reflexives (see **5.4.1**), *hacerse* may still have a nuance of 'to make oneself': *la princesa se hizo rana* means 'the princess turned herself into a frog'.

A more restricted verb is *ponerse*. This is available only with adjective complements, and is broadly parallel to the copula *estar*, as can be seen in (5.77a–b). (It will be remembered that *estar* similarly cannot be used with noun complements – see **5.5.1.2**.) The implication accordingly is that adjectives used with *ponerse* are not inherent properties of the subject of the verb:

(5.77) a. *Se puso muy contento*
'He became very happy'

b. *Estaba / *Era muy contento*
'He was very happy'

A number of periphrastic constructions also express the notion of becoming. *Llegar a (ser)* 'to get (to be)' and *venir a (ser)* 'to come (to be)' are the most versatile of these, the first carrying the nuance of achievement (5.78a) and the second the nuance of more casual evolution (5.78b); they are not restricted to use with *ser* (*estar* can also be used), and with *ser* they can take both adjective and noun complements. But although they are in some ways 'safe' translations of English *become*, they are not especially frequent in Spanish; *venir a ser* in particular is somewhat archaic. The verb *convertirse en*, on the other hand, which takes only noun complements, is so frequent that it seems to be losing something of its literal meaning of 'to be converted into', and is much more freely used in Spanish than this English equivalent.

(5.78) a. *El orfelinato llegó a ser escuela*
'The orphanage became a school'

b. *–Mire, señor – observó sorpresivamente la vieja–, la historia viene a ser como un bife con papas fritas, uno lo pide en cualquier lado y siempre tiene el mismo sabor.* (Julio Cortázar, *Fantomas contra los vampiros multinacionales* Buenos Aires: Gente Sur, 1989)
'"Look, sir," the old woman observed out of the blue, "history is getting to be like steak and chips; you can order it anywhere and it always tastes the same."'

c. *Su rivalidad se convirtió en amistad*
'Their rivalry became friendship'

We have not exhausted all the possibilities for the translation of English *become* in Spanish. Some Spanish verbs have 'to become' as part of their meaning, e.g. *oscurecer* 'to become dark', *envejecer* 'to become old', *mejorar* 'to become better', *enfermar* 'to become ill'. The suffix *-ecer*, which derives from the Latin **inchoative** suffix -ESCĔRE, which had the meaning of 'to begin to', is, not surprisingly, especially associated with this value. The middle and ergative functions of the reflexive (see **5.4.1**) also sometimes express 'becoming': *agrandarse* 'to become bigger', *alargarse* 'to become longer', *ensancharse* 'to become wider', *entristecerse* 'to become sad'. We can also widen the range of verbs of 'becoming' to include *caer*, which can be used in contexts which denote a misfortune. such as *caer enfermo* 'to fall ill', and *quedar* and *quedarse* have the closely related senses of 'to be left' (e.g. *quedar huérfano* 'to become / be left an orphan', and (5.50a) above). As we examine the various nuances of all these verbs, we realise that there are other verbs and expressions in English which are very close in meaning to *become*: *get*, *grow* and *turn* are particularly common, especially in speech, and so in this respect Spanish and English are not so dissimilar. The crucial difference between the two languages is that the latter verbs are in a hyponymic relation (see **3.4**) with *become*, while in Spanish there is no such over-arching term.

EXERCISES

1. Apart from reference to sex (e.g. *empleado/a*), is there any semantic basis for the distinction between masculine and feminine in the suffix *-do*? Consider at least the following examples:

batido 'milkshake' / *batida* 'beating, searching'
calzado 'footwear' / *calzada* 'road'
helado 'ice-cream' / *helada* 'frost'
pasado 'past' / *pasada* 'wipe (effect of passing a cloth over something)'
peinado 'hairstyle' / *peinada* 'quick combing'
picado 'act of grinding, mincing or chopping' / *picada* 'bite, sting'
pisado 'treading (of grapes)' / *pisada* 'footstep, footprint'
planchado 'ironing (as task)' / *planchada* 'a single application of the iron'
puñado 'handful' / *puñada* 'blow with the fist'
tostado 'toasting' / *tostada* 'slice of toast'

2. Try and find examples of pairs of sentences which are discriminated in meaning only by the personal *a*. An example is the title of Rosa Montero's novel *Te trataré como a una reina* ('I will treat you like a queen', i.e. as if <u>you</u> were a queen): as *Te trataré como una reina* the meaning would be 'I will treat you as if <u>I</u> were a queen'. Can you identify any recurrent patterns?

3. Investigate how the 'nuance' reflexive changes the meaning of sentences in Spanish by collecting examples of their use and non-use and asking native speakers for their reactions. You will find a great deal of information on this subject in Moreira Rodríguez & Butt (1996).

4. We have identified a number of verbs which take either the indicative or subjunctive in their complements (*decir, pensar, sospechar, temer*). How many further examples can you find? What is the basis for the difference between the indicative and subjunctive?

5. We have not looked at prepositional phrase complements of *ser* and *estar* (apart from those which have a locative meaning, in **5.5.1.3**). Some examples are:

(a) *Estamos de vacaciones*
(b) *Esta mesa es de madera*
(c) *Mi amigo es de Costa Rica*

(d) *Estas fuentes no son de fiar*

(e) *Antes de encontrarse un trabajo permanente, mi novia estaba de camarera en un hotel.*

(f) *Estás de broma*

(g) *Estamos a dieta*

(h) *El nuevo colegio está todavía en proyecto*

(i) *La pared está sin pintar*

Make a study of these and other prepositional phrase complements. Do they bring any new information to the question of the distribution of *ser* and *estar*?

6 | Regional and social variation

6.1 Standard written language

6.1.1 Standardisation

In Chapters 3, 4 and 5 we have mainly been addressing features of the standard, written language. As we saw in Chapter 1, this is what many people understand by 'the Spanish language'; but the existence of an agreed written standard is not an essential feature of language: human languages are primarily means of oral communication and writing is a relatively recent phenomenon in human history. Indeed, we might put it even more strongly and say that a standard language is an artifice, the result of sometimes arbitrary decisions by language planners which are then imposed on the speech-community, through education and official usage, often with the political motive of centralisation (though there are also practical communicative advantages in an agreed standard). Standardisation may be a more or less conscious process. We saw in Chapter 1 how in the Spanish-speaking world this is achieved through the RAE today. However, even before this, in the 13th century a degree of standardisation was achieved in early written Castilian through the Royal Scriptorium usage known as 'castellano drecho' which developed under the aegis of Alfonso X, and from the late 15th century onwards humanist interest in the vernacular meant that there was an increasing concern with linguistic conformity. For Spanish speakers of the 21st century, a tradition of standardisation is therefore well established and taken for granted. But, as it happens, Spain in recent years has given us some interesting insights into rather more sudden processes of standardisation as a result of the encouragement of languages other than Castilian, which it is worth pausing briefly to examine.

   Catalan, Galician and Basque, the three languages which have been given co-official status with Castilian within the *autonomías* of Catalonia, Galicia and the Basque Country respectively, are the best developed in this respect, but there have also been attempts to provide standardised forms of Asturian and Aragonese. The standardisation of Catalan and Galician makes an interesting contrast. Both Catalan and Galician had continued to be widely used within Catalonia and Galicia despite their demise as written languages as they were overshadowed by Castilian (see **6.2.3.4**). In Catalonia in particular, there had been a considerable rekindling of interest in Catalan as a literary language during the 19th century (the *Renaixença*). Modern standard Catalan was largely the creation of one man, Pompeu Fabra (see Badia Margarit (1975 [1964]: 87–92). In 1913, the Institut d'Estudis Catalans, founded six years previously with sponsorship from wealthy industrialists, adopted the spelling system (the *Normes ortogràfiques*) which Fabra had already largely worked out in previous publications. Fabra remained the guiding spirit behind the *Gramàtica catalana* of

1918 and the *Diccionari general de la llengua catalana* of 1932. Fabra's concern was to create a universal form of the written language which would satisfy speakers from all regions, and so a kind of average, or **diasystem** (Weinreich 1954), informed by both the medieval and the modern literary languages, was taken. Thus the letters *a*, *e*, *o* and *u* are all used in the spelling of unstressed syllables, although a distinction between /a/ and /e/ and between /o/ and /u/ is not univerally made in this context; for many speakers, therefore, including *barcelonins*, the spelling system is etymological in this respect. Where a variety of morphological forms exist, more than one standard is often admitted: thus both *el* and *lo* are given as forms of the masculine definite article. Choice of words for the *Diccionari* was governed by a desire to 'restore' native Catalan words in preference to Castilian borrowings. Overall, however, the language of Barcelona, which was the centre of cultural activity in both the Middle Ages and the modern period, is the most significant ingredient in the creation of the new standard.

By contrast, Galician had no such obvious focus for the standard. The development of modern standard Galician thus began as an essentially academic endeavour: it may be reckoned to have begun with the publication in 1933 of *Algunhas Normas pra a Unificazón do Idioma Galego* by the Seminario de Estudos Galegos at the University of Santiago, originally drawn up for use within the Seminar. The standard that has eventually emerged is eclectic in nature and cannot be associated with any one pre-existing variety of Galician, though the morphology is most often that of the Galician southwest, while the phonology (reflected in the spelling) is largely that of the Galician centre. This is illustrated in Table 6.1, where a range of regional variants (Southwestern, Northwestern, Central and Eastern) is shown, with the chosen standard form underlined.

6.1.2 The spoken language

Whereas the standard written language is by definition invariable (except by conscious language planning decision), the spoken language varies in a number of ways. It is such variation in the spoken language that is the subject of this chapter. Although in the last analysis variation is infinite, since no two people speak in exactly the same kind of way (cf. **2.3.1**), variation can also frequently be seen to be systematic; we can make a number of generalisations about variation in the spoken language according to the geographical origins of speakers, their social class and their network of friendships and other associations, their age and their sex.

6.2 Regional variation

The best known kind of linguistic variation is geographical, or diatopic, variation. The way in which a person speaks (unless modified for some reason) associates them, sometimes very precisely, with a particular geographical location. George Bernard Shaw's depiction of the phonetician Henry Higgins in *Pygmalion*, who purports to be able to identify the exact

Table 6.1 Choices in the formation of standard Galician (adapted from Carballo Calero 1976 [1966]: 81).

	SW	NW	C	E
Development of Lat. -ANU: 'brother'	irmán	irmá	irmao	irmao
Development of Lat. -ANA: *irmá* (corresponds to Cast. *hermana*) 'sister'	irmán	irmá	irmá	irmá
Plural of nouns ending in a nasal consonant: *cans* (cf. O. Cast. *canes*) 'dogs'	cans	cas	cas	cais
Plural of nouns ending in -*l*: *animáis* (corresponds to Cast. *animales*) 'animals'	animás	animás	animás	animáis
Principal diminutive suffix: *paxariño* (corresponds to Cast. *pajarito*) 'little bird'	paxariño	paxariño	paxariño	paxarín
Apical [s] or coronal [s]	[s]	[s̺]	[s̺]	[s̺]
seseo: *moça* (Cast. *moza*) 'girl'	['mosa]	['moθa]	['moθa]	['moθa]
Distinction between /s/ and /θ/ in syllable-final position: *luz* (Cast. *luz*) 'light'	[lus]	[lus]	[luθ]	[luθ]
geada (pronunciation of *g* before *a*, *o* or *u* as [x] rather than [g] or [ɣ]): *agulha* (Cast. *aguja*) 'needle'	[a'xuʎa]	[a'xuʎa]	[a'ɣuʎa]	[a'ɣuʎa]

street where a Cockney speaker lives on the basis of their pronunciation, is a popular, if exaggerated, representation of this phenomenon.[1]

6.2.1 Linguistic atlases

The late 19th and early 20th centuries saw the awakening of interest in **dialect geography**, the result of which was that the compilation of many large scale linguistic atlases was undertaken, one of the earliest and most famous being Jules Gilliéron's *Atlas Linguistique de la France*. Such projects are still under way. Spain still awaits the publication of a comparable overall survey: work on the *Atlas lingüístico de la Península Ibérica* (*ALPI*), covering the whole Peninsula, was interrupted by the Civil War and only a part of the first planned section, on phonetics, has been published. More circumscribed atlases have been produced, however, under the direction of the late Manuel Alvar: for Andalusia the *Atlas lingüístico-etnográfico de Andalucía* (*ALEA*) (Alvar *et al.* 1961–73), Aragon, Navarre and La Rioja (Alvar *et al.* 1979–83), the Canary Islands (Alvar 1975–8) and, most recently, Cantabria (Alvar *et al.* 1995). A linguistic atlas of Castilla-La Mancha (García Mouton & Moreno

---

[1] Henry Higgins is generally thought to have been modelled on Henry Sweet, one of the founders of modern phonetics.

Fernández, forthcoming) is to be published shortly. Latin America offers more problems, partly due to the vastness of the areas involved, and partly to the fact that most of the population lives in large cities, for which geographically-based surveys are inappropriate. Alvar himself, together with Antonio Quilis, was editing a macro-atlas of the whole region (Alvar & Quilis forthcoming); there are atlases already in existence for Puerto Rico (Navarro Tomás 1948), Southern Chile (Araya 1973) and Colombia (Buesa Oliver & Flórez 1954, and Flórez 1981–3), and projects in progress for Mexico (Lope Blanch 1990–) and Uruguay (Thun & Elizaincín, forthcoming).

Linguistic atlases are impressive and admirable projects, and many have recorded data which would otherwise have been totally lost to scholarship as the result of changes in the nature of society. It is important, however, to be aware of their limitations. A typical enquiry consists of seeking responses to a fairly lengthy preconceived questionnaire and so there is a considerable danger of a field-worker receiving atypical responses because of the rather artificial nature of such an enquiry (the so-called 'observer paradox'). Another usual, but problematic, technique has been the formal interviewing of a single informant, selected because he or she was born in the locality, has always lived there and ideally has rarely travelled far afield. The following is the description of informants for the *ALPI*:

> Tenían que ser naturales del pueblo estudiado, y se procuraba que
> también lo fuesen sus padres y esposas. Eran preferidos los que habían
> viajado poco y no habían residido fuera del lugar, y también los
> analfabetos o muy poco instruidos, a fin de que se viesen exentos de la
> influencia de los dialectos de otras localidades y de la lengua culta.

The linguistic situation recorded in such an enquiry is therefore very different from the kind of situation we encounter today, where the vast majority of speakers are literate, mobile and aware, if only passively, of many other linguistic varieties within their speech-community through the broadcasting media.

The snapshot of usage obtained by the atlases is actually very partial: the method is designed for the recording of the speech of rural communities, and it does not extensively reflect kinds of variation other than diatopic, such as age, sex and social class (it would be unfair to say that dialect geographers were not aware of other kinds of variation, but extensive investigation of these across the vast areas they covered in the interests of recording diatopic variation was clearly impractical). Even the selection of localities can be an issue: the *ALPI*, for instance, has a dearth of localities in Old and New Castile, reflecting the expectation (false, as it has turned out) that these would not be significantly different from standard Castilian. The data obtained does not necessarily provide us with a structural view of language: for example, while considerable phonetic detail is likely to be recorded, the phonological system of a particular speaker does not necessarily emerge, although many atlases also provide synoptic interpretative maps. Most of the questions are lexically- or phonetically-orientated, the ethnographic/linguistic atlases directed by Alvar being also concerned to capture a full lexicon for each locality, especially vocabulary which relates to agriculture and local customs. This is not to say that there has been no attempt to elicit morphological and syntactic data as well, but such data has tended to be restricted to features which are anticipated to be of interest; in syntax, for instance, it is usual to enquire about such things as the choice of verb form in conditional sentences or the use of second-person pronouns, but it is not usual to attempt the systematic study of complementation patterns or the use of the subjunctive. Another rather frustrating feature of linguistic atlases is that they often do not provide examples of the continuous speech of the localities they have investigated, so the user has no real idea of what the speech of a particular locality is like in this respect.

Despite these caveats, the work of the linguistic geographers has naturally given extremely valuable insights into the nature of linguistic variation. Perhaps its most valuable achievement is the demonstration that certain areas exhibit a particular linguistic feature while others do not, and that in many cases there is a clear geographical divide between these areas. The boundary that can be drawn between such areas is known as an **isogloss**. Isoglosses are often included in one way or another on the maps drawn by dialect geographers, or can be inferred from them: Figure 6.1 shows a map of Aragón, taken from Alvar (1996), in which a series of different symbols has been used to make generalisations about the raw individual results obtained, together with an alternative isogloss representation.

However, another important result of dialect geography was the realisation that such isoglosses do not always cluster together and that in many areas there is essentially a continuum of features, with the geographically closest areas sharing the most features. This has the interesting consequence that the traditional notion of 'dialect' as applied to particular geographical areas (e.g. the Galician 'dialect', the Leonese 'dialect') is untenable, since such 'dialects' could only be delimited by the arbitrary selection of one isogloss. An example of this is given in Figure 6.2, where it can quickly be seen that there are no coherent linguistic boundaries which will delimit the 'Leonese' dialect.

6.2.2 'Dialects'

The term '**dialect**' has also suffered from being commonly used as a pejorative term for any non-standard language; within Spain it has caused particular offence when applied to languages other than Castilian, such as Catalan and Galician. The Spanish Constitution of 1976 is careful to use terms such as 'lenguas españolas' and 'modalidades lingüísticas' rather than 'dialectos'. Linguists have tended to use the term in two ways.

The first is essentially synchronic (pertaining to the present-day; see 10.1): to distinguish between a standardised national language ('language') and what may be regarded as variants of that language ('dialects'): in this sense the speech of an Argentine farmhand, for example, is a 'dialect' of Spanish. In particular there has been a strong association between 'dialect' in this sense and the notion of 'diatopic variant', the dimension of variation investigated by the 'dialectologists'. According to this view, all speech represents a particular 'dialect', one of which may happen to be favoured as the standard 'dialect' (indeed, a famous characterisation of the term 'language' is that it is 'a dialect with an army and a navy').[2] This synchronic definition of 'dialect' assumes that we know what the limits of a particular speech-community are. When there is a strong sense of speech-community, as in the case of the Spanish-

---

[2] Usually attributed to the Yiddish scholar Max Weinreich.

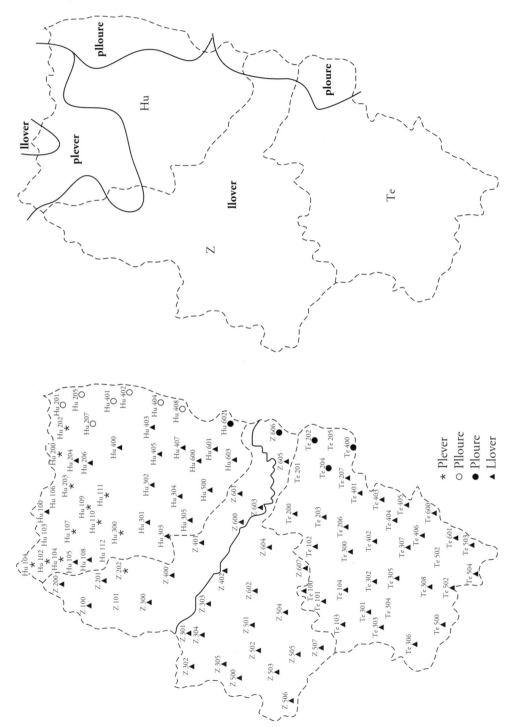

Figure 6.1 Two ways of showing isoglosses (left: based on Alvar 1996: 280)

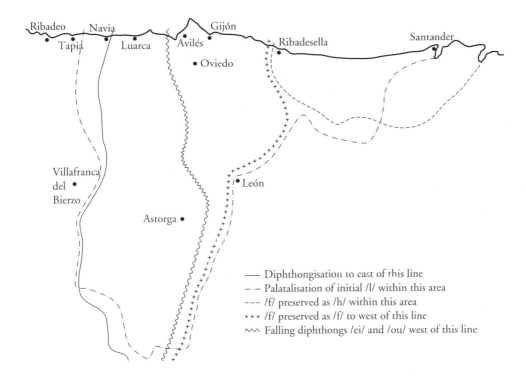

Figure 6.2 The isoglosses of 'Leonese'

speaking world, this seems to be a relatively straightforward matter, though we shall see in Chapter 9 that there are initially problems as regards what can and cannot be considered 'Spanish': no one is in any doubt that our Argentine farmhand referred to above speaks a form of 'Spanish' (including the farmhand himself). But what about subjects interviewed for the *ALPI* who gave the responses in Table 6.2, do they speak a 'dialect' of Spanish, of Catalan or of something we might call 'Aragonese'?

Table 6.2 Responses from speakers of 'aragonés' (*ALPI*)

		ALPI map number					
		29	64	73	44	48	32
ALPI location	606	*caballo*	*dreita*	*endo*	*cerrojo*	*clau*	*caxa*
	607	*caballo*	*drecha*	*an*	*ferrollo*	*clau*	*caxa*
	610	*caballo*	*drecha*	*nonde*	*cerrollo*	*clau*	*caxa*
	611	*caballo*	*drecha*	*ande*	*cerrojo*	*clau*	*caxa*

most 'Castilian'   most 'Catalan'

Castilian	*caballo*	*derecha*	*dónde*	*cerrojo*	*clavo*	*caja*
Catalan	*cavall*	*dreta*	*on*	*forellat*	*clau*	*caxa*

According to the *ALPI*, they call their language *aragonés*, which might suggest that this is a sufficient criterion; but then many inhabitants of Andalusia consider that they speak *andaluz* (see **6.2.3.2**), though their 'dialect' is recognised by many other members of the Spanish speech-community as being 'Spanish' in a way that the speech of Upper Aragon is not. It is not surprising, then, that the apparently more objective criteria of political and geographical boundaries have sometimes replaced the rather more nebulous awareness of speech-community, so that the Aragonese informant is deemed to speak *aragonés* solely by dint of living in Aragon. (It is in fact interesting to see how, correspondingly, there have recently been moves to create non-Castilian speech-communities on a territorial basis, Aragon being a case in point: see Green 1994.)

The second way in which linguists have used the term 'dialect' is diachronic in nature: in the course of time a language may come to be spoken over a broad area across which variation is intensified, sometimes to the point of mutual incomprehensibility. This is what has happened with the Romance family of languages, for example: modern French, Spanish, Portuguese, Catalan, Italian, etc. are all recognisably developments from their common ancestor, Latin, and it is common to speak of them as 'dialects' of Latin, and the process of fragmentation as 'dialectalisation'. (We must not make the mistake, however, of imagining that in such a scenario the parent language is monolithic and uniform in nature: there is no reason to suppose that parent languages are any less variable than their present-day descendants.)

This, however, is an over-simplistic view. In describing the linguistic geography of the Iberian Peninsula, it is convenient to distinguish between the 'primary' variation which is the result of the ongoing fragmentation of Latin and the 'secondary' variation observable in Castilian (and Portuguese), the two national standardised languages, as they have diffused over territories where 'primary' varieties were originally spoken, or, indeed, continue to be spoken. We must also bear in mind the more recent propagation of standard forms of Catalan and Galician. This produces a potentially complex picture: it is not inconceivable, for instance, that a young inhabitant of rural Pontevedra will speak a 'native' variety of Galician, be able to use the standard Galician now taught in schools, besides what may be described as a Galician-coloured variety of Castilian. In some areas the situation is even more complex than that, with 'mixed' languages and code-switching attested (see **6.2.3.4**, **9.5**). But this complexity is not reflected in the linguistic atlases; where there is such multilingualism (or diglossia), only the local 'native' response is recorded. There is a tacit assumption by dialect geographers that these responses represent a 'purer', more authentic kind of language – but they do not reflect the linguistic realities of today.

Despite such limitations, linguistic atlases have provided a great deal of raw material which is still being fully digested and interpreted. One interpretational strand is what we might call archaeological: the possible relation of isoglosses to old tribal territories or administrative boundaries of one kind or another, to movements in population, or to trade routes. These in turn often correlate with natural geographical boundaries such as rivers and mountains. Another strand is more linguistic in nature: isoglosses may reveal such phenomena as the irradiation of a feature from a prestige centre, the extent of the survival of a feature of a **substrate** language (that is, a language used before the language of the colonisers) or of the presence of an **adstrate** borrowing (that is, a borrowing from the language of a neighbouring culture). In the next two sections we will look at some of the isogloss patternings that are found in Spain and Latin America in this light, as well as providing some examples of regional variation.

6.2.3 Spain

The dialect geography of the Iberian Peninsula clearly mirrors its political history. In 711 the Visigothic kingdom of Spain, which covered the entire Peninsula, was invaded from north Africa by Muslim peoples generally known in history collectively as the Moors, and almost totally occupied (the area of the Peninsula in Moorish hands can be conveniently labelled Al-Andalus, the Arabic name for Spain, which is the origin of the modern name Andalusia). The Moorish presence in the Peninsula formally came to an end nearly 800 years later in 1492 with the taking of the Kingdom of Granada by the forces of the Catholic Monarchs, Ferdinand and Isabella, which marked the culmination of a gradual process of 'reconquest' by the Christian states of the north. The isoglosses which tend to run north-south (Figures 6.2 and 6.3) reflect the expansion of the northern Christian states southwards. In the centre, Castile came to occupy a pre-eminent position, and was the spearhead of the reconquest of the whole of the southern half of the Peninsula, precluding southerly expansion by León and Aragon. In the west, the county of Portugal gained political inde-

Figure 6.3 Some isoglosses of the Iberian Peninsula

pendence of Castile/León in 1143 and expanded due south in parallel with Castile, while in the east, Aragon/Catalonia made similar but rather slower progress, reaching as far south as Alicante.

The diphthongisation isogloss (Figure 6.3) marks out almost exactly the territorial limits of Castile in the centre and south of the Peninsula in the late Middle Ages. Another feature of Peninsular isoglosses is the lack of coincidence of isoglosses in the northern part of the Peninsula as against the clustering of these isoglosses further south (Figure 6.2). Again this is indubitably the consequence of history: the north exhibits a continuum of features typical of the 'primary' variation of Latin and very similar to what we find throughout France and Italy, while the greater uniformity of the centre and south show the territorial expansion of the northern kingdoms, the linguistic consequence of which was the effacement of the 'primary' variants of Latin in Al-Andalus (collectively known as 'Mozarabic'). The process involved a number of elements: first, the resettlement of the southern lands by northern speakers; second, possibly a certain linguistic **levelling** (the suppression of minority or irregular forms) as a result of the movement of speakers from a number of different northern areas; third, the setting of new political boundaries which inhibited movement and contact in the newly occupied zones (Penny 2000: 108). However, the south does have differentiating isoglosses which reflect the 'secondary' dialectalisation of Castilian as it came to be adopted in the reconquered territories. The isoglosses interestingly sometimes coincide with the 'primary' variation of other areas, so that the absence of an opposition between /θ/ and /s/ in the south of Spain is shared with areas of Galaico-Portuguese and Catalan, and the maintenance of /f/ as [h] is shared with a small area of the north immediately around Santander.

6.2.3.1 THE CHARACTERISTICS OF CASTILIAN

As we have seen, it is impossible to delimit a 'Castilian' dialect area in the north of the Peninsula, unless by this we mean the speech of the medieval county of Castile (though its frontiers were constantly changing). However, certain features of modern standard Castilian distinguish it from the Romance varieties of originally neighbouring territories, and in this section we shall look at some of these. In most cases the individual features we identify are not unique to modern Castilian, though their overall configuration is. These features are well-known from historical studies of Castilian. We shall then look at something which is not so widely appreciated: how some of the features of modern standard Castilian differ from variants in the speech of the geographical areas of Cantabria, Old and New Castile, which are often reckoned as constituting the homeland of Castilian. In carrying out this study, we shall inevitably have to pay some attention to the history of the Romance languages.

6.2.3.1.1 Castilian in contrast with other Peninsular Romance varieties

There are a number of phonetic developments which are characteristic of Castilian. The diphthongisation of Latin Ĕ and Ŏ evident in Castilian *tierra* < Lat. TĔRRA and *muerte* < Lat. MŎRTE [MŎRS] is shared with areas of Asturias/León and Aragon, but is absent from the extreme west and east of the Peninsula (contrast Pg. *terra, morte*, Cat. *terra, mort*); Castilian contrasts with its immediate neighbours in that this diphthongisation does not take place before a palatal consonant: so Cast. *ojo* < OCast. ['oʒo] < Lat. ŏcŭLU[s], where diphthongisation of ŏ is prevented by the developing palatal consonant /ʒ/, contrasts with such results as the modern Asturian *güeyo*, in which diphthongisation to /we/ has taken place unimpeded). There are some palatalisations which are characteristic of Castilian: the /li/ of Lat. MŬLĬĔRE [MŬLĬĔR], which remains as a lateral palatal [ʎ] in most Peninsular varieties (cf. Pg. *mulher*), has become [x] in modern Spanish *mujer*, having passed through the stage [ʒ] in the medieval language; and the /kt/ group of Lat. OCTŌ develops to the palatal affricate [tʃ] in Spanish *ocho* (contrast Pg. *oito*, Cat. *vuit*). These changes already distinguished Castilian from its northern neighbours in the Middle Ages and today are common to all varieties of the Spanish-speaking world, even though they may have undergone subsequent further modification. Since the 15th century, there have been other consonantal changes which have been adopted in the standard Peninsular language, though they do not characterise all varieties of modern Spanish. Latin initial /f/ before a vowel weakened to /h/ and subsequently fell altogether in most areas (the so-called 'f > h change'), so Lat. FĪLĬU[s] yields modern *hijo* /ixo/ (by contrast with Pg. *filho*, Cat. *fill*); however, the sound [ɸ] or [h] is retained in southwest Andalusia (Figure 6.4).

Figure 6.4 Maintenance of initial /h/ in Andalusia: realisations of *horno* (< Lat. FURNU(S)).

Spanish now has no distinction corresponding to Latin /b/ and /w/; so in Sp. *bien* /bien/ < Lat. BĔNE /bene/ and *viene* /biene/ < Lat. VĔNIT /wenit/ the initial consonants are identical, while in the Portuguese **cognates** (parallel forms) *bem* /bẽ/ and *vem* /vẽ/ they are different. (Some varieties of Judeo-Spanish do preserve such a contrast: see **9.1.4.1.**) There has been extensive change since the medieval period in the sibilant consonant system of Spanish. In Old Castilian, it is generally reckoned that there were seven sibilant phonemes: /ts/, /dz/,

/s/, /z/, /ʃ/, /ʒ/ and /tʃ/. In the development of Castilian, a series of phonemic mergers took place to produce the following standard Peninsular phonemic system (/tʃ/ was unaffected by this development and so is omitted):

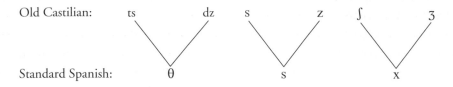

Figure 6.5 The development of the Spanish sibilants

Although all Romance Peninsular varieties, which originally had similar medieval sibilant systems (though not necessarily deriving from Latin sources in quite the same way), experienced some merger in this area, the characteristic feature of Castilian is that it ended up with a set of exclusively voiceless consonants: Portuguese and Catalan still have contrasts between /s/ and /z/ and between /ʃ/ and /ʒ/. This change has been the basis for considerable variation within the Spanish speech-community: Judeo-Spanish (see **9.1.4.1**) has a quite different set of mergers which do not involve devoicing, and Andalusian and Latin-American varieties, though sharing devoicing, show further mergers (see **6.2.3.2.1** and **6.2.4.2.1**).

6.2.3.1.2 'Innovating' and 'conservative' varieties

Linguists have often characterised varieties as 'innovating' or 'conservative'. There are perhaps two senses in which a variety can be thought of as 'innovating'. In the first place, an innovating variety shows a relatively greater degree of difference from its ancestor, while 'conservative' varieties appear to maintain more features of their ancestor. All the changes we have considered in the previous section are innovating in this sense in Castilian: the change of initial /f/ to /h/ followed by the fall of /h/ appears to represent a conspicuous movement away from Latin, whereas Portuguese and Catalan, which still have the initial /f/ in all environments, preserve the Latin phoneme. Secondly, in this particular feature, Castile can be seen to be the area of origin of this change, since it does not propagate beyond Castilian territory.

Castilian has often been represented as a particularly innovating Peninsular Romance variety; such innovation being associated, often somewhat nationalistically, it has to be said, with the role of Castile as the vigorous spearhead of the Reconquest – even such an authority as Lapesa (1980: 173) wrote:

> El dialecto castellano evoluciona con más rapidez que los otros y... se
> muestra distinto de todos, con poderosa individualidad. Castilla,
> levantisca y ambiciosa en la política, revolucionaria en el derecho, heroica
> en su epopeya, fue la región más innovadora en el lenguaje.

But while Castilian (or, more accurately, its speakers) might be thought of as innovating in certain respects, it is rash to think of innovation as being characteristic of the language as a whole. We can instantly think of Castilian features which are rather conservative: unlike some of its immediate neighbours in the north, there is no palatalisation of Latin initial /l/ (compare such results as Cat. *llop*, Asturian *chobu* < Lat. LŬPU[S]); intervocalic /l/ and /n/

which have been lost in Portuguese and Galician are preserved (Sp. *dolor* but Pt./Gal. *dor* < Lat. DOLŌRE[M], Sp. *luna* but Pt./Gal. *lua* < Lat. LŪNA); nasalisation of vowels has generally not taken place in Castilian (certainly not to the extent of creating new nasal vowel phonemes, as has happened in Portuguese), and final vowels have not fallen in Castilian as extensively as in Catalan. Moreover, some features of Castilian which might be seen as innovating in the context of the Iberian Peninsula are shared with other Romance languages. The monophthongisation of Latin /au/ is innovating by comparison with Portuguese and Galician, which maintain /au/ as a falling diphthong [oṷ] (Pg. *ouro* < AURU[M]); but the movement of /au/ to /o/ is not restricted to Castilian. It is a change which is widely shared throughout the Romance languages, and its distribution suggests that if anything it may have irradiated from the centre of the Latin-speaking world to include the east and centre of the Iberian Peninsula, but not the extreme west.

In conclusion, while individual changes (indeed all changes!) may be thought of as 'innovating', it is probably misleading to claim that one particular diatopic variety is more or less 'innovating' than another overall.

6.2.3.1.3 Differences between the modern standard and the speech of Old and New Castile

There is a common perception that standard Spanish (often referred to as the 'best' Spanish) is spoken in Old Castile. It is not the only prestige norm in the Peninsula: Andalusian *seseante* speech and the educated speech of Madrid are also esteemed; but it is notable that the educated speech of Burgos and especially Valladolid have a prestige value which is quite disproportionate to the social or economic importance of these localities (see Williams 1987: 19–21). One reason for this perception is the knowledge that, historically, it was the Romance of Castile which provided the basis for standard Spanish. This occurred first in the Middle Ages, when the output of the Royal Scriptorium of Alfonso X at Toledo established a norm for written chancery Castilian; the speech of Toledo was regarded as the most prestigious into the 16th century. In the mid-16th century, the establishment of the capital in Madrid by Philip II led to a shift in standard, with the incorporation of a number of features which appear to have had their origin in Old Castile (Philip himself was born and brought up in Valladolid), most notably the further weakening and loss of initial /h/ and the devoicing of the medieval sibilants (see Figure 6.5). Another reason is no doubt that many speakers from Castile preserve features which are reflected in the standard spelling of Spanish but have been lost in other regional varieties, most obviously the distinction between /s/ and /θ/.

As we saw in **6.2.1**, the expectation of the identity of the standard with the regional speech of Old and New Castile led to the neglect of these areas in the *ALPI*. However, more recent investigations have revealed considerable variety in the speech of Castile as well as lack of conformity with the standard. *Yeísmo* (see **2.3.4**) is widespread: Hernández Alonso (1996: 200) reports that 60% of speakers in the city of Burgos are *yeísta* and that the figure is higher for Valladolid, Palencia, Zamora, Ávila and Segovia, though the higher proportions of non-*yeísta* speakers in older age-groups suggests that this may be a fairly recent phenomenon. Intervocalic /d/ is very widely lost, especially in past participles in *-ado*, to yield pronunciations such as [ao], [au] or even [aṷ], and intervocalic /ɾ/ is similarly prone to loss (so, for example, *para* is pronounced [pa] and *parece* [pa'eθe]). The weakening of final /d/

is also widespread; sometimes it falls completely, giving pronunciations such as *ciudad* [θjuˈða] and *salud* [saˈlu], and sometimes it devoices to [θ] ([θjuˈðaθ], [saˈluθ]), the latter being peculiar to Old Castile.

Consonant groups involving a syllable-final plosive are very frequently simplified in speech. Table 6.3 shows some examples: in the first two, the plosive is completely lost and in the second two the plosive is converted to a fricative:

Table 6.3 Syllable-final plosives in Castilian speech

	Standard	Castilian speech
doctor	[dokˈtoɾ]	[doˈtoɾ]
examen	[ekˈsamen]	[eˈsamen]
directo	[diˈɾekto]	[diˈɾeθto]
digno	[ˈdigno]	[ˈdixno]

Another phonetic feature of the speech of Castile, widely encountered in the popular speech of the Spanish-speaking world as a whole, is the pronunciation of initial /bwe/ and /we/ as [gwe], e.g. *bueno* [ˈgweno], *huella* [ˈgweja]. In New Castile there is some weakening of syllable-final /s/ and some use of /s/ for /θ/ and vice versa; also, the opposition between /ɾ/ and /l/ is often neutralised in syllable-final position (Moreno Fernández 1996: 219). These features are more thoroughly realised in Andalusia (**6.2.3.2**).

The phenomenon of *leísmo* (the use of *le(s)* as a masculine direct object pronoun referring to people) is a well-known characteristic of Castilian which is admitted by the Real Academia as standard, alongside the rigorous distinction between *lo(s)*, *la(s)* for direct object, whatever its nature, and *le(s)* for indirect object that is typical of Andalusia and Latin America, that is to say, of the overwhelming majority of the Spanish-speaking world. Also widespread, but not admitted as standard, is *laísmo*, the use of *la(s)* as a feminine indirect object pronoun. A schematic representation of these different systems is given in Table 6.4 (though there is a good deal of variation within *leísta* and *laísta* systems).

However, recent investigations have revealed considerable variation in third-person pronoun usage in Castile which is not standard (Fernández Ordóñez 1994). The principal patterns observable are (a) *la(s)* is used as a feminine indirect object pronoun (*laísmo*), (b) a distinction is made between **mass** nouns (nouns denoting a quantity, such as *azúcar*, *leche*; mass nouns do not retain such a meaning if they are pluralised, but then denote a 'type of' the substance, e.g. *quesos españoles* 'Spanish cheeses' = 'Spanish types of cheese') and **count** nouns (nouns denoting individual entities, which can be pluralised without such a change in meaning), (c) *lo(s)* is used as a masculine indirect object pronoun. For example, in Palencia, northeast Burgos and Valladolid, *lo* is used to refer to mass direct and indirect objects of whatever gender, while *le(s)* refers to masculine count direct and indirect objects and *la(s)* to feminine count direct objects and indirect objects: an example of this use of *lo* is

(6.1) a. *La sangre hay que revolver<u>lo</u> para que no se cuaje* (Fernandez Ordóñez 1994: 84)
'You have to stir the blood so it doesn't congeal.'
(*Lo* refers to the mass concept *sangre*, which is a feminine noun; it is used as the direct object of *revolver*.)

b. *Lo eché, lo di una vuelta, lo amasé bien la carne* (*ib.*, 85)
'I laid the meat out, turned it over and kneaded it well.'
(*Lo* refers to the mass concept *carne*, which is a feminine noun; it is used as the direct object of *eché* and *amasé* and as the indirect object of *di*.)

Table 6.4 *Leísmo, loísmo* and *laísmo*

loísmo

	direct object	indirect object
m.sg.	*lo*	*le*
f.sg.	*la*	
m.pl.	*los*	*les*
f.pl.	*las*	

Example: *—¿Dónde está Miguel? —Lo vi en la biblioteca.*

leísmo

	direct object		indirect object
	animate	inanimate	
m.sg.	*le*	*lo*	*le*
f.sg.	*la*		
m.pl.	*les*	*los*	*les*
f.pl.	*las*		

Example: *—¿Dónde está Miguel? —Le vi en la biblioteca.*

laísmo

	direct object	indirect object
m.sg.	*lo*	*le*
f.sg.	*la*	
m.pl.	*los*	*les*
f.pl.	*las*	

Example: *La dices que no vaya* (standard *Le dices que no vaya*).

Such variation has a number of intriguing aspects. The third person pronouns form a number of different referential systems in the regional varieties of Castile, and so differences in meaning which are not represented elsewhere in the Spanish-speaking world are encoded in Castile. The distinction made in the alternative standard *leísta* system between *le* and *lo* encodes animacy vs. non-animacy in masculines; *laísmo* encodes a gender distinction in the indirect object (between *le* and *la*), and the use of *lo* as in (6.1) encodes a distinction between mass and count noun reference. In fact, variation between *lo* and *le* means that the distinction between direct and indirect object is not always easy to substantiate (see also **5.2**).

A feature of northerly areas of Old Castile, particularly associated with the Spanish of the País Vasco, is the use of the conditional in place of the past subjunctive, giving usages such as

> **(6.2)** **a.** *Si tendría tiempo, iría al cine* (standard *si tuviera tiempo, iría al cine*)
>
> **b.** *Y para que no los cogerían los ladrones su madre y él se subieron a un árbol* (Espinosa 1930: 446)

6.2.3.2 FURTHER VARIATION IN SPOKEN PENINSULAR CASTILIAN: ANDALUSIA

There is quite a widespread popular concept of 'Andalusian' amongst Peninsular Spanish speakers, not least among Andalusians themselves (so much so that there have even been serious proposals to establish *andaluz* as an official language of the autonomy of Andalusia in much the same way as Catalan, Basque and Galician have been established.[3] Even those concerned professionally with the Spanish language often promote this view by using the blanket term *andaluz* prodigally. However, as we have already seen, there is no possible linguistic definition of an Andalusian 'dialect' or 'dialect area': all that can be meant by such a notion, in fact, is the range of varieties of Castilian spoken in the autonomous region of Andalusia. Having said that, there are some isoglosses which set off parts of that area from the rest of Spain.

6.2.3.2.1 Phonetic features

Most obviously, and best-known, is the absence of opposition between /θ/ and /s/, a phenomenon generally referred to as either *seseo* (if the neutralisation is in favour of /s/, see **2.3.4**) or *ceceo* (if in favour of /θ/). These may be seen as the different results of the historical devoicing of the medieval sibilants described above, as shown in Figure 6.6:

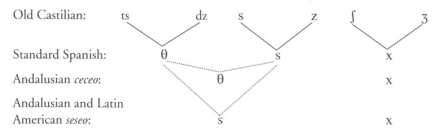

Old Castilian /s/ and /z/ were probably articulated as apico-alveolar [ş] and [ẓ]

Figure 6.6 The development of the medieval Castilian sibilants

---

[3] See, for example, *El Adarve: Revista de estudios andaluces* (http://www.andalucia.cc/adarve/).

(This is a very much simplified representation of the actual historical developments: it is likely that the order of the changes was broadly (1) devoicing of /z/, /dz/ and /ʒ/, (2) deaffrication of /ts/, (3) development of the pronunciation [θ], (4) movement of [ʃ] to [x]: for a convenient account, see Lloyd 1987: 328–44.) As can be seen from Figure 6.7, however, the political boundary of Andalusia does not at all coincide with the isogloss delimiting the presence or absence of this opposition. The isogloss is also not very clearcut, and this is also true of the isogloss separating *seseo* and *ceceo*. The discontinuity of the latter isogloss is rather important: it may seem surprising at first sight that the area covered by *seseo* is relatively smaller than that covered by *ceceo* when *seseo* is regarded as such a stereotype of Andalusian speech; but we must note that the city of Seville forms an island of *seseo* in an otherwise generally *ceceante* area. It is this fact that has probably given *seseo* its higher social prestige, a difference which of course the dialect map does not represent.

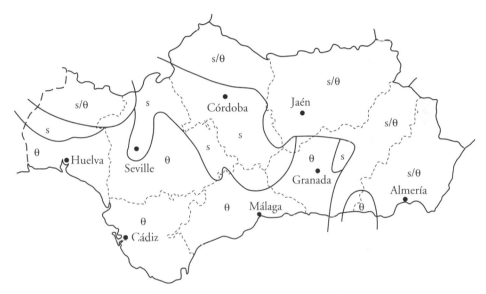

Figure 6.7 *Seseo* and *ceceo* in Andalusia

Moreover, Andalusia is by no means a homogeneous area from the linguistic point of view. As already noted (6.2.3.1.1), quite extensive areas of the southwest preserve the /h/ phoneme deriving from Latin initial /f/, so there are pronunciations such as [ha'rina] for *harina* and [ha'βlar] for *hablar* (this might, incidentally, be a good reason for standard Spanish orthography keeping the initial *h-* in such words, see 2.4.1). There are also two principal articulations of /s/ observable in *seseante* areas, coronal and predorsal (see 2.1.2), the latter pronunciation being typical of the more southerly areas of Andalusia; we should also note that much of the north of Andalusia shares the apico-alveolar articulation of central and northern Castilian. For other phonetic features, it is even difficult to establish continuous isoglosses. Syllable-final /s/ is frequently weakened to the point of aspiration (realisation as [h]) or disappears totally, the phoneme /x/ also undergoes weakening to [h], /r/ and /l/ are often neutralised in syllable-final position and vowels before a syllable-final nasal /n/ often show quite a high degree of nasalisation.

The aspiration of syllable-final /s/ has far-reaching consequences. It has led to the lowering (opening) not only of the immediately preceding vowel, but also of other vowels in the same word. *ALEA* Map 1644 records pronunciations of *¡Buenos días!* such as [ˈbwɛnɔ ˈθᵟia], where it can be seen that both the /o/ and the /e/ of *buenos* are open. It may also cause the assimilation of a following consonant (see **2.3.1**), examples being *las botas* [la ˈɸota] (*ALEA* Map 1638), *¡buenos días!* [ˈbwɛnɔ ˈθia] (*ALEA* Map 1644), *los garbanzos* [lo xaɾˈβanθɔ], [lo ɣaɾˈβanθɔ], [lɔ haɾˈβanθɔ] (*ALEA* Map 1661) and *los/las mimbres* [lɔh ˈβimbrɛ], [la ˈfimbre] (*ALEA* Map 1633). Here, the consonant following the former /s/ assimilates regressively to the new aspiration (a) by becoming a fricative instead of a plosive and sometimes (b) by losing its voicing (so [b] → [ɸ], [d] → [θ], [g] → [x]); but the aspiration itself also assimilates progressively to the following consonant by adopting its point of articulation (so [h] → [ɸ] or [θ]). The net effect of this is to produce the unusual phonetic combinations illustrated above. Assimilation of the /s/ may also sometimes produce a **geminate** (double) fricative consonant, e.g. *las botas* [laᵝˈβota], [bwɛnɔᶿˈθiaʰ], [loˠɣaɾˈβanθɔ], [laᵝˈβimbre].

Intervocalic consonants are very prone to weakening. We have already seen that [ð] is universally weakened, especially in words ending in *-ado*, but in Andalusia it can be completely lost in a much wider range of environments. The other voiced fricatives, [β] and [ɣ], as well as [ɾ], are also prone to loss. Thus pronunciations such as [peˈir] *pedir*, [xuˈar] *jugar*, [toˈijo] *tobillo* and [kje] *quiere* are commonly encountered.

In some areas syllable-final /n/ has nasalised the preceding vowel and has then been virtually lost, e.g. *fueron* [ˈfwerõ⁽ⁿ⁾], so that a series of nasal vowels is being created.

The problem with describing many of these phenomena is that it is difficult to represent the results in terms of the simple presence or absence of a feature, which is the basis for an isogloss, since the phonetic realisations of these mergers are spread along a continuum. Indeed, the accurate phonetic representation of Andalusian articulations poses a severe problem for dialectologists: the *ALEA* makes distinctions along the articulatory continuum from [j] to [ʒ], as shown in Figure 6.8 (*RFE* symbols, rather than the IPA symbols, see Tables 2.1–2.3, are used):

[y]	palatal central fricativa sonora
[y̓]	prepalatal central fricativa sonora
[y̦]	palatal central sonora muy abierta con tendencia a semivocal
[y̆]	palatal central sonora ligeramente rehilada
[y̌]	alvéolo-prepalatal central muy rehilada y sin labialización
[y̥]	alvéolo-prepalatal central rehilada semisorda
[y̥]	alvéolo-prepalatal central fricativa semisorda con tendencia a la asibilación
[y̌]	alvéolo-prepalatal central fricativa sonora con tendencia a la asibilación
[ŷ]	palatal central africada sonora
[ŷ̥]	palatal central africada semisorda
[ŷ̊]	palatal central africada sonora con el momento fricativo prolongado y rehilado
[ŷ̥]	palatal central africada semisorda con el momento fricativo prolongado y rehilado

Figure 6.8 Phonetic discrimination in the *ALEA*

6.2.3.2.2 Phonemic consequences of Andalusian phonetic changes

In some areas of eastern Andalusia, where syllable-final /s/ weakens to the point of complete loss, there is the interesting consequence that crucial contrasts which in the standard language depend on the presence or absence of /s/ come to be signalled instead by vowel quality: Figure 6.9 shows an idealised scheme, though it is typical of many eastern localities:

Standard Spanish	/s/-dropping varieties
bueno ['bweno] vs. *buenos* ['bwenos]	*bueno* ['bweno] vs. *buenos* ['bwenɔ]
come ['kome] vs. *comes* ['komes]	*come* ['kome] vs. *comes* ['kɔmɛ]

Figure 6.9 Vowel quality in eastern Andalusia

This means that there is a phonemic contrast between open and close vowels, or at least between /e/ and /ɛ/, /o/ and /ɔ/, and /a/ and /ɑ/, which are the most frequently occurring and easily discriminated vowels (/i/ and /u/ are much less frequent, and hardly occur at all in final syllables; it is in any case difficult to make distinction of openness in these areas, though *ALEA* does make some distinctions here too). Thus the vowel system of such varieties is as in Figure 6.10 (compare **2.2.1**):

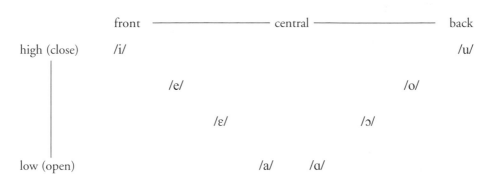

Figure 6.10 The eastern Andalusian vowel system

In western Andalusia, where in general there is no such distinction in vowel quality (see Figure 6.11), the loss of /s/ is sometimes compensated for phonemically in a different way. In the sequence *las botas*, for instance (*ALEA* Map 1638), the initial /b/ may be devoiced by assimilation to the preceding /s/, which is realised as an aspiration or in extreme cases completely deleted. In the latter circumstance the phonetic realisations of *la bota* and *las botas* are as follows:

la bota	[la 'βota]
las botas	[la 'ɸota]

This means that there is a new phonemic opposition between /β/ and /ɸ/ (see Penny 1986). The other changes observed above produce more neutralisation in certain positions, and occasionally this leads to homonymy between pairs of words which are distinguished in the standard language, e.g. *abrir/abril*, which may be pronounced [a'βril].

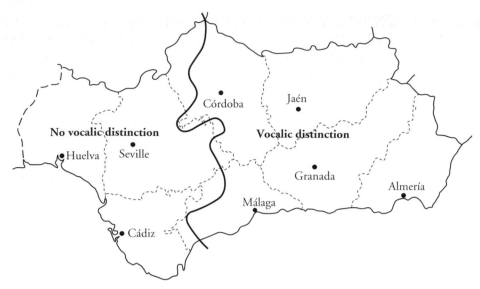

Figure 6.11 Phonemic distinction between open and close vowels in Andalusia

In some areas syllable-final /n/ has nasalised the preceding vowel and has then been lost, so that plurality in the third person is often signalled by the nasal vowel rather than by the /n/ itself. Thus we find contrasts of the type *cogía* [ko'hia] vs. *cogían* [ko'hiã] (Mondéjar 1970: 66).

6.2.3.2.3 Morphological and syntactic features

Phonetic changes have brought about important morphological consequences in Andalusian varieties. As we have seen, where syllable-final /s/ is lost, the signalling of plurality in nouns and adjectives is carried out through vocalic distinctions rather than by the addition of /s/ or /es/, which is a major difference from the standard language, and typologically resembles the ***umlaut*** phenomenon in the Germanic languages (cf. German *Apfel* (sg.) / *Äpfel* (pl.), English *goose* (sg.) / *geese* (pl.)). Weakening of other final consonants contributes another source of new plural types: the loss of final /d/ creates singular/plural pairs such as *pared* /pa'ɾe/, *paredes* /pa'ɾɛ(ð)ɛ/, and similarly the loss of final /l/ produces *papel* /pa'pe/ vs. *papeles* /pa'pɛlɛ/. The consequence of all this is that from the point of view of the spoken language the plural is not regularly formed from the singular in such cases; why should /pa'ɾe/ add /ðɛ/ but /pa'pe/ add /lɛ/? (The problem is of course obscured by the use of conventional spelling, which represents the lost phoneme.)

The fall of final /s/ also has an impact on the verb system, since /s/ is a marker of the second person singular in a number of tenses. This, coupled with nasalisation, can produce such contrasts as *come* ['kome] / *comes* ['kɔmɛ] *comen* ['komẽ] (see Mondéjar 1970: 66). In western Andalusia *vosotros* and the corresponding second person plural verb forms are often not used (see Figure 6.12), with the result that there is no distinction of formality in the second person plural and hence a reduction in the number of inflectional verb forms, though there are also 'mixed' situations such as the use of *ustedes* with a second person plural verb, e.g. *ustedes hacéis* (Mondéjar 1970: 128). Overall, then, there are a number of points at which the standard Spanish verb-system is severely undermined through phonetic erosion and loss. An extreme example is the speech of Cabezas de San Juan in Seville province, where the following paradigm for the present subjective of *salir* can be observed (Mondéjar 1970: 65):

(yo) [ˈθarɣa]	*(nosotros)* [θarˈɣamɔ]
(tú) [ˈθarɣa]	no *vosotros* form
(él, usted, etc.) [ˈθarɣa]	*(ellos, ustedes, etc.)* [ˈθarɣa]

We shall have more to say about the possible structural consequences of the fall of /s/ in **10.2.1**.

Figure 6.12 Use of *vosotros* and *ustedes* in Andalusia

As we have seen, another morphological characteristic of Andalusian speech is the case-based third person pronoun system. In contrast to the *leísmo* and *laísmo* which are features of Castilian speech, *le(s)* in Andalusia is used exclusively for indirect objects and *lo(s)*, *la(s)* for direct objects. There is a good deal of variation in the use of first and second person plural object pronouns, however. The first person plural (standard *nos*) sometimes has the form *mos* or *mus* (presumably as a result of analogy with the first person plural verb inflection *-mos*) or even *los*; the second person plural object pronoun, no doubt as a corollary of the variation observable in the subject pronoun, takes such forms as *se*, *sos* and *sus*.

There is a great deal of less systematic variation. The gender of some nouns differs from the standard: *puente*, *azúcar* and *almíbar* are generally feminine in Andalusia, though they are masculine in the standard language. There are also differences in verb forms: *entregar* is widely treated as a radical-changing verb, with forms such as *entriego* and *entriega*); *vido* is general in eastern Andalusia as the 3rd person singular preterite of *ver*, and the subjunctive form *haiga* corresponding to standard *haya* is widespread.

6.2.3.2.4 Vocabulary

It is not possible to characterise differences in vocabulary systematically. In some instances Andalusian speakers seem to give a higher frequency to words which are part of standard Castilian, or they are used in a slightly different way. Thus *cacho* 'piece', which in standard usage is mainly restricted to colloquial register, tends to be preferred to *trozo*; it is also used in the sense of 'horn' (standard *cuerno*) (Álvarez Curiel 1991: 18). Some words which are archaic in the standard language survive, e.g. *cabero* 'last' (standard *último*), *hacer mala orilla* (standard *hacer mal tiempo*). There are also neologisms such as *tabaquear* (standard *fumar*) and in popular speech some borrowings from *caló* or Romany Spanish, e.g. *menda* as the first person pronoun (Zamora Vicente 1960: 256–9 and De Bruyne 1995: 261).

6.2.3.2.5 An example of Andalusian speech

The following text was collected by Manuel Alvar on 19 July 1956. (Word stress is not shown in this transcription.)

TEXT A

[la ɟjehta ðeᵈ dia ðel santo kriʰto ɛ el katoɾθe ðe setjembɾe ‖ el treθe pol la
taɾde etʃan una relaθjõŋ | aθen un tablao i se pone unọ eŋ kaða punta ðel
tablao ‖ la relaθjõᵑ eʰtá ʰkɾita i se laprenden de memoɾja | kwentan loʰ
milagɾoᵈ del kɾiʰto i ðɔ xweɣan la βandera i lɔ otɾoʰ ban tokandọ el pitọ
jel tambol i ðe βɛ eŋ kwando | le:tʃan um biβa i tiɾaŋ ketɛ | ke tiɾam   5
mutʃisimo | jel dia treθe pol la notʃe etʃan el kaʰtijọ ‖ el dia katoɾθe se
saka el santọ kɾiʰtọ pa jeβaˈlọ a la ehmita | seʰta:ji una oɾa o asi | bwerben
otɾa βɛ al kaminọ alante pa traeˈlo a la iglesja ‖ ese ðia etʃan la relaθjõᵑ
una oɾa o ðɔ anteᵈ de sakaˈlọ ‖ lo θo ðiạ se βiʰten de moɾɔ unɔ ɔmbɾɛ a
loʰ ke se lɛ θan la kolaθjɔnɛ | ke kaða uno ða ɣarbanθɔ toʰtaɔ i βino i roʰkaʰ   10
pa la eʰkwadɾa | ke son loʰ ke aθen la ɣerija esa jeʰtan apuntaɔ poɾ el
majoɾdomọ ‖ son loʰ ke xweɣan lɔ sablɛ komo pelẹ andọ | mjentɾaʰˡ lɔ ɔtɾọ
ðiθen la relaθjõŋ | el dia kinθe akaβan | alguna ɟeθɛ emɔ tɾaiðo tɾɛ o kwatɾo
βakɔ pa la xente ðel pweblo | ke ja eʰtamɔ solɔ | jɛɛl dia mexol pa lo θel
pweblo]   15

Alvar 1960: 580–1. The original has been converted into IPA script; [s] is coronal. A narrower phonetic transcription may be consulted in Alvar, Llorente & Salvador 1995: 379–81.

Version in standard orthography:

La fiesta del día del Santo Cristo es el catorce de setiembre. El trece por la tarde echan una relación, hacen un tablado y se pone uno en cada punta del tablado. La relación está escrita y se la aprenden de memoria. Cuentan los milagros del Cristo y dos juegan la bandera y los otros van tocando el pito y el tambor, y de vez en cuando le echan un viva y tiran cohetes, que tiran muchísimos. Y el día trece por la noche echan el castillo. El día catorce se saca el Santo Cristo para llevarlo a la ermita; se está allí una hora o así, vuelven otra vez al camino adelante para traerlo a la iglesia. Ese día echan la relación una hora o dos antes de sacarlo. Los dos días se visten de moros unos hombres a los que se les dan las colaciones, que cada uno da garbanzos tostados y vino y roscas para la escuadra, que son los que hacen la guerrilla esa y están apuntados por el mayordomo; son los que juegan los sables como peleando, mientras los otros dicen la relación. El día quince acaban; algunas veces hemos traído tres o cuatro vacos para la gente del pueblo, que ya estamos solos, y es el día mejor para los del pueblo.

The first thing to notice is that the distinction between /s/ and /θ/ is preserved, so this is neither a *seseante* nor a *ceceante* variety. *Yeísmo*, however, is a feature: *castillo* [kaʰˈtijo̜] (l.6), *guerrilla* [ɣeˈrija] (l.11). Syllable-final /s/ is either aspirated or lost completely; where it is lost, there is usually a noticeable compensatory opening of the preceding /o/ and /e/, and sometimes of /a/ (*tostados* [toʰˈtaɔ], l.10, *tres* [trɛ], l.13, *días* [ˈðiạ], l.9), and this opening can affect other vowels in the same word too, as the /o/ of *colaciones* [kolaˈθjonɛ] (l.10). Conversely, final /o/ in a non-plural word is sometimes closed (*castillo* [kaʰˈtijo̜], l.6). Loss of /s/ at the end of a word extends even to intervocalic contexts: *unos hombres* [unɔ ˈɔmbrɛ] (l.9). Final /θ/ appears to be lost in much the same way (*vez en cuando* [βɛ eŋ ˈkwando], l.5). Word-final /s/ assimilates to the following consonant, though the results are interestingly variable: /s/ + /d/ yields [θ] (*les dan* [lɛ θan], l.10) or [ðd] (*milagros del* [miˈlagroˊ del], l.4). Syllable-final /l/ and /r/ are consistently neutralised, generally in favour of a lateral pronunciation (*tambor* [tamˈbol], l.5) which results in the creation of a geminate [l] where /l/ follows (*traerlo* [traˈeˈlo], l.8), though there are also examples of the maintenance of /r/ (*catorce* [kaˈtorθe], l.6) and neutralisation to [r] (*vuelven* [ˈbwɛrben], l.7); there is also evidence of an aspirate articulation of syllable-final [r] in the context of a following /m/ (*hermita* [ehˈmita], l.7) and /d/ (*del día* [ðeˊ ˈdia], l.1). Intervocalic /d/ is always lost between /a/ and /o/ (*apuntados* [apunˈtaɔ], l.11), though it appears to be retained in other contexts (*cada* [ˈkaða], l.2, *traído* [traˈiðo], l.13). Word-final /n/ is velarised to [ŋ] (*relación* [relaˈθjõŋ], l.2).

Although the general picture is clear, detailed examination of this text shows that there is much contextual variation in the behaviour of sounds, and also probably variation within the speech of the same individual, even in exactly the same phonetic context, as the various realisations of the /s/ + /d/ group show.

6.2.3.2.6 The 'Andalusianisation' of Castilian

An interesting dialectological question at present is whether features of Andalusian Spanish are propagating beyond Andalusia, and, if so, why. Salvador (1964) called attention to the existence of stereotypical 'Andalusian' features in the speech of parts of New Castile. The propagation of *yeísmo* from urban centres in the north (we have already seen more recent evidence that *yeísmo* is indeed a feature of a majority of speakers in a number of northern cities) which, as he puts it, acts as a 'fifth column' for the diffusion of this feature. Syllable-final /s/ is also present in many northern areas, especially in the 'difficult' contexts /sg/, /sb/ and /sθ/. The loss of intervocalic /d/, as we have seen, is widespread. Salvador attributes the 'Andalusianisation' of the centre and north of Spain to the prestige of Andalusia, which began in the 19th century, and to the fact that Andalusians themselves regard their speech highly. The migration of Andalusian workers to northern cities, especially Barcelona and Madrid, is also an important factor to be considered.

However, all these changes can be seen as part of the natural and inevitable evolution of Spanish: it is just that Andalusia (and Latin America) have been more 'innovating' in these respects than other areas. The fact that they are all attested to a certain extent in the speech of Old Castile probably means that they have developed independently there. It is also important to stress that certain Andalusian features do not appear to have propagated in the same way: while *yeísmo* is extremely common everywhere in the Peninsula, for example, *seseo* is not adopted widely outside Andalusia, nor are the morphological features of Andalusian speech which we examined above. Another factor to be borne in mind is the possibility of a new levelling with greater social mobility within Spain and with greater awareness of the broader Spanish-speaking world through the media, which may be encouraging simplification in directions which are embryonically already present in northern Peninsular speakers.

6.2.3.3 THE SPANISH OF THE CANARY ISLANDS

The speech of the Canary Islands has often been thought of as representing an 'intermediate' variety between Peninsular and Latin American Spanish. While the importance of the Canaries in the discovery and colonisation of the Americas cannot be denied, such a view is intrinsically inappropriate. Canaries Spanish shares many features with Seville and southwestern Andalusia (*seseo*, aspiration of syllable-final /s/, the weakening of /x/ to [h], neutralisation of syllable-final /ɾ/ and /l/), which is not surprising in view of the fact that the Canaries were largely colonised from these areas in the 15th century. Some Canaries variants have retained certain features which have generally changed elsewhere: the distinction between /ʎ/ and /j/ is often maintained, as is the /h/ deriving from Latin initial /f/. Because of this, Canaries Spanish is sometimes characterised as 'conservative'; but again, such a label is inappropriate, because it has also has 'innovatory' features. One such is that syllable-final /ɾ/ is realised as [h] before /n/ and /l/ (e.g. *carne* ['kahne], *darle* ['dahle]. But the most striking is the voicing, or **lenition**, of /p/, /t/, /k/ and /tʃ/ in intervocalic position, which has been recorded extensively in Gran Canaria by Oftedal (1985). This happens word-internally or when an initial consonant is preceded by a vowel, as illustrated in the following examples:

típico	['tibigo]	*una pluma*	[una 'bluma]
frutero	[fru'deɾo]	*una tienda*	[una 'djenda]
música	['musiga]	*la cama*	[la 'gama]
flecha	['fledʒa]	*una chica*	[una 'dʒiga]

Note that the results of the lenition of /p/, /t/, /k/ are not the intervocalic fricatives [β], [ð] and [ɣ] which are familiar from standard Spanish (and are in fact the historical developments of Latin intervocalic /p/, /t/ and /k/), but are indeed plosives. This has the interesting phonological consequence that there are potentially phonemic oppositions between /b/ and /β/, /d/ and /ð/ and /g/ and /ɣ/, e.g. *ropa* /roba/ vs. *roba* /roβa/, *nata* /nada/ vs. *nada* /naða/, *placa* /plaga/ vs. *plaga* /plaɣa/ (there are extremely few plausible candidates for this last opposition, however), and that [β], [ð] and [ɣ] cannot be regarded as allophones of /b/, /d/ and /g/ as they are in standard Spanish (see **2.3.1**). Furthermore, when syllable-final /s/ falls completely, plurality in nouns and adjectives may be signalled by the same opposition word-initially, which significantly increases the functional load on these phonemic contrasts: thus *su baño* [su ˈβaɲo] but *sus baños* [su ˈbaɲo].

6.2.3.4 THE CASTILIAN OF NON-CASTILIAN REGIONS

The attention of present-day dialectologists is largely concentrated on either the 'primary' dialects of Latin or on the 'secondary' dialects of Castilian. Relatively little attention has been paid to the Castilian of regions which are 'primary' dialect areas but where Castilian has subsequently been adopted or imposed (e.g. Catalonia, the Basque Country, Asturias and Galicia). The linguistic atlases (see **6.2.1**) do not record such varieties at all. Yet the Castilian of these 'non-Castilian' regions has quite individual characteristics which are often the result of contact between Castilian and another language. A well-known feature of the Castilian of many Catalans is the pronunciation of final /d/ as [t]: this parallels the availability of final /t/ in Catalan, and the correspondence of Catalan [t] to Castilian [d] in many cognate words, e.g. Cat. *ciutat* [sjuˈtat] / Cast. *ciudad* [θjuˈðaᶞ]. In Asturias it is common to hear clitic pronouns following a finite verb, e.g. *Fuime a la playa* rather than *Me fui a la playa* (see 1.4), and *ye* for the third person singular of the verb *ser* (Castilian *es*), even on the lips of those who are apparently monolingual speakers of Castilian: both these are features of the 'primary' *asturiano* or *bable* dialects.

A phenomenon which has often been noted but rarely studied closely is the existence of 'mixed' languages. A question which it would be very interesting to address in connection with such languages (but which is beyond the scope of this book) is whether these are linguistic hybrids or whether they represent examples of code-switching (see **9.5**). Piñán (1991: 49–50) is firmly of the opinion that such 'mixed' languages in Asturias are hybrids and are effectively learned as native languages by successive generations, rather like creoles which have derived from pidgins (see **9.4**). However, there is also a common perception (even amongst native speakers) that some 'primary' dialects are hybrids; speakers refer to them by such adjectives as *chapurrao* (the verb *chapurr(e)ar* means to speak a 'broken' language) or *amestao* or 'mixed'. In some cases this label is almost certainly inaccurate: the *fala* of Valverde del Fresno, Eljas and San Martín de Trevejo (Cáceres), for example, is often thought of such a language because it is not identifiable with either Castilian or Portuguese, but in fact it is in origin most probably a form of one of the northwestern 'primary' dialects. On the other hand, there are examples along the border between Spain and Portugal of speech which genuinely code-switches between one language and the other, even though it is sometimes argued that such switching is an inherent feature of these varieties (see Elizaincín 1992: 216–23).

The following is a well-known example of code-switching between Catalan and

Andalusian Spanish. It is taken from Juan Marsé's novel *El amante bilingüe*, in which the central character, a Catalan, cuckolded by an Andalusian migrant worker, gradually adopts features of Andalusian speech.

TEXT B

> Pué mirizté, en pimé ugá me'n fotu e menda yaluego de to y de toos i així
> finson vostè vulgui poque nozotro lo mataore catalane volem toro
> catalane, digo, que menda s'integra en la Gran Encisera hata onde le
> dejan y hago con mi jeta lo que buenamente puedo, ora con la barretina
> ora con la montera, o zea que a mí me guta el mestizaje, zeñó, la barreja   5
> y el combinao, en fin, s'acabat l'explicació i el bròquil, echusté una
> moneíta, joé, no sigui tan garrapo ni tan roñica, una pezetita, cony, así
> me guta, rumbozo, vaya usté con Dió i passiu-ho bé, senyor …

> Juan Marsé, *El amante bilingüe* (Barcelona: RBA Editores, 1993).

In the following version, standard Castilian and Catalan forms are used with the Catalan underlined; meanings of unfamiliar words appear in square brackets:

> Pues mire usted, en primer lugar <u>me'n fotu</u> el menda [= *yo*; *menda* is in origin a Romany *caló* term meaning 'I, myself', used with a third person verb form, but it now has some currency in colloquial Andalusian usage] de todo y de todos <u>i així fins on vostè vulgui</u> porque nosotros los matadores catalanes <u>volem</u> toros catalanes, digo, que menda se integra en <u>la Gran Encisera</u> [lit. 'the great enchantress', a designation of Barcelona originally coined by the poet Joan Maragall] hasta donde le dejan y hago con mi jeta lo que buenamente puedo, ora con <u>la barretina</u> [Catalan woollen cap] ora con la montera [bullfighter's hat], o sea que a mí me gusta el mestizaje, señor, la <u>barreja</u> [a drink consisting of a mixture of *aguardiente* and wine] y el combinado [cocktail], en fin, <u>s'ha acabat l'explicació i el bròquil</u> [phrase used to indicate that a conversation is at an end], eche usted una monedita, joder, <u>no sigui</u> tan garrapo [pig] ni tan roñica [miserly], una pecetita (diminutive of *pieza* 'coin'), coño, así me gusta, vaya usted con Dios <u>i passiu-ho bé, senyor</u>...

6.2.3.5 STEREOTYPES

Modern sociolinguistics has coined the notion of a **stereotype**, i.e. a marker which a speech-community consciously recognises as being an identifying feature of a particular variety, but which does not necessarily correspond to the real linguistic performance of speakers. We can exemplify this notion in respect of some of the data which has been given above. For example, *seseo* is usually thought of as stereotypical of Andalusian speech, though it is by no means universal in Andalusia. Deletion of intervocalic /d/ and *yeísmo* are similarly regarded as stereotypes of Andalusian, although these features are extremely common in Castile too. Stereotypes are often reflected in literary authors' representations of local speech (see 7.1 and Carrillo Herrera 1964: 25). A related phenomenon is the attitude of speakers towards particular stereotypes: not only do speakers make value judgements about the beauty or otherwise of regional varieties, but they often endow the users of such varieties with particular personal characteristics: Bennett (1982) reports an experiment in which young *granadinos* rated a speaker with a Castilian accent highly in terms of intelligence, wealth, self-assertiveness and hard work, and a speaker with a *granadino* accent most highly in terms of generosity, friendliness, lack of irritability and sense of humour.

6.2.4 Latin America

6.2.4.1 ISOGLOSS PATTERNING

In the Iberian Peninsula we were able to identify two quite distinct types of isogloss patterning: the continuum of the north and the projection of northern features southwards to give sharp differentiation ultimately in the clustering of isoglosses between Castilian in the centre, Portuguese to the west and Catalan to the east. Within the southerly Castilian area (Andalusia), we have been able to identify something of a new continuum of isoglosses (e.g. *seseo / ceceo*, *yeísmo*, the use of *ustedes* instead of *vosotros*), but equally a number of isoglosses have proved to be discontinuous. Latin America overall is characterised by isogloss discontinuity: its isogloss patterning has been described by one dialectologist as presenting a 'leopardlike picture' (Canfield 1981: 1). If we examine the use of *voseo* (the replacement of *tú* as a familiar second person person singular by *vos*: see below), for instance, we find that not only is this a feature of the River Plate region and Chile but also of parts of Central America (see Figure 6.13).

There have nevertheless been a number of attempts to establish dialect zones for Latin America, the most appropriate of which simply characterise individual regions in terms of their distinctive linguistic features: Zamora Munné & Guitart (1982: 182–3) propose nine different regions on the basis of three features: (a) loss of syllable-final /s/, (b) weakening of /x/ to [h] and (c) *voseo*. But there is really only one very general pattern of isogloss clustering that emerges, between highland and lowland speech.

6.2.4.2 THE FORMATION OF THE LATIN-AMERICAN VARIETIES

Many factors have been adduced as being responsible for regional variation in Latin-American Spanish.

6.2.4.2.1 The Andalusian base

The coincidence of many features in Latin American Spanish and Andalusian Spanish is striking, though on closer scrutiny some of the parallels are not always exact. *Seseo*, with /s/

Figure 6.13 The distribution of *voseo* in Latin America

realised as coronal [s], is universal in Latin America, but does not characterise the whole of Andalusia (**6.2.3.2.1**). *Yeísmo* is not universal in Andalusia and is not restricted to Andalusia; velarisation of final /n/ is not limited to Andalusia but is also a feature of Galicia, León and Extremadura, and *seseo* is not universal in Andalusia.

Nevertheless, such linguistic similarities would seem to correlate with the high degree of direct contact between Latin America and Andalusia and the Canaries throughout the colonial period.

6.2.4.2.2 Correlation with external factors

Phases in the exploration and settlement of the New World also correlate with linguistic features to a certain extent. The isoglosses observable in Argentina are a good example of this. Two major isoglosses reflect the areas first settled from Bolivia and Chile on the one hand and those settled later from Buenos Aires on the other. The former are characterised by the neutralisation of /ʎ/ and /j/ as [j] (*yeísmo*) and by the pronunciation of /r/ as an assibilated [ɹ] (this sound lies between [z] and a standard southeast British English [ɹ]), while the latter neutralise /ʎ/ and /j/ as [ʒ] (a characteristic of the River Plate area which is often referred to by Spanish linguists as ***rehilamiento***) and have a trilled [r]. The province of Santiago del Estero, in northwestern Argentina, has a number of very individual features which are probably explained by the fact that it was a very early settlement which was then eclipsed by other

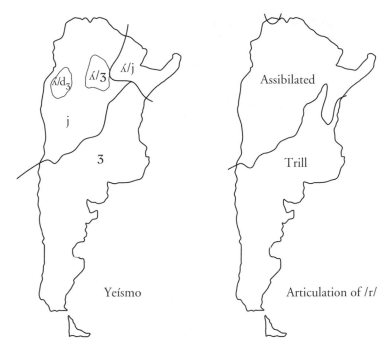

Figure 6.14 Argentine isoglosses

cities (Lipski 1994: 164). Here, syllable-final /s/ is generally retained as [s] and the opposition between /ʎ/ and /j/ is preserved (though /ʎ/ is realised as [ʒ]).

   External factors may also explain the broad differences between highland and lowland speech. The trade system between Spain and its colonies was based for greater security on a biennial convoy whose destinations were Cartagena de Indias, Portobelo, Veracruz and a number of other Caribbean ports. From Portobelo, goods were transferred by mule train to Panama City and thence to the Pacific ports of Guayaquil and El Callao; Havana formed the assembly point for the return voyage. These coastal areas were thus the ones that kept in closest contact, both with each other and with Spain, and were therefore likely to have been most open to linguistic innovation. Canfield (1981: 9) proposes on this basis a very general chronological classification of Latin-American speech, associating highland areas, Guatemala, Costa Rica and northwest Argentina with mid-16th-century Andalusian Spanish, the River Plate area, western Argentina, Chile, El Salvador, Honduras, Nicaragua and New Mexico with the mid-17th century and Mexico and other coastal areas, as well as central Chile, with the mid-18th century. Another important factor was perhaps the location of the viceregal administrative centres (Mexico City and Lima) in which there would have been a higher concentration of Peninsular officials, clergy and military personnel.

A great deal of research has taken place on the geographical origins of the settlers (see, for example, Boyd-Bowman 1972) in order to assess the 'Andalusian base' hypothesis, though statistics based on public records tend to be skewed by the fact that many emigrants appear to have given their place of residence as the port from which they embarked. Such figures as we have suggest that while Andalusians were a sizeable proportion of immigrants, they did not constitute the majority. What is actually most likely is that immigrants to the New World represented a fairly heterogeneous assortment of regional varieties, and not only of Castilian, but of other Peninsular Romance languages. But as in Spain itself, Castilian was the language of administration and must also have been the only possible candidate as a common language for Spain's overseas empire. The forces operating on Castilian in the formation of Latin-American varieties were most probably levelling in the adoption by many different speakers of such a common language and contact with the substrate Amerindian languages.

6.2.4.2.3 Levelling

While the linguistic parallels between Andalusian and Latin-American speech are obvious, there has been a great deal of debate concerning the extent to which Latin-American Spanish had an Andalusian base or developed independently. The balance of opinion is now clearly in favour of the Andalusian hypothesis, but as we have already seen, 'Andalusian' is very far from being a well-defined concept. Latin America is universally *seseante*, but Andalusia is not; we must therefore seek some explanation as to why *seseo* rather than *ceceo* or the preservation of a distinction of the more northerly Castilian type eventually prevailed. One answer could be geographically-based: that Latin-American Spanish is associated with a particular area of Andalusia. As we noted, although *seseo* is not as widespread as *ceceo*, it is today a feature of the speech of the city of Seville, which was the centre of trade with the New World and which certainly set, and continues to set, its own regional norm; we may imagine, then, that it was Seville that in an important sense set the standard for Latin America in the first place. Another answer could be chronological: that Andalusian *ceceo* is a development subsequent to *seseo* which was therefore not a feature of any variety of Spanish at the time of the early settlement of Latin America. A third answer is that Latin-American *seseo* is the result of **levelling**, the common adoption of a feature which then became a stereotype of Latin-American speech, thus reinforcing it even more. *Seseo* might have been favoured in such a scenario because it represented the simplest of a number of alternatives (see Penny 2000: 142).

Some Latin-American developments, however, are likely to be independent innovations, or at least more localised levellings. One such is *voseo*, the use of *vos* as a familiar second person singular pronoun, which is widespread in Latin America. There is a ready Peninsular antecedent for this: in medieval Castilian, *vos* had a double function as a second person plural and a polite second person singular, rather like modern French *vous*, but in the course of the 16th and 17th centuries in the Peninsula it became a casualty of a very extensive remodelling of the system of second person address, the catalyst for which was the appearance of a number of honorific morphologically third person forms such as *vuestra merced* and *vuestra señoría*, the first of which has yielded by a sequence of substantial phonetic erosion modern *usted*. *Vos* is no longer used as a singular in the Peninsula, a simple two-way contrast now being made between *tú* (familiar) and *usted* (polite), and as a plural it has been replaced by the form *vosotros* which has the advantage of explicitly marking plurality by the ending *-otros*, a feature it shares with the first person plural pronoun *nosotros*, which similarly replaced older *nos*. In Latin-American *voseo*, *vos* appears to have survived to the exclusion of *tú*; indeed forms morphologically related to *tú* combine **suppletively** with *vos*, which is used only as a subject and prepositional object form: thus *te* is the verbal object pronoun corresponding to *vos*, and *tu(s)* and *tuyo/a* its possessive forms, as the following example shows:

> **(6.3)**   <u>Vos</u> que sos golosa acá estarías en <u>tu</u> elemento. ¿Mañana domingo
> vas a ir al cine?   ¿quién <u>te</u> va a comprar los chocolatines?
> Manuel Puig, *Boquitas pintadas* (Barcelona: Seix Barral, 3rd ed.,
> 1989), p. 107.

This is a prima facie case of simplification of categories as a result of levelling, but it yields a result which is not paralleled exactly in the Peninsula. The form *vosotros* exists nowhere in Latin America, a feature that Latin-American Spanish (not only the *voseante* varieties) has in common with much of Andalusia (see **6.2.3.2.3** and Figure 6.12); it may be that the 'new' form *vosotros/as* did not diffuse to these areas. However, the equally new form *nosotros/as* did, as did the even later *usted(es)*, which is used throughout the Spanish-speaking world with essentially the same form of phonetic contraction from *vuestra(s) merced(es)*, suggesting a very successful diffusion indeed. In some ways it is rather surprising that nowhere in Latin America has adopted *vosotros/as*, which must have been familiar to Peninsular emigrants from the early 16th century onwards, while *nosotros/as* and *usted(es)* have been taken on, and again it is possible to see this as a kind of levelling, a cutting down on distinctions of formality. Indeed, the economies in this area are actually rather wider-ranging, since distinctive second person plural verb forms are not used either in Latin America. In some areas, the old second person plural forms supply the verb form for *vos*, but as a singular: thus Chilean *(vos) hablái(s)*, which corresponds to the modern Peninsular form, and Argentine *(vos) hablás*, which derives from a form of the second person plural which was common in the 15th century. Nowhere is the standard Peninsular distinction between *habláis* (second person plural familiar) and *hablan* (second person plural polite) made.

6.2.4.2.4 Substrate influence

The possibility of substrate influence on the development of a language (that is, influence from the language of a culture which is inferior in status on one which is superior) is one which has been extensively used by historical linguists to explain changes which at first sight may seem rather unusual. A famous example in the Peninsular Hispanic context is the change in Castilian of Latin initial /f/ to /h/, which it has been suggested is due to the absence of a labiodental /f/ phoneme in earlier Basque, which was the substrate to Latin in the part of northern Spain immediately bordering on the Castilian hinterland; the hypothesis runs that the consequent difficulty encountered in the pronunciation of Latin [f] led to its articulation in a different way. This is not the place to discuss the detailed case for and against this hypothesis; suffice it to say that as more and more comparative data on language change has been assembled, and more idea gained of what is more or less likely in change, the necessity of having recourse to substratist explanations has substantially diminished.[4] It must also be said that many substratist explanations are based on shaky knowledge of the

---

[4] An important assessment of some of the issues involved is given by Jungemann (1955).

supposedly substrate languages themselves, and pertain to changes which are relatively remote in time. In Latin America, however, where Amerindian languages were (and are) substrate to Spanish, we are looking at a more recent period of change and, even though many of these languages are disappearing, we have detailed knowledge of those still currently spoken. However, and perhaps most crucially, there is still a reasonable degree of bilingualism. Latin America therefore makes an interesting modern testing ground for substratist hypotheses of language change.

One aspect of the question of 'influence' which immediately becomes apparent is that features possibly associated with the substrate have different degrees of diffusion. Some lexical borrowings from the Amerindian substrate languages have diffused very widely and become part of the standard language: for example, Taíno *maíz* and Arawak *canoa, hamaca, sabana, tabaco,* Aztec *chocolate, chile, tomate,* Quechua *cóndor,* Guaraní *tapioca,* have generalised throughout the Spanish-speaking world and beyond (cf. Eng. *maize, canoe, hammock, savannah, tobacco, chocolate, chile, tomato, condor, tapioca*). Others, however, are much more localised, and reflect borrowing from different substrates: names for a turkey include *guajolote* (Mexico), *chompipe* (also Mexico and Central America) and *pisco* (Colombia). It is such localised usages that perhaps foreshadow the fragmentation of Spanish (see **10.3.3**) and are the bane of dictionary-makers, whose task in charting these words and meanings and in attaching to them an exact geographical and social characterisation is truly daunting; a very interesting project currently in hand is VARILEX, which aims to create a dictionary of 'geosynonyms', i.e. different words used in the Spanish-speaking world to express the same notion.[5] Another important consideration in assessing substrate influence is to what extent features supposed to be due to the substrate have been adopted by monolingual Spanish speakers. Paraguayan Spanish is well-known for the high incidence of Guaraní features, even in its syntax (Granda 1979), but the vast majority of the Spanish-speaking population are bilingual in Spanish and Guaraní. There is evidence that the introduction of a glottal stop at a word boundary between vowels in Yucatecan Spanish, which is very likely to be due to Maya (as the same phenomenon in Paraguay is likely to be due to Guaraní), e.g. *tu hija* [tuʔˈixa], while most frequent among Maya-Spanish bilinguals, has also extended to monolingual Spanish speakers, and has indeed become a stereotype of the Spanish of this region (Lope Blanch 1987: 115–24).

While there can be no doubt about the reality of lexical borrowing from the substrate languages of Latin America, convincing examples of substrate influence on monolingual speakers at the phonological, morphological or syntactic level remain very limited, even if we restrict our attention to the speech of lower-class monolinguals. Even the degree of adoption of indigenous words can be overstated: see Lope Blanch (1965). Mostly the search has been on for substrate language features which are imitated directly in Spanish, as in the case of the Yucatecan glottal stops discussed above. However, there is a possibility that substrate influence may act in a more indirect fashion. Lipski (1994: 82–9) discusses the phenomenon of clitic doubling, whereby an apparently 'redundant' direct object pronoun (in Spanish terms) is used when an overt direct object noun follows the verb, e.g. *lo compramos*

---

[5] VARILEX was pioneered by Hiroto Ueda at the University of Tokyo and is now run by Signum in Quito, Ecuador.

la harina, a construction which is unacceptable in standard Spanish (**la compramos la harina* is also unacceptable in the standard). The phenomenon is encountered, in slightly different ways, in speakers who are bilingual in Spanish and Nahuatl (in Mexico) or in Spanish and Quechua (in the Andes); among Nahuatl speakers, the pronoun is invariably *lo*, whatever the gender and number of the direct object noun, and it is also used with intransitive verbs in the preterite. However, neither Nahuatl nor Quechua has an exactly parallel construction. Lipski argues that in the case of Nahuatl, use of the *lo* may be parallel to the use of the direct object prefix *qui(n)-* and the past tense prefix *o-*, while in the case of Quechua, *lo* may have been the consequence of a calque of the direct object inflection *-ta*, which stands immediately before the Quechua verb in the same way as *lo* does in Spanish. (It must be stressed once again that Lipski's study does not concern monolingual Spanish speakers, and that the 'influence' of such clitic doubling on Spanish is probably nil; but it is extremely valuable in focusing on the detail of how such substrate influence might occur.) At the same time, however, the phemonenon of clitic doubling is already regularly present in standard Spanish with indirect objects (*le enviamos una tarjeta a María*), and there is evidence that in cultured Latin-American usage clitic doubling is used with personal direct objects as well: Kany (1951: 116–17) cites such examples as *¿Lo ha visto a Lucas?* from a wide range of authors and countries. Such clitic doubling in the speech of monolinguals is much more likely to be the result of the analogical extension of the standard doubling of indirect objects than of any substrate influence. It has also perhaps been facilitated by the use of the 'personal *a*' with personal direct objects, which makes these superficially indistinguishable from indirect objects. Clitic-doubling in monolingual speakers is also different in that it is limited to personal direct objects and that gender and number agreement is observed.

6.2.4.2.5 Regional norms

So far we have said nothing about prestige norms in Latin America. We saw that in Spain there is an over-arching notion of 'correct' usage, and a strong, if not altogether accurate, association of Old Castile with the geographical locus of this prestige norm; at the same time, the educated speech of Seville provides the locus for another prestige norm which is widely recognised in Andalusia. In Latin America there is the sense of what we may call a 'pan-American' prestige norm, the feeling being that the most 'correct' pronunciation is the one which has the most regular relation with the standard orthography, and that on the whole the educated speech of cities is preferable to rural usage. Thus the retention of syllable-final /s/, the distinction between syllable-final /l/ and /r/ and the maintenance of intervocalic /d/ are all highly regarded. But this principle does not extend as far as equivalence to the Peninsular standard: *seseo* and *yeísmo* also form part of this 'pan-American' norm. It can quickly be seen that such a norm is effectively the highest common denominator of all the Latin-American varieties, and it interestingly comes close to the notion of a diasystem (see **6.1.1**). It is also a tangible manifestation of the unity of Spanish on at least one level, an issue which we will return to in **10.3.3**.

Apart from this supranational norm, each of the Latin-American countries appears to have its own slightly different prestigious usage based on the educated speech of its capital city, an important factor in which is the capital's control of the broadcasting media. This means that essentially the same linguistic features may have a different prestige value within different countries, a well-known case being the Andean areas of Venezuela and neighbouring Colombia. In Colombia highland features have a high prestige because they are closer to the speech of the highland capital Bogotá, while in Venezuela the same features are regarded poorly by speakers of the lowland Caracas prestige norm. In Argentine Spanish, *voseo* is accepted to the point of regular use in print because of its growing acceptance in educated speech, while in Chile, though it is currently on the increase amongst younger generations of speakers, it is prescriptively castigated: even more particularly in Chile, use of the *-ái(s)* verb form is more acceptable than the *vos* pronoun itself. A change in social or political conditions can also bring about a change in the prestige norm: in Nicaragua, the public use of previously lower-class *vos* became a stereotype of the Sandinista Revolution, and so more highly regarded (Stewart 1999: 123).

6.3 Sociolinguistic variation

In much of the foregoing discussion we have often referred to variation along parameters other than the diatopic. Such variation may broadly be categorised as diastratic, and will include at least the parameters of social class, age and sex. In examining the work of the dialect geographers, we saw how attempts were made to limit the possible variables under consideration to the purely diatopic, with the selection of similar speakers for all localities. However, it proves much more difficult to separate out the variables of social class, age and sex. Objective categories are sometimes difficult to establish. Ages must be grouped along a continuum in a fairly arbitrary way: does 30–39 form a natural category, or 35–44, for example? Social class is altogether more difficult to characterise objectively, since it is often subtly determined by a number of other variables, such as income, occupation and family background; furthermore, classification of social class may be vitiated by the individual aspirations of individuals (the desire, for example, to belong to a higher group than the apparently objective criteria of one's occupation and income suggest). A very important insight into the nature of class-based variation has been the notion of social networks developed by Milroy (1980), according to which the different social groups to which speakers belong (e.g. workplace, leisure activities) also correlate with linguistic variation; furthermore, she has shown that where such networks are dense, with strong social ties, there will be a higher degree of linguistic conformity. In the light of the foregoing, it is not surprising that methodology is of prime importance in sociolinguistic investigation; we cannot pursue this matter further here, but readers are urged to find out more on their own account.[6]

It must also never be forgotten that difference from the standard may reflect a rather different conceptual system altogether, which makes straightforward comparison with the standard difficult. A study of counterfactual conditional protasis verb forms in Buenos Aires Spanish by Lavandera (1984) at first sight reveals variation between the *-ra* form of the imperfect subjunctive (as in the standard language) and the conditional, e.g. *Si tuviera*

---

[6] A very readable account is to be found in Hudson (1980: 143–57).

dinero iría al cine. But on closer inspection, these protasis forms cooccur consistently with different apodosis verb forms, yielding the following overall patterns, with the meanings shown, whereas the standard language has only two meaning possibilities:

Table 6.5 Counterfactual conditional protases

Protasis verb form	Apodosis verb form	Example	Meaning
Buenos Aires:			
-ra subjunctive or conditional	present	*Si tuviera/tendría dinero, voy al teatro*	no probability (counterfactual)
conditional or present	conditional	*Si tendría/tengo dinero, iría al teatro*	some probability
present	present	*Si tengo dinero voy al teatro*	total probability (open)
Standard language:			
-ra (or *-se*) subjunctive	conditional	*Si tuviera/tuviese dinero iría al teatro*	no probability (counterfactual)
present	present	*Si tengo dinero voy al teatro*	total probability (open)

The conclusion must therefore be that there is not simple variation between *-ra* subjunctive and conditional; the variation is not only between different verb-form sequences in protasis and apodosis, but also between different systematic semantic distinctions.

6.3.1 Social class

We cannot give an overview of diastratic variation in the Spanish-speaking world, not least because the collection of compendious data of the kind now available for the study of diatopic variation is not being undertaken, and is not likely to be. In the following sections we give some indication of observable diastratic variation based on recent research. (We shall also return to some issues concerning diastratic variation in **10.2.2**.)

Social class has not always been recognised as an important factor in linguistic variation in Spain, an impression that has been resoundingly corrected by sociolinguistic investigation. Williams (1987) found a good deal of evidence for such variation in a study of Valladolid speakers, where, for instance, the pronunciation of *muy* proved to correlate very clearly with social class, the lower classes tending towards the pronunciation [muị] or [mu] and the middle and upper classes to the standard [mwi]. Since social class is not an easy parameter to define objectively, a number of studies have used level of education as a parameter: thus Silva-Corvalán (1989: 76–7) reports on the behaviour of two groups of male speakers in

Santiago de Chile with regard to the pronunciation of /f/, one with three years' education or under and one with 12 years or more. Speakers in the first category consistently show a higher incidence of the velarised (and socially stigmatised) pronunciation [x], e.g. ['xweɾsa] *fuerza*.

6.3.2 Age

Silva-Corvalán's (1987) study of the neutralisation of syllable-final /l/ and /ɾ/ in Chilean Spanish revealed that speakers in higher age groups (30–45 and 50+) had a higher incidence of exchange of liquids (the use of /l/ for /ɾ/ and vice versa) than speakers in lower age groups (young children and teenagers).

6.3.3 Sex

Salvador (1952), in a study of the villages of Vertientes and Tarifa in the north of Granada province, found that men used the coronal [s] while women used the apical [ş], and that men had a higher incidence of aspiration of /s/, *yeísmo* and the neutralisation of syllable-final /l/ and /ɾ/. This is a typical pattern insofar as women's speech is usually more 'conservative' and men's speech more 'innovating'. Williams (1987: 137) in his survey of Valladolid speech, comes to the same conclusion for several of the variables he investigates, but observes that a relatively higher proportion of female than male middle-upper class speakers adopted non-standard pronunciations of 'learned' words (e.g. *examen* [e'samen] rather than [ek'samen], *acción* [a'θjon] rather than [ak'θjon]), which goes against the general pattern. He suggests that this may be attributable to the greater demand for freedom by Spanish middle-class women at the time of his study (the 1970s).

6.3.4 Other factors

There are yet other parameters of linguistic variation. Some are essentially internal to the structure of language: phonological variables are conditioned by phonetic context (see **2.3.1**) and also by the speed of speech, for example. Others are to do with the external situation in which language is being used: all variables may be conditioned by such factors as the formality of the interview situation and the degree of confidence or spontaneity on the part of the informant. Politeness and formality have long been recognised as important conditioning factors and sometimes correlate with deep-rooted structural features of a language (for example, the use of second-person pronouns and their corresponding verb-forms in Spanish, and a whole range of differences in vocabulary, which will be further examined in Chapter 7). We rapidly realise that even the speech of the same individual can vary considerably from situation to situation.

6.3.5 Covariation

Setting all these difficulties aside, however, sociolinguistic investigations have yielded a number of consistent patterns. It turns out that a feature which shows variation along one parameter may show similar variation along another, a phenomenon known as **covariation**. The following pattern is not at all atypical for Spanish, for example: looking at *yeísmo*, we tend to to find (Table 6.6) that the opposition is maintained more amongst upper-class speakers than amongst lower-class speakers, more by older speakers than by younger, and more by women than by men. From this there follows the significant fact that the lower classes and men are on the whole more 'innovative' in their speech than the upper classes and women.

Table 6.6 A possible covariation pattern for *yeísmo*

Opposition between /ʎ/ and /j/	Absence of opposition
Upper classes Older speakers Women	Lower classes Younger speakers Men

Fontanella de Weinberg (1979) found in a study of the speech of Bahía Blanca (Argentina) that there was variation between [ʃ] and [tʃ] in the pronunciation of everyday words such as *chalet*, *shampoo*, etc., with [ʃ] characterising the speech of better educated speakers and women; it was also more frequent in reading than in spontaneous conversation. Covariation follows a number of patterns. Variables which covary for class, age, sex, ethnic group, etc., but not for situation or style, are known as indicators; those which also covary for situation or style are known as **markers**. Stereotypes, a term which we have already informally introduced, are markers which are associated with particular speech communities (because such variables in fact often do not have a consistent value throughout the speech community, the investigation of stereotypes relies on the eliciting of subjects' opinions). When the social factors which are relevant to variation can be hierarchically ordered, indicators are said to be **stratified**.

There is thus also likely to be a close relation between the features which covary along the parameters of social class, age and sex and those which are the basis of diatopic isoglosses. For example, the fall of syllable-final /s/ is an 'innovatory' feature occurring in many areas of the Spanish-speaking world; similarly, the typically 'conservative' groups (upper classes, older speakers, women) are likely to preserve the /s/ to a greater extent than the typically 'innovating' groups (lower classes, younger speakers, men). But occasionally this pattern is broken in a way which permits interesting conclusions to be drawn.

Klein (1980) reports on three aspects of pronoun usage in Castile (see also **6.2.3**): the use of *le(s)* with masculine animate reference, the use of *le(s)* with masculine inanimate reference, and the use of *la* as a feminine indirect object pronoun. Comparing results obtained for men in Valladolid and Logroño, she shows (Figure 6.15) that for upper-middle-class speakers the use of *le(s)* with masculine animate reference is approximately as high as for middle- and working-class speakers in Valladolid and higher than in Logroño (though in Logroño the overall percentage of usage is much lower). For the use of *le(s)* with masculine inanimate reference and the use of *la* as a feminine indirect object pronoun, the upper-middle classes score less highly in Valladolid and about the same as the middle and working classes in Logroño (with negligible usage all round). This rather unusual distribution, in which the upper-middle classes use an innovating feature as much as or more than the middle and working classes, points to the greater prestige which *leísmo* which masculine animate reference enjoys in Castile.

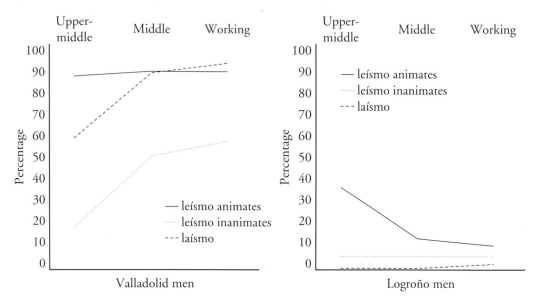

Figure 6.15 *Leísmo* and *laísmo* in Valladolid and Logroño as a function of social class (from Klein 1980: 64–65)

EXERCISES

1. The following table compares developments of four Latin words in Castilian, Portuguese and Catalan. Which do you think shows the most 'innovating' changes?

Latin[7]	Castilian	Portuguese	Catalan
JANŬĀRĬU[S] [janu'aːriu]	*enero* [e'neɾo]	*janeiro* [ʒɐ'nɐi̯ɾu]	*gener* [ʒə'ne]
PLĒNU[S] ['pleːnu]	*lleno* ['ʎeno]	*cheio* ['ʃɐju]	*ple* [ple]
ANNU[S] ['annu]	*año* ['aɲo]	*ano* ['ɐnu]	*any* [aɲ]
MULTU[M] ['multu]	*mucho* ['mutʃo]	*muito* ['mwĩtu]	*molt* [mɔɫ]

---

[7] Phonetic representations of Latin are of course conjectural and reflect the most likely common source of these Romance words.

2. What is the likely phonemic status of [h] and [ɸ] in Andalusian Spanish? (A first step is to research the pronunciation of words which begin with /f/ and /x/ in the standard language.)

3. Use your knowledge of the isogloss patternings of Andalusia (see Figures 6.4, 6.7 and 6.11) to pinpoint the area of origin of the speaker of the Text A. (Look particularly at the isoglosses relating to *seseo/ceceo*, differentiation of vocalic opening and *yeísmo*.)

4. This text was written by a Latin-American author who was trying to represent features of local speech. What are these features, and where do you think the text comes from?

> –¿Y qué'stay haciendo aquí vos?
> –Esperándote.
> –¿Cómo supiste ...?
> –Oyí cuando la fiera'e tu mamá te dijo anoche que teníay qu'ir a las casas del jundo.
> –¿Y no saliste a trabajar?
> –Aunque me hubieran pagado en oro. Hace dos semanas que no te doy un beso.
> Ha avanzado unos pasos, y sin aguardar mucho, coge a la muchacha por el talle.
> –Y estay más rebonita – dice.
> –Y vos más entraor ...
> –Te quiero.
> –¿Y yo...? ¡Creís que a palos van a sacarme del corazón el cariño!
> –¡Así me gusta oírte!

5. Get native speakers you know to talk about their 'accent' and their attitude towards other native speakers' 'accents'.

7 | Register

In Chapter 6 we looked at diatopic and diastratic variation in modern Spanish. In this chapter and the next we will consider what is sometimes called **diaphasic** variation. First of all we look at **register**, i.e. variation according to the situation in which language is used, or the purpose for which it is used. As with diatopic and diastratic variation, it turns out that such external circumstances can often be correlated with internal, structural features of language. Native speakers can make judgements about what is appropriate and inappropriate linguistically in a particular situation, an ability which is sometimes called **communicative competence** (Hymes 1974: 75), just as surely as they can recognise the acceptability or unacceptability of grammatical forms. Unlike diatopic and diastratic linguistic variation, however, register has primarily been studied as a property of written texts, and while the geographical and social variation observable in speech is largely subconscious on the part of the speaker, written register is often a more consciously cultivated phenomenon. Furthermore, the characterisation and classification of situation and purpose cannot by its very nature be as rigorous as identification of such variables as sex, age, or even social class, and it is rarely possible to say that a particular text uniquely exemplifies one particular register. Certain situations of use in fact demand and exploit register-switching (e.g. quoted conversational forms in a newspaper report, allusory language, parody).

We must distinguish between categorisation of the situation or purpose of a text and the identification of its characteristic linguistic features. Register is often characterised (following Halliday 1978: 31–5) according to the parameters of **field**, **tenor** and **mode**. Field relates to the subject-matter of the discourse, tenor to the relation between the participants (e.g. speaker and hearer, writer and reader) and mode to the medium employed (e.g. speech or writing). In a political speech, the field might be the national economy, the tenor would be a single speaker trying to persuade a mass audience of a particular point of view, and the mode would be spoken, but usually on the basis of a written script. From the linguistic point of view it is common to use general terms such as high or low register, high register being generally correlatable with an abstract or intellectual field, a formal or conventional tenor, and non-spontaneous written mode. In the last thirty years or so it has become more common for dictionaries to give some indications of register when a word is restricted in use from this point of view: *OSD*, p.xxxvi, for example, uses the following labels:

> formal
> colloquial
> language used by or to children
> slang
> vulgar (coarse or offensive)
> euphemistic

humorous
ironical
pejorative
literary
poetic
journalistic
dated (but still used by older people)
archaic (no longer in common use, but familiar from literature or used
    humorously)
historical (obsolete term)
criticised (deemed incorrect)
set (set phrase)
technical

Some words and constructions are marked in the sense that they are particularly associated with certain registers, while others are unmarked, carrying no such associations. To express the notion 'dirty', for example, the Spanish adjective *sucio*, which is unmarked for register, can be used in all situations. *Guarro*, by contrast, is restricted in usage to colloquial register (informal tenor and spoken mode), while *inmundo* is more likely to be used in high registers (formal tenor and written mode). We shall therefore be especially interested in the marked forms, since these may be potentially taken as indicators of particular registers. In looking at the linguistic correlates of particular registers, we should distinguish between features which are determined pragmatically by the field and tenor of the discourse and features which are apparently independent of such pragmatic motivation. Pragmatic factors actually determine rather more than might initially be suspected: for example, a camera instruction manual would naturally be rich in the semantic field of photography; spoken discourse usually shows a high frequency of constructions associated with characteristic speech acts such as questions and commands; spontaneous speech will contain hesitations, and there will be a high premium on economy of expression and clarity of anaphoric reference in journalistic writing.

7.1 Register variation in the spoken language

As a convenient illustration of variation within the same speaker according to situational context, we begin by examining the following passage, which is taken from Rafael Sánchez Ferlosio's *El Jarama*, a novel which pays considerable attention to the stereotypical representation of Madrid speech (cf. **6.2.3.5**) – note the *laísmo* of *la dices a la telefonista* in Text C(i), l.4. The novel relates a day excursion by a group of young people to the countryside in the course of which one of the girls in the party is drowned in the river whilst bathing. Here one of the Civil Guards reports the drowning. This incident is set in the days of operator-connected calls, and he has to speak first to the operator, a girl much younger than himself whom he knows well (Text C(i)), and then to his superior, whom he naturally treats with extreme deference (Text C(ii)). The mode of discourse is the same, that of a telephone conversation. The tenor, however, is quite different, the first being informal and the second more formal. There is also a slight difference in field: the conversation with the operator is to do with making the telephone connection and deliberately avoids giving details of what has happened, while the conversation with the superior is limited to terse reporting of the incident. The linguistic features of each conversation are strikingly different.

TEXT C (i)

Mira, aquí es Gumersindo, el guardia, al aparato –se tapó con
un dedo el oído libre. Mira, Luisa: me vas a dar, pero urgente, Alcalá de
Henares, llamada oficial, con el Señor Secretario del Juzgado; escucha, si
no contestan en su casa, la dices a la telefonista que te lo localice como
sea por ahí, ¿entendido? –hizo una pausa–. ¿Qué? Ah, eso a ti no te   5
interesa; ya lo sabrás –volvió los ojos hacia la gente de las mesas–.
¡Pues claro está que algo habrá pasado! ¡No va a ser para felicitarle las
Pascuas! –se reían en las mesas, volvió a escuchar–. ¿Quéeee? –
escuchando de nuevo, esbozó poco a poco una sonrisa–. Mira, niña,
podía ser yo tu padre un par de veces; de modo que no juegues con los   10
cincuentones y espabílame rápido la conferencia, anda. Me la das aquí
mismo, ¿eh?, donde la Aurelia, ya sabes. Cuelgo.

TEXT C (ii)

¡Diga! ¿Es ahí el Señor Secretario? ...
–Mire usted, Señor Secretario, aquí le llaman desde San
Fernando de Henares, el guardia civil de primera Gumersindo
Calderón, para servirle ... ! ¡Cómo dice? –escuchó–. Sí, señor –asentía
con la cabeza–. ¡Sí, sí señor; la pareja de servicio en el Jar ... ¿Diga?   5
–Pues mire usted –continuó Gumersindo–, o sea que en la
tarde hoy se ha producido un ahogamiento, de cuyo ahogamiento ha
resultado siniestrada una joven, según indicios vecina de Madrid, que se
sospecha asistía a los baños, en compañía de ... ¡Diga, Secretario! –
escuchaba–. ¡En la presa, si señor, en las inmediaciones de ...! –se   10
interrumpió de nuevo. Bien, Secretario! –otra pausa–. ¡De acuerdo, sí
señor, conforme! ¿Mande ...? –escuchaba y asentía–. Sí señor, sí, sí
señor ... Hasta dentro de un rato, señor Secretario, a sus órdenes.

Rafael Sánchez Ferlosio, *El Jarama* (Barcelona: Destino, 9th ed., 1969), pp. 289–91.

The contrasting tenor of the two extracts is reflected most obviously in address features. In Text C(i), Gumersindo addresses the telephone operator, Luisa, as *tú*, and calls her by her first name or by the term *niña*, stressing his seniority; he also identifies himself to her by using his first name, Gumersindo, showing that there is a degree of familiarity between them. In Text C(ii), he uses *usted* to his superior and the respectful terms *(Señor) Secretario* or *señor*; he identifies himself by his rank and full name as *el guardia civil de primera Gumersindo Calderón*. There are other indications of a difference in the level of politeness in the two conversations: in Text C(i), Gumersindo announces himself rather abruptly as being *al aparato* and similarly terminates the conversation by with a curt *cuelgo*; in Text C(ii), apart from fuller information, he uses the phrase *le llaman* (use of the third person plural implies that it is the pair of civil guards who are making the call and distances Gumersindo from direct personal involvement) and concludes with the polite (and rather antiquated) formula *para servirle*. To request repetition or further explanation, he uses *¿Qué?* in Text C(i) by contrast with the more polite *¿Cómo dice?*, *¿Diga?* and *¿Mande?* of Text C(ii). Text C(i) contains a high number of imperative expressions, since here Gumersindo is giving the instructions (*me vas a dar, la dices, no juegues, espabílame, anda, me la das*, as well as the confirmatory *escucha, ¿entendido?, ¿eh?*), while in Text C(ii) he is presumably receiving them.

In addition to this, Text C(i) contains many linguistic features which are typical of informal conversational register whilst Text C(ii), though spoken, has features which could be used in formal written register, especially the language of official documents or the press. In Text C(ii), adjectives are used as adverbs (*urgente*, l.2, *rápido*, l.11, see **1.1**) and *pero* is used as an intensifier (*pero urgente*, l.2). *Donde* is used as a preposition (*donde la Aurelia*, l.12), and in this phrase the typical rural use of the definite article with a name can also be observed. The imperfect is used for a conditional (*podía* for *podría*, l.10). Topicalisation is used: *eso a ti no te interesa* (ll.5–6). *Espabilar* (lit. 'to awaken', l.11) is common in colloquial usage in the meaning of 'hurry along, get a move on'. In Text C(ii) there is a considerable use of circumlocutory phrases involving nominalisations: *se ha producido un ahogamiento* (l.7) (= *alguien se ha ahogado*), *asistía a los baños* (l.9) (= *se estaba bañando*), *en las inmediaciones de* (l.10) (= *cerca de*). The use of *cuyo* (l.7) as a transition relative (see **4.6.2**) rather than in its possessive relative function meaning 'of whom' and the omission of the complementiser *que* in *se sospecha asistía a los baños* (ll.8–9) are syntactic features which are very strongly associated with highly formal written language. The word *siniestrada* 'involved in an accident' (l.8), a euphemism for *muerta*, is similarly formal, as are the phrases *en la tarde hoy* (= *esta tarde*) (ll.6–7), *según indicios* (= *al parecer*) (l.8) and *en compañía de* (= *con*) (l.9).

7.1.1 Politeness

Tenor is thus an extremely important determinant of variation in the spoken language, and interacts very closely with politeness. We can in fact make some fairly specific correlations between degrees of politeness and formal features of the language, especially the use of second person pronouns and imperative constructions.

7.1.1.1 SECOND PERSON PRONOUNS

All varieties of Spanish appear to make a distinction of formality in singular second person pronouns, though, as we have seen (**6.2.4.2.3**), only Peninsular speakers do so in the plural. The basis for the distinction varies very considerably throughout the Spanish-speaking world and is quite difficult to systematise. In Spain, the use of *tú* and *vosotros/as* gained in frequency in the second half of the 20th century, to such an extent that it is probably appropriate to say that *usted/es* is now the marked form, used only when it is intended to signal politeness. The loosest perception of belonging to the same social group as one's interlocutor seems to be enough to favour the use of *tú* and *vosotros/as*: age (not only young people in general but increasingly amongst older people too), similar social background or job, colleagues at work. On the other hand, in Colombian Spanish, there seems to be the opposite situation: here *usted* is the generalised default address form, while *tú* or *vos* marks a definite intimacy. The contrastive marking of formality or informality sometimes produces results which break the general association of *usted/es* with formality and of *tú/vosotros* and *vos* with informality: a parent may use *usted* to a child in anger, for example. There are even more striking instances of such distinctions: Kany (1951: 93–4) records a number of 'affectionate' uses of *usted* in Spanish America, and Keller (1975), in a study of speakers in New York and Mexico City, notes the change from mutual *tú* to *usted* which denotes the passage of a *cuate* (buddy-to-buddy) relationship to the apparently more intimate one of *compadre* (parent-to-godfather). 'Idiomatic' uses of the second-person pronouns are another example of such distinctiveness: *vos* was for a long time used to the king in Spain even when otherwise it was generally regarded as pejorative, and *vosotros* is regularly used oratorically to a mass audience.

The values of the second-person pronouns may also be described not by trying to attach any meaning to them as such but rather by looking at the significance of particular patterns of usage between speaker and addressee. The now famous proposal by Brown & Gilman (1972) concerning 'power' and 'solidarity' hypothesised that the use of any informal/formal distinction implies relations of 'power' and 'solidarity' rather than simply politeness (though politeness is an aspect of 'power'), and that the use of the same form of address between speakers implies a 'solidarity' relationship, whereas the use of a different form implies a 'power' relationship. The 'power' and 'solidarity' parameters seem to offer a good explanation of the use of *tú* and *usted* in modern Spanish advertisements, for example, where *tú* expresses an attitude of 'matiness' (solidarity with the advertiser) and *usted* that of 'esteemed customer' (implying that the customer has power over the advertiser) – see **7.2.3**. The local and generational variation observable within the Spanish-speaking world is similarly explicable in terms of the Brown & Gilman hypothesis: their contention that asymmetric 'power' patterns are increasingly giving way to symmetric 'solidarity' patterns aptly explains some of the recent moves in Peninsular Spanish. On the other hand, Schwenter (1993), who has also used 'power' and 'solidarity' as parameters for differentiating Castilian dialects, concludes that, while *tú* forms are used much more widely in Spain than in Mexico, Spanish speakers are motivated by 'power' in their choice of *tú* or *usted* according to age, sex or social class, while Mexicans are motivated by the degree of familiarity or 'solidarity' they have with a person.

7.1.1.2 IMPERATIVES

The plain imperative verb form comes towards the very bottom end of the politeness scale; its use is typical of orders being given by a superior to an inferior, for example, military commands (*¡Presenten armas!*), or in an informal situation among speakers who know one another well. If a superior is being addressed, or if a favour is being asked, a more polite mode of formulating a command is adopted. There are a number of strategies for signalling politeness in this way, generally involving a lengthening of the utterance:

● Use of *usted* with the bare imperative form
● The addition of the adverbial *por favor*
● Using a modal auxiliary such as *poder* or *saber* in the conditional tense (a protasis can even be supplied for such a construction, such as *si no le molesta*)
● Embedding the command as the complement of another verb
● Formulating the whole sentence as a question
● Suggesting that the speaker is also involved in the action, e.g. by using the first person plural or a phrase such as *yo que tú* 'if I were you'
● Using an explicit verb of requesting

Another strategy is to use the present tense rather than the imperative itself. A combination of a number of these strategies is common. Thus a simple command to open the window might be expressed in the following (and more) ways:

(**7.1**) **a.** *¡Abra la ventana!*
   b. *¡Abra (usted) la ventana, por favor!*
   c. *Por favor, ¿me abre la ventana?*
   d. *Podría abrir la ventana*
   e. *¿Podría abrir la ventana?*
   f. *¿Le importa abrir la ventana?*
   g. *Haga el favor de abrir la ventana*
   h. *¿Abrimos la ventana?*
   i. *¿Tendría la amabilidad de abrir la ventana?*

7.1.2 Conventionalised and real spoken language

Texts C(i) and (ii), though fictional, are convincing because they include a number of features which are typical of spoken language but which are not usually encountered in written registers. These are:

● The use of **fillers** (*muletillas*), which have little or no semantic content, but which have the function of giving the speaker time to think: *mira, mire usted, escucha, ah, o sea que*.
● Truncated sentences, shown by suspension marks (...) in punctuation.
● Formulae which check that the addressee can hear or is still paying attention (*¿entendido?*, *¿eh?*), or which ask for repetition or clarification of something the addressee has said (*¿Qué?*, *¿Cómo dice?*, *¿Mande?*).

● The high frequency of questions, answers and commands and responses to questions and commands (*sí, de acuerdo*)

7.1.2.1 Spoken language transcribed from a recording

However, we still have not examined real spontaneous speech. The following is an extract from a transcript of a recorded interview made in Seville as part of a major investigation of the cultured norm in a number of cities in the Spanish-speaking world.

TEXT D

–¿Qué es lo que hace la gente los fines de semana aquí?

–Bueno. Aquí yo creo que el cine, el cine de invierno. Bueno, verás tú, según. Es que está el problema de gente casada o de gente soltera. La gente casada o con hijos suele salir fuera. Si hace buen tiempo, pues va a chalets de los alrededores, o a la playa en verano. Y   5
después, al cine. Yo creo que se va mucho. Y además, ahora mismo en Sevilla, con relación a los cine clubs, hay bastantes. Está bastante bien, porque hay cuatro o cinco cine clubs que están bastante bien organizados, ¿no? Contando lo de Ingenieros Industriales, de Arquitectura, el Club Vida, el Universitario. Por lo menos entre los   10
estudiantes tienen bastante, sí, si, aceptación.

–Respecto a la vida de Sevilla, ¿alguna cosa que le guste especialmente?

–Quizás me guste la gente, ¿no?, de Sevilla. Yo no sé si es porque soy de aquí, pero me gusta que sean abiertas. No sé, yo es que   15
estuve, por ejemplo, unos años estudiando fuera. Luego, cuando volví, que preguntaras a una mujer dónde estaba la calle tal y te dijera "Sí, sí, yo voy para allá, yo mismo te llevo". Y que te llevaran ellos mismos a los sitios. Muy abiertas. Esto es una cosa ... . Por ejemplo, yo en Madrid he estado muy poco, pero no existe esto que parece muchas veces un tópico   20
en Sevilla, pero yo creo que no. Sí. Incluso dentro de Andalucía, yo creo que es la que más. Porque Granada, que yo voy bastante porque estoy haciendo allí la tesis, es más cerrada.

Miguel Ángel de Pineda, *Sociolingüística andaluza 2. Material de encuestas para el estudio del habla urbana culta de Sevilla.* (Seville: Universidad de Sevilla, 1983), pp. 158–9.

The features we have already noted are clearly present. Amongst the fillers is *sí* (l.21), which is even interposed within a noun phrase (*bastante, sí, sí, aceptación*, l.11). Another is *por ejemplo*, which often seems not to have its literal meaning, as in l.19. However, a number of features strike us particularly about this transcript. The first is that there is a great deal of repetition, which is another strategy which allows a speaker time to think. More exactly, what happens is that the speaker begins with basic information which is then progressively elaborated. In ll.2–11 she develops her basic answer to the interviewer's question, that the most frequent leisuretime activity at weekends is going to the cinema. Qualification of this answer builds up in the following way:

(1) People go to the cinema.
(2) People go to the cinema in winter.
(3) But it depends on (a) whether people are married or single: married people go out, (b) the weather: if it's fine people go to their houses in the country, (c) the time of year: in summer they go to the beach; they then go to the cinema afterwards.
(4) There are a lot of film clubs in Seville, which also favours cinema-going.
(5) The film clubs are well-organized.
(6) She lists four of them.
(7) She comments that film clubs are especially popular with students.

In fact, the development of this information is not very coherent (see 8.1): we do not learn what the difference in cinema-going habits between married and single people actually is. In a written text we expect greater economy in expression and a tighter logical relation between clauses: otherwise material rapidly becomes tedious and confusing to read, not to mention the inevitable editorial constraints on expensive space. So a written answer to the question, using the same information, might read as follows:

> *Va al cine, sobre todo en invierno, y sobre todo los estudiantes, porque hay en Sevilla bastantes cine clubs muy bien organizados, por ejemplo, el de Ingenieros Industriales, el de Arquitectura, el Club Vida y el Universitario. A los casados con hijos les gusta salir fuera: suelen ir a los chalets de los alrededores, o a la playa en verano, pero aun así van al cine después.*

The second prominent feature, related to the first, is topicalisation (see **4.4.3**), or the mention in first position of the theme of the sentence, after which supplementary comments are placed, sometimes with a syntax that is 'loose', that is to say, anomalous in the standard language. In the speaker's second answer, where she is asked for a personal opinion, several sentences begin with the first person pronoun *yo*. The sentence on ll.15–16 shows *yo* separated from the verb *estuve*; compare also *yo en Madrid he estado muy poco* (ll.19–20). The very last sentence (ll.22–23) has as its topic *Granada*; the relative clause that is added as the first comment (*que yo voy bastante*) has a relative element that is strictly speaking inexact: in the written language *adonde* would be preferred. Lastly, we should note the frequency of ellipsis: *según* (l.3) implies *según la estación*; *la que más* (l.22) means *la ciudad que es más abierta*.

7.1.2.2 SPOKEN LANGUAGE BASED ON A WRITTEN TEXT

Many manifestations of spoken language are not spontaneous but are based on written texts, either totally or partially. A speech or lecture may be written out in full or based on notes, with important passages often read verbatim. In the broadcasting media much use is made of scripts, although these are usually invisible to the viewer. However, materials designed to be read aloud usually pay attention to the demands of speech, so that the result is as 'natural' (i.e. appropriate to the apparent situation) as possible. Text E is a transcript of part of a television news bulletin:

TEXT E

La investigación judicial descubrió que algunos guardias civiles utilizaban droga para pagar a sus confidentes. El juez Garzón inició unas diligencias que han culminado con la detención de cinco guardias civiles y dos mandos. Un escándalo que según Luis Roldán implica únicamente a los acusados, que no compromete una eficaz trayectoria 5
del Servicio Antidroga y que pone de manifiesto la necesidad de mayores medios.

    Hoy el Director de la Guardia Civil, Luís Roldán, ha hablado extensamente de este asunto y lo ha hecho en una entrevista concedida a Radio Televisión Española en la que precisa varios aspectos del caso. En 10
primer lugar, ha sido rotundo al asegurar que ningún superior jerárquico conoció o autorizó las actuaciones irregulares de los guardias acusados. Pero ha dicho más. Pese a la polvareda levantada, ningún mando se lucró o consumió droga y las irregularidades afectan a una parte mínima del Servicio Antidroga. 15

Informe del día, RTVE, 8.1.93

This passage has no hesitations, repetitions or fillers. It contains a number of characteristics of the written language: nominalisations (*detención*, l.3, *actuaciones*, l.12), use of an adjective before the noun (*eficaz trayectoria*, l.5) and a good deal of vocabulary (*iniciar*, l.2, *diligencias*, l.3, *trayectoria*, l.5, *concedida*, l.9, *jerárquico*, l.12, *pese a*, l.13). On the other hand, it differs from very formal language in that the sentences are relatively short and, perhaps more importantly, comprise short phrases or clauses. They generally have a straightforward subject-first, verb-second structure and marked topicalisation is avoided; only adverbials precede the subject. Although there is a good deal of subordination, there is also coordination of clauses, especially with *y* (ll.6, 9, 14). One sentence is 'incomplete' by prescriptive standards (see **4.2**), containing only a noun phrase as a **head** or main element (*Un escándalo…*, ll.4–7), though ellipsis is otherwise absent.

7.1.3 Jargon and slang, special language and cryptolects

The English terms 'jargon' and 'slang' are used quite widely in everyday speech to denote what we may now think of as special registers, but their meanings are somewhat vague. In

Spanish the terms *argot*, *jerga* and *jerigonza* are perhaps even less clearly delineated. The *DRAE*'s definitions are as follows:

> argot:
> 1. m. Jerga, jerigonza.
> 2. Lenguaje especial entre personas de un mismo oficio o actividad.

> jerga:
> 1. f. Lenguaje especial y familiar que usan entre sí los individuos de ciertas profesiones y oficios, como toreros, estudiantes, etc.
> 2. jerigonza, lenguaje difícil de entender.

> jerigonza:
> 1. f. Lenguaje especial de algunos gremios, jerga.
> 2. fig. y fam. Lenguaje de mal gusto, complicado y difícil de entender.

In fact, these definitions do not conform to actual usage: *Clave* points out (p. 148) that *argot* is used socially for the purposes of differentiation or unintelligibility (what we will call below a **cryptolect**) while *jerga* corresponds more to the English 'jargon' and *jerigonza* is used pejoratively in the English sense of 'gobbledygook'. If such terms are to be used with any accuracy in linguistic description, there is thus a need for rigorous definition, and we will distinguish the notions of **jargon** and **slang**. By jargon we will understand the use of vocabulary which is restricted to a specialised field of discourse necessitating the labelling of concepts which are not regularly expressed in everyday usage, often through the more nuanced discrimination of a semantic field. The use of jargon is of course common in written technical language, though spoken discussion of a technical field also encourages its oral use. In Text F, for example, a sailor is talking about the characteristics of different winds:

TEXT F

–Sí. Los sudoestes, que allí llamamos lebeches, entran a menudo
por la tarde y a veces se mantienen durante la noche, como fue, según tú,
el caso durante la persecución del *Dei Gloria*. En invierno el viento suele
rolar luego al noroeste para venir de tierra por la mañana ... Un
poniente o un mistral pudieron empujarlo hacia el sudeste.   5

Arturo Pérez-Reverte, *La carta esférica* (Madrid: Alfaguara, 2000, p. 178).

The special terms *lebeche* 'warm southeasterly wind of the Mediterranean', *poniente* 'west wind' and *mistral* 'cold northeasterly wind' (also specific to the Mediterranean) cover a field which mariners clearly need to discriminate very precisely but which land-dwellers might not. The verb *rolar* 'to back, veer' is also, in Peninsular Spanish at least, specific to such a field of discourse. All these terms might be said to form part of a maritime or meteorological jargon. Slang, on the other hand, is more a matter of alternative ways of expressing notions which belong to a more generalised field of discourse, and is predominantly a spoken register. The following conversation between two men in their early twenties, reported in a Caracas newspaper, contains a number of slang words and expressions which reflect their uninhibited, spontaneous speech; their meanings and standard equivalents are shown in the table following:

TEXT G

– Si pana, es que te lo digo lo peor que puede pasarte es que rebotes con una jeva, es la sensación más horrible que puede haber, tienes que estar más o menos seguro se que le gustas a la jeva.

– Otra son las buenas labias, labias que les gusten a las jevas, como todas son unas interesadas, tienes que hablarles de que las vas a poner,   5
en un video, les vas a tomar una foto y esas muerden. No puedes caerle de una a las jevas diciéndoles cosas románticas y eso, las asustas, tienes que tener una excusa perfecta e irrefutable para acercarte.

– Pero lo más importante brother es la seguridad, sentirte seguro de lo que eres, incluso superior a ellas, que para veneno, veneno y medio   10
¿entiendes?, si no que estás frito, puedes estar bueno, tener real y un carrote y nada. En cambio, si tienes confianza y eres feo y pelabola, vas a tener éxito.

– Mira, hay dos tipos de cacería, una la del barranco, una jeva con la que te quieres divertir y tal, y otra la seria, la jevita, la legal, tienes que   15
estar pilas.

– Sí, yo creo que la relación entre hombres y mujeres en Caracas es buena, las jevas echan palante, y hay un culero, hay encuentro y tal y ¿sabes?

Planeta Urbe (http://www.planetaurbe.com)[1]

Slang term	Meaning	Standard words
pana	'mate, buddy'	amigo, compañero
jeva	'(young) girl'	chica
rebotar	lit. 'to bounce'; here 'to fail, not to score'	no tener éxito
labias	labia (singular) means 'gift of the gab'; here the plural means 'chatting up'	most equivalents are circumlocutory, e.g. tratar de ligar
muerden	lit. 'they bite'; here, 'they accept, are attracted'	aceptan
frito	'to be done for'	estar en una mala situación
real	'money'	dinero (LA plata)
carrote	'car'	coche (LA carro)

[1] I am grateful to Nick Roberts for this example.

pelabola	'having no money'	*no tener dinero*
de barranco	*barranco* has the literal meaning of 'ravine'; here, the phrase means 'casual'	*superficial*
estar pilas	'to be alert, careful'	*tener cuidado*
culero	This word has a variety of pejorative meanings including 'bugger' (from the root *culo* 'arse'), but here means 'boy, likely lad'	*chico*

One extremely interesting phenomenon in spoken language is the use of **cryptolects**, or modes of communication used within a particular community which are intended not to be readily understood outside that community. This, as we saw above, is essentially the common meaning of Spanish *argot*, though in the Spanish-speaking world many cryptolects exist and are referred to by different names in different areas. *Germanía*, the language of the Peninsular criminal underworld, is documented since the 16th century, and *caló*, the language of the Spanish gypsies, has also been extensively studied. The best-known of the Latin-American cryptolects is perhaps Argentine *lunfardo*, but there are also Mexican *caliche* and *sirigonza*, Chilean *coa*, Peruvian *replana* and Venezuelan *coba*. The following is an example of the speech of Nicaraguan young male gangs:

TEXT H

–¿Te has peleado por una mujer?
–Una vez por una ñora tuani, pero calzón flojo. Miguel estaba en un cuateturco y un frix me avisó que mi ñora estaba afincando en la carpa con el dañino. Me safé de volar pimpón y cuando la vicentié la agarré de la tuza, pero no hay más el comanche me echó el papo y me pegó la   5
mazorca en el parlante; entonces yo lo rayé con el puyón y cuando me soltó todo churretiado me hice alkaseltzer. Por eso ya no volví a llegar a la carpa. ¿Para qué? ¿Para que me meta el purgante ese pintón? Nelson Mandela.

Version in 'standard' Spanish:
–Una vez me peleé por una novia bonita, pero coqueta. Yo estaba en un prostíbulo y un amigo me avisó que mi novia estaba romanceando en nuestro sitio con el jefe. Corrí rápido y cuando la vi la agarré del cabello, pero el jefe me agarró del cuello y me mordió la oreja; entonces, yo lo herí con la navaja y cuando me soltó, todo ensangrentado me corrí. Por eso ya no volví al sitio. ¿Para qué voy a ir? ¿Para que me apuñale ese delincuente? Nunca.

Róger Matus Lazo, *El lenguage del pandillero en Nicaragua (estudio léxico-semántico)* (Managua: Editorial CIRA, 1997), p. 150[2].

[2] I am grateful to Joel López Ferreiro for drawing this source to my attention.

What strikes one immediately about this language is the degree of lexical difference from the standard, contrasting with the syntactic and morphological similarity. The lexical creations are unknown outside this register and many are likely to be ephemeral: the use of such words as *Nelson mandela* (l.8) and *alkaseltzer* (l.7) show the recency of their creation. A number of strategies have been used in word creation. *Nelson mandela* (ll.8–9) and *vicentié* (l.4) are phonological lengthenings of the initial /n/ of *nunca* and the initial /b/ of *ver* respectively; the first person pronoun *Miguel* (l.2) is similarly probably a lengthening of *mí*; in each case, an existing proper name has been exploited for the ultimate word. Standard words may be used with related but different meanings: *carpa* 'tent' (l.3) signifies 'dwelling' (*casa*), *afincar* 'to settle, be established' (l.3) means 'to court' or 'to have sexual intercourse with', *rayar* 'to scratch' (l.6) is used in the more general sense of 'cut, wound with a knife'. *Churretiado* (l.7) is a member of a whole morphological set of words based on *churrete* 'blood' which probably derives from *chorro* 'stream, jet' (as blood flowing). Some transfers of meaning can be rather more distantly connected and based on appearance or function: *mazorca* 'corncob' (l.6) becomes 'mouth' and *parlante*, 'loudspeaker' (l.6) in Latin America, becomes 'ear'; *calzón flojo* 'loose knickers' (l.2) expresses the notion of 'flighty, an easy lay'; *purgante* 'something which purges', is 'knife' (which lets blood). *Dañino* (l.4), literally 'harmful', is used in both a pejorative way ('hateful, repugnant') but also as a positive term ('bold, daring' – because damaging to other people) and hence as a noun 'leader of a gang'. Metaphorical expression can be seen in *volar pimpón* (l.4), lit. 'to fly like a pingpong ball', hence 'to move quickly, to run' and *me hice alkaseltzer* (l.7), lit. 'to dissolve like an Alka-Seltzer tablet', hence 'to disappear quickly, get out of the way'.

The rapidity of change in such cryptolects is reflected in a number of general features. A number of common semantic fields show a great many synonyms. In the passage above, for example, both *dañino* (l.4) and *comanche* (l.5) denote the leader of the gang. Matus Lazo records no fewer than twenty terms for the notion 'to eat': *bajonar, carpetear, charbasquear, gamelear, garatosar, machacar, melcoquear, merusear, ñequear, plenfiar, venadear, chamolear, chancletear, chupetear, empacar, jamar, jamear, yamar, merolear, tamaguear.* Conversely there is a high degree of polysemy of individual words: thus *peluche* (standard 'felt', as in *oso de peluche* 'teddy bear' – see also **3.2**) has developed meanings which reflect both the positive and negative connotations of such objects: (a) 'member of a gang', (b) 'stupid', (c) 'outsider, foreigner', (d) 'sensitive, softy' (e) 'decent person'. Lastly, many forms show phonetic variation. *Frix* 'friend, mate' (l.3) is a variant form of *prix*, which probably derives from *primo,* standard 'cousin'; *puyón* 'knife' (l.6) is an augmentative form of *puya*, which also has the forms *puña* and *poya*, the former no doubt associated with *puñal.*

7.2 Register variation in the written language

So far we have been tending to characterise written register as universally 'formal' by contrast with speech. However, the purposes for which written language is used are tremendously varied, and hence so are its registers. In this chapter we shall set aside creative literature, since that will be the special subject of consideration in Chapter 8. We shall examine, somewhat arbitrarily, three kinds of written language which have very distinctive registers: journalism, legal and administrative documents, and advertisements.

7.2.1 Journalism

The individual register of journalistic reporting is illustrated by the injunction of *El País*'s *Libro de estilo* (*El País* 1990), to which we will refer on a number of occasions in this section: 'Los periodistas han de escribir con el estilo de periodistas, no con el de los políticos, los economistas o los abogados' (p. 23). The same publication (p. 30) demonstrates the difference by giving information in a 'legal register' and then rewriting it in 'journalistic register', commenting that the journalist must be more imaginative and point out the possible consequences of an event:

> 'Legal register':
> *El Consejo de Ministros decidió ayer, 30 de diciembre, conceder una ayuda de 1.000 millones de pesetas para los damnificados por las últimas inundaciones...*

> 'Journalistic register':
> *Los damnificados por las últimas inundaciones podrán reparar sus casas sin recurrir a créditos bancarios, merced a la ayuda aprobada ayer por el Consejo de Ministros, que consiste en subvenciones de 1.000 millones de pesetas.*

However, any unitary notion of 'journalistic register' is probably much too broad to be useful, though in practice the term relates primarily to the register of news reports (see below). The written media comprise many different registers: in addition to 'plain' news reports there are main headlines, the expository prose of leading articles and essays, and the specialist registers associated with particular fields: the reporting of sports, fashion, the weather forecast, and so on. In this section we will look at a selection of these.

7.2.1.1 HEADLINES

Although other kinds of written text may have section or paragraph headings (e.g. travel guides, books such as this one), headlines are a distinctively journalistic feature. While some headlines simply summarise the report to which they pertain (we will look more closely at this technique in the following section), others seek first and foremost to attract the reader's attention and give little or no concrete information.

Even informative headlines often use a distinctive syntax. Especially common is the use of a verb-first construction which gives its subject noun more prominence as the 'new' information (see 4.4.3):

> **(7.2)** *Muere un granjero blanco de Zimbabue tras ser asaltado por 'veteranos de guerra'* (*El País*, 8.8.01)

When the full verb would have been passive, a past participle is used:

(7.3) **a.** *Detenida una pareja por dejar al hijo encadenado a una cama (El País*, 8.8.01)

b. *Desarticulada una organización que estafó 100 millones con prácticas de santería* [idol worship] (*Faro de Vigo*, 17.8.01)

The techniques used in more eye-catching headlines are various. A selective quotation from the report itself may be used:

(7.4) «¿Qué dejamos de propina» (article on the introduction of the euro in Spain, *El País*, 3.1.02)

or the selection of apparently irrelevant detail which will capture the reader's interest:

(7.5) **a.** *Llamadme Penti* (*El País*, 8.8.01) [sketch of Antonio Jiménez, Spanish athlete]

b. *Canguro Edwards* (*El País*, 8.8.01) [Jonathan Edwards, British triple jump athlete]

Rhetorical figures of speech (see **8.2**) are also used to catch the eye, such as this oxymoron:

(7.6) *Pequeño gran actor* (*DeViD*, El Corte Inglés, 3, Jul/Aug 2001)

Another device is the use of intertextual reference:

(7.7) **a.** *Ser o no ser periodista* (*El País*, 8.8.01)

b. *Benidorm: grúa eres y en grúa te convertirás* (*El País*, 19.8.01)

(7.7a) was the headline for a report on the case of Vanessa Leggett, who had claimed journalistic immunity under the First Amendment of the US Constitution and refused to give information about a murder case, but who had never formally worked as a journalist; it raised the important question of the basis on which someone could be deemed to be a journalist. The reference is to Shakespeare's *Hamlet* ('To be or not to be'), a quotation as familiar to the Hispanic world as to the English-speaking one. (7.7b) headed a report on Benidorm, featuring the difficulties of parking due to the massive influx of holidaymakers in August; the reference is Biblical: 'Dust thou art and to dust shalt thou return' (*Genesis*, 3: 19).

7.2.1.2 NEWS REPORTS

The characteristics of news reports are the result of a number of conflicting requirements. On the one hand there is a demand for economy, which means that the maximum information has to be packed into the shortest space, yet at the same time events must be made to sound important, which means that circumlocutory 'high' register is often employed; articles must also be attractive to the readership, which means that some variety in vocabulary and structure must be achieved. Clarity is also a prime requirement, which may involve a concentration on accuracy of anaphoric reference, and prevents the language used from straying too far from the cultured spoken norm: 'El estilo de redacción debe ser claro, conciso, fluido y fácilmente comprensible, a fin de captar el interés del lector'; 'Los términos empleados deben ser comunes, pero no vulgares' (*El País* 1990: 23, 24).

Text I is a fairly typical example of such a report:

TEXT I

Detuvieron a dos delincuentes que hirieron a un hombre

Uno de los ladrones resultó herido tras un fuerte tiroteo con la policía en la localidad bonaerense de Villa Tesei

Dos delincuentes que habían robado a dos personas y herido a una de   5
ellas fueron detenidos hoy tras tirotearse con policías en Morón, al oeste
del conurbano bonaerense.

El hecho comenzó esta madrugada cuando dos hombres fuertemente
armados asaltaron en Morón a un hombre, a quien le robaron dinero, lo
despojaron de un vehículo Renault 19 y en el forcejeo le dispararon en el   10
rostro.

Los ladrones emprendieron la fuga hacia la localidad bonaerense de
Bella Vista, en donde abandonaron el vehículo.

Luego de caminar unos metros por la misma calle donde abandonaron el
Renault 19, los asaltantes abordaron a otra persona, a quien le   15
sustrajeron dinero y otras pertenencias y le robaron su auto Fiat Uno,
con el que huyeron hacia la localidad de San Miguel, en el noroeste del
conurbano.

La policía, que ya estaba alertada, avistó a los delincuentes en la avenida
Gaspar Campos, de San Miguel, y luego de una intensa persecución y ya   20
en jurisdicción de Villa Tesei, los asaltantes dispararon sobre efectivos del
Comando Patrullas de San Miguel, que los perseguían.

Ya en la calle Villegas, de Tesei, los ladrones fueron interceptados por
personal de la Dirección de Investigaciones de Morón, que se unió al
operativo, y allí se produjo un fuerte tiroteo.   25

Tras el enfrentamiento, los delincuentes bajaron del Fiat Uno e
intentaron fugar a pie, pero a los pocos metros fueron detenidos por la
policía, que identificó a los ladrones como M.C., de 23 años, y H.R.G., de
18 años, quien resultó herido y fue trasladado a una clínica de Haedo
para su atención.   30

En tanto, se informó que el propietario de Renault 19 herido por los
delincuentes, que no fue identificado, fue trasladado de urgencia al
Hospital Municipal de Morón, donde fue intervenido quirúrgicamente y
se repone de las heridas.

La Nación, 9.6.01(Argentina)

One immediately striking feature of news reports is presentational. The piece begins with a headline and a subheading in different points of type, the advantage of this being that a reader can skim through the paper reading the individual headlines, which give an outline of the events reported, and then return to read items that are of particular interest. (According to Martín *et al.* (1996: 199–200), this 'inverted pyramid' structure for news reporting began during the American Civil War when war correspondents, fearful that the telegraph might not work, developed the strategy of sending the crucial information first and elaborating it only afterwards; previously, reporting had been chronologically rather than hierarchically structured.) In this case, the headline reports the information that two men have been arrested after wounding another man; the subheading adds the information that one was himself wounded after a shoot-out with police, and gives the location of the incident. In the body of the article, the first paragraph repeats this information (it is on the basis of such an introductory paragraph, giving the essentials of the incident, that the headlines would have been written by a copy editor). Only in the second paragraph of the article does a chronological and more extended account of the events begin, signalled by *comenzó* (l.8). Each sentence constitutes a paragraph, which is easier on the reader's eye.

As regards the field of the passage, great attention is paid to the provision of details: the exact location of the incident down to the identification of particular streets and the position of Morón and San Miguel within the Buenos Aires conurbation, the police units involved, the make of the cars which were stolen, the names of the perpetrators (given as initials here, but full names were given in the original) and their ages, and the hospitals to which the wounded were taken.

The formal tenor of the passage is reflected in a number of features. The *ser*-passive is extensively used, especially in the final paragraph (ll.31–34). There is some use of nominalisation: *tiroteo* (ll.3, 25), *persecución* (l.20), *enfrentamiento* (l.26), and some circumlocution: *conurbano bonaerense* (= *Buenos Aires*), l.7, *emprendieron la fuga* (= *(se) fugaron*), l.12, *se produjo un … tiroteo* (= *se tirotearon*), l.25, *fue intervenido quirúrgicamente* (= *le operaron*), l.33. In other respects, however, the structures used are straightforward and very similar to those of Text E: sentences generally have a subject-first, verb-second order and subordination is limited to relative clauses and adverbial phrases. ('Las frases deben ser cortas, con una extensión máxima aconsejable de 20 palabras. Sujeto, verbo y predicado es regla de oro': *El País* 1990: 24.) Only short adverbial constructions of time or place precede the subject (*Luego de caminar* …, l.14, *Ya en la calle Villegas* …, l.23, *Tras el enfrentamiento*, l.26, *En tanto*, l.31), which is consistent with the concentration on a chronological account and accurate situation of the incident. ('Una información no debe comenzar con un adverbio o locución adverbial – excepto el adverbio "sólo" si su cambio de orden modificase el sentido – ni con un complemento circunstancial. No porque sea algo incorrecto gramaticalmente, sino porque dificulta la lectura precisamente en el momento en que ha de producirse el *enganche* del lector': *El País* 1990: 30.)

There is some attempt to vary vocabulary denoting theft and personal attack in order to avoid the excessive repetition of one word: *robar* (ll.5, 9), *despojar de* (l.10), *sustraer* (l.16); *asaltar* (l.9), *abordar* (l.15).

7.2.1.3 SPORTS REPORTS

Sports reports are rarely a simple factual account of an event. The reporting of football matches in particular has developed a register all of its own which is rich in figures of speech whilst at the same time communicating the excitement of the game.

TEXT J

Un Athletic desdibujado y con un flojo balance defensivo cae con merecimiento ante el Middlesbrough en su peor partido de la gira inglesa

JUANMA VELASCO

<u>ENVIADO ESPECIAL MIDDLESBROUGH</u>   5

Jornada de reflexión en Middlesbrough. El Athletic, después de encajar
su primera derrota de la gira inglesa, ha descubierto que es vulnerable.
En Birmingham y Bolton ofreció un buen apunte de ilusión. Ayer, en el
Riverside Stadium, el 'Boro' le grabó con goles el decálogo de aspectos
en los que debe mejorar.   10
    En el encuentro frente al rival más fuerte el Athletic fracasó. Fue fácil
presa del 'Boro', que homenajeaba a Colín Curtis por sus diez años
vistiendo la camiseta del club. Un reconocimiento a la fidelidad que
agradeció muy pronto. En el minuto seis. El curtido lateral mandó un
balón largo hacia la posición de Job. El fino delantero se coló entre   15
Carlos García y Larrazabal, se adelantó a Lafuente en su salida y marcó
a puerta vacía. 1-0, el primer gol que encajaban los de Heynckes en
Inglaterra.
    El principio de una mala tarde. El equipo escogió el día de Curtis para
ejercitarse en los errores. Los tuvo en ataque y en defensa. El Athletic se   20
ofuscó en jugar por el centro. Y hacerlo contra un equipo inglés es
sinónimo de fracaso. Así, el único temblor para Schwarzer se produjo en
disparos fuera del área. Las bandas se asemejaron aun espejismo. A los
de Heynckes les costó un mundo abrir el balón. El técnico lo tiene como
un objetivo de obligado cumplimiento, pero no se hizo. Aunque las   25
mejores ocasiones – remates de Guerrero y Urzaiz – estuvieron
precedidas de centros realizados desde la cal por Etxeberria y Javi
González, la experiencia no debió satisfacer lo suficiente porque apenas
se repitió.
    Heynckes intentó un golpe de efecto con el partido ya avanzado. Colocó   30
a Cuéllar en la derecha y envió a Etxeberria a la otra banda. Dos cebos
para recoger balones. El cambio no tuvo consecuencias. Era como si los
dos laterales del Middlesbrough exigieran un peaje a todo aquel que se
acercara por sus dominios.

El Correo, 6.8.01

Much of the vocabulary is technical and is determined by the field: *gol, balón largo, abrir el balón, salida* (in the sense of a goalkeeper coming forward), *marcar* 'to score', *puerta* 'goal', *disparo* and *remate* 'shot' *área* 'penalty area', *banda* 'line, wing', *cal* '(white) line', *lateral* 'winger', *delantero* 'forward'. A number of words also have to do with the notion of competition (*rival*) and, more strongly, though commonly used with reference to competitive sport, to warfare (*derrota, vulnerable, ataque, defensa*) and hunting (*presa*). There is some variation in vocabulary in making anaphoric reference: Athletic is also referred to as *los de Heynckes* and Middlesborough is also called *el 'Boro'*.

Amongst the figures of speech used (see 8.2) are hyperbole (*les costó un mundo* 'it cost them the earth (i.e. a lot)', l.24; *ejercitarse en los errores* 'to exercise in (i.e. to make) mistakes', l.20; *se ofuscó* '[the team] was blinded, went to pieces' *en jugar por el centro*, ll.20–1) and circumlocution (*vistiendo la camiseta del club* 'playing for the club', l.13; *es sinónimo de fracaso* 'it was a disaster', ll.21–2; *no debió satisfacer lo suficiente porque apenas se repitió* 'they didn't repeat it', ll.28–9). There are also similes (on l.23 the lines are likened to mirages (*espejismos*) and on ll.32–4 the Middlesborough wingers are likened to toll collectors) and metaphors (on l.9 Middlesborough is said to have carved out with goals the ten commandments of Athletic's mistakes, and on ll.31–2 the Athletic players are described as bait for the ball). These similes and metaphors are also a form of hyperbole.

The reporter uses short sentences, often consisting only of a noun phrase (l.1, ll.13–14, l.19 and ll.31–2), in a way which recalls an oral commentary and hence the excitement and pace of the actual match.

7.2.2 Legal and administrative language

The language of law and administration has a number of characteristics which make it different from the registers we have been looking at so far. Explicitness is a prime requirement, and this may be achieved at the expense of repetition which would be considered undesirable in other registers, especially those registers in which there is some observation of the rules of classical rhetoric (see **8.2**), in which variation, especially in vocabulary, is highly rated. However, subject to the requirement of explicitness, concision is also important. Another consideration is consistency of meaning, so that the same word always means the same thing. The consequences of this requirement are that words which are very wide-ranging in their reference, or which have a marked connotative meaning (see **3.4**) are avoided. The pursuit of consistency leads to the adoption of certain formulae which are particular to this register, and even sometimes to the coining of new words or phrases. There is clearly the danger that legal and administrative register can differ very considerably from other registers if these considerations get out of hand, and indeed a current problem is how to keep such documents intelligible to speakers at large.

TEXT K

1. Sólo se podrán recoger datos de carácter personal para su tratamiento automatizado, así como someterlos a dicho tratamiento, cuando tales datos sean adecuados, pertinentes y no excesivos en relación con el ámbito y las finalidades legítimas para las que se hayan obtenido. En su clasificación sólo podrán utilizarse criterios que no se presten a prácticas   5
ilícitas.
2. Los datos de carácter personal objeto de tratamiento automatizado no podrán usarse para finalidades distintas de aquellas para las que los datos hubieran sido recogidos.
3. Dichos datos serán exactos y puestos al día de forma que respondan   10
con veracidad a la situación real del afectado.
4. Si los datos de carácter personal registrados resultaran ser inexactos, en todo o en parte, o incompletos, serán cancelados y sustituidos de oficio por los correspondientes datos rectificados o completados, sin perjuicio de las facultades que a los afectados reconoce el artículo 15.   15
5. Los datos de carácter personal serán cancelados cuando hayan dejado de ser necesarios o pertinentes para la finalidad para la cual hubieran sido recabados y registrados.
No serán conservados en forma que permita la identificación del interesado durante un período superior al necesario para los fines en   20
base a los cuales hubieran sido recabados o registrados.
Reglamentariamente se determinará el procedimiento por el que, por excepción, atendidos sus valores históricos de acuerdo con la legislación específica, se decida el mantenimiento íntegro de determinados datos.

Ley Orgánica de Protección de Datos de Carácter Personal, *Boletín Oficial de Estado* 298, 14.12.99.

The field of this document is the expression of rules or commands, and so every sentence is imperative in modality: the verb-form used to express the imperative is the future indicative (*podrán*, l.1 and throughout). The field also requires the expression of eventuality or hypothesis, rendered by the present subjunctive in temporal clauses (*cuando tales datos sean adecuados …*, ll.2–3; cf. also l.16) or relative clauses (*criterios que no se presten a prácticas ilícitas*, ll.5–6; cf. also ll.9, 8–9, 16, 17–18 and 22–4). There is one conditional sentence beginning with *si* (l.12) which, rather unusually, contains an imperfect subjunctive in the protasis (the more usual sequences would be either *si resultan … serán* or *si resultaran … serían …*); until relatively recently in legal documents the now obsolete future subjunctive (*si … resultaren …*) was common in such a context (and still appears sporadically: elsewhere in this same law is the construction *reanudándose el plazo de prescripción si el expediente sancionador estuviere paralizado durante más de seis meses*), and the use of the imperfect subjunctive in its place is clearly an attempt (ironically, not altogether successful) to bring legal register closer to the cultured norm. Indefinite subjects are also a part of such hypothesising, and this encourages the use of passive constructions, both the reflexive passive (*Sólo se podrán recoger* …, l.1; and cf. also ll.5, 8 and 22) and the more frequent *ser* passive (*Dichos datos serán … puestos al día* …, l.10; and cf. ll.13, 16, 17–18, 19 and 21). A final feature intimately connected with the field of the document is the predominance of generalisation: there are no concrete examples given here of what might or might not constitute an infringement of the law. This last feature in particular often makes the text difficult to understand: the last paragraph (ll.22–4) is particularly obscure in this respect, since to understand its implications we need to envisage a situation in which there might be a historical reason for the maintaining of personal data and how those historical reasons might be enshrined in another law: it begins to make sense only when we think perhaps of statistics collected in a census, which the laws governing the census would no doubt deem should be kept for posterity in digital format.

The pursuit of clarity can be observed in a number of cases. The notion of incorrectness of electronic data is expressed by the phrase *inexactos, en todo o en parte, o incompletos* (ll.12–13) and correction by *rectificados o completados* (l.14). 'Electronic data' is a concept which has to be defined explicitly, and to do this there is the rather cumbersome phrase *datos de carácter personal objeto de tratamiento automatizado* (l.7), which has a syntax (two noun phrases with the same function placed one after the other, a phenomenon known as **apposition**) which is not altogether usual in Spanish (see also **10.4.3.3**) but which certainly makes the notion very clear. Anaphoric reference is signalled by the use of *dicho* (ll.2 and 10) and *tales* (l.2).

Some other features are typical of 'high' written register. The use of nominalisations (already discussed, see commentary on Text I) can be seen in *su tratamiento automatizado* (ll.1–2), *clasificación* (l.5), *identificación* (l.19) and *mantenimiento* (l.24). The long adverb *reglamentariamente* (l.22) and the absolute construction (*atendidos sus valores históricos*, l.23, see **4.5.3**) are also associated with this register. Simple sentence structures are complicated in three principal ways. The first is by the addition of conjoined elements which typically express alternatives or further qualification (examples are the definition of *inexactos*, l.12, discussed above, the addition of *así como someterlos* …, l.2, and the phrase *recabados y/o registrados*, ll.18 and 21). The second is by the addition of adverbial phrases and clauses (*sin perjuicio* …, ll.14–15, *por excepción*, ll.22–3). Lastly, as already noted, there is a high incidence of relative clauses in this text: in a number of these, the relativised element is the prepositional object of the relative clause (e.g. *el procedimiento por el que … se decida* …, ll.22–4); there is also a recurring formula in which such a relative clause also has a prepositional object as its antecedent (e.g. *para los fines en base a los cuales hubieran sido recabados* …, ll.20–1: *los fines* is the antecedent and is the object of *para* in the main clause and of *en base a* in the relative clause).

Some vocabulary belongs to legal jargon. *Afectado* (ll.11 and 15) and *interesado* (l.20) denote people whose personal data is collected; words relating to legal procedures are *procedimiento* itself (l.22), *de oficio* 'by court order' (ll.13–14) and *reglamentariamente* 'by regulation' (l.22); there are also the formulaic expressions *sin perjuicio de* (l.15) and *el ámbito* 'area' (ll.13–14), widely used in legal phrases such as *en el ámbito de sus competencias*.

7.2.3 The language of advertising

Advertising plays subtle games with field, tenor and mode. Superficially, these might appear obvious: the field must be the product being advertised, the tenor is the addressing of a mass audience and the mode is written (or spoken on the basis of a written text). But in practice things are much more complicated. Although the field may consist of the simple description of a product, it is quite possible for the text of an advert apparently to have nothing, or little, to do with the product, or to be related in subject-matter in a very unobvious way: this has the effect of stimulating the reader's curiosity. The tenor of an advert can simulate a conversation between friends or it can be very formal indeed; it may resemble a number of special registers, such as a scientific report or a work of creative literature. Although language plays an essential role in the vast majority of advertisements, the mode usually involves other visual material such as pictures or graphic design in material designed to be seen, and music or other background sound effects in material designed to be heard. The reason for these unexpected relationships is that the business of the advertisement is first and foremost to seize attention, and only then to represent the product in such a way that the overall aim of persuading people to buy it is achieved. By way of introduction we will consider the following advertisement for a *cava* sparkling wine which appears on p.190.

The linguistic material is inseparable from the visual, which shows the bottle of wine protruding above the background of a sky, obscuring the sun so that a kind of aureola appears to shine around it. The text is set in small capitals in the same font as the brand label, thus reinforcing visual recognition of the label. A characteristic of advertising is the use of slogans or easily memorable phrases which can be associated with a product: in this case the slogan, set in larger type at the head of the page like a title, and further subtly emphasised by the use of larger initial capitals, is NO TOQUE EL CIELO ANTES DE HORA. The theme of the advert is that of waiting to achieve the ultimate satisfaction, suggested by the product name NON PLUS ULTRA, the meaning of which is duly explained. The notion of waiting allows another essential ingredient of adverts, namely, comparison with rivals, explicit or implicit, to the advantage of the product: paradoxically (and hence intriguingly) the text begins by apparently encouraging people to try other brands of *Cava*, which are characterised as being *de moda*, with the implication that what is popular with other people is not necessarily the best – there is also the flattering suggestion that the drinker of NON PLUS ULTRA will be asserting his or her individuality and standing out from the crowd (as the bottle stands out from its background). Preferring NON PLUS ULTRA is portrayed as the product of education gained in this process and the moment of becoming a real expert, beyond which no further education is possible. The final statement that NON PLUS ULTRA has been waiting for the reader for more than a hundred years (although the brand has existed for this length of time, the bottle the reader will drink of course has not) implicitly refers to another element that is common in advertisements: an assurance of the quality of the product gained through years of experience.

The tenor of the advert is therefore pitched as if addressing a single person of refinement and education, and the *usted* form of address is used. The polite imperative is not brusque in this case because pragmatically it expresses an invitation or suggestion rather than a command; its use also contributes to the directness of the advertisement's impact.

TEXT L

NO TOQUE EL CIELO
ANTES DE HORA

NO TENGA PRISA. INÍCIESE CON LOS CAVAS DE MODA . JUEGUE A CAMBIAR DE MARCA CADA NOCHE. LOS GOURMETS Y LOS BUENOS CAVAS NO SE IMPROVISAN. NECESITAN TIEMPO Y CULTURA. YA LE LLEGARÁ EL MOMENTO DE PREFERIR NON PLUS ULTRA. EL CAVA PARA TODA UNA VIDA. SERÁ UN FELIZ ENCUENTRO. ESTÉ PREPARADO PARA CONVERTIRSE EN UN AUTÉNTICO ENTENDIDO. ES EL FINAL DEL CAMINO. NO HAY NADA MÁS ALLÁ . ESTE ES EL REAL SIGNIFICADO DE NON PLUS ULTRA. LA PRIMERA JOYA DE LA CORONA DE CODORNIU. NO TENGA PRISA EN TOCAR EL CIELO. NON PLUS ULTRA LE ESPERA DESDE HACE MÁS DE CIEN AÑOS.

NON PLUS ULTRA

1872 1897

CODORNÍU

EL PRIMER CAVA

Muy interesante, 211, December 1998

The text comprises a number of very short sentences (an average of just six or seven words per sentence) with no subordinate clauses; straightforward syntactic structures are preferred in advertising because they are easily comprehensible, but here the excessive shortness of the sentences, because of the frequent full final cadences, also contributes to the expression of the notion of gradualness, and their resemblance to the syntax of moral maxims imparts a serious tone. Two of the sentences consist just of noun phrases, with no verbs: they refer directly to the wine (*El cava para toda una vida* and *La primera joya de la corona de Codorníu*). The repetition of *no tenga prisa* reinforces the message. There is a good deal of exploitation of imagery (the main image of *tocar el cielo*, which suggests not only achievement in terms of height ('sky') but also happiness ('heaven'), and also *el final del camino, la primera joya en la corona*) which raises the level of expression above the everyday to the more literary or poetic, again suggesting refinement and beauty, and capturing the reader's attention because it is unexpected. The use of the adjective before the noun in *feliz encuentro, auténtico entendido* and *real significado* is typical of advertising, where this position gives the reader to understand that the quality in question is an expected property of the noun.

Text M uses a number of strategies to engage the reader's attention. Its primary aim is to encourage Sunday shopping, which it does by subverting normal expectations about holidays. The sign *Abierto por vacaciones*, set at an angle, is the opposite of the usual sign seen in shops during the holidays, *Cerrado por vacaciones*. The text to the right of the notice presupposes that Sunday is a busy shopping day (*día de compras*) for the reader which can be converted into a period of rest (*respiro*) by going to the Corte Inglés. This tongue-in-cheek humour is separated by a double line from the essentially factual information given at the top of the page. The difference is also signalled typographically, the information about opening hours and offers being typeset to resemble a newspaper, using headlines, subheadings, block titles and columns (note, however, how the 'bullet point' triangle is in fact the same shape as the Corte Inglés logo). The contrast between the two sections is further emphasised by the choice of second-person forms, *usted* being used at the top of the page to indicate seriousness of purpose and respect for the customer, while *tú* is used in the lower part to suggest a more intimate tenor in which the joke can be shared; it also suggests the family atmosphere that might be associated with a holiday excursion.

7.2.3.1 PERSONAL ADVERTISEMENTS

Personal adverts are formulaic, with a premium on economy (in Text N below, only the contact details have been left out). Articles are omitted (e.g. *vendo piso*), as is any material which can be inferred on the basis of pragmatic expectation: thus *Urge 52.000* means that a property is being offered for 52,000 euros with the aim of making a quick sale; 150 € implies the weekly rent; and the description of the apartment is simply a series of nouns and adjectives.

TEXT M

EL CORTE INGLÉS
Noticias

Venga a conocer lo nuevo para este otoño

▶ Las últimas tendencias de moda. Lo nuevo de las grandes firmas. Los nuevos colores. Los nuevos diseños. No se pierda las colecciones de este otoño. Le esperamos.

Vuelta al cole... con muchas ventajas

▶ Cuando compre los uniformes, la ropa, los zapatos... le obsequiamos con el **10%** del importe en Corticoles, para canjear, a partir del 1 de octubre, por ropa, zapatos y complementos de la Planta Infantil.

HOY DOMINGO ABRIMOS EN MADRID.
EL CORTE INGLÉS DE 11 A 21 H.
TIENDAS EL CORTE INGLÉS DE 10 A 22 H.

Precios válidos del 5 de julio al 31 de agosto.

Date un respiro y ven hoy a El Corte Inglés.
Hacemos, de tu día de compras,
todo un día de fiesta.

QUINCENA FINAL de rebajas

El País, 19.8.01, p.7

TEXT N

VENDO piso amueblado. Teléfono...
URGE 52.000. 3 dormitorios, vistas, terraza, luminoso, amplio, financiamos,...
150€ Apartamento totalmente amueblado, 2 habitaciones. Electrodomésticos, buena zona...
SE necesita chica para bar. Buena presencia.
EMPLEADA fin de semana "Bar..."
SE necesita cocinera, turno de mañana...

Selected and adapted from *La Voz de Galicia*, 14.8.01

EXERCISES

1. The following is an extract from an open letter written by the Sindicato Unitario de Trabajadores de Telefónica del Perú S.A. to the Spanish Prime Minister. What are the distinctive features of the register of a formal letter? How is politeness signalled here? How would you characterise the register of the letter in general?

Lima, 16 de setiembre de 1,998

Excelentísimo Señor Jefe de Gobierno del Reino de España Don José María Aznar

LIMA.-

Excelentísimo Señor: 5

Reciba el saludo respetuoso del Sindicato Unitario de Trabajadores de Telefónica del Perú S.A. Vemos con expectativa el desarrollo de la industria española y el despliegue de sus inversiones en Latinoamérica, especialmente en telecomunicaciones, así como los importantes avances en el campo social. En particular, seguimos con interés las relaciones laborales entre empresas y   10 sindicatos en la tierra de Cervantes.

De nuestra parte, Señor Jefe del Gobierno español, no podemos expresar igual sentimiento de satisfacción, respecto a la política laboral que viene aplicando Telefónica del Perú S.A.A., filial de Telefónica Internacional de España, porque hiere nuestra sensibilidad humana de peruanos. Esto parece   15 no tener importancia para los funcionarios de la Empresa, sin embargo para los trabajadores peruanos tiene un significado discriminatorio.

El sindicato de trabajadores telefónicos no tiene ninguna controversia con la inversión española en nuestro país, pero estimamos señor Jefe de Gobierno de España, que esta no debe desarrollarse a costa de perjuicios que afectan   20 derechos inalienables que las leyes peruanas contemplan a favor de los trabajadores. Lamentablemente esta es la situación que venimos confrontando con Telefónica del Perú.

La jornada de las ocho horas diarias se ha ampliado ilegalmente de dos a cuatro horas adicionales sin compensación del sobretiempo correspondiente,   25 en calidad de "trabajo voluntario", para apoyar su manejo operativo. Los trabajadores peruanos tienen que soportar un lenguaje inapropiado y humillante para no ser calificados como "excedentes" y sufrir la pérdida inmediata del puesto de trabajo. Este trato inhumano crea resentimiento e impide la identificación de los trabajadores con la Empresa y con el pueblo   30 que usted dignamente representa. Los convenios colectivos, que tienen fuerza de ley entre las partes, son transgredidos con frecuencias y obligan a nuestros sindicatos a entablar engorrosas demandas judiciales para rescatar el derecho vulnerado. Aparte que Telefónica aparece atentando contra el principio básico de seguridad jurídica.   35

...

Apreciaremos, señor, se sirva considerar la posibilidad que sus asesores más cercanos tomen nota de esta misiva respetuosa, para que usted pueda interceder en el tema que preocupa a los trabajadores telefónicos del Perú, toda vez que las soberbias actitudes de la empresa nos hacen recordar la etapa colonialista nada edificante, que nuestro propio presidente el Ingº. Alberto Fujimori ha mencionado expresando que para él "España evoca el colonialismo y la injusticia social", en entrevista concedida al diario "El País" de Madrid, el año 1996.   40

Hacemos propicia la ocasión, excelentísimo señor presidente, para expresarle nuestra estima y consideraciones más distinguidas.   45

Atentamente,

SINDICATO UNITARIO DE TRABAJADORES DE TELEFONICA DEL PERU S.A.

http://www.labournet.net/spanish/1998/peraznar.html

2. This is an extract from *El condado de Belken. Klail City.* by Rolando Hinojosa (Tempe, Arizona: Bilingual Press, 1994). It portrays the slang of the spoken Spanish of Texas. What are the features of this slang?

Amigo de la raza, ¡ya quisieran, raza! Choche Markham es bolillo y rinche. ¡Qué va a ser amigo de la raza! No me anden ustedes a mí con eso. Si fuera amigo no le hubiera rajado la cabeza a Olegario Gámez con las cachas de la 45. ¡Amigo de la raza! ¡Díganmelo a mí! Choche Markham está casado con mujer mexicana y deje usted de contar: la trata peor que a una perra y Dios   5 sabrá por qué vive con ella. Choche Markham es un aprovechado y montonero. Flacocabróndehuesocolorao, a mí no me la da. ¡A ver! ¿Por qué no se entra en esta cantina cuando hay pedo? ¡A ver! ¿Por qué? Pos, porque le faltan tanates – sí, cuñao – le faltan huevos. Le faltan los morenos, raza. ¿Ehm? ¿Qué chingaos pasa cuando viene aquí don Manuel? Se acaba el   10 pedo, ¿verdá? Pos sí; pero don Manuel se entra aquí y cuídate con cabronearle porque te da en la madre – pero lo hace cara a cara – y solo; y sin ayuda de nadie. Por las buenas o por las malas – pero te arreglas o te arregla. ¿Y con el otro? ¡Mierda, cuñao! Te pega allá. Afuera. En plena calle; pa avergonzar a uno y para qué? Pa que lo vean. Pa que le diga a su vieja que   15 allí andaba muy macho. ¡Chingue a su madre, ¡Choche Markham! Don Manuel no. Don Manuel te echa al bote y ya. Un huerco suyo viene, te trae café y sanseacabó. ¡Y qué pasa con el famoso Choche Markham, palomilla? Te cañonea en la calle, en el carro, y, para acabarla de arruinar, en la misma cárcel – Ah, y con otros pa que le ayuden porque lo que es solo el muy hijo   20 de su chingada madre no va. Ni en sueño, cuñao, ni en sueño.

8 | Style

'Style' is a concept which has been understood in a wide variety of ways. In this book we shall understand style as comprising those linguistic features of texts which are used to create particular effects, and stylistics as the study of those features. We shall *not* be equating 'style' with the notion of 'good style', the sense in which the word *estilo* is used in several so-called *Manuales de estilo*. However, so-called 'good style' may be regarded as just one particular kind of style, and we shall look at it first of all (**8.1**). Nor shall we use the term 'style' in the way in which it has sometimes been used in linguistics, to refer simply to the speech of an individual for a particular purpose (according to this view a speaker's styles would make up his or her **idiolect**, or individual manner of speech).[1] We will also distinguish between style and register (see Chapter 7): while the characteristic features of a register tend to be accepted convention (this is why we can instantly recognise a text as 'journalistic', 'legal', etc.), style is more likely to be recognised as a **deviation** from an expected pattern, and in extreme cases is deliberately innovative and creative.

In stylistics there is a natural overlap between the concerns of the linguist and those of the literary critic. But there need not be any conflict between the two: the linguist's task is primarily to explain and quantify how a particular stylistic effect takes place, while value judgements are left to the critic's sensitivity (see Chatman, 1971 xiv–xv; and more particularly Halliday 1971: 358–60).

8.1 'Good' style

The notion of 'good' style is often presented as simply an extension of prescriptive grammar. A well-known *Manual de redacción* (Alvar Ezquerra 1999: 9) declares: 'Nuestro repertorio intenta recoger los vicios lingüísticos más usuales, explicar el porqué de su incorrección y formular su buen uso.' 'Good' style often castigates the deviation which we have suggested characterises individual authors' styles. For example, reference is often made to the avoidance of 'cacophony' in prose, by which is usually meant the use of a series of words that rhyme or repeat the same sequences of sounds – a feature which, however, might be considered desirable in verse. Jauralde Pou (1973: 125) castigates (8.1) on the grounds that the word *de* occurs three times in close proximity and (8.2) because *ilusión* rhymes with *excursión*:

---

[1] See, for example, the distinctions made by Robins (1964: 50–53).

(8.1)   Viene de fuera de parte de Antonio

(8.2)   Tengo ilusión por ir de excursión

Sequences of adverbs ending in *-mente* come in for especial criticism in Spanish, again because of their supposed cacophony. There is a certain objective basis for this: adverbs in *-mente* are some of the longest words in Spanish, particularly when they are formed on the basis of long adjectives (such as *premeditada+mente*, *impaciente+mente*, both of which appear in the *DRAE*) and in that sense are somewhat atypical of the language; they are also somewhat unusual in having, as well as a main stress, a secondary stress which follows the stress pattern of the adjective component and is reflected in the written accent (e.g. *fácilmente* is stressed [ˌfaθilˈmente]). Yet long adverbs in *-mente* are regularly to be found in technical and formal registers of the language. Colloquial register, as we have seen (**7.1**), is prone to repetition, the use of fillers (*muletillas*), clichés (*frases hechas*) and a high incidence of words of very wide applicability, such as *cosa, problema, interesante, guapo, bonito* (known in Spanish as **comodines**, lit. 'wild-cards'), all of which are prescriptively castigated in 'good' style. The concern here may be interpreted as the pursuit of economy and exactness in expression, as well as the creation of reader interest by the use of varied vocabulary (variation is also a valued rhetorical feature, see **8.2**). Conversely, the overuse of figures of speech (see **8.2**), which is sometimes a feature of literary register, is criticised: *MEU* (p. 19) suggests rewriting (8.3a) as (8.3b):

(8.3)   a.   *La magna conferencia o sesión especial sobre el desarme comenzó en la ONU el pasado 23 de mayo, y ha producido un verdadero torrente de discursos, propuestas, advertencias, súplicas, manifiestos y predicamentos sobre el mayor escándalo de un holocausto nuclear a escala global por la loca carrera armamentista que se lleva al año la astronómica cifra de 400.000 millones de dólares.*

b.   *En la conferencia sobre el desarme iniciada en la ONU el pasado día 23 se han producido numerosas intervenciones, proclamando el escándalo y el peligro que para la humanidad representa el derroche anual de 400.000 millones de dólares destinados a comprar armamento.*

The revised version removes a good deal of hyperbole. *Verdadero torrente* is changed to *numerosas*; the quantifying adjectives *magna, mayor* and *astronómica* are omitted or moderated; *un holocausto nuclear a escala global* becomes *peligro*, and *la loca carrera armamentista* is re-expressed in *comprar armamento*.

The notion of 'good' style is also addressed more positively, especially as regards the overall structure of a text. Great store is set by the **coherence** of a text, that is to say, its unification around a central theme, its relevance and clarity. Major ingredients in achieving coherence are **cohesion**, or the way in which a passage holds together in the sense of conveying a logical argument which is clearly expressed, and the avoidance of ambiguity. A particular problem in achieving coherence lies in accurate anaphoric reference, especially the 'recoverability' of the subject of the sentence, which is made even more difficult in Spanish by the fact that it is a pro-drop language. Reyes illustrates this with the following extract from a student essay:

TEXT O

Los países extranjeros no deberían intervenir en conflictos de
otros países. Muchas veces tendemos a mirar al extranjero y no al
propio país donde deberían solucionarse muchos problemas.
   De todas formas, no hablamos de países sino de las personas que
los gobiernan. Estos no suelen intervenir en los asuntos ajenos de   5
manera filantrópica. Por otra parte, los países desarrollados han estado
colonizando durante siglos a los subdesarrollados, y quedan sin recursos,
y luego intervienen en sus asuntos.

Graciela Reyes, *Cómo escribir en español: Manual de redacción*, 2nd ed. (Madrid:
Arco, 1999) p. 155.

In the first sentence, *extranjeros* is logically superfluous and the preposition *de* is vague: the
meaning is simply that one country should not interfere in the affairs of another (*Un país no
debe intervenir en conflictos entre otros países*). The exact meaning and hence relevance of the
second sentence are unclear, partly because of the switch of subject to the first person plural,
and partly because of the imprecise meaning of *propio*, but also because the perspective of
extranjero has changed. What seems to be implied is that countries sometimes intervene in
conflicts to divert attention from their own internal problems; but this is not a supporting
argument for the judgement expressed in the first sentence. In the second paragraph, the
anaphoric reference of *estos* is unclear: grammatically, it appears to refer to *países*, but logically it must refer to *personas*. *Por otra parte* is used inappropriately: the exploitation of
underdeveloped countries by developed countries does not stand in contrast to the assertion
that governments do not act out of philanthropic motives, but is an example of this. The
subjects of the verbs *quedan* and *intervienen* must be different (*los países subdesarrollados
quedan sin recursos; los países desarrollados intervienen en los asuntos de los países subdesarrollados*), even though they are grammatically conjoined as if they had the same subject, and the
reference of *sus* is also unclear.
   However, because of the strong traditional association with prescriptive grammar, recom-
mendations about 'good' style can devolve into arbitrary prescriptive rules. Alvar Ezquerra
et al. (1999: 223–8) list a number of phrases which in their opinion contain 'redundancy'
and so should be avoided. However, the grounds for establishing such redundancy are sometimes purely etymological. They criticise the expressions *aterido de frío*, *lapso de tiempo* and
divisas extranjeras on this basis, since *aterido* in itself means 'frozen', *lapso* can mean a 'period
of time', and *divisa* is necessarily 'foreign currency'. But etymologically redundant or not,
the fact of the matter is that these expressions are in common use in modern Spanish, perhaps, we might speculate, because the common words *frío*, *tiempo* and *extranjeras* make the
meaning of the other, rare, words more transparent. *MEU* (p. 43) insists on the revision of
(8.4a) as (8.4b) on the grounds of lack of coherence, claiming that it is not clear to which
noun *con las puertas abiertas* pertains:

> **(8.4)** **a.** *El taxi se encontraba en las afueras de la ciudad, cerca de un edificio destinado a almacén con las puertas abiertas*
>
> **b.** *El taxi se encontraba con las puertas abiertas en las afueras de la ciudad*

Actually, for (8.4b) to convey exactly the same information as (8.4a), it should read *El taxi se encontraba con las puertas abiertas en las afueras de la ciudad, cerca de un edificio destinado a almacén*; but (8.4a) could be adequately clarified by the use of a comma after *almacén*, and even without the comma, it is unlikely that a reader would really suppose that the warehouse rather than the taxi had its doors open.

8.2 Rhetorical style and figures of speech

A good place to start our study of other kinds of style is to look at some of the **figures of speech** which are associated with classical rhetoric. They were extensively studied and catalogued by classical grammarians, and indeed still form a part of many traditional grammars, since the model for grammars of the Western European languages was Latin grammar. Although we often take the use of such rhetorical figures for granted, they were introduced into the languages and literatures of Western Europe as a result of the imitation of classical models which culminated in the Renaissance. Some of the principal types are given in Table 8.1.

Poetry is especially rich in such figures of speech. In the following short stanza from the *Rimas* of Gustavo Adolfo Bécquer (1836–70), we can observe metaphor (the poet is saying that he is the golden fringe of the distant star and the gentle light of the moon), the use of epithets (*lejana* and *alta*) and hyperbaton (*de la alta luna la luz* ... instead of the normal order *la luz* ... *de la alta luna*).

> **(8.5)** *Yo soy el fleco de oro*
> *de la lejana estrella,*
> *yo soy de la alta luna*
> *la luz tibia y serena.*

The following quatrain from Lope de Vega's (1562–1635) play *Fuenteovejuna* illustrates antithesis: *cortesía* is counterposed to *descortesía* and *voluntad* to *enemistad*. The structure of the third and fourth lines is an inversion of the first and second. Here again a metaphor is used, politeness being said to be the key of goodwill.

> **(8.6)** *Es llave la cortesía,*
> *para abrir la voluntad,*
> *y para la enemistad*
> *la necia descortesía.*

The next extract, from Juan Ramón Jiménez's (1881–1958) poem *Intelijencia*, is an apostrophe, and the sequence of possessive pronouns is polysyndetic:

Table 8.1 Common rhetorical figures of speech

English term	Spanish term	Meaning	Spanish example
alliteration	*aliteración*	repetition of word-initial consonants	*Tres tristes tigres comieron trigo en un trigal* (a well-known tongue twister; the first three words are the title of a novel by Guillermo Cabrera Infante)
anadiplosis	*anadiplosis*	consecutive repetition of a word or part of a phrase	*Y en mi corazón ardiente llueve, llueve dulcemente* (Juan Ramón Jiménez)
anaphora	*anáfora*	repetition of a word at the beginning of a sentence within the same sentence OR repetition of a word at the beginning of consecutive sentences	*encinas, pardas encinas* (Antonio Machado)
antithesis	*antítesis*	contraposition of a word and its opposite	*Los de dentro no podían salir; los de fuera no podían entrar*; see also (8.6) and Text P.
antonomasia	*antonomasia*	a kind of synecdoche (see below) in which a proper name, usually seen as a prime example of the substituted word (Sp. *por antonomasia* = Eng. *par excellence*)	*Es un verdadero Salomón* (i.e. a very wise person, like Solomon)
apostrophe	*apóstrofe*	address usually interposed in the middle of a sentence	*Tal es, ¡oh pueblo grande! ¡oh pueblo fuerte! el premio que la suerte y tu valor magnánimo destina.* (Manuel José Quintana) See also (8.7).

Table 8.1 continued

English term	Spanish term	Meaning	Spanish example
asyndeton	*asíndeton*	omission of conjunctions to give a sense of drama or urgency	*Los manifestantes gritaban, echaban insultos, amenazaban a las fuerzas del orden;* see also Text P.
circumlocution, paraphrase	*circunloquio, perífrasis, rodeo*	an indirect or roundabout way of expressing a simple concept	*La (dulce) lengua de Cervantes* is a circumlocution for *el español*
enumeration	*enumeración*	a sequence of words which have the same grammatical function	*Ya no pasaba nadie por la Plaza Nueva, ni lacayos, ni curas; ni chiquillos; ni mujeres del pueblo* (Leopoldo Alas); see also Text P.
epithet	*epíteto*	the addition of an adjective to a noun; in Spanish, this term is reserved for adjectives which precede the noun and express a well-known, often conventional, attribute (see **1.7.1**)	*la muy leal y heroica ciudad de Burgos* (see also (8.5))
euphemism	*eufemismo*	use of an expression which does not have unpleasant or embarrassing connotations	*Hacer sus necesidades* is a euphemism for *orinar* 'to urinate' and *defecar* 'to defecate'; see also Text P.
hyperbaton	*hipérbaton*	separation of a grammatical unit which is normally inseparable	*De este, pues, formidable de la tierra bostezo el melancólico vacío* (Góngora) = *El melancólico vacío de este formidable bostezo de la tierra* See also (8.5).
hyperbole	*hipérbole*	exaggeration	*Tengo mil cosas que hacer* (meaning simple that I have a lot of things to do – perhaps literally seven or eight); see also (8.3) and Text P.

Term	Spanish	Definition	Example
inversion	*inversión, anástrofe*	changing the usual order of grammatical elements	*Cerrar podrá mis ojos la postrera sombra* (Quevedo) = *La postrera sombra podrá cerrar mis ojos* See also (8 6).
irony	*ironía*	saying the opposite of what is meant, though the intended meaning is usually clear from the context	*¡Valiente amigo eres tú!* (cf. Eng. 'You're a <u>fine</u> friend!', meaning that the friend has proved unreliable). In Spanish the irony is partly signified by the position of the adjective before the noun (see **1.7.1** and Text P).
litotes	*litotes*	understatement, most usually achieved through negating the opposite	*Es un asunto de <u>no pequeña</u> importancia* (meaning that it is of great importance: *de mucha importancia*)
metaphor	*metáfora*	like simile (see below), except that in a metaphor one term is equated with another	*estos arroyos, <u>jirones de cristal</u> en campo verde* (Tirso de Molina); see also (8.5) and Text P.
metonymy	*metonimia*	a word is used with the meaning of another (with which it is usually obviously related)	*¡Oh siempre gloriosa patria mía tanto por <u>plumas</u> cuanto por <u>espadas</u>!* (Luis de Góngora) *plumas = escritores, espadas = soldados* See also Text P.
oxymoron	*oxímoron*	a special case of paradox (see below) in which the contradiction is between two juxtaposed elements, usually a noun and its adjective	*gritos mudos*
paradox	*paradoja*	an apparent logical contradiction	*el mayor bien es pequeño* (Pedro Calderón de la Barca); see also Text R.

Table 8.1 *continued*

English term	Spanish term	Meaning	Spanish example
paraphrase	*perífrasis*	see circumlocution	
parenthesis	*paréntesis*	the intercalation of a sentence or phrase within another: in parenthesis the intercalated material is not signalled by a conjunction	*Y por fin llegué sano y salvo – ¡gracias a Dios! – a Nueva York*
paronomasia	*paronomasia*	the placing in close proximity of words which have a similar sound pattern	*Abandoné las carambolas por el calembur, los madrigales por los mamboretás, los entreveros por los entretelones, los invertidos por los invertebrados* (Oliverio Girondo)
personification	*personificación, prosopopeya*	typically, when an abstract notion is endowed with animate properties	*La niebla tiene sal y tiene prisa* (Miguel Arteche)
polysyndeton	*polisíndeton*	proliferation of conjunctions, most usually *y*.	*Y emponzoñé cuanto vi, Y a las cabañas bajé y a los palacios subí, y los claustros escalé.* (José Zorrilla) See also (8.7).
pun, play on words	*calambur, retruécano, juego de palabras*	use of a sound sequence that can be interpreted in two different ways	*Entre el clavel blanco y la rosa roja su majestad escoja* (Quevedo) = ... *su majestad es coja*

rhetorical question	interrogación retórica	a question which is not meant to be answered, but is used to make a strong affirmation	¿Y se perdió aquel tiempo que yo perdí? La mano dispone, dies ligero, de esta luna sin año. (Jorge Guillén)
simile	comparación / símil	a word is likened to another	Platero... como un alacrán cercado por el fuego, intenta, nervioso, huir por doquiera (Juan Ramón Jiménez); see also Text P.
synaesthesia	sinestesia	a kind of metaphor (see above) in which a term belonging to one semantic area is applied to another	Mil panderos de cristal / herían la madrugada (Federico García Lorca); see also Text R.
synecdoche	sinécdoque	a special case of metonymy (see above) in which a word expressing a feature or part of something is used to mean the whole concept	Le gustan las faldas (= las mujeres)
pleonasm, tautology	pleonasmo, tautología	use of words or phrases which are strictly redundant	volar por el aire

(8.7)   *¡Inteligencia, dame*
el nombre exacto, y tuyo,
y suyo, y mío, de las cosas!

However, figures of speech are far from being the exclusive preserve of creative literature. Many semantic figures of speech are a part of normal oral expression, and no doubt reflect the universal creativity of the human mind, as is evident from a consideration of the following extract, taken from an archive of recordings of colloquial Spanish:

TEXT P

... referente a cosas de los hombres, pero... eh... muchas cosas nos
ocurren porque nosotras tenemos la culpa. Porque es que nosotras no
nos damos a valer y no plantamos cara a las cosas. Pero la sociedad
hasta ahora ha estado hecha para los hombres. Las mujeres no hemos
tenido nada que pintar. Y tienen que llevar en cuenta una cosa los   5
hombres, porque antes ha dicho uno que si las mujeres no hacen la mili.
Las mujeres hacemos: de pediatra, de geriatra, porque ¡ay cuando los
padres se nos ponen viejos! Nos tenemos que hacer cargo de ellos, el
hombre se va a trabajar fuera de casa, y la mujer se queda con el
mogollón. Tenemos que gestionar todas las cosas burocráticas de   10
colegios, de papeleos de 40.000 cosas. Eso todo lo hace la mujer. Y
muchas veces no sabemos ni de dónde sacar tiempo, es correr de un
lado, y correr para otro; y que éste viene, y que éste hay que darle la
comida a una hora, y que al otro hay que darle a la otra. Que parece una
mujer en la casa como un guardia de tráfico dirigiendo toda la orquesta.   15
Y muchas cosas de estas, pues...

LOLA Archive, file adeb001a.asc

The word *cara*, literally 'face', has undergone both metonymic and metaphorical extensions in its meaning. It has come to signify 'cheek' or 'nerve' (the meaning of these English words has been similarly metonymically extended), and the idiomatic expression *plantar cara a* (l.3) has the meaning 'to stand up to'. (In passing, notice that *cara* in its sense of 'side (of a coin)', 'face (of a round object)' is a metaphorical extension of its basic meaning.) Another metonymic extension is to be seen in the colloquial use of *pintar* (l.5) 'to have a say (in something)'. The beginnings of an asyndetic enumeration are seen in *de pediatra, de geriatra* (l.7), which is also something of an exaggeration, or hyperbole, a phenomenon more clearly seen in *papeleos de 40.000 cosas* (l.11). Antithesis is used in the sentence beginning on l.11: *correr de un lado, y correr para otro..., que éste hay que darle la comida a una hora, y que al otro hay que darle a la otra.* There is a mixed simile in the penultimate sentence, where the housewife is likened to both a traffic policeman and to an orchestral conductor.

Some of the rhetorical figures of speech also appear to correspond to historical processes of change in the meaning of words. Metonymy, or association with a closely related concept, is very often involved; an example of this is to be seen in one of the Spanish words for 'brown', *castaño*, which is the name of the sweet-chestnut tree with its typically brown fruit. Metaphor is also common: *gemelos* 'twins' is also used in Spanish with the meaning of 'cufflinks', which are typically a matching pair. Hyperbole leads to semantic weakening, so that the Spanish verb *salir* derives from Latin SALĪRE, which had the stronger meaning of 'to jump, leap'. It is possible that even a kind of irony is involved in changes such as the evolution of Latin CĂBAL-LUS 'nag', a pejorative term, perhaps a self-deprecating or familiar way of referring to one's horse, to Sp. *caballo*, which is not at all pejorative. Euphemism can be seen in words for notions which have a superstitious or embarrassing connotation, a very clear example being the use of *fallecer*, which formerly meant 'to be lacking', in the meaning of 'to die'.

8.3 Literary style – some examples

While, as we have seen, figures of speech are not absent from everyday expression, the most striking examples of deviation are to be found in creative literature. We will begin by looking at an extreme example of innovatory literary style, Carlos Fuentes's novel *Aura*. The following is the first paragraph of the work:

TEXT Q

Lees ese anuncio: una oferta de esa naturaleza no se hace todos los días. Lees y releps el aviso. Parece dirigido a ti, a nadie más. Distraído, dejas que la ceniza del cigarro caiga dentro de la taza de té que has estado bebiendo en este cafetín sucio y barato. Tú releerás. Se solicita historiador joven. Ordenado. Escrupuloso. Conocedor de la lengua   5 francesa. Conocimiento perfecto, coloquial. Capaz de desempeñar labores de secretario. Juventud, conocimiento de francés, preferible si ha vivido en Francia algún tiempo. Tres mil pesos mensuales, comida y recámara cómoda, asoleada, apropiada estudio. Sólo falta tu nombre. Sólo falta que las letras más negras y llamativas del aviso informen: 10 Felipe Montero. Se solicita Felipe Montero, antiguo becario en la Sorbona, historiador cargado de datos inútiles, acostumbrado a exhumar papeles amarillentos, profesor auxiliar en escuelas particulares, novecientos pesos mensuales. Pero si leyeras eso, sospecharías, lo tomarías a broma. Donceles 815. Acuda en persona.   15 No hay teléfono.

Carlos Fuentes, ed. Peter Standish, 1986 [1962], *Aura* (Durham: University of Durham), p. 24

Pragmatically, the reader expects a narrative to be situated in past time and to be in the third person (if the writer is telling a story about other people) or in the first person (if the writer is purporting to be telling an autobiographical story). Fuentes goes against both these expectations with two very obvious deviations: first, by using the second person (*Lees* ..., l.1, etc.) and, second, by using the future tense (*Tú releerás*, l.4) and a sequence of tense in the conditional sentence in ll.14–15 (*si leyeras eso, sospecharías* ...) which is most naturally intepreted as future-referring ('if you were to read this, you would suspect ...'). The use of the present tense, incidentally, is not so surprising, since this tense is often used with past time reference in narrations, especially in spoken Spanish; but the perfect tense (*que has estado bebiendo*, ll.3–4) is not so usual in such a context. Another kind of deviation employed by Fuentes is the use of very short sentences which consist only of nouns or adjectival phrases (ll.5–9 and l.15) and display a high degree of ellipsis, or omission of expected words, e.g. *apropiada estudio* = *apropiada al estudio* (l.9), *novecientos pesos mensuales* = *que gana novecientos pesos mensuales* (l.14). This is a feature strongly associated with the register of personal adverts, where economy is of the essence (see **7.2.3**), and so we naturally conclude that this forms part of the text of the advert that has caught Felipe's eye. It makes a particularly sharp contrast (sometimes called **internal deviation**) with the sentence which begins on l.11 (*Se solicita Felipe Montero* ...), which is more conventionally constructed and fuller in information, representing Felipe's own response to the advert. The distinction between Felipe's response to the advert and the advert itself is also signalled by the second person form, *tú* being used for Felipe's internal monologue and *usted* for the advert (*acuda en persona*, l.15).

Another interesting feature of this text is the ordering of information. The reader might have expected to be introduced to the protagonist first of all, or at least for the protagonist to be named, followed by a chronologically sequenced account of his going into a café, ordering a cup of tea, opening the newspaper, reading the text of the advert and then responding to it. Instead, the paragraph begins with Felipe's reading the advert (the text of which is not yet revealed) and his immediate response. The event is then situated in the café. The majority of the text of the advert is then given, and Felipe's more detailed response given in such a way that it informs the reader of his name and background. Lastly, the final details of the advert (the address) are given. This is a deviation from the normal concerns of cohesion (see **8.1**), but cohesion is achieved by a number of repeated features. *Lees* (l.1), *lees y relees* (l.2), *tú releerás* (l.4) stress the process of first notice, casual reading and detailed reading and re-reading by which Felipe takes cognisance of the contents of the advert (this is also in accord with the kind of account Fuentes has chosen to give of the incident, since it is clear that reading and response are not discrete sequential activities but that there is movement back and forth between the two). This impression is strengthened by the repetition of *sólo falta* ... (l.10) and the parallel between *Se solicita historiador joven* (ll.4–5) and *se solicita Felipe Montero* (l.11).

Another comment that we might make as linguists about this passage is that it represents a mixture of points of view. On the one hand, it seems to be a narrative as perceived by a third party (*Lees ese anuncio* ... (l.1), *distraído, dejas que la ceniza del cigarro caiga dentro de la taza de té* ... (ll.2–3)); but at the same time it represents the thoughts of Felipe (*Parece dirigido a ti, a nadie más* (l.2)). We can now see that this ambiguity is compounded precisely beause of the use of *tú*: compare a more conventional (and therefore less striking) way of expressing the first three lines:

(8.8) *Felipe leyó el anuncio. «Una oferta de esa naturaleza no se hace todos los días», pensó. Leyó y releyó el aviso. «Sí, parece dirigido a mí, a nadie más». Distraído, dejó que la ceniza del cigarro cayera dentro de la taza de té …*

In the above, I have not made any comment about the content of the text as such (e.g. what general philosophy of life is being advocated, how realistic or convincing the characterisation of Felipe is, etc.), and I have attempted to steer clear of any judgement concerning the literary merits of this text, although I have identified some features of form and meaning which correspond in an interesting way, which is often the mark of a skilful writer. Essentially, the commentary has been linguistic in nature, providing an objective account of some of the features of this text.

The next text we shall examine presents deviation of a different kind. It is a poem from César Vallejo's anthology *Trilce (1922)*.

TEXT R

> ESTE PIANO VIAJA PARA ADENTRO.
> viaja a saltos alegres.
> Luego medita en ferrado reposo,
> clavado con diez horizontes.
>
> Adelanta. Arrástrase bajo túneles,   5
> más allá, bajo túneles de dolor,
> bajo vértebras que fugan naturalmente.
>
> Otras veces van sus trompas,
> lentas ansias amarillas de vivir,
> van de eclipse,   10
> y se espulgan pesadillas insectiles
> ya muertas para el trueno, heraldo de los génesis.
>
> Piano oscuro, ¿a quién atisbas
> con tu sordera que me oye,
> con tu madurez que me asorda?   15
> Oh pulso misterioso.

César Vallejo, 1967 [1961], *Trilce*, 2nd ed. (Buenos Aires: Losada), p. 74

What we notice immediately here is a good deal of synaesthesia, or the breaking of the normal semantic constraints which hold between different parts of speech, especially between a verb and its arguments and a noun and its dependent adjectives. The poem is a series of predicates concerning *este piano*. Let us look first of all at the verbs of which *piano* is a subject: *viaja* (ll.1–2), *adelanta* and *arrástrase* (l.5), *atisbas* (l.13) and *medita* (l.3). The pragmatic expectation on the first three of these verbs is that they take a subject which is capable of movement; whereas *viaja* and *adelanta* can denote movements initiated by an external force, *arrástrase* requires the motion to be supplied by the subject itself. *Atisbas* must take a subject which is capable of sight, and *medita* an animate subject capable of thought. *Piano* would meet the requirements of the first two verbs if it were being moved, but it cannot under normal circumstances meet the requirements of the last three. However, if we thought that *viaja* was a plausible predicate for *piano*, we would be challenged by the manner adverbial *a saltos alegres* that modifies it: pianos may travel in removal vans, but not in this fashion, and the adjective *alegre* again presupposes an animate quality. In ll.8–16 the piano is represented as possessing certain attributes, *trompas* (l.8), *sordera* (l. 14) and *madurez* (l.15), all of which are pragmatically impossible. I will not examine exhaustively all the other broken selectional restrictions in the poem (in fact, it is difficult to find any that are actually observed), but we might note the pragmatic oddity of *ferrado reposo* (l.3) where an adjective normally pertaining to a physical property qualifies an abstract noun and *lentas ansias amarillas* (l.9) where again an abstract noun is qualified by inappropriate adjectives of speed and colour. A special kind of semantic inconsistency is the paradox *tu sordera que me oye* (l.14).

Having taken the poem apart in this way (and once again it must be remembered that we are making no value judgement about the poem as a literary work), we might now notice some consistencies. If we ignore the fact that the subject of the sentences in ll.1–7 is a piano, we in fact have a coherent representation of movement starting and stopping, and the manner or mood of the movement: *viaja a saltos alegres, medita en … reposo, adelanta, arrástrase*. *Trompas* (l.8) is consistent with *amarillas* (l.9), the expected colour of brass instruments, and the notions of *se espulgan*, *insectiles* and *muertas* (ll.11–12) are semantically related in that delousing involves the death of an insect. The final unanswered question (ll.13–15) is consistent with the description of the piano as *oscuro* (l.13) and its being addressed as *pulso misterioso* (l.16). There are more indirect consistencies too. *Ferrado* (l.3) is consistent with the material of which piano frames are made, *lentas* (l.9) and *pulso* (l.16) relate back to the movement represented by the verbs of ll.1–7. Even less directly we can relate the form of the words *clavado* (l.4) with the *clavi-* element present in the names of many keyboard instruments (e.g. *clavicordio, clavicémbalo*) and the verb *fugar* (l.7) with the musical form *fuga*. Once again I have attempted to be objective in the tracing of these semantic relationships; it may be (though it is unlikely) that none of these associations is significant from the literary point of view (according to Martos & Villanueva 1989: 231, the theme of the poem is poetic creation, the piano being the symbol of poetic writing).

8.4 Statistics and the use of concordances

Computers have made the statistical study of texts a relatively easy task. **Concordances** which when produced manually were once the herculean labour of a lifetime can now be generated in seconds; moreover, it is straightforward to extract information about the distribution of words in a text, the length of words, the number of different words used and the contexts in which they occur. In this section we shall look in this way at two well-known 20th-century texts: Federico García Lorca's play *Yerma* and Gabriel García Márquez's short novel *El coronel no tiene quien le escriba*, analysed with the program WordSmith Tools.

Before looking at the results of statistical analysis it is worth pausing to mention some problems in the preparation of electronic text. If our interest, as here, is in the plain text itself, material which is extraneous to the text is obviously not to be included, most obviously such information as page numbers, chapter numbers, publishing details, indices and editorial footnotes (if present). The choice of what to omit is fairly clear in the case of a novel, but it is less clear in the case of a play: for example, I have chosen to omit not only the *dramatis personae* list but also stage directions and the identities of the speakers, so that the text I am examining is only the actual dialogue. But for other purposes the stage directions might be of interest (for example, how many times does Lorca refer to colours in his stage directions?), and retaining information about which character says what would permit a study of the language of each character individually as well as that of the text as a whole. For these reasons, the most complete preparation of electronic texts will **mark up** such significant features so that different users can exploit them accordingly, the acknowledged international standard for this being Standard Generalized Markup Language (SGML). SGML provides for the representation of features of the organization of a text such as chapters, paragraphs and sentences, its typographical layout and the characteristics of different types of text (e.g. prose, verse, drama, dictionaries, legal documents, spoken texts, etc.). It can quickly be appreciated that SGML markup has the potential for being very detailed indeed: in the markup of the stage directions of a play, for instance, the SGML *Guidelines* (Sperberg-McQueen & Burnard 1994) provide for categorising stage directions as having to do with delivery (how a character speaks), location, entrance, business, exit, modifier (giving some detail about a character), setting, novelistic (narrative, motivating stage direction) and mixed (more than one of the above). For the purposes of a quick comparison of features of plain text it is clearly not worth using SGML extensively.

However, some markup is essential. For example, the word *saco* may function as a noun ('bag') or as a form of the verb *sacar* 'to take out', and these two functions must clearly be distinguished, since in an important sense *saco* is not always the same word: it has two different functions and two different meanings. The verb form *siente* has different functions according to its meaning: it can be either a present indicative form of *sentir* or a present subjunctive form of *sentar*. *Muerto* has two different functions, although its meaning is constant: a verbal function as the past participle participating in compound tenses (e.g. *ha muerto*) and an adjectival/noun function (e.g. *el día de los muertos*). *Había* is consistently an imperfect indicative verb form of *haber*, but it may function as a perfective auxiliary (*había salido*) or as an **existential** verb (meaning 'there is/are': *había mucha gente en la sala*). Different functions can be indicated by Part of Speech (POS) tagging (e.g. *saco<v>* and *saco<n>*); different meanings are perhaps best dealt with by numerical tagging (e.g. *haber<1>*, *haber<2>*).

Another desirable feature of an electronic text is **lemmatisation**, which can be done in

SGML but is often handled (as it was in this case) through the creation of word-lists which are then read by the concordancing program. Lemmatisation allows different words to be counted as instances of the same word, a procedure that is particularly appropriate for inflected languages like Spanish. Thus verb-forms such as *hago, haces, hace, hacemos, haga, hice, hizo, hecho*, etc. can be lemmatised as forms of *hacer*, and in any study of *hacer* all its inflectional forms can be inspected at once. Lemmatisation makes clear the need to distinguish the two meanings of *siente* discussed above, since they must be lemmatised as forms of two different verbs.

The overall statistics for the two texts are shown in Table 8.2. The two texts are rather different in length, *El coronel* being nearly twice as long as *Yerma*, so another column (*El coronel 2*) gives statistics relating to the first 8,831 words of the novel to give a sample comparable to the length in words of *Yerma*.

What is initially most striking about these general statistics is their similarity, given that *El coronel* and *Yerma* are very different in type. Even the distribution of words by length follows the same pattern, as is shown by presenting the same data in the from of a graph (Figure 8.1):

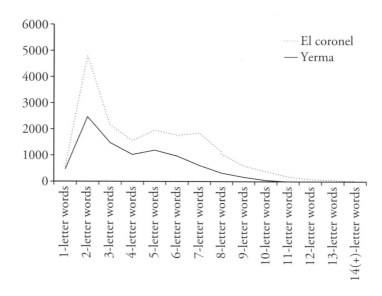

Figure 8.1 Word lengths in *Yerma* and *El coronel no tiene quien le escriba*

Having said that, we can see some differences. The average sentence length is slightly higher in *El coronel*, which probably reflects the fact that it is a prose narrative; there is also a sharper falling off in the numbers of 'long' words (seven letters and above) in *Yerma*, which may be a characteristic of the predominantly spoken nature of this text. It is difficult to conclude much from the slight difference in type/token ratio. The lower ratio of *El coronel* would at first sight suggest a less varied vocabulary, but conversely we might expect that the longer the text the lower the variation: this is confirmed by the statistics of *El coronel 2*, which in fact shows a higher type/token ratio, and hence a richer vocabulary, than *Yerma*.

Table 8.2 Comparative statistics of words occurring in *El coronel no tiene quien le escriba* and *Yerma*

	El coronel	*El coronel 2*	*Yerma*
Tokens (number of words)	17,395	8,831	8,835
Types (number of different words: not lemmatised)	3,491	2,308	1,964
Type/token ratio	20.07	26.14	22.23
Average word length	4.61	4.64	4.02
Sentences	914	483	429
Average sentence length	11.65	11.89	7.81
Paragraphs	701	294	974
Average paragraph length	24.81	30.02	9.01
1-letter words	635	309	456
2-letter words	4,811	2,437	2,467
3-letter words	2,192	1,111	1,448
4-letter words	1,545	789	1,030
5-letter words	1,990	921	1,208
6-letter words	1,789	947	989
7-letter words	1,858	975	624
8-letter words	1,094	564	336
9-letter words	622	327	167
10-letter words	421	224	72
11-letter words	209	103	20
12-letter words	105	62	16
13-letter words	80	39	0
14(+)-letter words	18	9	2

Looking at the frequency and distribution of individual words as revealed in the concordance is more rewarding. After lemmatisation, the 200 most frequently-occurring words in the two texts were scrutinised and compared with two other frequency lists: Juilland & Chang-Rodríguez (1964) and Chandler-Burns *et al.* (1992). If a word is in, say, the top 200 in one text but is much lower down or non-existent in the other as well as in the frequency lists, then it is likely that the word is a **keyword**, belonging to the distinctive vocabulary of that text. The words which meet these criteria in *Yerma* and *El coronel* are shown in Tables 8.3 and 8.4:

Table 8.3 Keywords in *Yerma*

Yerma (all): Rank (Occurrences)	*El coronel* (all): Rank (Occurrences)	Juilland (first 1000 words only): Rank (Occurrences)	E92 (first 1000 words only): Rank (Occurrences)
alegría 123 (11)		700 (63)	
arroyo 156 (8)			
cantar 101 (13)	350 (6)	630 (59)	
carne 130 (10)	596 (3)	779 (57)	
comida 174 (7)			
criatura 174 (7)			
cuidar 174 (7)	1216 (1)		
guardar 156 (8)	239 (9)	607 (71)	
hermoso 156 (8)		581 (74)	
honra 111 (12)			
Juan 130 (10)			364 (236)
llenar 147 (9)	811 (2)	779 (57)	
marchita 130 (10)			
monte 174 (7)			
oscuro 130 (10)			
oveja 156 (8)			
pan 174 (7)	483 (4)		834 (118)
pastor 101 (13)			
pecho 101 (13)		929 (48)	
rama 147(9)			
romería 174 (7)			
rosa 101 (13)	483 (4)		821 (119)
rosal 174 (7)			
seco 130 (10)	596 (3)		
vientre 156 (8)	811 (2)		

Table 8.4 Keywords in *El coronel no tierne quien le escriba*

El coronel (all): Rank (Occurrences)	*Yerma* (all): Rank (Occurrences)	Juilland (first 1000 words only): Rank (Occurrences)	E92 (first 1000 words only): Rank (Occurrences)
abogado 100 (22)			
acordar 177 (12)			
administrador 100 (22)			
Agustín 123 (18)			
Álvaro 149 (14)			
bolsillo 133 (16)			
café 164 (13)	599 (1)	832 (53)	789 (124)
cama 177 (12)	275 (4)		1000 (98)
cerrar 112 (20)	234 (5)	719 (61)	
compadre 48 (42)			
coronel 6 (358)			
correo 116 (19)			
cuarto 123 (18)		501 (86)	561 (164)
cuello 177 (12)			630 (148)
descubrir 164 (13)		602 (72)	
dormitorio 142 (15)			
esposa 83 (25)	599 (1)		
gallo 26 (103)			
Germán 164 (13)			
hamaca 149 (14)			
hoja 177 (12)	337 (3)	870 (51)	*hoja* 917 (107) *hojas* 764 (127)
interrumpir 177 (12)			
lancha 149 (14)			
llover 177 (12)			
muerto[n] 112 (20)	431 (2)		*muerto* 747 (129) (*muertos* 1114 (89))

continued

Table 8.4 *continued*

El coronel (all): Rank (Occurrences)	*Yerma* (all): Rank (Occurrences)	Juilland (first 1000 words only): Rank (Occurrences)	E92 (first 1000 words only): Rank (Occurrences)
octubre 149 (14)	599 (1)		
oficina 105 (21)			
paraguas 149 (14)			
periódico 116 (19)		559 (77)	*periódico* 592 (157) *periódicos* 812 (121)
peso 86 (24)			*peso* 943 (105) (*pesos* 1270 (78))
reloj 100 (22)			
replicar 149 (14)			
responder 86 (24)	599 (1)	700 (63)	
rostro 164 (13)		889 (50)	991 (99)
Sabas 32 (60)			
saco[n] 177 (12)			833 (118) ? (No part of speech tag given)
sentar 105 (21)	275 (4)	443 (96)	
silencio 177 (12)	275 (4)	630 (69)	525 (177)
veinte 133 (16)	599 (1)	575 (75)	
vender 66 (30)		677 (65)	
ventana 164 (13)		594 (73)	
zapatos 177 (12)	599 (1)		

A number of these words quite obviously owe their high frequency to the fact that they are closely connected with the subject-matter of the work concerned. In *El coronel*, this explains the figures for *coronel* (the central character), *gallo* (the fighting cockerel on which his hopes are pinned), for *administrador*, *correo*, *saco* and *lancha*, which are all to do with the postal service, *oficina*, *bolsillo*, *peso* and *vender*, which are to do with money, and the names of the characters *Agustín*, *Álvaro*, *Germán* and *Sabas* (plus *compadre*, the relationship between the colonel and Don Sabas), as well as *abogado* and *esposa*. The colonel's house, where he and his wife spend most of their time inactive, is reflected in *cama*, *cuarto*, *dormitorio*, *hamaca* and *ventana*, as well as in the verb *sentar*. The time of year, *octubre*, has an unexpected prominence which is of special significance, as a KWIC (Key<u>W</u>ord <u>I</u>n <u>C</u>ontext) concordance reveals. It represents the rainy season (cf. the frequency of *llover* and *paraguas*) that the colonel finds it most difficult to survive (*Más dura que las cuatro semanas de octubre a las cuales el coronel no creyó sobrevivir. / El coronel sintió un ligero malestar en los intestinos. Pero no se alarmó. Estaba a punto de sobrevivir a un nuevo octubre.*) and for which he and his wife feel distaste (*«Debe ser horrible estar enterrado en octubre», dijo*). It also represents the years going by as the colonel vainly awaits his pension (*Octubre era una de las pocas cosas que llegaban*) and the colonel's rekindled hope as it passes (*El viscoso aire de octubre había sido sustituido por una frescura apacible*). *Reloj* is also associated with the theme of passing time, the clock that the colonel repeatedly winds up; it is also an asset which the colonel unsuccessfully tries to sell (suggesting that the time he spends in waiting is worth nothing). *Periódico* also reflects time (the doctor gets the papers with the mail on Friday), poverty (the colonel borrows them from the doctor) and, indirectly, the political situation (via clandestine supplements which the doctor gives the colonel with the papers). In *Yerma*, *criatura*, *pecho* and *vientre* reflect directly this text's concern with childbearing, as more obliquely may the verb *cuidar* (though a KWIC concordance of this word shows that it is not always used to refer to caring for children), and *guardar* and *honra* reveal the pervasive theme of concern for the opinion of others. Natural features of the rural environment are also represented in the keywords of *Yerma*: *arroyo*, *monte*, *oveja*, *rama*. A stylistically significant difference between the two texts is that some of the keywords of *Yerma* are adjectives (all the keywords in *El coronel* are nouns or verbs): *hermoso*, *marchita*, *oscuro* and *seco*. The frequency of *marchita* and *seco* especially reflects Yerma's barrenness. If we look at the **collocates** of these adjectives, we can see the nouns they most frequently qualify. The following tables (8.5 and 8.6) show the words occurring immediately before *marchita* and *seco/a* respectively: *carne* is the noun most commonly qualified by *marchita* and *casada*, *carácter*, *cuerpo* and *vientre* are qualified by *seco/a*.

The reason for the frequency of some of the other keywords is less obvious. In *El coronel*, *replicar* and *responder* are frequent because they are used to indicate replies in direct speech, a phenomenon which is of course totally absent in *Yerma*. The frequency of *silencio* reveals the extent to which activities are carried out in silence in *El coronel*, indicative of its generally gloomy atmosphere; *café* is associated with the struggle for the basic everyday necessities of life experienced by the colonel and his wife (the novel opens with the colonel finding that there is no coffee for breakfast). In *Yerma*, *cantar* is occasioned by the frequency of songs and poetry in the play. Especially striking in *Yerma* is the frequency of *rosa* and the much more unusual *rosal*. A glance at the distribution of *rosal*, however, shows that all its occurrences cluster closely together, and that the reason for its frequency is the repetition of the lines in the poem in the final scene; such distributional patternings are more typical of poetry than prose.

(8.9)   *El cielo tiene jardines*
    con rosales de alegría:
    entre rosal y rosal,
    la rosa de maravilla.

Table 8.5 Collocates appearing immediately before *marchita* in *Yerma*

ay	1	*marchita*	1
carne	3	*marchita*	3
marchita	1	*marchita*	1
pinchosa	1	*marchita*	1

Table 8.6 Collocates appearing immediately before *seco* in *Yerma*

casada	3	*seca*	3
estaba	1	*seca*	1
verano	1	*seca*	1
yo	1	*seca*	1
campo	1	*seco*	1
carácter	1	*seco*	1
cuerpo	1	*seco*	1
vientre	1	*seco*	1

Use of a KWIC concordance can facilitate examination of the contexts in which a particular word is used by an author. As an example, let us look at Lorca's use of the word *oscuro* in *Yerma*:

(8.10) *Tu colcha de **oscura** piedra, pastor, y tu camisa de escarcha, pastor, juncos grises del invierno en la noche de tu cama.*

(8.11) *Pero que está **oscura** y débil en los mismos caños de la sangre.*

(8.12) *Muchas noches bajo yo a echar la comida a los bueyes, que antes no lo hacía, porque ninguna mujer lo hace, y cuando paso por lo **oscuro** del cobertizo mis pasos me suenan a pasos de hombre.*

(8.13) *Pero el cementerio estaba demasiado **oscuro**.*

(8.14) *Dejarme libre siquiera la voz, ahora que voy entrando en lo más **oscuro** del pozo.*

(8.15) *Te desnudaré, casada y romera, cuando en lo **oscuro** las doce den.*

(8.16) *El año pasado, cuando se hizo **oscuro**, unos mozos atenazaron con sus manos los pechos de mi hermana.*

(8.17) *Y en el vientre de tus siervas la llama **oscura** de la tierra.*

(8.18) *Mirad qué **oscuro** se pone el chorro de la montaña.*

(8.19) *Ha llegado el último minuto de resistir este continuo lamento por cosas **oscuras**, fuera de la vida, por cosas que están en el aire.*

The dark is very clearly associated with a world which reaches out beyond the mundane and normal. It provides an opportunity for sexual contact: explicitly in (8.15), (8.16), (8.17) and (8.18) (the latter from the pilgrimage chorus evoking the prelude to the impregnation of the *triste casada*) and more indirectly in (8.10), in which Yerma echoes the words of Víctor's song, *¿Por qué duermes solo, pastor?*. It represents the superstitious world of the *conjuradora* in (8.13) and (8.14), and the unconventional activity of Yerma feeding the oxen in (8.12). For Yerma, darkness is the means of fulfilling her ambition to have a child. For Juan, on the other hand, darkness is something to be avoided as contrary to convention: (8.11) refers to *honra* which passion (*sangre*) can compromise, and in (8.9) he is referring to Yerma's longing for a child, a desire which is quite outside his own comprehension.

EXERCISES

1. Alvar Ezquerra *et al.* (1999: 238–9) suggest rewriting sentence (a) as (b):

(a) La noticia repercutió negativamente en la economía, y en los medios políticos no se habló de otra cosa cuando el ministro anunció su dimisión.

(b) Cuando el ministro su dimisión, la noticia repercutió negativamente en la economía, y en los medios políticos no se habló de otra cosa cuando el ministro anunció su dimisión.

What is 'better' about sentence (b)?

2. The same authors (94–7) castigate the following constructions involving relative pronouns:

(a) Se ha publicado un artículo que su autor es conocido en el campo de la fisiología

(b) Este libro que lo estoy escribiendo parece no tener fin

(c) El pastel el que me compraste ayer estaba buenísimo

(d) El 24 de junio pasado hubo un accidente en el mismo tramo de carretera, que tampoco se enteró SUR

(e) Aquí tienes el libro, la historia del cual tanto te gusta

(f) Tu cara de pena fue quien me hizo cambiar de idea

(g) Leí una novela de Cervantes, cuyo autor nació en Alcalá de Henares

What are the 'correct' versions? Do the 'correct' versions have any advantages over the original?

3. The following is a short extract from Luis Martín-Santos's novel *Tiempo de silencio* (Barcelona: Seix Barral, 1966). What are the stylistic strategies used by the author?

> No, no, no, no es así. La vida no es así, en la vida no ocurre así. El que la hace no la paga. El que a hierro muere no a hierro mata. El que da primero no da dos veces. Ojo por ojo. Ojo de vidrio para rojo cuévano hueco. Diente

por diente. Prótesis de oro y celuloide para el mellado abyecto. La furia de
los dioses vengadores. Los envenenados dardos de su ira. No siete sino 5
setenta veces siete. El pecado de la Cava hubo también de ser pagado. Echó
el río Tajo el pecho afuera hablando al rey palabras de mane-tecel-fares.
Cuidadosamente estudió el llamado Goethe las motivaciones del sacrificio de
Ifigenia y habiéndolas perfectamente comprendido, diose con afán a ponerlas
en tragedia. El que la hace la paga. No siempre el que la hace: el que cree 10
que la hizo o aquel de quien fue creído que la había hecho o aquel que
consiguió convencer a quienes le rodeaban al envolverse en el negro manto
del traidor, pálida faz, amarilla mirada, sonrisa torva.

9 | Spanish or not?

In this chapter we will examine a number of languages which may in some respects all be considered varieties of Spanish, but which to a greater or lesser extent are further removed from the various Spanish standards (whether in the Peninsula or Latin America) than any of the regional varieties we have so far considered. What they all have in common is that they have either developed or have come to be spoken in situations where access to native speakers of what we might view as a 'mainstream' variety is not available. This has happened in a number of ways, which are individual to each case.

A. A group of speakers becomes separated from the main speech-community; in time, their language develops in a way which is significantly different from that of the main speech-community, where, despite variation, there is also a centripetal tendency towards unity, especially among educated speakers and in written registers. This is the case of Judeo-Spanish (**9.1**).

B. A group of speakers become bilingual in Spanish and another language, which eventually becomes dominant. In such a situation Spanish enters a stage of incipient language death, and a number of characteristic changes which tend to distance it from the main speech-community take place. This is the case of the vestigial varieties of Spanish (**9.2**).

C. Spanish is learned imperfectly by native speakers of another language, and is typically used as a **lingua franca** (a common language) to enable communication between people whose native languages are not mutually intelligible. In the initial stages this may produce a pidgin language. The degree of contact maintained with native speakers will determine what happens next. Maintenance of some contact may result in a language which is somewhat simplified by comparison with the language of the main speech-community, which seems to be the case of the Afro-Hispanic or *bozal* varieties (**9.3**). Such languages are often characterised as being partially creolised. But if contact with native speakers is looser, then the pidgin, learned by succeeding generations as a native language, undergoes restructuring and becomes a full creole (**9.4**), though it is lexicalised by another language or languages. If, on the other hand, Spanish is more thoroughly taught and assimilated as a second language, it will approximate more closely to the language of the main speech-community (the case of the Spanish of Equatorial Guinea, see Lipski 1985).

D. Speakers are bilingual in Spanish and another language and oscillate between the two languages, in some circumstances (notably when speaking to other bilinguals) often in mid-sentence, a phenomenon known as code-switching. The most extensive studies of code-switching have been on the use of Spanish and English in the US (**9.5.1**), but the phenomenon is also important for an understanding of 'frontier' speech (**9.5.2**).

9.1 Judeo-Spanish

9.1.1 The relation of Judeo-Spanish to Castilian

Judeo-Spanish is the generic term now generally used amongst Hispanic linguists for the language of the Sephardic ('Spanish') Jews, who were expelled from Spain in 1492 and settled in various parts of Europe, North Africa and the Middle East (see Figure 9.1), so giving rise to the existence of a number of Spanish-speaking communities which were separated both geographically and politically from the rest of the Spanish-speaking world.[1] There has been a great deal of debate as to whether the language of the Sephardic Jews was differentiated in any way from the language of the Christian inhabitants of Spain at the time of the expulsion, and, if it was already differentiated, whether it had arisen in Jewish communities for what we might term sociolinguistic reasons (such as the marking of a cultural or community identity) or whether it was an essentially different kind of Romance variety, perhaps formed from a 'Judeo Vulgar Latin' (see Wexler 1977). The matter is extremely difficult to judge, because much of the textual evidence on which the arguments are based is literary or religious in nature, and it is to be expected that religious texts especially would employ a linguistic register which was not typical of everyday speech. One particularly misleading kind of text is the translation of holy writings into Spanish, which is made word for word: Sephiha (1986) labels this *ladino*, and describes it as a calque language, distinct from the spoken language (*judezmo* in his terminology) which in his view only begins to be differentiated from Peninsular Spanish in the first half of the 17th century. However, we must also bear in mind that although by 1492 Castilian was in the ascendant as the national language of the newly-unified Spain, it was far from standardised and clearly had many local variations (Andalusian speech was already different from the speech of Old Castile in a number of important respects, for example); furthermore, other local Romance varieties, such as Catalan and Aragonese, still survived strongly. There is no reason to suppose that the Jewish communities stood apart from that linguistic diversity, and so the idea of a unified 'Judeo-Spanish' dating from this time is probably in itself quite erroneous, as indeed is the notion of a unified 'Spanish' at all. Another factor in an assessment of the Peninsular origins of Judeo-Spanish is the fact that many Sephardim sought refuge in Portugal before being expelled from there too. Penny (1992) is of the opinion that the later Judeo-Spanish varieties were formed as local *koine* languages with input from a number of Peninsular Romance sources; indeed, it has been claimed that Judeo-Spanish exhibits no feature which is not paralleled somewhere in Peninsular regional varieties (and, conversely, most of the Peninsular varieties appear to have had some impact on Judeo-Spanish, though its basis is definitely Castilian). Finally, we must remember that a good many of the differences between Judeo-Spanish and modern standard Spanish are due to the immunity of the Sephardic communities from the later emergence of metropolitan and regional standards in the main Spanish-speaking world.

---

[1] Other names in common use are *ladino* and *judezmo* (see below).

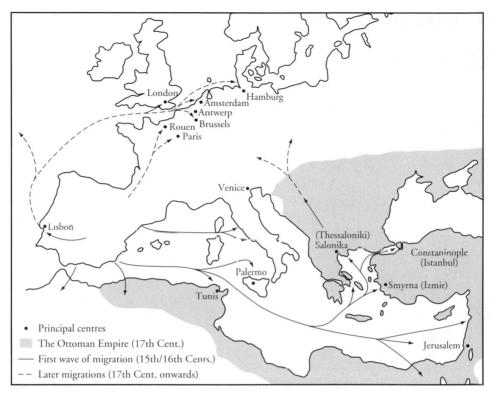

Figure 9.1 The Sephardic diaspora

If we take the view that the starting-point for Judeo-Spanish is the Peninsular Romance of the late 15th century, we must then ask when exactly it began to be differentiated from Castilian. This also is not an easy question to answer. Contemporary observations are not totally helpful: Harris (1994: 39 and 62) cites the testimony of Gonzalo de Illescas (1565–1633), a traveller who observed that the language of Jews in Venice was no different from the Castilian he himself spoke, and that of Bernardo Aldrete, who in 1614 commented that the language of Jews in Italy, Salonika and Africa was different from Castilian, displaying features he recognised as archaic (we should of course bear in mind that in the early 17th century the speech of Toledo in Spain was generally thought to be archaic by comparison with that of the new capital, Madrid, so this judgement may not mean that the Judeo-Spanish he heard was any more different from his own Spanish than some other Peninsular varieties). To complicate matters even further, there is considerable evidence that Judeo-Spanish was used as a lingua franca of commerce in the Eastern Mediterranean, since the Sephardic Jews enjoyed considerable prestige as the merchant class of the Ottoman Empire, and established important communities in such important trading centres as Venice, Livorno and Naples; it is very likely, therefore, that Sephardic traders were **diglossic**, using one Romance variety in this international context and another in a domestic environment. The process of differentiation, which was probably embryonic from a relatively early stage, was eventually intensified by a number of factors. Borrowings from languages with which the exiled communities came into contact was an inevitability, so the Judeo-Spanish of

Turkey had borrowings from Turkish, that of Bucarest from Romanian and that of Serbia and Bosnia from Italian, the latter due to prolonged contact with Venice. In North Africa a rather more thoroughgoing merger took place with the development of *hakitia*, a mixture of Spanish and Arabic. A decline in the fortunes of the most significant group of Judeo-Spanish speakers, the Sephardic Jews of the Ottoman Empire, meant that they ceased to be a force in international trade, and thus were culturally isolated from the European Renaissance, the Enlightenment and the Industrial Revolution, all of which led to innovations in the vocabulary of Spanish and other western European languages. The 16th and 17th centuries were also a time during which a number of phonetic and morphological changes took place in Peninsular and Latin-American Spanish, in which Judeo-Spanish did not share. Later, in the 19th century, the dominant western cultural and linguistic influence on educated Judeo-Spanish speakers of the Ottoman Empire was French, as the French-based Alliance Israélite Universelle intervened in Jewish education in the Levant, leading to the use of French rather than Judeo-Spanish as the medium of instruction. Increasing demands for the Jewish communities to surrender the independence they had originally been granted in large measure and to integrate into the national community meant in the 20th century that the number of monolingual speakers of Judeo-Spanish became increasingly smaller.

9.1.2 Judeo-Spanish communities

In the original diaspora following the expulsion of 1492, by far the most important destination was the Ottoman Empire, to which the Sephardic Jews had been invited by the Sultan, Bajazet II, where they were generally made welcome and held in high regard as a new merchant class, exercising considerable political influence as advisers to the Sultan; they also introduced printing in the Levant. Indeed, Judeo-Spanish came to be a language of some prestige, and even as late as 1970 Sephiha (1986: 30) recalls how on a visit to Istanbul older Greeks, Armenians and Muslim Turks were able to speak to him in the language. In the city of Salonika (modern Thessaloniki), Sephardic Jews came to constitute the majority of the population. Constantinople (modern Istanbul), Smyrna (modern Izmir) and Monastir (modern Bitola) were other important settlements. Palestine also proved a focus of initial emigration, since there was a history of a Sephardic community in Jerusalem going back to pre-expulsion days. Still others settled in the trading cities of North Africa, such as Tangiers and Oran.

The survival of Judeo-Spanish is due largely to the favourable conditions under which the Sephardim lived under Ottoman rule. Jews were able to live in their own quarters (*juderías*) as they had done in Spain (the preference for this was to facilitate religious observance, in particular being within walking distance of the synagogue), and so maintained their own culture and lifestyle. Judeo-Spanish was also of some importance as a liturgical language alongside Hebrew, which was generally not understood. There was a tradition of printed books: by far the most important work in Judeo-Spanish was the *Me'am Lo'ez* of 1730, a popular Sephardic encyclopedia, and there were many periodicals.

But the history of the Sephardic Jews has been one of ongoing fragmentation in the wake of economic difficulties and persecutions. In the 17th century there were important Sephardic communities in England, the Low Countries and France as a result of the late 16th-century Marrano diaspora of crypto-Jews from Portugal. The Sephardic communities underwent further diaspora through the Balkans as the Ottoman Empire progressively destabilised in the course of the 18th and 19th centuries; the language of a number of these communities was recorded in detail: see Wagner (1914), Luria (1930) and Crews (1935). The effects of the Second World War and the Holocaust on the Balkan Sephardim were catastrophic: many communities were completely annihilated, most notably the city of Salonika itself, which had been the Sephardic city *par excellence*. Only in neutral Turkey did significant Sephardic communities survive. There was also emigration to the Americas, where a considerable number of refugees from the Turkish revolution of 1908 had settled in New York and Los Angeles (there had in fact been a Sephardic community in New York since the 17th century, following flight from persecution in Brazil, cf. also **9.4.1**). With the formation of the state of Israel in 1948, many Sephardim moved to join fellow-Jews there.

9.1.3 Judeo-Spanish today

There seems little doubt that Judeo-Spanish is now in terminal decline, despite intense academic interest in the language and the strenuous efforts of a number of people to maintain interest in the language among younger generations of Sephardim. There have been a number of important initiatives in recent years: in Israel, the Autoridad Nasionala del Ladino i su Kultura was created in 1996 by the Israeli government and the international journal *Aki Yerushalayim* is published by Kol Israel (Israeli radio), which also transmits a daily broadcast in Judeo-Spanish; in France, the *Association Vidas Largas* has been in existence since 1974; in Belgium, the magazine *Los Muestros* began publication in 1990. In Spain, the Instituto Arias Montano was founded just after the Civil War; it is primarily an academic institution, publishing the journal *Sefarad* and, perhaps most significantly, Joseph Nehama's *Dictionnaire du Judéo-Espagnol* (1977). The Internet is an ideal medium for contact between widely separated groups. However, the prospects for Judeo-Spanish depend on its popularity among the younger generations and perhaps in part too on its being standardised. Harris (1994: 197–224) lists a number of reasons for its decline, including the reduction in numbers of speakers, lack of prestige, assimilation into other language communities, the lack of a body of literature, lack of use in education, lack of a standard language and reduction of contexts of use. Even within the Jewish world the prospects are bleak: Sephardim living in Israel adopt Hebrew rather than Judeo-Spanish, and there is much intermarriage between Sephardic and Ashkenazi Jews, with the consequent abandoning of Judeo-Spanish.

Standardisation is an unlikely prospect without a single national base or official status for the language. Even within the same community, there is much linguistic variation, especially lexical; and there are a number of different spelling systems currently in existence (see Table 9.1). The obvious solution is some kind of '**supralect**'; but that stands no chance of adoption unless it is imposed through education or official requirements.

Table 9.1 Spelling systems for Judeo-Spanish today (based on *Aki Yerushalayim*)

IPA symbol	*Aki Yerushalayim*	Nehama dictionary	*Şalom*	*Vidas largas*
b	balansa	balansa	balansa	balansa
β	saver, alavar	savér, alaƀar	saver, alavar	saver, alavar
tʃ	chiko	čiko	çiko	tchiko
d	demanda	demanda	demanda	demanda
ð	dado	dađo	dado	dado
f	famiya	famíya	famiya	famiya
g	gato	gáto	gato	gato
ɣ	agora	aǵóra	agora	agora
dʒ	djudio	ǧudio	judio	djudio
x	hazino	jazíno	hazino	hasino
ɦ	es.huenyo	esjwéño	eshuenyo	eshuenyo
k	kaza	kaza	kaza	kasa
l	ladino	lađíno	ladino	ladino
m	meter	metér	meter	meter
n	no	no	no	no
ɲ	anyo	áño	anyo	anyo
p	poko	póko	poko	poko
ɾ	ora	óra	ora	ora
r	gerra	gérra	gerra	gerra
s	paso	páso	paso	passo
ʃ	shavon	šavón	şavon	chavon
t	topar	topár	topar	topar
v	venir	venír	vinir	venir
ks	aksion	aksyón	aksiyon	aksion
gz	examen	egzámen	egzamen	egzamen
j	eyos	éyos	eyos	eyos
z	koza	koza	koza	cosa
ʒ	ojos	ožos	ojos	ojos
we	muevo	mwévo	muevo	mwevo
je	siempre	syémpre	syempre	syempre

The pressures on the younger generations away from Judeo-Spanish are immense. By the 20th century it had already become a predominantly domestic language, the preservation of which relied on strong family and community ties. Decline in religious observance, a falling birth rate and a move towards greater integration into the local speech-community all militate against its use. It is also held in low esteem, the cultivation of 'international' languages (especially English) being perceived as having more importance.

9.1.4 The linguistic characteristics of Judeo-Spanish

Because there is a good deal of diversity within Judeo-Spanish, this section will deal with only the most generalised and distinctive features of the various dialects. Several of the characteristics of Judeo-Spanish are best appreciated from a diachronic perspective, since in a number of respects they reflect Peninsular Castilian of the late 15th century. However, it is important not to overstate the archaic nature of Judeo-Spanish, since it also shows a number of innovatory features.

9.1.4.1 PHONOLOGY

The most obvious phonological difference between Judeo-Spanish and all other Spanish varieties is the different development undergone by the sibilant consonants of the medieval language since the 16th century (see **6.2.3.1.1**). It is this feature, more than any other, which is responsible for Judeo-Spanish being considered 'archaic', since it indeed preserves some consonantal sounds which have been lost elsewhere. However, in Judeo-Spanish the pattern looks rather different:

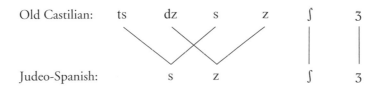

Figure 9.2 The origins of the sibilant consonants of Judeo-Spanish

Thus we have the following parallels between Modern Spanish and Judeo-Spanish:

Old Castilian	Modern Spanish	Judeo-Spanish
cerca [tserka]	*cerca* [θerka] or [serka]	*serka* [serka]
dezir [dedzir]	*decir* [deθir] or [desir]	*dizir* [dizir]
casa [kaza]	*casa* [kasa]	*kaza* [kaza]
dexar [deʃar]	*dejar* [dexar]	*deshar* [deʃar]
fijo [ɸiʒo]	*hijo* [ixo]	*(f)ižo* [(f)iʒo]

But it would be erroneous to claim that Judeo-Spanish preserves the system of Old Castilian intact. Although the voiced/voiceless opposition between /s/ and /z/ has been preserved, the oppositions between /ts/ and /s/ and between /dz/ and /z/, which are the basis of the modern opposition between /θ/ and /s/, have been lost, a feature Judeo-Spanish shares with the more 'advanced' varieties of Spanish.

There is a similar kind of balance-sheet between archaism and innovation overall in phonology. Some variants of Judeo-Spanish retain initial /f/ in words in which this changed first to /h/ and then was completely lost in most areas, e.g. *fierro* ['fjero] corresponding to Sp. *hierro* ['jero], and some still have a distinction between /b/ and /v/, which has been abandoned everywhere else in the Spanish-speaking world (this could be the consequence of contact with languages such as French which have /v/). Another source of /v/ in some areas was the original back semivowel in the rising diphthongs /au/, /eu/ and /iu/, giving results such as *Evropa* (Sp. *Europa*) and *sivdad* (Sp. *ciudad*), which may also be a remnant of earlier variation within Castilian itself, since spellings such as *cibdad* are found in Old Castilian texts. An innovation shared widely with regional varieties of Spanish is *yeísmo* (*kavayo* corresponding to Sp. *caballo*). Less widespread is the raising of atonic vowels: in Judeo-Spanish, /o/, /e/ and /a/ all tend to raise to [u], [i] and [e] (e.g. *sinku* corresponding to Sp. *cinco*, *sieti* to Sp. *siete* and *mansane* to Sp. *manzana*); while the raising of /o/ is extremely common regionally in Spanish, the raising of /e/ is more infrequent and the raising of /a/ very unusual (it is a feature of Asturian Spanish, where it is a legacy of the 'primary' Romance of Asturias). Judeo-Spanish, like many regional varieties of Spanish, is resistant to vowels in hiatus, but tends to have replaced hiatus groups and even diphthongs by inserting the semivowel [j] between the two original vowels, e.g. *veyo* for Sp. *veo* (original hiatus) and *diyente* for Sp. *diente* (original diphthong). This strategy is particularly unusual where the second vowel is /i/, e.g. *oyí* corresponding to Sp. *oí*. Neutralisation of the opposition between /r/ and /ɾ/ has taken place in some varieties of Judeo-Spanish, a development otherwise only familiar from *bozal* (see **9.3**). Other innovatory changes have been the widespread change of /n/ to /m/ before the diphthong /ue/ (e.g. *mueve* for Sp. *nueve*) and the frequent **metathesis** (exchange of places of two sounds) of the /rd/ sequence to /dr/, e.g. *akodrar* for Sp. *acordar*.

9.1.4.2 MORPHOLOGY

There are a number of differences in the derivational morphology of Judeo-Spanish which involve diphthongisation, especially in radical-changing verbs (cf. Andalusian, **6.2.3.2.3**). To Sp. *quiero* corresponds JSp. *kero*, while to *poder* corresponds *pueder*: the motivation for these developments was no doubt the morphological regularising of these verbs. The verb system also shows other kinds of analogical levelling, for example, the use of the older first person singulars *estó*, *do*, *vo* and *so* instead of Modern Spanish *estoy*, *doy*, *voy* and *estoy*.

As we might expect, pronouns of address, which underwent such great changes in the 16th century, have a different complexion in Judeo-Spanish, the third person forms *el* and *eya* being used as polite forms, as well as *vos*.

Again, we can draw up a balance sheet of archaism and innovation. A number of gender differences reflect Old Castilian (e.g. feminine gender for the majority of nouns in -*or*, such as *la kalor*, *la kolor*). Derivational creations, on the other hand, have often yielded different results from Spanish, e.g. *justedad* rather than the learned Sp. *justicia*, *malazedor* rather than *malhechor, orasyionar* 'to pray' rather than Sp. *orar*. Hypercharacterisation of gender is a common phenomenon, with adjectives which are invariable for gender in Spanish showing the addition of *-o* and *-a*, e.g. *mondiala* for Sp. *mundial*, *sosyala* for Sp. *social*; Sp. *cual*, which is used adjectivally in Judeo-Spanish, has developed the forms *cualo/a*.

9.1.4.3 VOCABULARY

This, as usual, is the most volatile area of language. Judeo-Spanish has preserved older forms of some words (e.g. *agora* for *ahora*, *ansí* for *así*) and archaisms such as *menester* 'necessity' and *trokar (trocar)* 'to change' (both still in the *DRAE*, but *menester* has been generally replaced by *necesidad*, the phrase *es menester* 'it is necessary' having been superseded by *es necesario, es preciso*; and *trocar* has given way to *cambiar*). Another archaism is *embezar* or *ambezar* 'to teach, to learn', which corresponds to Old Castilian *avezar* 'to teach, to accustom', which now exists in Spanish only in its past participle form *uvezado* 'seasoned, experienced'. Words have sometimes been preserved with, or have developed, meanings which are different from those of their corresponding forms in Spanish: *alguno* retains the meaning of 'someone' (MSp. *alguien*); *(f)echos*, which as MSp. *hechos* has the general meaning of 'actions, facts', has the more specialised meaning of 'business affairs', a sense it had in the 16th century, and *enchir* retains the meaning 'to fill', while in Modern Spanish it has somewhat specialised to mean 'to swell'.

Judeo-Spanish has words which appear to emanate from non-Castilian Peninsular sources, reflecting the multiple origins of the Sephardic communities: *ainda* (Castilian *todavía*) is likely to be of Portuguese or Galician origin, while the expression *kale (ke)* (Castilian *hay que*) derives from Catalan or Aragonese. There are numerous later borrowings from other languages, especially from French, e.g. *avenir* 'future', *buto* (< *but*) 'goal, end', *suetar* (< *souhaiter*) 'to wish', and Italian, e.g. *kapo* 'chief, head', *perikolo* 'danger', as also from the languages of the countries in which the Sephardim settled: Turkish, for instance, has contributed many words to the Judeo-Spanish of that area.

9.1.4.4 AN EXAMPLE OF JUDEO-SPANISH

The following is an extract from a short story by Sara Benzon Ruso, which appeared in the Istanbul newspaper *Şalom* on 23 May 2001. This newspaper, which has a history of over fifty years, still carries a regular page in Judeo-Spanish.

TEXT S

> El Sinyor Avram de la Kasturia era el givir de la sivdad. Muy
> riko ma muy eskaso. Kuando murio su mujer i kedo solo en la
> grande kaza, los ijos le tomaron un moso, ma el no keria pagar.
> Alora le dizia al moso: "Mira yo kero todo kon lo de detras, si
> una koza vyene a mankar, pisin te meto a la puerta i no te pago
> nada."   5

> Venia un moso, la demaniana ya le aparejava las pantoflas i el
> kurdi, la leçe, la asukar i el pan tostado, i mizmo le aprontava la
> agua kayente para el banyo ma si se olvidava una koza, por
> egzempio la tovaja al punto ke salia del banyo, pisin se arravyava 10
> i lo metia a la puerta. Ya tomava alora un otro moso ma despues
> de un mes i el muevo se iva por ke no le avia dado "lo de detras."
> Ansina kada mes se ivan los mosos sin ser pagados i el sinyor Avram
> estava muy kontente de azer ekonomias.
>
> *Şalom*, 23.05.01

Many of the general features that we have described above are illustrated here. The sibilant system is shown by *s* /s/ and *z* /z/, both corresponding to Spanish /s/ and /θ/ (*moso* = Sp. *mozo*, *koza* = Sp. *cosa*, *dezir* = Sp. *decir*), and by *j* /ʒ/, corresponding to Spanish /x/ (*mujer* = Sp. *mujer*). (*Ç* represents /tʃ/, so *leçe* is identical with Sp. *leche*.) *Yeísmo* extends to the realisation of the [lj] of standard *caliente* as [j]: *kayente*. Initial /f/ is not preserved in this variety (*ijos*, *azer*), but there is a distinction between /b/ and /v/ (*venir* but *banyo*: since Judeo-Spanish is written phonemically this is not just the etymological spelling of standard Spanish). The diphthong /iu/ has become /iv/ before a following consonant (*sivdad*). The distinction between /r/ and /ɾ/ is preserved (*arravyava* = Sp. *arrabiaba*), and /n/ before /ue/ has become /m/ (*muevo* = Sp. *nuevo*). Amongst morphological features, we may note the feminine gender of *asukar*, which is still encountered regionally in Spanish, the use of *la* rather than *el* before the stressed /a/ of the feminine noun *agua*, and the use of *un otro moso* rather than Spanish *otro mozo*. *Grande* does not **apocopate** (reduce in form) before *kaza* (cf. Spanish *gran casa*). Amongst vocabulary items of interest are *ma* 'but', probably an archaism corresponding to Spanish *mas*, which was current in Old Castilian and the Golden Age and is still used in some literary registers today. *Mancar* 'to be lacking' (MSp. *faltar*) is still listed as an archaism, with this meaning, in the *DRAE*. *Aparejar* 'to prepare, get ready' had this meaning in Old Castilian but now has the more specialised meanings of 'to rig; to saddle'. *Ansina* is an older form of *así* which is also found regionally. There are also borrowings: from Hebrew *givir* 'rich, notable man', from Turkish *pisin* 'immediately', from French *pantoflas (pantoufles)* 'slippers' and from Italian *per egsempio (per esempio)* 'for example'.

9.2 Vestigial Spanish varieties

A number of characteristic changes take place in language death, most notably accelerated simplification, often accompanied by the appearance of features of the dominant language. Unlike creoles, vestigial languages do not undergo a wholesale grammatical restructuring, and they still remain fairly readily comprehensible to speakers of the native standards. Impressionistically they often seem to be the standard language with 'mistakes' – the kind of mistakes that foreign learners would make in such areas as gender, agreements and verb inflections. On closer inspection, however, we can see that the simplification undergone by these languages is not completely arbitrary, but affects precisely those features which may be thought of being redundant within the standard language itself. Because a similar, but much more extensive, simplification is at the basis of a creole, a number of these features are shared with creoles, and because of this coincidence it is sometimes tempting to think of these 'vestigial' languages as having undergone a process of creolisation. This is not an appropriate conclusion, however, since, so far as we can see, there is no pidgin origin for 'vestigial' languages.

9.2.1 Isleño

The best studied Spanish variety of this type is the Isleño dialect of Louisiana. Its direct ancestry can easily be traced to Canaries immigrants who first settled in St Bernard Parish in Louisiana in the 18th century; there was a steady stream of immigration until the early 20th century. These Spanish-speaking communities were for many years relatively isolated, but in the 20th century better communications and the imposition of public education, coupled with emigration from the communities because of economic necessity, resulted in the increasing dominance of English and the relegation of Spanish to a subsidiary status. There has been some attempt at the maintenance of Spanish more recently (Coles 1999), but the days of its being actively spoken in this area are probably numbered.

The data described below is taken from Lipski (1990). Isleño Spanish, as is to be expected, shares a number of features with other non-standard varieties (e.g. the preservation of 16th-century initial /h/, verb forms such as *vide* for standard *vi* and *haiga* for standard *haya*, absence of *vosotros*, forms such as *naide(n)* for standard *nadie* and *a(n)sina* for standard *así*). But it is the specifically 'vestigial' features that will most interest us here, especially insofar as they can be compared with features of creoles.

Verbal morphology shows considerable simplification with a marked tendency to use the third person singular form, as in (9.1):

> **(9.1)** **a.** *Yo y mi ehposa no hablaba español*
> Standard: *Mi esposa y yo nos hablábamos en español*
> **b.** *No sé si tú lo vihto*
> Standard: *No sé si tú lo viste*

Use of a single verb form deriving from the third person singular of the standard verb is a consistent feature of Spanish creoles, which on the whole do not have any inflectional morphology; but, as will be seen in **9.4**, a characteristic feature of creoles is the development of a very individual tense-aspect system consisting of particles preceding the invariable verb. In Isleño there is no sign of the development of such a system, and although the person-number inflectional features of the verb have been heavily eroded, neither they nor the tense inflections have been totally lost.

There is also simplification of noun morphology, with apparently arbitrary and inconsistent gender assignment and failure to make gender agreements:

(9.2) a. *Era cosa serio*
    b. *la casita ese*

This is indeed a feature paralleled in creoles, where the category of gender simply does not exist, and nouns and adjectives which are the product of lexification (see **9.4**) from Romance languages appear to bear little relation to their original gender marking. Creoles also eliminate number inflections in nouns and adjectives. Neither of these features has developed to the same extent in Isleño. Although gender agreements are not always made, nouns retain gender marking and both masculine and feminine forms of adjectives and articles are used; and although it may appear that number inflections are suppressed (often because of the aspiration or loss of final /s/), marking of number in articles (e.g. by the use of *lo(s)* rather than *el* in the plural) has not been lost.

Prepositional usage is reduced, *de* and *a* being especially prone to elimination:

(9.3) a. *Ya recibirá carta Ehpaña*
       Standard: *Ya recibirá una carta de España*
    b. *Comenzaba setiembre*
       Standard: *Comenzaba en setiembre*
    c. *Tú jura un isleño*
       Standard: *Tú juras a un isleño*

Creole languages similarly show a good deal of restructuring in their prepositional systems, and *a* is generally completely lost (though a number of the functions of *de* survive in Papiamentu *di*). But once again, the movement in Isleño is nowhere near as extreme or as thoroughgoing as in a creole.

Subordinating constructions are simplified, the subordinating conjunction being eliminated and the verb often appearing in the infinitive form:

(9.4) a. *Hay mucha manera loh muchacho salí*
       Standard: *Hay muchas maneras para que los muchachos salgan*
    b. *No faltó nada no morimo*
       Standard: *No faltó nada para que nos muriéramos*

The simplification of subordination in favour of **parataxis** (the use of clauses without conjunctions) is a feature not only of creoles but also of spoken registers of the standard language.

Articles are frequently omitted:

(9.5) a. *No ponen zapato en la mesa*
    b. *la gente que viene de ehcuela*

In Papiamentu, by contrast, the articles are reasonably strongly maintained.

Subject pronouns are used with a greater frequency than in the standard language:

(9.6) a. *Yo tengo a dos hijo; yo tengo a Al y yo tengo a Paul*
       = *Tengo dos hijos: (tengo) Al y (tengo) Paul*
    b. *Él decía que el podía para una manguera*
       = *Decía que podía parar una manguera*

Creoles do share this feature, but to a much more intense degree: the expression of a subject is obligatory in a creole.

Perhaps most strikingly, *tener* is used as an existential verb (see **8.4**), corresponding to standard *haber*:

> **(9.7)** *A casa loh muchacho tiene una harmónica*
> Standard: *En casa de los muchachos hay una harmónica*

This is also a feature of all Spanish creoles.

9.3 Afro-Hispanic varieties

Throughout the history of Spanish over the last 500 years we find ample testimony of the speech of negros who have apparently imperfectly learned the language (for a sample, with commentary, see Pountain (2001: 237–41)). We can think of these manifestations as a form of pidgin Spanish, and certainly not necessarily as the speech of all negros, who were often distinguished by Spaniards from the linguistic point of view as *bozales* (pidgin-speaking) or *ladinos* (Spanish-speaking) – see Lipski (1998: 299). It must be remembered that black slaves continued to be transported to the Americas until the 19th century, when slavery was finally abolished, and so there would have been a steady stream of native speakers of African languages who became such speakers of a pidgin Spanish over a long period of time. In fact, the period of most intense transportation was from the 18th century, when workers for the Caribbean sugar plantations were needed in large numbers. There was also some movement of slaves within the Caribbean area, and within the Spanish-speaking world especially to Cuba, where memories of the speech of former generations still persist, confirming that a kind of Spanish somewhere between a pidgin and a creole was still being spoken until relatively recently.

Such forms of Spanish are usually referred to collectively as *bozal*, and they have become the subject of intense linguistic interest. Part of this interest is stimulated by the realisation that while *bozal* as a living form of communication has practically died out, recovery of data is still possible (see, for example, Ortiz López 1998). Another reason for concentration on *bozal* has centred on the hypothesis that it may have been a formative factor in Caribbean Spanish. Intimately connected with this question is that of where *bozal* stands with respect to other creoles, and here there is a considerable amount of difficulty because of terminology which is perhaps unduly restrictive. *Bozal* is not at all a constant language but is a generic term to include negro speech of many different centuries and localities. Its manifestations are exclusively spoken, typically unstable, languages which are not at all standardised. *Bozal* varieties certainly exhibit some features that are shared with creoles, yet at the same time they typically remain closer to Spanish, having a number of features which are also attested in regional varieties of Spanish. They also in some ways resemble Spanish learned as a second language (see **9.5**). They thus sit rather uneasily between a pidgin and a creole, and commentators have therefore sometimes dubbed them 'semicreoles', that is to say, pidgins which have to a certain extent stabilised and undergone some restructuring by successive generations of speakers. The complex social conditions under which *bozal* developed, which are also not easily recoverable in detail, no doubt explain this complexity. We are looking at communities of black slaves to which there has been constant immigration, and what seems most likely is that the process of creolisation in such communities has not been as thoroughgoing as in the case of Papiamentu and Palenquero, which we shall examine in some detail in **9.4.2**. Contact with native Spanish speakers using varieties with Andalusian and Canary characteristics may have provided another input into the development of *bozal*, and it is striking how many phenomena, because they represent simplification by comparison with standard Spanish, coincide. It is even possible that some *bozal* varieties were influenced by the better-established creoles, especially Papiamentu, in view of the heavy involvement of the Dutch Antilles in the slave trade. In short, creolisation is possibly better envisaged as being a matter of degree, with those creoles which have achieved the greatest prestige within their communities representing the extreme known point in this direction of development.

The following text, from Ortiz López, is a reconstruction, by a present-day descendant of a Cuban negro slave, of the speech of his forbears.

TEXT T

Entonce ya tá decí pa'ti. Niño, tú tá queré que lo negro áa decí
cuanto yo vá hacé, si me tá acodá. Cuando to tá vení de lo tiera
mío sí poqque yo tá sé negro de nación. Entonce, yo branco tá
cojé a toitico lo negro de lo de lo monte en baracón grande,
grande. Y que tá metío dentro de lo mimo má. Negro tá   5
soprendío sí señor. Otro negro etá juí juí po lo monte paque lo
branco no lo tá podé cojé. Yo era un peque un piquinine e niño,
como utede. Asi mimitico. Taita mío etá peliá y peliá con lo
branco y tá morí. Sí. Mi amá, mi amá etá traé a mí mucho día
sin que lo ve el só(l). No lo la quiera branco no no sé malo malo   10
no sé malo con lo negro. Da mucho cuero y si negra tá revirá lo
tá matá como pe(r)ro mimo, sí señó. Uni día blanco tá decí que
salí de lo baracón entonce el negro etá mirá una tiera muy
bonito. ¡Linda tierra carai! Y tá creé que sotro mundo. Branco
tá jabla que te jabla, jabla que te habla, no entendé, poqque el   15
negro no jabla como lo branco.

Luis Ortiz López, *Huellas etno-sociolingüísticas bozales y afrocubanas* (Frankfurt:
Vervuert, 1998) p. 140.

This fragment must be treated with some caution, since although it has a number of the features which have been observed to be typical of *bozal* speech, there is probably also a certain intereference from the speaker's own Spanish (we must remember he is not a native *bozal* speaker). It also reflects some features of Cuban Spanish, such as the preservation of the intial /h/ which has generally ceased to be pronounced in Spanish (*juí* = *huir* (l.6), *jabla* = *habla*, l.15), the diminutive suffix *-ico* (*toitico* = *toditico*, l.4), the elision of intervocalic /d/ (*metío* = *metido*, l.5) and the fall of syllable-final /s/ (*mimo* = *mismo*, l.5). But some widely attested features of *bozal* speech are clearly present. There is no phonemic contrast between /r/ and /ɾ/ (*tiera~tierra*, l.2, *per(r)o*, l.12, *bar(r)acón*, l.13); /ɾ/ and /l/ appear to be neutralised before a vowel (*branco*, l.3), and are regularly lost in syllable-final position (*soprendío* = *sorprendido*, l.6, *só(l)*, l.10, *seño(r)*, l.12, *poqque* = *porque*, l.3) and possibly all the 'infinitive' verb forms, such as *entendé(r)*, l.15). Indeed, there is some tendency to avoid closed syllables altogether (*utede* = *usted*, l.8, *uni* = *un*, l.12, *que sotro* = *que es otro*, l.14). Gender and number inflection in nouns and adjectives is generally absent (*lo tiera mío*, ll.2–3). Articles are not always used (*negro tá soprendío*, ll.5–6), though they are not systematically absent (*el negro no jabla como lo branco*, ll.15–16). Absence of any verbal inflection and use of the tense-aspect markers *tá* and *va* is especially noticeable here (*tá queré*, l.1, *va hacé*, l.2); note also that there is no subjunctive marking in *paque lo branco no lo tá podé cojé* (ll.6–7), and *sin que lo ve el só(l)* (l.10). The incidence of repetition as an intensifying device is high (*etá juí juí*, l.6, *etá peliá y peliá*, l.8, and the formula *jabla que te habla*, l.15).

Other features which regularly occur in *bozal* are the obligatory use of a subject pronoun when the verb has no other subject (thus, like creoles, *bozal* is resistant to the pro-drop feature of Spanish), the omission of the copular verb, the loss of the prepositions *a* and *de* and the introduction of the preposition *na* for *en*, the omission of the complementiser *que* and the use of double negation – all features which are also evidenced in creoles (see **9.4**).

9.4 Spanish creoles

Creole languages were once much misunderstood as being imperfect, substandard versions of the languages of the imperial powers. Even today, creole data rarely figure in cross-linguistic studies, as if creoles were in some way not quite 'proper' languages. Yet in terms of everyday use, creoles are the principal means of communication in many communities and so function in just the same way as non-creole languages. However, creoles are now the subject of intense linguistic interest for a number of reasons.

First, what exactly is the relation between creoles and other languages? Linguistic study has revealed that creoles are very far from being simply varieties of other languages. The grammars of 'Spanish' creoles, for example, as we shall see, differ typologically in a number of important respects from the grammar of Spanish, even though Spanish has clearly supplied most of their vocabulary. Accordingly, what we might mean by a 'Spanish' creole is a language which has been **lexified** (has words supplied) by Spanish. But in that case, what was the underlying grammatical system on to which Spanish words were grafted? The idea that the starting-point could have been a system of empty grammatical slots waiting to be filled is patently absurd, so where does the grammar of a creole come from? There seem to be three possible answers to this question. Maybe the grammar is in origin the native grammar of early speakers – in the case of Latin-American creoles, this means the West African languages of the black slaves. Or perhaps the grammar is the result of **pidginisation**, that is to say, basically the grammar of a Western European language (Portuguese is the obvious choice here, since it was the main language of the slave trade) which was highly simplified for use as a language of basic communication. The last possibility is that some features of the grammar are the result of borrowing from the lexifying language. As we shall see, the Spanish creoles provide evidence of all these processes, which perhaps indicates that the grammatical complexion of a creole is the result of a number of factors. In Creole studies, the pendulum has swung back and forth, it currently being thought that perhaps the African element has been insufficiently recognised.

The scenarios outlined here in turn raise interesting linguistic issues. The simplification of grammar envisaged in pidginisation and the subsequent development of a creole raises questions about redundancy in language. We might expect *a priori* that creoles will lack precisely those features which seem to contribute little or nothing to efficient communication. English-speaking learners of Spanish will therefore not be surprised to find that the following are often lost in Spanish creoles: the complex and often irregular verbal inflectional system, grammatical gender, the subjunctive, the distinction between *ser* and *estar*. They are all features which English speakers, for instance, manage perfectly well without. Since such simplification is often a feature of the diachronic development of non-creole languages, a number of linguists have envisaged the development of creoles as an accelerated process of language change; it may be no accident, therefore, that some of the changes we see in modern Spanish (for example, the erosion of verb-inflection) are anticipated in creoles. The question of contact borrowing is also a subject of great current interest. The borrowing of words is a patent feature of language contact, but can languages actually borrow grammatical features from one another? Creoles offer us a number of important insights on this matter: some grammatical features of creoles seem to be the product of essentially lexical borrowing (e.g. derivational morphology in Papiamentu), while others (especially the apparently more recent phenomena) appear to offer quite clear evidence of syntactic **calquing** or imitation of a foreign construction (e.g. the passive in Papiamentu).

The second general issue of interest in the study of creoles regards their origin. Two theories have been proposed and are the subject of extensive debate. The **monogenesis** theory hypothesises that all creoles derive from a common ancestor, possibly a Portuguese pidgin used along the African coast where slaves were assembled for exportation; differences among the creoles would then be explained by differential relexification. The **bioprogram** hypothesis is that the development of creoles is due to 'natural' evolutionary processes in language, and that any similarities among the creoles simply reflect these universal tendencies. One of the themes I shall focus on, therefore, is how similar the Spanish creoles in fact are, the provisional conclusion being that while at first sight they appear to coincide remarkably in a number of general features, especially by contrast with Spanish, on closer inspection they turn out to be quite different in detail.

Another general issue takes us back to the discussion in Chapter 1 concerning the nature of languages. Some creoles (and this is not a phenomenon restricted to creoles) are different from many Western European languages in that they exist primarily, sometimes exclusively, in spoken form and do not have many of the characteristics of an official language: hence they are not standardised; they are not the vehicle of a written literature (we must not confuse this with the absence of literature altogether, since there may well be an oral literary tradition), and they are not used for specialised purposes – legal, administrative or scientific, for example. In the case of the Spanish creoles, it is likely that there are nowadays no monolingual speakers of these languages; in particular, some creole speakers also speak Spanish. This means that the collection of data is no easy matter. It is often difficult to detect codeswitching between the creole and Spanish, so that assessing what constitutes a lexification, a borrowing or a code-switch is highly problematic. Furthermore, because creoles are largely unstandardised, they are characterised by variability which makes clearcut native-speaker judgements sometimes difficult to obtain – indeed, most creole linguistic studies are essentially corpus-based, i.e. derived from the analysis of field recordings.

Spanish creoles are relatively few in number. In the Americas, by far the strongest in terms of future prospects is Papiamentu (spelt Papiamento in Aruba), with over 200,000 speakers; this is spoken in the Dutch Antilles, notably on the islands of Aruba, Bonaire and Curaçao. Although the official language of these islands is Dutch, Papiamentu is spoken by the vast majority of the population (estimated at 84 per cent in 1995 by Ethnologue) across all sectors of society, and is used even for official government communications; it is also widely used in the media. It has a written literary tradition dating back to the 19th century. It is even making progress in the traditionally Dutch-based educational system, and the Curaçoan Minister of Education, Martha Dijkhoff, has plans to extend its use as a language of instruction (Perl 1999). Its prestige is unusual for a creole language. The other generally recognised Spanish creole of the Americas is Palenquero (called 'lengua' by its speakers, as opposed to 'kasteyao'), which is spoken in El Palenque ('the stockade') de San Basilio, located to the south of Cartagena in Colombia. It is now restricted, in active use at least, to older speakers, since the younger generations tend to adopt Spanish exclusively; it has perhaps only survived because of the very remoteness of the community, which had its first dirt road to the outside world only in 1967. The other area of interest for Spanish creoles is the Philippines, where a number of '**contact vernaculars**' survive; the strongest of these, Chabacano, is spoken in Zamboanga on Mindanao by some 155,000 inhabitants of the city and extends to other nearby communities (other enclaves of Spanish creoles in the Philippines are Cavite and Ternate near Manila and Cotabato on Mindanao, the latter being a variety of Zamboangueño), giving a total of 292,630 speakers in all (1990 census figures, reported by Ethnologue). A 'contact vernacular' is strictly speaking the product of contact between speakers of two different languages: in this case the process is complex and involves Spanish, a Portuguese-Malay pidgin, Malay and Tagalog (Whinnom 1956: 1–17).

9.4.1	The historical background to the formation and present-day use of the Spanish creoles

To understand the basic linguistic complexion of these creoles, we need to look both at their history and at their current situation.

The establishment of the community of Palenque was the result of an escape in 1603 by a small group of slaves who were working on the fortifications of Cartagena, though it also became a refuge for other runaway slaves over the following century. Palenquero would therefore probably have had a mixture of black creole inputs and have developed in isolation; however, as early as the end of the 18th century the community was described as also being Spanish-speaking (Bickerton & Escalante 1970: 255), and any outside contact Palenquero speakers had would have been, as today, with Spanish. What is likely is that the maintenenance of Palenquero had advantages as the private language of the fiercely independent El Palenque community, a need which is today receding. All Palenquero speakers are therefore bilingual (or diglossic), and there is typically much code-switching in Palenquero speech. Today, Palenquero is not used for any purpose other than that of local oral communication within a country whose national language is Spanish, which there is every incentive – educational, economic and social – to know and use.

Papiamentu developed against a much more complex linguistic background which reflects the turbulent history of the region down to the 19th century. Curaçao became the centre of the Dutch slave trade in the mid-17th century, and several factors seem to have favoured the development of a Portuguese/Spanish lingua franca there. It is not impossible that Spanish continued to be used on the Dutch Antilles by the remnants of the Spanish-speaking Indian community who remained there after the annexation by the Dutch of Curaçao and Bonaire in 1634 and of Aruba in 1688. In 1659, Sephardic Jews from north-eastern Brazil sought Curaçao as a refuge from the Portuguese, who had retaken this part of Brazil from the Dutch, and became involved in the new slave trade. So into the linguistic melting-pot went (a) Spanish as used among and to the Indians, (b) whatever language was spoken among the Sephardic Jews (perhaps Portuguese or Judeo-Spanish) and (c) the West African Portuguese pidgin spoken among the slaves. To this must be added the proximity of the Spanish-speaking mainland and contact with Spanish as an important language of trade, especially the slave trade (the Dutch held the monopoly in supplying the Spanish-American colonies with slaves until the end of the War of the Spanish Succession in 1713). Papiamentu has emerged with very definite traces of a Portuguese pidgin ancestry but with the majority of its lexification being from Spanish (though there is extensive lexification from Dutch too, especially in Curaçao itself). Constant contact with Spanish, which has intensified with the advent of broadcasting from nearby Venezuela, has no doubt led to what looks at first sight like the **decreolisation** of Papiamentu in the direction of Spanish. However, most authorities today regard the role of Spanish as a means of enriching expression rather than as a target of convergence: that is to say that Spanish borrowings add to the existing lexical stock of the language rather than relexifying it.

Papiamentu is today undergoing the interesting stage of development towards what is sometimes known as an *Ausbau*-**language** (see Kloss 1967), in which, as a written language and as a medium of culture and, in effect, of administration, its language-planners seek to coin new words for concepts not previously expressed in the language, the obvious direction in which to look being Spanish (we may compare this with borrowing from Latin in the Western Romance languages from the Middle Ages to the present day as these erstwhile vernaculars underwent what was in many ways a similar process of enrichment); it was for this purpose that the Komishon di Standarisashon di Papiamentu was founded in Curaçao in 1984. In this process, however, Papiamentu does not really run any risk of losing its separate and very distinctive identity. And although contact with Spanish is extensive, Papiamentu exists against the background of an officially Dutch-speaking environment, the majority of speakers being bilingual in Papiamentu and Dutch. Another way in which Papiamentu has come to be more like a non-creole language is in its diatopic and diastratic variation, which is extensive. Curaçao and Aruba have slightly different standards (and significantly different spelling systems); within Curaçao, it is the speech of the middle and upper classes of the capital, Willemstad, that provides the basis of the standard, which is a very similar situation to that obtaining in many Western European countries.

We now turn to the Philippines. To understand the origin of Zamboangueño we must work backwards from 1719, when this garrison town was significantly strengthened by Spanish-speaking American Indians and *mestizos* married to Filipinas. The creole which developed there was probably in origin a military pidgin which had developed as a result of Moluccan creole speakers' extensive involvement in the Spanish navy (Moluccan creole, now extinct, was probably based in origin on a Malayo-Portuguese pidgin). There is evidence that Spanish was quite extensively used in Zamboanga in the late 19th century, and certainly during the American colonial period it seems to have undergone something of a revival, possibly as the result of resistance to English on the part of the native middle classes. Spanish, which had never been extensively used in the Philippines, has now largely died out, as a consequence of English (under American occupation) and subsequently Tagalog having been cultivated as national languages and lingua francas of this multilingual state.

A diglossic situation seems to have ensued, in which 'high' and 'low' varieties of Zamboangueño creole, or Chabacano as it is generally known, developed, the 'high' style increasingly approximating to Spanish though retaining significant creole features, and the 'low' style remaining much more creole-like with many borrowings from Tagalog and the surrounding Philippine languages.[2] (One problem in describing Chabacano is that most written texts are in the 'high' style, which is not typical of present-day speech.) The Second World War completely destroyed Zamboanga City and with it much published material in Chabacano, and after the war English became the dominant language. In the Philippine civil war Zamboanga became a refuge for many outsiders who were not Chabacano-speaking. However, Chabacano still continues as the primary language of everyday communication in Zamboanga, where it has a status approaching that of Papiamentu in the Antilles, and is used as a lingua franca in a more extended region around the city. Unlike Papiamentu, however, there is no possibility of its aspiring to the status of a national language. Contact with Spanish is now also limited, although recently the Philippine creoles have received the unexpected backing of the Academia Filipina, who, faced with the prospect of the total annihilation of Spanish in the Philippines (Spanish disappeared as an obligatory subject in the school curriculum in 1987), have seen the possibility of the cultivation of Chabacano as a means of revitalising Spanish – a somewhat utopian prospect, it has to be said.

---

[2] For a definition of the notions of 'high' and 'low' varieties, see Ferguson (1959). In a creole context, it is appropriate to speak of a continuum between the creole variety which most closely approximate to an established language (basilect) and the one which is most distant from it (acrolect), intermediate varieties sometimes being known as mesolects.

It is quite beyond the scope of this book to give a comprehensive description of the Spanish creoles, but bearing in mind the issues raised above, I shall try to point out the principal differences and similarities of these three creoles, as well as their relationship with the mainstream varieties of Spanish.

9.4.2.1 PHONOLOGY

The creoles differ substantially from the phonological point of view, due no doubt in part to their contact history. The exact phonemic system of Papiamentu is in fact difficult to ascertain, since some sounds, whilst frequent, appear to be limited to Dutch and English borrowings which do not enter into functional oppositions with other words in the language. It distinguishes in its orthography rather more sounds than Spanish. The phonology of Chabacano is closer to that of Spanish, though there are some sounds which appear to be due to Tagalog and others which may be the result of contact with English. Palenquero phonology does not differ very substantially from that of neighbouring Spanish varieties, though it has some distinctive phonological groupings.

Papiamentu has two central vowels, /y/ and /ø/ (written *ü* and *ù*) and two half-open vowels, /ɛ/ and /ɔ/ (written *è* and *ò*) in addition to the five Spanish vowels (represented, as in Spanish, by *i, e, a, o* and *u*). However, /y/ occurs only in words which derive from Dutch and is often replaced by /i/ in popular speech (e.g. *hür* [hyːr] or [hiːr] 'rent' < Du. *huur*), while /ø/ occurs in Dutch or English words and is often commutable with *e* (e.g. *bùs* [bøs] or [bes] 'bus' < Eng. *bus*); there do not seem to be any minimal pairs based on oppositions with other vowel phonemes. /ɛ/ and /ɔ/ are similarly most common in words of Dutch and English origin, and they cannot occur in final position unless the same vowel appears in the stressed syllable. The sound [ə] may occur in unstressed final syllables which end in a liquid consonant, though it is often replaced by [u] (and in Aruba [o]): thus *dòkter* ['dɔktər] ~ ['dɔktu] ~ ['dɔkto]. Vowels are heavily nasalised before a nasal consonant.

The vowels distinguished in Chabacano are the five of standard Spanish, with some tendency to raise /e/ and /o/ to [i] and [u], especially in unstressed syllables (thus *dispierto* < Sp. *despierto*, *cugí* < Sp. *coger*); this is in line with the three-term vowel system of Tagalog, but, equally, such raising is also widespread in the mainstream varieties of Spanish.

As far as consonants are concerned, all three creoles appear to inherit the *seseo* of most American Spanish varieties (e.g. Pap. *kuminsá* 'begin' < Sp. *comenzar*, Pal. *ndose* 'twelve' < Sp. *doce*, Cha. *lus* 'light' < Sp. *luz*) and have weakened /x/ to [h] (e.g. Pap. and Pal. *hende* 'person' < Sp. *gente*, Cha. *hunto* 'together' < Sp. *junto*) or to nothing (e.g. Pap. *wega* 'game' < Sp. *juega*). Papiamentu and Palenquero additionally have *yeísmo* (Pap. *yama* 'call' < Sp. *llamar*, Pal. *ayá* 'there' < Sp. *allá*), a feature which is interestingly absent in Chabacano (e.g. *lyama* 'call' < Sp. *llamar*), the more so since in many early Tagalog borrowings from Spanish [ʎ] is replaced by [j] or [l]. On the other hand, the voiced intervocalic plosives /b/, /d/ and /g/ do not appear in Papiamentu and Chabacano to be fricativised to [β], [ð] and [ɣ] as they are universally in Spanish, though there is a good deal of variation observable in this respect.

Palenquero does have fricatives in such environments, and has developed a phonological contrast between these and the corresponding plosives as a result of the avoidance of sylla-ble-final consonants: thus /kaβo/ < Sp. *cabo* vs. /kaːbo/ < Sp. *calvo*, /seðo/ < Sp. *cedo* vs. /seːdo/ < Sp. *cerdo* and /aɣo/ < Sp. *hago* vs. /aːgo/ < Sp. *algo*.

It is a moot point as to the extent of the debt of creole phonology to the antecedents of the pidgins from which they sprang. Palenquero has initial consonant clusters *mb-*, *nd-* and *ng-*, which are shared with a number of West African languages (though they regularly appear in words of Spanish origin, e.g. *ndoló* 'pain' < Sp. *dolor*, *ngande* 'big' < Sp. *grande*). Chabacano similarly has /ŋ/ in positions which are impossible in Spanish, but here the sound is limited to words it has borrowed from Tagalog (e.g. the emphatic particle *ñga* [ŋga]); /ŋ/ is also found in final position (e.g. *camantíng* 'sweet potato') in Tagalog bor-rowings, and is distinguished from /n/. At the same time, final [ŋ] is a frequent regional fea-ture in Spanish, and is the regular pronunciation of the final -*n* of Spanish lexifications in Papiamentu (Papiamentu now has final /n/ as a result of Dutch and English borrowings, such as *pèn* 'ballpoint pen' < Eng. *pen*). Also in Chabacano, a glottal stop [ʔ] is often pres-ent after a word-final vowel (e.g. ['bwɛnoʔ]), a feature of Tagalog. Chabacano shows evi-dence of a former resistance to /f/, which is absent in Tagalog, replacing it with /p/ (e.g. *plores* < Sp. *flor*), although /f/ has now been introduced through borrowings from Spanish. Another feature of creole languages which may be due to the pre-creole stage is that their words tend to be disyllabic and have a strong tendency towards a consonant + vowel syllable structure. This is very noticeable in Palenquero, where final consonants regularly have a **par-agogic** vowel added, and initial vowels and syllable-final consonants are eliminated, thus:

> *kiene* < Sp. *quien*
> *kabá* < Sp. *acabar*
> *aggo* < Sp. *algo*

A similar feature is observable in Papiamentu words which may be taken to be part of the original lexification:

> *mucha* 'child' < Sp. *muchacho/a* 'boy/girl'
> *kuchú* 'knife' < Sp. *cuchillo*
> *muhé* 'woman' < Sp. *mujer*
> *awor* 'now' < Sp. *ahora*

but extensive borrowing, especially from Spanish and Dutch, and more recently from English, has led to complication of this pattern, a feature which is symptomatic of the *Ausbau* nature of the language (see **9.4.1**):

> *buskuchi* 'biscuit' < Du. *biscuitje*
> *pòstbùs* 'postbox' < Du. *postbus*
> *projekto* 'project' < Sp. *proyecto*
> *solamente* 'only' < Sp. *solamente*
> *wikènt* 'weekend' < Eng. *weekend*

In Papiamentu, borrowing from Dutch and English has led to some degree of adoption of /v/ (orthographic *v*) and the fricative /x/ (orthographic *g*, used only before a front vowel). However, there is a strong tendency for /v/ to alternate with /f/ (e.g. *vris* or *fris* 'freeze' < Eng. *freeze*) or for /f/ to be used instead of /v/ (e.g. *fèrt* 'speed' < Du. *vaart*), and /x/ with /h/. (The /v/ cannot be any remnant of Spanish, incidentally – and in this Papiamentu shows its allegiance to Spanish rather than Portuguese, since Portuguese does have an opposition between /b/ and /v/ – since Papiamentu has such developments as *bende* 'sell' < Sp. *vender* and *bini* 'come' < Sp. *venir*.) /v/ is also present in Chabacano, where it is distinguished from /b/ in a way which generally follows Spanish orthography. This is a much more mysterious feature, however, since for the reasons already given it does not seem possible that it can derive from Spanish itself, though it is a feature of words inherited from Spanish. Whinnom (1956: 104) postulates that the influence of the pre-war written language may have been an important factor; the sound [v] may also have been familiar from some of the southern Philippine languages. Another sound which must be the product of borrowing in Papiamentu is /z/: *zòm* 'hem' < Du. *zoom*, *zür* 'acid' < Du. *zuur* (again, /z/ cannot be inherited from Spanish, where today [z] only appears as an allophone of /s/ before a voiced consonant: *casa*, though pronounced [kaza] in the medieval language, has yielded *kas* [kas] in Papiamentu, showing lexification from the modern pronunciation ['kasa]). Chabacano has a 'dark' (velarised) *l* [ɫ] in syllable-final position, most probably as the result of contact with English.

Some differences from Spanish in consonantal phonology seem to be the result of the natural phonetic evolution of the creoles themselves. There is no echo of the Spanish opposition between the flap /ɾ/ and the trill /r/ in either Papiamentu or Chabacano, a feature shared with *bozal*, and in Palenquero, both are often realised as /l/ (thus *loyo* < Sp. *arroyo*); however, in Palenquero, /ɾ/ often substitutes initial /d/, thus producing an opposition between /ɾio/ 'God' (< Sp. *Dios*) and /rio/ 'river' (< Sp. *río*) (Bickerton & Escalante 1970: 256). In Papiamentu, /s/, /t/ and /d/ followed by an original /i/ in syllable-initial position have palatalised to [ʃ], [tʃ] or [tj] and [dʒ] or [dj] respectively: *bishitá* 'visit' < Sp. *visitar*, *tienda* ['tʃenda] < Sp. *tienda*, *dies* [dʒes] < Sp. *diez*. These have been reinforced by borrowings: *klèsh* 'dispute, clash' < Eng. *clash*, *djèk* 'jack (of car)' < Eng. *jack*, *choka* 'strangle' < Eng. 'choke', *sunchi* 'kiss' < Du. *zoentje*.

A feature of Papiamentu and Palenquero is that tone appears to be phonemic. One important tone pattern, common to both languages, is that two-syllable verbs end on a high tone whereas the corresponding noun ends on a low tone: thus *kaska* ['ka̱skā] 'peel (verb)' versus *kaska* ['kāska̱] 'peel (noun)' (note that the stress is on the same syllable in these two words). Other distinctive functions of tone have been identified in Papiamentu, the best studied of the creoles: Maurer (1998: 169) points to the fact that *ta* as a tense/aspect marker (see below) always has a high tone while *ta* as a copular verb ('to be') varies in tone according to the context.

9.4.2.2 MORPHOLOGY

Absence of inflectional morphology (often to the point of complete elimination) is a hallmark of creoles, though here too Papiamentu shows a greater movement in the direction of inflectional devices than the other creoles, a development which has come about largely through the borrowing of Spanish and Dutch words which incorporate inflections of those languages. ('High' Chabacano preserves many features of Spanish inflectional morphology, though this may be interpreted as the legacy of former code-switching.)

9.4.2.2.1 Nouns

None of the creoles shows systematic gender distinctions, though some varieties of Papiamentu have adopted Spanish nationality nouns and adjectives such as *colombiano/a*. Where not pragmatically obvious, plurality is marked **analytically** (i.e. by the use of separate words rather than inflected forms – see **3**): in Papiamentu by the postnominal particle *nan*, which is also the third person plural pronoun and possessive, in Palenquero by the prenominal particle *ma*, and in Chabacano by the prenominal plural particle *mana* or *maga*. All these elements appear to be pre-creole: *nan* and *ma* are African in origin, and *mana~manga* is Tagalog. However, Papiamentu *nan* now seems to have an almost inflectional status (plurals are usually written as one word, e.g. *ladron* 'thief' / *ladronnan* 'thieves'). In Chabacano the Spanish *-s* inflection (sometimes in combination with the *mana* particle) is also found.

9.4.2.2.2 Verbs

The creoles have no person/number or tense inflections in verbs. Tense and aspect are denoted by a system of preverbal particles used with an invariable verb-form, and person is indicated by an obligatory subject. Although the particles and their exact semantic values differ, there is a remarkable typological similarity among creoles in this respect, which can perhaps be interpreted as the rejection of inflectional morphology in favour of analytic constructions, though on closer inspection the systems do not correspond in detail. Although this is probably the best-known feature of creole grammar, it is still not fully understood or documented. There is considerable debate as to what constitutes a tense/aspect marker, and what their precise semantic values are. One problem is that it is almost certainly inappropriate to try and describe the conceptual framework of the creole verb in terms of Western European languages, and that it owes more to pre-creole origins. Yet having said that, the strategy used to simplify the verb-system is remarkably like the use of auxiliaries in the Romance languages, especially modern Spanish, where it can similarly be argued that the conceptual framework behind the verb-system is changing as a result of new morphological possibilities (Lorenzo 1980: 127–42). A tabular comparison is given in Table 9.2.

Most of the tense/aspect markers can easily be derived from Spanish or Portuguese verbs or adverbs. *Ta* is from Sp./Pg. *está*, *a* < *ha*, *taba* < *estaba* n *estava*. Pal. *tan* is probably from the Palenquero verb *tando* 'to go', which in turn perhaps derives from Sp. *estando*; Pal. *ase* has been associated with Sp. *hacer*. Pap. *lo* is from Pg. *logo* (= Sp. *luego*) and Cha. *ya* from Sp. *ya*; the etymology of Cha. *ay* is, however, unknown.

All three creoles make use of the Spanish gerund form in *-ndo* and the past participle in *-do*. The gerund is used with the imperfective aspect marker to create a verb form that closely resembles the Spanish progressive expressed by *estar* + *-ndo*, both formally and semantically; literary Papiamentu also uses the gerund to constitute a manner adverbial clause, as in Spanish:

Table 9.2 The tense-aspect systems of the Spanish creoles

Papiamentu		Palenquero[4]		Chabacano	
lo (…) V[1]	posteriority; probability	tan V	future; intention	ay or de V	future / contingent
(bai V)[3]		(bae V)[3]	future		
		tan-ba or tamba V	irrealis (future in the past)		
		aké or á-ké V	future (subjunctive); conditional (hypothetical)		
		aké-ba V	conditional (counterfactual)		
ta / zero V or ta V-ndo	simultaneity	ta V or ta V-ndo	progressive	ta V	present / progressive
a V[2]	perfective anteriority	á V[2]	completive	ya V[2]	past / perfective
		asé or á sé V	habitual		
(sa V)[3]	repeated or habitual	(sabé V)[3]	habitual		
tabata~tawata V	imperfect anteriority / past habitual	ta-ba V or ta V-ba	progressive + anterior		
zero	restriction of assertion (subjunctive)	zero			
		asé-ba V, asé V-ba or sabé V-ba	habitual + anterior		

[1] *Lo* may precede *no* or a pronominal subject.

[2] There is no distinction between 'present perfectivity' (Sp. *he visto*) and 'punctual past' (Sp. *vi*). The value of *á* is difficult to establish, since it is also used with verbs in a clearly present-referring sense: it has been proposed (Bickerton & Escalante 1970: 285) that it is a reduced form of *ta* in this usage.

[3] Usually regarded as an auxiliary.

[4] There has been considerable discussion over the composition of the Palenquero tense/aspect markers, especially with regard to the independence of *á*. *Ké* is difficult to disentangle from the complementiser *ke*, though Schwegler (1998) is convinced of its independence as a tense/aspect marker. *Ba* resembles the imperfect inflection of Spanish *-ar* verbs and is always postposed to a verb or another of the tense/aspect markers (which derive from verbs), and so is unlike the other markers.

(9.8) *Kanando lihé nos por yega na tempu* (Maurer 1998: 169)
walking light 1pl be-able arrive in time
'By walking quickly we can arrive in time'

The past participle of Papiamentu is formed in two ways, generally according to the ety-mology of the verb concerned, which suggests a purely lexical origin: in verbs deriving from Spanish, there is a shift in stress to the final syllable, thus *morde* (verb), *mordé* (participle), and in verbs deriving from Dutch, the prefix *(h)e-* or *(d)i-* (< Du. *ge-*) is used, e.g. *wèlder* 'solder', *hewèlder* 'soldered'. The past participle is also used in Papiamentu to form a passive construction, a rather remarkable development in a creole language. The existence of a pas-sive construction in Papiamentu at first sight suggests a marked convergence with Spanish, although the source of the construction is almost certainly Dutch, where it is much more frequent in informal registers. It is formed from the invariable verbs *wordu* (< Du. *worden*) or *ser* (< Sp. *ser*) used in apparently free variation (*ser* is not otherwise used in Papiamentu, the verb 'to be' being *ta*: there is no *ser/estar* contrast); the agentive phrase is introduced by the complex preposition *dor di* (a combination of *dor* < Du. *door* and *di* < Sp. *de*) or *pa* (a preposition which has several other functions, roughly corresponding to Sp. *por* and *para*).

9.4.2.2.3 Suffixation

In Papiamentu, there is also evidence of inflectional elements in borrowed words becoming productive in the formation of neologisms. The nominal suffixes *-mentu* (< Sp. *-miento*), which forms a noun from a verb, and the agentive suffix *-dó* (< Sp. *-dor*) are very productive, to the extent that they are used in the formation of derivatives which have no parallel in Spanish as well as with borrowed Dutch lexical stems. From *dal* 'to hit' < Sp. *dar* is formed *dalmentu* 'collision' and from *papia* 'to speak' *papiadó* 'speaker' (another coining from this stem is of course *papiamentu* 'conversation; the Papiamentu language'); from *fèrf* 'to paint' < Du. *verven* come *fèrfmentu* 'act of painting', *fèrfdó* 'house-painter'. Similarly, the occupa-tion suffix *-ero* (< Sp. *-ero/a*) and the establishment suffix *-eria* (< Sp. *-ería*) yield such for-mations as *shapero* 'bartender' (*shap* < Eng. *shop*) and *bukeria* 'bookshop' (*buk* < Du. *boek*). The adverbial suffix *-mente* has also been introduced, a feature which is generally absent from Chabacano except in patent borrowings, and apparently is totally absent in Palenquero. It does not therefore seem extravagant to speak of some convergence between Papiamentu and Spanish in such use of inflectional morphology, in the first place as a result of extensive lexical borrowing, followed by analogical creation.

9.4.2.2.4 Personal pronouns

The creole personal pronoun systems differ a good deal, the main forms being given in Table 9.3.

The first thing to notice about the creole personal pronouns is the relatively high inci-dence of pre-creole forms: Pap. *nan*, Pal. *enu* and *ané*, which are of African ancestry, and the plural forms of Chabacano, which are entirely Visayan. These systems look different from Spanish, and yet the distinctions they make are not particularly unusual in Romance per-sonal pronouns, even within the history and varieties of Spanish itself. The distinction of an

Table 9.3 The personal pronoun systems of the Spanish creoles

	Papiamentu	Palenquero	Chabacano[1]
1sg.	*mi / ami* (emphatic)	*yo* (clitic) / *i~y~yo* (free)	*yo* (subject) / *conmigo* (**'oblique'**, i.e., general object function)
2sg.	*bo / abo* (emphatic)	Familiar:*bo* (clitic) / *bo~o* (free) Polite: *uté~te*	*tú~vos* (subject) / *contigo~con vos* (oblique)[2]
3sg.	*e~el*	Specific: *ele~eli* (clitic) / *ele~el'~e* (free) General: *hende* (free)	*ele* (subject) / *con ele* (oblique)
1pl.	*nos*	Exclusive: *suto~uto* Inclusive: *ma hende~ende*	Exclusive: *kamí* (subject) / *kanamon* (oblique) Inclusive: *kitá* (subject) / *kanaton* (oblique)
2pl.	*boso~bosonan~bosnan*	*utere~utée* *enu* (archaic)	*kamó* (subject) / *kaniño* (oblique)
3pl.	*nan*	*ele~eli* *ané* (distinctively plural) *enu* (archaic)	*silá* (subject) / *kanila* (oblique)

[1] The plural forms given here are 'low' Chabacano; the 'high' variety uses Spanish forms (even *vosotros*).

[2] Apparently used in free variation with no distinction of formality.

'emphatic' pronoun in Papiamentu resembles the Romance distinction between tonic and atonic forms, e.g. Sp. *me* and *mí*, though it is not identical, since the emphatic forms of Papiamentu can be used in subject or object function and the non-emphatic forms are not clitic (a property which, however, does find some parallel in Palenquero). The distinction between inclusive and exclusive 1st person plural was probably the basis of the late medieval difference between *nos* and *nosotros* in Spanish (compare *nous* and *nous autres* in modern French), though it is implausible that this stage of Spanish had any direct influence on the creoles. The lack of formality distinctions is unsurprising in what must have been predominantly domestic languages (the same phenomenon has been noted in some varieties of Spanish in the US), and the adoption of a derivative of Sp. *vos* as a singular is in line with the extensive phenomenon of *voseo* in Latin America (see **6.2.4.2.3**). Although Chabacano is here represented (following Whinnom 1956: 88) as having **case** distinctions (i.e. distinctive inflected forms of a noun which correlate with such functions as 'subject of', 'direct object of', 'indirect object of'), the appropriateness of this depends on how these forms are construed and whether *kon-* is viewed as an inflectional part of the pronoun or as an independent preposition (McKaughan 1954: 205 proposed a third set of possessive case pronouns consisting of such forms as *dimio*, etc.). *Kon-* must in any case be thought of as an oblique marker with nouns:

(9.9) *Ya cucí con ele* (Whinnom 1956: 88)
PERF cook OBL 3sg
'He cooked it'

(9.10) *Cosa ba ta pasa con el mana mujer de ahora?* (Agustín Atilano, cit
Saavedra 1999)
What QU IMP happen OBL the PL woman of now
'What's happened to modern women?'

But even if we accept that Chabacano has case distinctions, we might bear in mind that the personal pronoun systems of all the Romance languages make distinctions of case which have otherwise been almost universally abandoned.

9.4.2.2.5 Demonstratives

Spanish (and Portuguese) differ from a number of other Romance languages in having a three-term demonstrative system (Sp. *este / ese / aquel*), and it might be assumed that this was an area ripe for simplification in the creoles. There is some sign that this is the case in Palenquero and Chabacano, where there is a marked tendency towards a two-way opposition between *ese* (common to both) and Pal. *aké*, Cha. *aquel*. Papiamentu has a three-term system, however, created in a very different way from the postnominal adverbs of place deriving from Sp. *aquí*, *ahí* and *allá* respectively: thus *e kas akí / e kas ei / e kas ayá*.

9.4.2.2.6 The articles

Although the category of article is familiar to speakers of most Western European languages, articles are by no means a universal category in the languages of the world – Latin, for example, is an example of a language which had no articles. We might expect therefore that creoles resisted the use of articles as well; but in fact the use of the definite and indefinite articles is fairly closely paralleled, Palenquero being the only one of the three which appears not to have a definite article as such at all:

Table 9.4 The articles in the Spanish creoles

	Papiamentu		Palenquero		Chabacano	
	def.	indef.	def.	indef.	def.	indef.
sg	*e* N	*un* N	zero	*un*	*el / si*[1]	*un*
pl.	*e* N *nan*	zero (N *nan*)	*ma*	*un ma*	*el*	zero

[1] Used with proper names; not a Spanish-derived form.

Superficially, other creoles give the impression of not using the articles as much as Spanish. One specific constraint on the use of the definite article in Papiamentu that contributes to this impression is that the article is not used with nouns used in a generic sense:

> **(9.11)** *E ta drumí abou ta wak strea* (Kouwenberg & Murray 1994: 184)
> 3sg IMP sleep below IMP look-at star
> 'He lay on the ground looking at the stars'

9.4.2.3 SYNTAX

9.4.2.3.1 Word order and basic constituent functions

Papiamentu and Palenquero appear to follow the pattern Subject-Verb-Object (SVO) without the Spanish possibility of verb-first order (see **4.4.3**). Another important difference from Spanish is that the subject is always expressed (hence, unlike Spanish, creoles are not pro-drop languages). Chabacano, similarly, is not a pro-drop language, but is unusual among creoles in having verb-first order as an alternative to SVO, verb-first order being especially favoured with personal pronoun subjects:

> **(9.12)** *Ya lyama el rey kon el kuray* (McKaughan 1954: 217)
> PAST call the king OBL the crab
> 'The king called the crab'

In Papiamentu and Palenquero, direct and indirect objects are not marked prepositionally but are distinguished by the strict ordering of the indirect object before the direct object:

> **(9.13)** *Maria a duna Margarita un buki* (Maurer 1998: 171)
> M. PERF give M. a book
> 'María gave Margarita a book'

Chabacano appears not to have such a strict constituent order rule, but, as we have seen, uses the preposition *kon* to make a number of oblique functions, which include direct and indirect object. The circumstances under which *kon* is used are not totally clear, however: it seems to differentiate function within the sequence of nouns which is often producd by verb-first word order:

> **(9.14)** *ya mira silá kon un pono de saging* (McKaughan 1954: 208)
> PAST see 3pl OBL a plant of banana
> 'They saw a banana plant'

> **(9.15)** *ya tira ele todo mana pelyeho kon kabáw* (McKaughan 1954: 209)
> PAST throw 3sg all PL peeling OBL monkey
> 'He threw all the peelings to the monkey'

Papiamentu permits the left-dislocation of one constituent to bring it into focus, e.g.:

> **(9.16)** *(Ta) mi brel so bo por wak un tiki* (Kouwenberg & Murray 1994: 36)
> (be/focus) 1sg glasses only 2sg can see a little
> 'It's only my glasses you can see a little'

This construction resembles, but is not the same as, two constructions in Spanish. It is like the cleft construction (*Son sólo mis gafas que puedes ver un poco*, see **4.4.3**) except that there is no relativiser corresponding to *que*, and the 'focus marker' *ta*, which is formally identical with the verb 'to be', is, unlike Spanish *son*, optional. Without *ta*, (9.16) is like the Spanish *Mis gafas las puedes ver un poco*, where the direct object is moved to the left of the verb in a similar way to achieve focus; but in Spanish the resumptive pronoun *las* (see **4.4.3**) is normally needed. In Papiamentu, a resumptive pronoun is only used when the focused element is part of a prepositional phrase, and even there it is probably optional (Kouwenberg & Murray 1994: 37):

> **(9.17)** *(Ta) ku Wito ela papia (kuné) awe* (Kouwenberg & Murray 1994: 37)
> (be/focus) with Wito 3sg+PERF talk (with+3sg) today
> 'It's to Wito that he spoke today'

An interesting possibility in Papiamentu is that a single verb can be focused in the same way, an option which is not available, at least not in the same way, in Spanish. Thus in

> **(9.18)** *(Ta) pòst mi no a pòst e karta* (Kouwenberg & Murray 1994: 36)
> (be/focus) mail 1sg not PERF mail the letter
> 'It's just that I hadn't mailed the letter)

the verb is obligatorily repeated. The nearest formal parallel in Spanish

> **(9.19)** *Enviar la carta es lo que no hice*
> 'What I didn't do was mail the letter'

as well as being different in syntax (in particular, the verb slot in the main clause is filled by the 'pro-verb' *hacer*), does not have the same meaning, as can be seen from the English gloss.

9.4.2.3.2 Questions

Questions in Papiamentu and Palenquero simply involve a different intonation, which is also one of the possibilities in standard spoken Spanish (see **2.7** and **4.4.1**). Even when an interrogative element is used, the basic Subject-Verb-Object word order does not change apart from the left-dislocation of the interrogative element itself, which is markedly different from the usual order in standard Spanish, though it is a feature of some Caribbean Spanish varieties (Lipski 1994: 60):

> **(9.20)** Pap. *Ki dia bo ta kere bo ta haya bo outo bèk?* (Kouwenberg & Murray 1994: 36)
> which day 2sg IMP believe 2sg IMP get 2sg car back
> 'When do you think you are getting your car back?'

> **(9.21)** Pal. *¿Ké enú ta asé?* (Friedemann & Patiño Rosselli 1983: 169)
> what 2pl IMP do
> 'What are you doing?'

In Chabacano, on the other hand, a question marker *ba* (from Tagalog) is used to signal a question, and can be optionally used even when an interrogative element is present; word order is variable as in delarative sentences:

> **(9.22) a.** *Ya mirá ba vos con ele?*
> PERF see QU 2sg OBL 3sg
> 'Have you seen him/her?'
> **b.** *Dónde (ba) vos ya andá?*
> where (QU) 2sg PERF go
> 'Where did you go?

9.4.2.3.3 Negation

Negation in Papiamentu and Chabacano is like that of Spanish in that a negative particle precedes the verbal group. In Papiamentu, the particle is *no* postvocalically and *un* postconsonantally; in Chabacano it is *no* or *hende'* (the latter from Tagalog *hindi*). Palenquero is conspicuously different in having three possibilities: the particle *nu* is placed at the end of the sentence (regarded as the unmarked, 'native' variant); *nu* is placed before the verbal group (possibly as the result of Spanish influence), or a double negative is used for emphasis, a construction which is particularly associated with imperatives:

> **(9.23)** *nu nda Purita ndulo nu* (Friedemann & Patiño Rosselli 1983: 172)
> NEG hit P. hard NEG
> 'Don't hit Purita hard'

9.4.2.3.4 Reflexive

The creoles do not have a distinctive reflexive personal pronoun corresponding to Spanish *se*. There is nothing like the passive, indefinite subject or 'nuance' uses of the Spanish reflexive (see **5.4.1**), and even some verbs which are literally reflexive in Spanish, e.g. *bañarse*, are not reflexive in the creoles even though they are reflexive in meaning – this reduction in redundant morphological marking may be compared with English 'intransitives' with reflexive meaning (cf. Eng. *bath, wash*, see **4.3.6**). The literal reflexive in Papiamentu is expressed analytically, either by the use of *mes* < Sp./Pg. *mismo/mesmo* with the personal pronoun, or by the personal pronoun, presumably used as a possessive, followed by *kurpa* 'body' < Sp./Pg. *cuerpo/corpo*; the reciprocal can be expressed by *outo* (< Sp./Pg. *o(u)tro*). Palenquero also uses *memo*, but examples of the literal reflexive often seem to code-switch to Spanish syntax:

> **(9.24)** *Si bo no me paga, yo me pago yo memo* (Friedemann & Patiño Rosselli 1983: 226)
> 'If you don't pay me, I'll pay myself'
> (Note the Spanish inflected verb forms, the form and position of the pronoun *me*, and the close correspondence to normal Spanish word order.)

9.4.2.3.5 Complex sentences

The creoles make no distinction between either finite verb and infinitive or indicative and subjunctive mood, and so although complementation patterns are generally modelled on

Spanish, they cannot always be described in the same terms. Creoles are able to make some temporal and modal distinctions through the use of verbal particles. The use of the particles *(a)ke* and *(a)keba* in Palenquero are especially striking in this regard and are used in future-referring time clauses and conditional sentences where Spanish would use the subjunctive or conditional:

> **(9.25)** *kuando Juan ké miní, Juan tan nda bo ata po jopo* (Friedemann &
> Patiño Rosselli 1983: 180)
> when J. KE come, J. FUT hit 2sg even round backside
> 'When Juan comes, he'll kick your ass'

> **(9.26)** *si Ana nu keba rregañalo, ané á keba aséloba* (Friedemann & Patiño
> Rosselli 1983: 181)
> if Ana NEG KE+BA scold+3sg, 3pl PERF KE+BA do+3sg+BA
> 'If Ana hadn't told them off, they would have done it'

The equivalent of a Spanish subjunctive is often expressed in Papiamentu by *pa*:

> **(9.27)** *Mi no kier pa hopi tempo mester pasa promé ku bo haya mi karta*
> (Kouwenberg & Murray 1994: 46)
> 1sg not want for much time must pass before that 2sg have my letter
> 'I don't want too much time to go by before you get my letter'

But relations between clauses are often not signalled very explicitly, as this example from Chabacano shows:

> **(9.28)** *si no sabe el hente kosa ay ase, ay mata le kon ese hente para saka*
> *su lugar y pwede ya le deskansa* (McKaughan 1954: 213)
> if NEG know the person thing FUT do, FUT kill 3sg OBL that person to
> take 3POSS place and be-able now 3sg rest
> 'If that person did not understand what he would do, he would kill
> that person in order that he might take his place and he could rest'

A very common pattern is for there to be no complementiser at all. There is extensive use in the creoles of what is known as a **serial verb** construction, which is a series of verbs denoting a related sequence of events or where the second verb qualifies the first, for example, by specifying the manner in which the first action is done.

> **(9.29)** *Tur mainta e tabata lanta traha kòfi, drecha mes, herebé webu, pone*
> *tur kos kla* (Maurer 1998: 170)
> all morning 3sg IMP get-up prepare coffee, lay table, boil egg, put all
> thing ready
> 'Each morning she would get up, prepare the coffee, lay the table,
> boil an egg and leave everything ready.'

> **(9.30)** *Ela kore bai su kas* (Kouwenberg & Murray 1994: 47)
> 3sg run go 3POSS house
> 'She ran home'

9.4.2.4 OTHER FEATURES

9.4.2.4.1 Copulas

The Spanish distinction between *ser* and *estar*, together with the existential verb *haber*, might seem to be a natural area of simplification in the creoles, and indeed Papiamentu uses *ta* exclusively as the copula. Palenquero, on the other hand, distinguishes *ta* and *se* very much along the lines of Spanish, and has even developed another copular verb, *sendá* (< Sp. *sentar(se)*):

> **(9.31)** *é monasita á ten ke sendá mu bonita* (Friedemann & Patiño Rosselli
> 1983: 132)
> DEM little-girl A must Ø be very pretty
> 'That little girl must be very pretty'

In Chabacano, the copula is regularly omitted, though *estar* survives, as everywhere, as the tense/aspect marker *ta*:

> **(9.32)** *Rabyaw gayót si komachíng* (McKaughan 1954: 209)
> angry very the monkey
> 'The monkey was very angry'

The existential notion is expressed by a derivative of the verb *tener* (Pap. *tin*, Pal. *tené*, Cha. *tiene*), e.g. (Palenquero):

> **(9.33)** *á tené un ma aló ke á se parí mucho akí* (Friedemann & Patiño Rosselli
> 1983: 129)
> A there-is a PL ricefield REL A SE produce much here
> 'There are some ricefields which produce a lot here.'

9.4.3 A written creole text

TEXT U

ORANJESTAD - Ayera tardi a tuma lugar e ceremonia di ponemento di prome piedra di e infraestructura of edificio nobo caminda lo wordo ubicá e ultimo adquisicion cu directiva di Horacio Oduber Hospital a haci, esta e aparato masha sofisticá di Magnetic Resonance Imaging (MRI).   5

E acto aki a wordo hací dor di sra. Marcia Bremo-Euton, kende pronto lo bai goza di su pension bon merecí. E tin 19 aña den servicio di Hospital y actualmente sra. Bremo ta ocupá e funcion di Hefe di Administracion di e departamento di Radiologia. Cu e gesto aki directiva di Hospital no solamente kier demostrá su gratitud y aprecio   10 pa e trabaonan cu sra. Bremo a cumpli cu nan cabalmente y na un manera ehemplar, pero tambe kier mustra su reconocimento na tur e empleadonan di e departamento di Radiologia pa nan aporte di calidad halto pa e cuido medico di nos hospital.

Bon Dia Aruba, 12.3.01

This passage exhibits many of the grammatical features of creoles we have identified above: the tense/aspect system, absence of gender, marking of number by *nan*, identity of personal pronouns and possessives, etc. However, this newspaper article shows very clearly the impact of the 'decreolisation' of Papiamentu. It contains a very large number of high register, typically abstract, words which have been borrowed directly from Spanish: *ceremonia, infraestructura, edificio, adquisicion, aparato, sofisticá, acto, pension, mercí, servicio, funcion, departamento, gratitud, aprecio, ehemplar, reconocimiento, empleado, Radiologia, calidad, medico, hospital.* There is also an example of an apparently independent derivation (*ponemento*: although *ponimiento* does exist in standard Spanish, it is restricted to technical registers, and in this context *colocación* would be the normal usage). This shows that Papiamentu is developing a facility for neologistic creations using the same inflectional suffixal means as Spanish (see Chapter 3), which is unusual for a creole. It has even borrowed some 'long' adverbs in *-mente* (*actualmente, solamente* and the 'learned' *cabalmente*), which are thought of as pertaining to formal register even in mainstream Spanish (see 7.1). There is inversion of subject and verb which is typical of Spanish but not of Papiamentu (*a tuma lugar e ceremonia*, l.1) and two passive sentences (*lo wordo ubicá*, ll.2–3, *e acto aki a wordo hací dor di sra ...*, l.6).

9.5 Code-switching

In simple terms, **code-switching** occurs when a speaker moves within discourse from one language to another.

9.5.1 *Spanglish*: Spanish – English code-switching in the US

Within the Spanish-speaking world, the phenomenon has been most extensively reported and studied in the United States, where switching between Spanish and English is extremely common among the Hispanic population. The following is an example of a natural conversation:

TEXT V

... yo voy comer allí poquito, y yo voy comer allá poquito so I can ... so
they can be happy. When we come here from California, we ... I ... eat
beans over here and chiles – same thing like back home pero porque
tienen papitas con chiles, papas – potatoes with chile and all that –
they think we don't like it because it's [fixed] that way. But I eat the   5
same thing over here because we like them that way. I don't like ... no
quiero venir a comer dicen, porque ... porque son papas con chiles, y no!
No! I eat that at home pero se les hace porque you just don't feel like

[eating] the food. They get mad, you know … you have to eat no matter
where, everywhere you go – just a little bit so they'll be satisfied.   10

Leonora Timm, 'Spanish-English code-switching: el porque and how not to' in
Romance Philology, 28, 1975, p. 482.

Code-switching has to be seen in the context of what is quite often an extremely complex
linguistic situation: Elías-Olivares (1979) describes the language of speakers in Austin,
Texas, as ranging over the following possibilities:

- Standard (Mexican) Spanish.
- Popular Spanish, which is characterised by phonological changes and morphological regularisations.
- *Español mixtureado* (*pocho, Tex-Mex*), which contains many English loanwords and loan translations of English syntactic patterns and idioms. It is characteristic of children who have not developed full competence in English, and appears to be actively cultivated by young people who are trying to shock. It is stigmatised by older speakers.
- *Caló* (*pachuco*), which is perhaps best described as a slang (see **7.1.3**). It is used especially by delinquent male adolescent groups. The origins of *caló* are in Spanish underworld slang, or *germanía*, and it has developed partly for cryptolectic purposes (i.e., to conceal meaning from those not familiar with it) and partly as a badge of group-membership (see Coltharp 1965).[3]
- Chicano English.
- Standard (American) English.

All of these must be set against a background of knowledge of English and high degree of
bilingualism. It is not always easy in practice to distinguish code-switching from borrowing.
The Spanish of speakers who are in close contact with another language will inevitably
include many borrowings at various degrees of assimilation. However, we would expect that
the hallmark of a borrowing would be that it shows some phonetic or morphological adaptation to the host language. For example, the word *chainear* 'to shine' is a widespread borrowing in US Spanish. Despite the obvious English origin, it shows the phonological
adaptation of English [ʃ] to Spanish [tʃ] and has all the morphological characteristics of a
regular Spanish *-ar* verb. On the other hand, in the sentence *El cabrón se puso jealous* (Pfaff
1979: 305), the adjective *jealous* shows no accommodation to Spanish and can be regarded
as a code-switch. However, not every case is as clearcut as these. Pfaff (1979: 296) distinguishes two kinds of borrowing: **integrated borrowings** of the *chainear* kind, and **spontaneous borrowings**, which show no integration into the system of the host language, but take
place within an exclusively Spanish discourse, e.g. *bussing* and *re-enlist* in the sequence *Los*

[3] *Caló* as applied to such jargons of the American South West is not to be confused with the same term used in a Peninsular context to denote the language of the Spanish gypsies, which contains many borrowings from Romany. Both have a cryptolectic purpose, and Spanish *caló*, perhaps unjustifiably, came to be associated with underworld slang (more properly *germanía*): hence the application of the same term to Southwest *caló*.

están bussing pa otra escuela – Va a re-enlist. Spontaneous borrowings typically occur where there is not a convenient Spanish term for the notion in question.

Another question concerning code-switching is whether it is appropriate to see one language or the other as somehow 'basic', with the other language simply exploited from time to time to fill structural gaps. This is extremely difficult to judge; but since typically it will seem that different sentences adopt different languages as 'basic' (probably according to the social factors described below), it is now generally agreed that code-switching is genuinely an oscillation between two languages in which the two languages have equal status. Thus code-switching between Spanish and English is not just Spanish with English words or English with Spanish words but is essentially a composite, a form of language which is different from either Spanish or English, though based on them both. This brings us on to another important point. Because code-switching strikes native speakers of the corresponding standard languages as neither one language nor the other, and because there are no immediate principles discernible for when code-switching takes place, it is tempting to think that such styles of communication are the consequence of insufficient familiarity on the part of speakers with either of the standard languages. Code-switching is often referred to and labelled in derogatory and undiscriminating terms: 'Tex-Mex', 'Spanglish', etc. However, a great deal of research has now shown that this impression is inaccurate: code-switchers are often the most competent speakers of standard languages (Poplack 1980: 615, Zentella 1982: 47) and code-switching constitutes a linguistic expressiveness of an interestingly different order from that available to a monolingual speaker.

Code-switching may be approached from both a linguistic and a social point of view. Linguistically, we may ask if a switch can take place at any point in the discourse or whether certain syntactic elements are more prone to code-switching than others. Sankoff & Poplack (1981: 5) proposed two contraints on code-switching. The **free morpheme constraint** states that a switch may not occur between a bound morpheme and a lexical form unless the latter has been phonologically integrated into the language of the bound morpheme. So **runeando* is ill-formed, since no verb **runear* has been borrowed into Spanish and would therefore involve an unacceptable code-switch between Eng. *run* and Sp. *-eando* (by 'Spanish' we of course mean the Spanish of US Spanish speakers, not the standard language), while *flipeando* is acceptable since *flipear* is a borrowed form which has been fully integrated into Spanish. The **equivalence constraint** states that the order of the elements immediately before and after a switch point must be grammatical in both languages. A good example of this is the constraints often observed on switching between noun and adjective within a noun phrase. Here a switch can only take place if the same order of noun and adjective obtains in both languages, i.e. only adjective-noun order is possible (since that is the only order acceptable in English) and this must be the natural order in Spanish (typically involving determining adjectives). So (Pfaff 1979) *el siguiente play* is acceptable because both *la siguiente comedia* in Spanish and *the following play* in English are acceptable, but we would expect that, for example, **la pared red* and **el rojo wall* are not, since **the wall red* is not acceptable in English and **la roja pared* is not acceptable under normal circumstancs in Spanish. But although it is possible to state in this way when switches will not happen, it is not so easy to say when they will. Poplack (1980) established the following frequency hierarchy for intra-sentential switches, which shows that the majority of switches involve nouns or noun phrases:

Table 9.5 Poplack's (1980: 602–3) frequency hierarchy for intra-sentential code-switches between Spanish and English

Single nouns	9.5%
Noun phrases	13.4%
Single adj	0.8%
Clauses	8.4%
Phrases (prepositional, adjectival, adverbial and infinitival)	5.1%
Single adverbs	2.6%
Single verbs	1%
Verb phrases	2.2%
Conjunctions (coordinating, subordinating and relative pronoun)	2.7%
Auxiliary, preposition, determiner	0.3%

(Intra-sentential switches account for 46% of the total number of switches: switches of complete sentences, interjections, etc., are more frequent.)

What this hierarchy suggests is that switches are most resisted by the deictic parts of speech (determiners and prepositions) and by the more grammatically significant elements (conjunctions). They are most favoured by nouns and noun phrases; this should not surprise us in that nouns are the most 'borrowable' of linguistic elements and therefore no doubt the category most readily replaced.

Looking at code-switching from the social or psychological point of view suggests that it is not random but reflects attitude and context of use. Fishman *et al.* (1971), describing the code-switching of Puerto Ricans in New Jersey, showed that Spanish was used for topics pertaining to the home or community while English was used for topics concerning work, education or other institutions. Gumperz & Hernández Chávez (1975) associated Spanish with personal or affective orientation and English with a more objective or impersonal orientation. It must be said, however, that it is extremely difficult to set up experiments to test such hypotheses rigorously.

An interesting question regarding code-switching is whether it will provide the basis for a new, consistent language variety which will eventually itself form the basis of a standard, or whether it will remain the exclusive preserve of competent bilinguals, who through code-switching achieve enhanced expressive possibilities. It is likely that the answer to this will depend on such factors as education (with the consequent pressures to adopt standard forms of Spanish and Portuguese, even if speakers retain a degree of bilingualism) and sense of community identity (which would tend to produce a more individual style of speech as a badge of the community). The latter is a distinct possibility amongst some Hispanic communities of the US, as the following quotation from a recent Hispanic author shows:

> "See, it's alive," he said, and right that minute, at a window next door to us, a woman yelled to her son down on the street. "*Mira*, Juanito, go buy *un mapo, un contén de leche*, and tell *el bodeguero yo le pago* next Friday. And I don't want to see you in *el rufo*!"
> We both laughed.
> "You know what is happening here, don't you? Don't you? What we just heard was a poem, Chino. It's a beautiful new language. Don't you see what's happening? A new language means a new race. Spanglish is the future. It's a new language being born out of the ashes of two cultures clashing with each other. You will use a new language. Words they might not teach you in that college. Words that aren't English or Spanish but at the same time are both. Now that's where it's at. Our people are evolving into something completely new."

> (Ernesto Quiñonez, *Bodega Dreams* (New York: Vintage Contemporaries, 2000), p.212)

9.5.2 *Fronteiriço*: Spanish – Portuguese code-switching in Uruguay

The Banda Oriental of the River Plate was territory long disputed between Spain and Portugal, a situation which ended only in 1825 with the creation of the state of Uruguay. The new country was home to large numbers of Portuguese-speaking settlers, who were not discouraged even after independence; it is estimated that in the mid-19th century 40 per cent of the population was Brazilian in origin. A series of frontier towns was established in the north, where Portuguese continued to be the language most frequently used, Spanish beginning to make an impact only in the 20th century with the introduction of primary education in Spanish and the development of communications with the rest of the country. The linguistic consequence of this has been that in the northern frontier zones a language which impressionistically consists of a mixture of Portuguese and Spanish is spoken. The following text, taken from Elizaincín (1992: 151–2), the story of Little Red Riding Hood as told by a little girl in Artigas, illustrates this phenomenon. *Ch* represents [ʃ]; *o* and *e* represent the open vowels [ɔ] and [ɛ] respectively. Forms which are clearly identifiable as Spanish are shown in bold while those clearly identifable as Portuguese are shown in italics; other material is attributable to either language.

TEXT W

Que *ela saiú, foi lá na* casa *da avó* y *veiu* y... y... **taba** sacando
flor*sinha*, **y** *u* lobo *veiu* **y preguntó** si *ela* non quiría, este... *corré a*
carrera, **y ela** decí que sí. **Preguntó** por qué cami... **camino** ela ía y *u*
lobo **dice** que... era... era... *aquele*, **y** *ele* por este *chegó na* casa *da*

> *avó*, y *batió* la *porta* y **mandó que entrase** y... y comió *a* **abuelita**, y   5
> *depós* a Caperucita *chegó* **y preguntó** "que *oreia* tan grande esa,
> **abuela**", y **después** "qué *oio* tan grande, **abuela**", y *ela respondeu*
> *"Eu so ansí"*, y... y a Caperucita **fue** y **alcanzó canasto** con **cosa** que
> *a... a mae dela tinha mandado*, y... y *eli depoi coméu* a Caperucita.
> Vinierun lenador **y cortaron** *a* barriga *du lobo*, y... *cheó* *a* barriga   10
> *deli* de *pedra*, y *eli caiú* dentro *duma* **cachimba**.
>
> (Adolfo Elizaincín, *Dialectos en contacto: español y portugués en España y América*
> (Montevideo: Arca, 1992) pp. 151–2

Spanish and Portuguese are much more closely related than Spanish and English, and, as can be seen from the portions of text in ordinary Roman type, it is much less clear when a switch from one language to the other has taken place. Moreover, although for the most part switching is between individual words and phrases, the free morpheme constraint is not observed, and a single word can show features of both languages: *chegó* and *batió* have Portuguese lexical stems (the corresponding full Spanish forms would be *llegó* and *golpeó*) but Spanish inflections (*-ó* and *-ió* rather than Portuguese *-ou* and *-eu*). (The equivalence constraint is of course not so likely to be broken between Spanish and Portuguese.) There are also switches of a kind that, as we have seen, are not at all favoured in 'Spanglish': for example, that between Spanish determiner (the definite article) and Portuguese noun in the noun phrase *la porta*. Another rather striking feature of this language which makes it different in kind from the code-switching of 'Spanglish' is that there are also apparently independent creations which are neither one code nor the other: *lenador* corresponds to neither Sp. *leñador* nor Pg. *lenhador*. A more complex case of such creativity is the verb-form *cheó*, which appears to be a Portuguese lexical stem with a Spanish inflection; however, the corresponding Portuguese verb-form is *encheu*. *Cheó* therefore must have been modelled on the Spanish verb *llenó*, but with a lexical stem based on the Portuguese adjective *cheio*, which is cognate with Sp. *lleno*. The form *decí* is a curious preterite form which corresponds exactly neither to Spanish *dijo* nor Pg. *disse* (nor is it an instance of analogical levelling, which would probably have produced **dició* or **decó*). Yet the fact that the same word can assume a Spanish or a Portuguese form, e.g. *abuela-avó*, *comió-comeu*, suggests that this language does in part constitute a kind of code-switching.

On the other hand, it may be more appropriate to regard such forms as evidence of variability within *fronteiriço*. Such variability is attributable to the fact that it is not a written language and has no standardised form; its speakers are also increasingly bilingual, or at least diglossic, in *fronteiriço* and Spanish, which means that there is plenty of scope for interference from Spanish. The syntax of *gustar-gostar* reported by Elizaincín (1992: 133) is especially interesting in this regard. The standard syntax of Sp. *gustar* is that it takes a subject infinitive complement and a personal indirect object, with the infinitive following the verb, while the standard syntax of Pg. *gostar* is that it takes a personal subject and an infinitive complement introduced by *de*:

> **(9.34)** Sp. *Me gusta bailar*
> Pg. *(eu) gosto de bailar*

In *fronteiriço* we find the following types of construction:

> **(9.35)** **a.** *Eu gosto de bailar* (standard Portuguese)
> **b.** *Eu gosto bailar* (Portuguese with interference from Spanish)
> **c.** *Me gusta de bailar* (Spanish with interference from Portuguese)

It is certainly a possibility that *fronteiriço* is not a random amalgam of Portuguese and Spanish, nor an example of code-switching, but that it is an emergent language variety with an identity of its own.

EXERCISES

1. This chapter has raised (but not answered) the question of which of the languages described here can be thought of as varieties of 'Spanish'. What is your view?

2. Edmundo Farolán, a member of the Academia Filipina, has written as follows:

> Uno de los fundamentos u objetivos de la RAE es enaltecer el idioma castellano, y los académicos filipinos tenemos esa responsabilidad de difundir el enaltecimiento del castellano en Filipinas.
>
> Pero el problema que existe en Filipinas es que el idioma español ya no se habla y entonces es necesario buscar medios de acercarse al castellano. Uno de estos medios es el chabacano, uno de los dialectos filipinos que se aproxima al español más que los demás dialectos hablados en Filipinas.
>
> Este acercamiento a un dialecto que podríamos calificar de español "aguado" es quiza la mejor posibilidad si queremos llegar a ese objetivo tan deseado por los hispanistas filipinos, o sea, hacer el castellano un idioma vivo en Filipinas.
>
> La Guirnalda Polar: Neoclassic E-Press, 1997

What do you think of this suggestion?

3. The following is a list of words borrowed from English into US Spanish. Why are they more likely to be borrowings than code-switches? How have they been assimilated into the structure of Spanish? Do these borrowings clash with words already present in Spanish?

la baica/baika: bicycle
el bas: bus
el bonche: handful
cachar: to catch
la cora: quarter (25 cent coin)
cuitear: to quit
chaineado: to shine, polish
cherapearse: to be quiet
el daime: dime (10 cent coin)
el dompe: rubbish dump

dropearse: to drop out, leave
la ganga: gang
el jira: heater
liquearse: to leak
el lonche: lunch
loquear: to lock
el lóquer: locker
mapear: to mop
la naifa: knife
la norsa: nurse
la ploga: (electric) plug

pompar/pompear: to pump
puchar: to push
el quequi: pie
el raite: lift
el saine: sign
la suera: sweater, jersey
el tíquete: parking ticket
la troca: truck
el troque: truck
la yarda: yard (place)
el zíper: zip

10 | Towards the future

10.1 Linguistic forecasting

Traditionally, linguists have not been much given to speculating about the future. The two dimensions of linguistic enquiry which defined linguistics in the 20th century, the Saussurean axes of **synchrony** and **diachrony**, envisaged the object of the study of language as either its structure at a particular moment in time (synchrony) or the changes which have taken place over time (diachrony). There came to be a high premium set on the scientific nature of linguistic enquiry, demanding that linguistics was an observational science with a rigorous empirical basis, which at its strongest even rejected the possibility of any diachronic study which was not based on directly observable data.[1] These strict demarcations have now been eroded to a certain extent because of the growing realisation that language is not a monolithic or stable structure but is subject to extensive variation even on the part of a single native speaker; and, as suggested in Chapter 6, the study of synchronic variation is inseparable from that of diachronic evolution. But linguistic forecasting is still not on many linguists' agendas. Nevertheless, in this chapter, I will suggest some ways in which forecasting might take place and what the limitations on such forecasting might be. I think this is important, because while descriptive linguists may be coy about predicting the future, there is no shortage of predictions emanating from prescriptivists, who tend to view future language change pessimistically, as some kind of threat to the established order.

10.2 Internal forecasting

There are in principle two kinds of forecasting which might be undertaken. The first, which we might label 'internal' forecasting, is a natural extension of the existing programmes for linguistics. Under this heading we could envisage forecasting on the basis of observed synchronic structure and variation, moderated by what we know, or have hypothesised, about linguistic evolution.

10.2.1 Forecasting on the basis of structure

In 6.2.3.2.1–6.2.3.2.3, we observed the tendency to aspirate or suppress syllable-final /s/ in a number of Spanish varieties, and we pointed out a number of phonological and morpho-

---

[1] See, for example, Lass (1980).

logical consequences of this development. Let us imagine for a moment that this feature diffused to such an extent that the fall of syllable-final /s/ became universal. The kind of structural impact that we have identified for some areas of Andalusia (also paralleled in parts of Latin America) would then become generalised, different diatopic variants of Spanish adopting one of the current possibilities identified in **6.2.3.2.2** (Table 10.1).

Table 10.1 Possible phonemic consequences of the fall of syllable-final /s/

Possible development	Modern *los buenos*	Modern *lo bueno*
(a)	Opposition between °/ɔ/[2] and °/o/	[lɔ ˈβwɛnɔ]	[lo ˈβweno]
(b)	Opposition between, for example, °/ɸ/ and °/β/	[lɔ ˈɸwɛnɔ]	[lo ˈβweno]
(c)	Opposition between °/ββ/ and °/β/	[lɔβ ˈβwɛnɔ]	[lo ˈβweno]

At present, these developments do not seem very significant, because they can all be regularly related to a common standard pronunciation which in an important sense 'underlies' them all. But if the suppression of syllable-final /s/ were to extend to the standard too, then this /s/ would no longer have any such reality. It would pose a considerable problem for the standard spelling system, since, if the present system were retained, *s* in this environment would become a redundant letter in much the same way as the *h* of *hacer* is today. If, on the other hand, the spelling system were changed in order to accommodate the new phonological situation, only one of the variants (a)–(c) could be successfully represented, to the exclusion of the others (there would also be problems in choosing a means of representing /ɔ/ or /ɸ/ in the spelling). These considerations reveal that the complete loss of syllable-final /s/ could result in a substantial fragmentation of Spanish if all the current variants were to persist.

We also saw that the complete fall of final /s/ has had important morphological consequences in Andalusia, since -*s* is a marker of plurality in nouns and of second person singular in verbs. If plurality and person are not so obviously marked, other ways of signalling them might become more important: for example, the use of determiners (especially since the masculine plural definite article *lo(s)* is quite distinct from singular *el*) and increased use of the subject pronoun *tú*. Again, French offers an interesting comparison, since final /s/ has fallen in these environments with, some linguists would claim, exactly these consequences (see Harris 1978: 75). There has been a considerable debate on the synchronic evidence for this which suggests that such a forecast is unsafe, however: Hochberg (1986) found evidence for exactly this scenario in the Spanish of Puerto Rico, but Ranson (1991) found no supporting evidence in the speech of Puente Genil, Córdoba, Spain.

The kind of predictions we have just been making have been a series of 'if-then' hypotheses, saying that if a particular change does occur, then certain consequences may result. But we have said nothing about their statistical likelihood. This forecast is therefore much more

---

[2] ° is used to indicate a hypothesised form.

non-committal than a weather forecast which states that there is a 50% chance of rain the day after tomorrow. The problem is that far too many variables are involved, even by comparison with weather forecasting, for any more significantly quantified prediction to be possible. Some of these variables are linguistic. In some varieties of Spanish, for example, there is a strong tendency for final vowels, especially /e/ and /o/, to raise to [i] and [u]. It might be, then, that the singular/plural and second/third person oppositions would be able to be marked in the following way: *libro* °/libru/ vs. *libro(s)* °/libro/, *come* °/komi/ *comes* °/kome/, and this complementary tendency would mean that the expression of plurality and person would not need to be extended by the development of new vocalic oppositions or of geminate consonants in the way we have envisaged.

10.2.2 Forecasting on the basis of variation

Other variables involved in linguistic forecasting concern the diffusion of incipient changes among native speakers. For a change to be realised (or **actuated** – see Weinreich, Labov & Herzog 1968: 102), a variable must be adopted by a significant majority of the speech-community; for this to happen, the variable must be well enough regarded to be imitated, usually because it has become associated with the speech of a prestigious group of speakers – it is not enough simply for a particular structural situation of the kind we have examined in **10.2.1** to apply. The forecasting of who will achieve prestige, and how, is an impossibly nebulous task, however, and is nothing to do with language as such. It is worth pointing out in this connection that 'prestige' is not necessarily equatable with the prescriptive standard or the speech of the upper classes. Prestige can be, and probably more often is, use by an admired social group (e.g. a school peer group, friends or work colleagues) or role-model (in modern western society we might think of figures or groups made popular through the entertainment industry or the media). Although we know that weakening and dropping of /s/ is quite widespread in the Spanish-speaking world, it is more difficult to assess the future prestige of /s/-dropping speakers and the consequent pattern of diffusion of /s/-dropping to other speakers. However, sociolinguistic techniques do allow us to make some general predictions about such questions.

Sociolinguists have identified certain distributional profiles which are associated with variation that is stable, variation which reflects changes in progress and variation which characterises a nearly completed change. Stable variation shows a good correlation between the linguistic variable, social class and style. Indeed, in such a situation, the linguistic variable is a good indicator of social class and is said to stratify speakers. Typically the upper-class variant will be the prestige variant which is imitated by lower-class speakers when they use more formal style (e.g. reading aloud). Speakers have a clear attitude towards the variable and will often correct themselves in favour of the prestige variant; and there is often **hypercorrection** (that is, inappropriate use of the prestige variant) by lower-class speakers – a well-known example of hypercorrection in Spanish is the insertion of [ð] between /a/ and /o/ in hiatus, as in [baka'laðo] for [baka'lao] (*bacalao*) by speakers who normally omit the intervocalic [ð] in such a context]. A change which is beginning or in progress shows similar correlation between the linguistic variable and social class, though it is usually possible to identify a particular set of speakers (typically lower middle-class speakers below the age of 40) as the innovating group. In any case, there is evidence of some groups of speakers showing greater advances than others in the use of the innovating variant. There is not, however, the clear correlation between the linguistic variable and style which is associated with stable variation. A change which is almost complete shows speakers in all social classes 'catching up'; a typical situation is that all but older upper-class speakers have more or less completely adopted the innovating variant. Another characteristic of an almost completed change is that a particular group of speakers may use the innovating variant in formal style to a much greater extent than a higher social group; this shows clearly the prestige achieved by the innovating variant and the desire of speakers to be seen to be adopting it.

Such profiles would be extremely difficult to work out in detail for the whole of the Spanish-speaking world; the sociolinguistic studies which employ them have typically been community-based (see Silva-Corvalán 1989: 151–69). But on the basis of the above, we might, for example, predict that *yeísmo*, the absence of opposition between /ʎ/ and /j/, represents the future direction of Spanish in Spain. Not only is it an extremely widespread phenomenon in the rest of the Spanish-speaking world; it has diffused within Spain from Andalusia to Madrid, where it is now adopted in the speech of all classes. Its prestige rating is thus high, and it can only be a matter of time before the endpoint of this change is reached.

Of course, it is not inevitable that changes will affect the whole of the Spanish-speaking world. We have already seen (**6.2.4.2.5**) how different prestige values may attach to the same variable in different parts of Latin America, a fact which seems to indicate that a more universal prestige rating will be difficult to achieve. This is especially true when a feature becomes associated with a particular country or group so that it becomes a stereotype of that country, with its prestige further enhanced as a result of patriotic or nationalistic feeling. Argentine *voseo*, which is examined in **6.2.4.2.3**, is a case in point. It is extremely unlikely either that *tuteo* will ever achieve prestige in Argentina or that *voseo* will achieve prestige in Spain. The consequence is that such a change will remain local and that there will be two coexisting norms (Alonso 1964: 261).

10.3 External forecasting

In recent years there has been a great deal of interest in linguistic forecasting of a quite different kind, informed by economic and demographic forecasting. At first sight, this is nothing to do with the future of languages as such, but rather addresses such questions as the projected number of speakers of a language and the status of a language internationally. Although such investigations can be purely academic, they are also motivated by economic concerns, since on their findings depend such questions as which languages should be used in international organisations, which should be taught in schools or learned by business employees, what the demand for teaching as a second language is, and which are viable languages for use in publishing. These questions may lead on to others which are linguistically significant: recurrent themes with regard to Spanish are to what extent linguistic unity will be maintained, and what the impact of foreign borrowing on the language, especially from English, is likely to be. It is interesting to compare Spanish with English in such forecasting (as also with French and Portuguese), because superficially at least these languages share a number of features. They are diasporic languages (see **1.4**), widely spoken in the world as the result of the European countries in which they originated having been imperial powers, and as a result of this territorial diffusion they have also diversified considerably. In the English-speaking world, the English 2000 Project and the Nuffield Languages Enquiry (Graddol 1997 and 1998; Moys ed. 1998) have yielded interesting results; in Spain, the Fundación Duques de Soria in Spain sponsored a similar kind of enquiry (Tamarón ed. 1995). We will now examine some of their findings.

10.3.1 Spanish as a native language

The league table of native speakers of the world's languages (see Table 10.2) is currently headed, by a considerable margin, by Chinese. English and Spanish come second or third, depending on the source consulted. Graddol (1998: 26) predicts that by 2050 (no one has the temerity to offer predictions beyond that date at present) the number of native Spanish speakers will have risen significantly, as will have that of Arabic and Hindi/Urdu. The growth of Spanish is dependent on the anticipated continued high birth rate in Latin America.

Table 10.2 Native speakers of the world's languages

Language Name	Rank 2000	Population 2000	Rank 2050 (projected)	Population 2050 (projected)
Mandarin Chinese	1	885,000,000	1	1,160,000,000
Spanish	2	332,000,000	4	475,000,000
English	3	322,000,000	3	480,000,000
Bengali	4	189,000,000	?	no figures
Hindi	5	182,000,000	2	520,000,000
Portuguese	6	170,000,000	5	220,000,000
Based on figures from Grimes ed. 1999 and Graddol (1997: 26)				

There are other important statistics in this connection, however. The raw figure of native speakers does not reflect the distribution of these languages throughout the world in terms of the number of countries in which they are spoken or the area of the earth's surface those countries occupy (see Figure 10.1). Nor does it say anything about the official standing of the language in those countries.

Figure 10.1 English, Spanish and French in the world

A significant contrast between English and Spanish is that whereas English is often an official language in countries where it is not widely spoken natively, Spanish is in the majority of cases the official language of those countries where it is spoken at all. A striking exception to this is the United States, which in terms of the number of speakers ranks as the third largest Spanish-speaking country after Mexico and Spain, but where Spanish is not an official language: indeed, some states have explicitly legislated against Spanish in various ways, and there is a vigorous ongoing debate about the relative merits of English-only and bilingual education.

10.3.2 Spanish as an international language

English appears to be well on the way to becoming the global language of international communication; indeed, this has already happened in such areas as air traffic control. English is spoken as a second language by as many people as speak it natively. Spanish does not compare at all in this respect. Except in Equatorial Guinea, it is not used as a lingua franca where it is not spoken natively. In terms of use in international organisations, however, Spanish has a substantial presence. It is one of the official languages of the United Nations and a working language of many of its dependent bodies (Ybáñez Bueno 1995). But within a European context the picture is rather different: Spanish is one of six working languages of the European Union, though English and French are the only languages actually used in most situations. Overall, it seems likely that the current position of Spanish will be broadly maintained.

10.3.3 Will the unity of Spanish be preserved?

Despite the occasional sounding of alarm bells about the possible fragmentation of the Spanish-speaking world, the fundamental linguistic unity that has been maintained is remarkable (Tamarón 1995: 53). It is important, however, to be exact about what is actually meant by unity. Unity is emphatically not equatable with lack of variation: the diatopic and diastratic variation discussed in Chapter 6 makes this quite clear. It does not mean that the language of the Nicaraguan street children described in 7.1.3 (Text H) would be instantly comprehensible to a Galician granny: at this level, fragmentation is extreme. It does not even mean that a cultured *porteño* and a cultured *madrileño* speak in exactly the same way. Unity is achieved by the broad acceptance of a written norm and by the continuing mutual intelligibility of cultured speech. As we have seen (**6.2.4.2.5**), in Latin America each country tends to have its own prestige norm (generally associated with the upper-class speech of the capital), as well as there being a notion of a supraregional cultured Latin-American prestige norm which consists of a 'lowest common denominator', i.e. an avoidance of regional indicators. A way of conceptualising the unity of the Spanish-speaking world is to think similarly of speakers as having individually a variety of usages, but with enough overlap to ensure substantial common ground and hence mutual comprehension. This is symbolised in Figure 10.2, where circles A, B and C represent three different speakers who individually have differences in their usage (the unshaded areas, which represent mutually unintelligible or unfamiliar usages), but overall share common, mutually intelligible usages (the central dark shaded area).

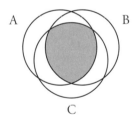

Figure 10.2 Linguistic unity (the shaded area represents overlap in usage among speakers A, B and C)

Historically, this situation was probably significantly encouraged by one rather important event: the publication of Andrés Bello's *Gramática de la lengua castellana destinada al uso de los americanos* in 1847 and its subsequent wide acceptance in Latin America. The emancipation of most of Spain's American colonies in the 1820s had threatened to sever cultural connections with the mother country, in particular with regard to the standards established by the Real Academia Española; indeed, in the mid-19th century the language of individual countries was sometimes dubbed *colombiano*, *venezolano*, etc. Bello, however, saw the value of the maintenance of linguistic unity, primarily in the context of contact among the newly independent American states. It is worth quoting from the prologue to his grammar:

No tengo la presunción de escribir para los castellanos. Mis lecciones se dirigen a mis hermanos, los habitantes de Hispanoamérica. Juzgo importante la conservación de la lengua de nuestros padres en su posible pureza, como un medio providencial de comunicación y un vínculo de fraternidad entre las varias naciones de origen español derramadas sobre los dos continentes. ... El mayor mal de todos, y el que, si no se ataja, va a privarnos de las inapreciables ventajas de una lengua común, es la avenida de neologismos de construcción, que inunda y enturbia mucha parte de lo que se escribe en América, y alterando la estructura del idioma, tiende a convertirlo en una multitud de idiomas futuros, que durante una larga elaboración reproducirían en América lo que fue la Europa en el tenebroso período de la corrupción del latín. Chile, el Perú, Buenos Aires, Méjico, hablarían cada uno su lengua, o por mejor decir, varias lenguas, como sucede en España, Italia y Francia, donde dominan ciertos idiomas provinciales, pero viven a su lado otros varios, oponiendo estorbos a la difusión de las luces, a la ejecución de las leyes, a la administración del Estado, a la unidad nacional. (Bello 1981 [1847]: 129)

Normativist teaching of a pan-Hispanic standard was therefore put in place relatively promptly. Each Latin-American country eventually established its own Academia, beginning with the foundation of the Colombian Academy in 1871, and in 1951, the Asociación de Academias de la Lengua Española was founded. This body has met every four years since 1961 and is dedicated to work for the 'unidad, integridad y crecimiento del idioma común'. The Latin-American Academies recognise the RAE as the natural body for directing linguistic regulatory activity; but at the same time, there is an agreement that any major policy proposal will be referred to each academy for comment. The Asociación de Academias has a Comisión Permanente which implements its decisions. The RAE, for its part, shows an increasing concern for admitting (cultured) Latin-American usage; this is dramatically illustrated by its comparison of *americanismos* in the 22nd edition of the *DRAE* as compared with the 21st edition of only nine years previously, shown in Figure **10.3**:

The prospects for the future unity of Spanish therefore seem good. They will be enhanced by judicious standardisation on the part of the Academies (the more judicious this is, the more it is likely to be respected), and indeed, we might go so far as to say that this is an advantage the Spanish-speaking world has over the English-speaking world. Globalisation is also likely to help in some respects: Alonso (1964: 266) makes the important point that unity in the labelling of new technological concepts has been facilitated by the fact that most are borrowed from English, a consequence of the economic and technological dominance of the US in the last part of the 20th century (the expectation that globalisation will lead to greater linguistic convergence *per se* is, however, probably erroneous; speakers remain just as likely to assert their individuality, or the individuality of their social group, through their language). The role of the broadcasting media is also likely to be significant, if only insofar as it makes speakers increasingly aware of and at least passively familiar with different varieties of Spanish. Urbanisation, especially in Latin America, is likely to produce linguistic levelling (see **6.2.3.2.6** and **6.2.4.2.3**).

The fundamental tasks of the Academies in this respect are (a) to maintain the common

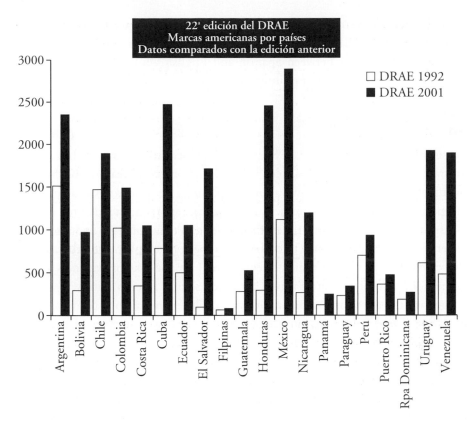

Figure 10.3 Comparison of the number of Americanisms in the 21st and 22nd editions of the *DRAE* (source: http://buscon.rae.es/diccionario/drae/ImgDRAE/marcasamericanaspaises.jpg)

spelling system (again, a point of contrast with English), and (b) to attempt to establish a common form for neologisms, especially in technical and commercial vocabulary. For the time being at least, it would appear that a common grammar can also be largely maintained for the educated written language. The Academies will only preserve respect and prestige, however, if, as also seems likely, they are prepared to bow to the inevitable and ultimately to respect the actual usage of speakers in their reference works (see **1.3**).

10.4 What will the impact of English on Spanish be?

I end this chapter, and this book, with some reflections on the possible impact of English on Spanish. This has been the subject of considerable alarmist disquiet amongst some prescriptivists, who tend to view foreign influence negatively (a view I shall not hesitate to oppose) and who have a mistaken view of the nature of *Spanglish* (see **9.5.1**), which is represented as the direction Spanish will take if allowed to assimilate anglicisms unchecked. Oddly enough, the matter has rarely been subjected to serious and rational scrutiny, precisely

[3] The highly objective account of Pratt (1980), for example, rejects any attempt at forecasting (pp. 239–40).

because of the reluctance of descriptive linguists to engage in linguistic forecasting.[3] It unites the areas of external and internal forecasting, since external circumstances determine the likely situations of contact between Spanish and English whilst the ways in English may affect Spanish are largely a matter of internal structure.

10.4.1 External factors

The reasons for English influence on Spanish may appear to be obvious, but we must take care to state them as exactly as possible. The two main external reasons for the widespread borrowing of English words are innovation and prestige. Because innovation in a number of areas (especially technological, commercial, the media, sport) has tended to come from the English-speaking world in recent times, the labelling of new concepts and artefacts has first of all been done in English. These terms have then been taken over into other languages not only for ease but also (a factor that is often ignored) for the sake of exactness and semantic discrimination; it is for the latter reason that the use of a foreign borrowing often has an advantage over the use of an existing native word. The economic prosperity of the English-speaking world, especially the United States, has also endowed English with prestige; it has become desirable to know, and to show that one knows, some English, and to imitate English-speaking instuitutions. The growth in the use of English as an international language referred to above has also contributed to this prestige; it has also meant that since the professional classes are often called upon to operate in English, there is perhaps room for English syntactic interference in Spanish, a phenomenon that can really only be brought about through more intimate knowledge of a foreign language. This is particularly apparent in journalism, where a Spanish reporter is often basing material on an English original which has had to be processed at high speed: the supposed over-use of the *ser*-passive in Spanish journalism has often been attributed to English influence of this kind (e.g. *MEU*, p. 47). To these reasons must be added more local factors: in Europe, Spain has since the 1950s been the willing host to mass tourism from Britain, which has resulted in the creation of virtual British enclaves and the consequent dissemination of their culture. In the Americas, the predominance of the United States since the 19th century and the contiguity of Spanish- and English-speaking communities in the US itself has meant that English is endowed with exceptional prestige and accessibility. Prestige encourages borrowings of different kinds, since the motivation is not so much exactness of reference but the communication of local colour or ostentation. For example, there is strictly no need for Peninsular Spanish to have borrowed the word *pub* ([puß] or [paß]), since it is essentially a *bar*; but *pub* communicates the distinctive features of a bar which emanates the atmosphere of an English pub, especially by selling draught beer.

10.4.2 Internal factors

Another very important factor favouring borrowing from English to Spanish is the structural similarity of the two languages in important respects. English words and phrases – even whole structures – easily find parallels in Spanish; this is partly because as Indo-European languages they have largely the same grammatical categories, but also because English borrowing from

French and the learned borrowing of both English and Spanish from Latin and Greek have already brought about a degree of convergence. A simple example is the English word *recycle*, which is formed from the Latin elements RE- and CYCLUS (the latter deriving from Greek *kyklos*). Since at least the early 18th century, Spanish has had in its learned vocabulary the word *ciclo*, and the prefix *re-* was familiar from long before, so the only adaptation necessary to accommodate this English verb into Spanish is to add a set of verbal suffixes to the stem *recicl-*, giving *reciclar*. Another example is Eng. *compact disc*, which becomes Sp. *disco compacto*; there are ready Spanish cognates for the two individual English words, and the only modification necessary in the new noun phrase is the change in order of noun and adjective. Even imitation of the English passive is facilitated by the availability in Spanish of the *ser* + past participle construction which is formally parallel to English *be* + past participle.

10.4.3 Assessment of the *status quo*

The possible future impact of English on Spanish can be judged by assessing the current situation. In this section I take each area of linguistic structure in turn.

10.4.3.1 VOCABULARY

I begin with this area because it is undeniable that English has contributed and will continue to contribute many words to the Spanish lexicon. A question we might ask is whether there is any possibility that English will 'colonise' Spanish to the extent of displacing native words and taking over lexical structures. To put anglicisms in context, we may consider the following etymological statistics for the 21st edition of the *DRAE* (the first to be available in electronic format), where we can see that the number of words of English origin is significantly less than those of French, or even of Italian, origin:

Table 10.3 Words of 'foreign' origin in *DRAE*, 21st ed.

Etymological source	Number of words in *DRAE*
Latin (includes 'learned' words, see 3.1)	19,501
Greek	4,298
French	1,785
Arabic	1,290
Amerindian languages (overall)	902
Italian	608
English	358
Germanic	134
Celtic	66
Dutch	45

Of course, such raw statistics say nothing about the frequency with which words are used, nor the familiarity of the concepts they represent. Also, the *DRAE* has a fairly conservative policy concerning the admission of neologisms, though one problem with assessing how many anglicisms there are in modern Spanish is that some of these borrowings will be of very short duration, and it is difficult to predict which will last and which are only ephemeral. Words denoting new concepts will last as long those concepts, so the *elepé* (Eng. *LP (record)*) is already giving way to the *minidisco* (Eng. *minidisk*). It is also the case that some anglicisms which appear in print are indeed the exoticisms of a particular writer (see England & Caramés 1978, Smith 1975).

Lexical borrowing takes place in two principal ways, by straight borrowing or by **calquing**. The difference between these two processes is that in borrowing the loanword is transplanted essentially as it stands, with differing degrees of phonetic adaptation (e.g. Eng. *software* becomes Sp. *software* ['sofwer], Eng. *standard* becomes Sp. *estándar* [es'tandar], Eng. *e-mail* becomes Sp. *emilio* – this last process, whereby an English word is reanalysed as a phonetically similar Spanish word, is called **folk etymology**), whereas in calquing a morphological or semantic equivalent is created in the host language (e.g. Eng. *photocopier* becomes Spanish *fotocopiadora*). Sometimes an existing word which is formally cognate with an English word is extended in meaning, a process which excites particular hostility from purists: an example is *sobrio*, which originally meant 'moderate, restrained', but now means 'sober' in the English sense of 'not drunk' (see Lorenzo 1996: 491, and my critique in Pountain 2000: 37). Calques merge almost imperceptibly into the language, since they do not display any marked 'foreign' features, while plain borrowings, as we shall see, may be instrumental in introducing new sounds, or combinations of sounds.

Plain borrowings and calques make different kinds of impact on the formal lexical structure of the language. Plain borrowings are often isolated terms in the sense that they have no formal parallels elsewhere in the host lexicon: they are morphologically unmotivated, and so constitute a kind of anomaly in the lexicon. It is clear that some anglicisms will continue to have precisely that status in Spanish, just as a number of Arabic borrowings from a much earlier time have remained in the language (e.g. *aljibe, aljaba, alforja*). What happens in a significant number of cases, however, is that the host language either ditches or more completely assimilates morphological isolates by creating new derivational forms, which sometimes are completely independent of the lending language. Examples of the abandoning of an anglicism in Spanish are *referee* and *basketball*, which, though retained in Latin America as *réferi* and *basket*, have been largely replaced in Spain by *árbitro* and *baloncesto*. Two striking examples of the creation of a whole series of related morphological derivatives are the words *líder* '(political) leader', which has yielded *liderar* 'to lead' and *liderazgo* 'leadership', and *gol* '(football) goal', from which we have *golear* 'to score a lot of goals against', *goleada* 'heavy defeat' and *goleador* '(high) goal-scorer' – note in this last example how English does not in fact have simple equivalents for the new Spanish words. Another mark of assimilation is when an English word is used in a rather different way: the word *off*, for example, is not used as a preposition but in the phrase *en off* 'offstage, offscreen'; *blíster* means 'blister pack' and *relax* 'relaxation' has has also become a euphemism for 'personal (i.e. sexual) services'.

From the semantic point of view, it is difficult to find convincing examples of a borrowing actually ousting a native word, which is one way in which the charges of the purists that English is 'colonising' Spanish might be said to have some substance. More usual in fact is that a borrowing is replaced, either by the use of an existing word which is given an extended meaning, or by a neologism coined from within the host language. The notion of 'sponsoring' in the sense of a company providing financial support of a sporting or cultural enterprise originally gave rise to the anglicisms *esponsorizar, esponsorización*, but these have now largely been replaced by *patrocinar, patrocinio* (*patrocinio* is attested in the 16th century – see Corominas & Pascual, IV: 336) and the noun *mecenazgo*, a noun originally used to refer to the notion of patronage by a nobleman. The calque of Eng. *test tube* as Sp. *tubo de ensayo* has been replaced by *probeta*, originally denoting a mercury pressure gauge, which is more transparently related to the verb *probar* 'to test'. The adoption of a loanword in an area already covered by a native word often results in semantic discrimination, which might in fact be seen as constituting enrichment of the language: thus Eng. *sandwich*, borrowed as Sp. *sándwich*, denotes a toasted sandwich rather than a filled roll, which is still *bocadillo*.

The answer to the question we posed at the beginning of this section is therefore that while English will make a significant contribution to the Spanish lexicon, the net impact will be one of enrichment and assimilation rather than displacement.

10.4.3.2 PHONETICS

A number of English borrowings appear to be introducing new sounds into Spanish, especially [ʃ] (*show* [ʃo(w)]~[tʃo(w)] and *short(s)* [ʃor]) and [(d)ʒ] (*jazz* [(d)ʒas], *jet* [(d)ʒet], *jeans* [(d)ʒins]). What is the likelihood that such sounds will become a permanent feature of the language? First, we should note that these sounds are passively familiar to many Peninsular speakers of Spanish from Catalan and Galician names; furthermore, [ʃ] is sometimes encountered regionally for [tʃ] and [(d)ʒ] for [ʎ] (see **6.2.4.2.2**). Such familiarity might well favour acceptance of the English pronunciation. However, the two current pronunciations for *show* indicate the possibility of [ʃ] being adapted to the native [tʃ], the strategy which eventually prevailed in the borrowing of many French words earlier in the history of Spanish: for example, *chimenea* < Fr. *cheminée, chal* < Fr. *châle*; compare also the older anglicisms *chelín* < Eng. *shilling* and *champú* < Eng. *shampoo*. [(d)ʒ] is perhaps more problematic, since there is apparently no similar native sound. On the other hand, the number of such words is relatively small: in addition to the above examples there are *jeep, jogging, juke-box* and *jumper*, some of which are already beginning to show their age (*footing* is generally preferred to *jogging*). Another strategy is that the *j* will be pronounced in the Spanish way, which can already be observed in *jersey* [xerˈsej] and *jungla* [ˈxuŋgla], or that it is substituted by [j] (*jeep* and *jogging* have the variant pronunciations [jip] and [ˈjoɣin]. In fact, the existence of variant pronunciations is itself an indication that the English pronunciations are not at all fixed, and the tentative conclusion must therefore be that they will not be lasting, despite some favouring circumstances.

Another question is whether English borrowings will introduce into Spanish unfamiliar combinations of existing phonemes or unfamiliar allophonic variation. Again, the indications are that this is being largely resisted. All borrowings from English words beginning with /s/ + consonant are usually pronounced with a prothetic /e/ in Spanish, e.g. Eng. *striptease*, Sp. [es'triptis] and final [ŋ] is adapted to [n], e.g. Eng. *camping*, Sp. ['kampin].

There is a challenge to Spanish from the pronunciation of English loanwords which we referred to in 2.4: the use of original English spellings which are not phonemic. This is an important issue for Spanish orthography (although it should be noted that once the Real Academia accepts a word into its Dictionary it usually imposes a Spanish spelling), but it is not necessarily relevant to the sound pattern of Spanish in itself. The spelling *whisky*, which is maintained for commercial reasons, is pronounced ['wiski] or ['gwiski], which while a little unusual, is none the less a plausible phonemic sequence in Spanish.

10.4.3.3 MORPHOLOGY AND SYNTAX

We should perhaps make a distinction in the first place between morphological and syntactic influence that takes place purely as a result of lexical borrowing and influence which can only be due to the wholesale imitation of structures. While the former is generally thought by historical linguists to be more likely, the latter is by no means impossible given the circumstances in which contact between English and Spanish takes place in the modern world (see above).

A very interesting speculation concerns plural morphology. With one or two exceptions, Spanish has a very straightforward process of plural formation which consists of the addition of /s/ to words which end in a vowel and of /es/ to words which end in a consonant; the problematic categories are words which end in a stressed vowel, such as *rubí (rubíes), tabú (tabúes or tabús)* and those which end in an unstressed syllable with a final /s/, such as *crisis (crisis)*. However, in English, words which end in a consonant simply add (in writing) *s*, and the imitation of such plurals is inconsistent with the existing plural rule of Spanish. What we find is that there is variation in this area, with Anglicisms of longer standing forming their plurals in the Spanish way while newer borrowings follow the English original: thus we have *cócteles, mítines, líderes* but *boicots, jeeps, suéters, pósters*. We can imagine two scenarios here. We may forecast that either the newer borrowings will eventually be assimilated into Spanish, to the extent of forming their plurals in the Spanish way, or that, if a very large number of such English words become established in Spanish, as may well be the case, their plurals will follow a separate rule and the rule for pluralisation in Spanish will be correspondingly complicated. The latter situation would have the interesting effect of marking out such words as being in some way special, or 'foreign', rather like words beginning with *al-* are often of Arabic origin (*al*, the Arabic definite article, was incorporated into such words).

Another feature of English is that nouns can quite freely be used as adjectives; this has led to the borrowing of a number of noun + noun set phrases: *canción protesta* (Eng. *protest song*), *fecha límite* (Eng. *date limit, deadline*), *ciudad dormitorio* (Eng. *dormitory town*), *hora punta* (Eng. *rush hour*). It will be noticed that these are morphological or semantic calques: the original words are translated and the adjectival noun follows the noun that it qualifies. There are two questions to be asked here: has this brought about a syntactic innovation in Spanish, and will this kind of structure become productive? The answer to the first question is certainly negative. While such calques have increased the repertoire of such constructions in Spanish, the possibility of using a noun as an adjective was not previously unknown. The nouns *macho* and *hembra* could be used in this way, as could a number of nouns denoting colours (usually now described as adjectives in dictionaries, though they were originally nouns, and many are still invariable, showing no agreement for gender or number with the nouns they qualify), e.g. *libros violeta*. Numbers might be included in the pattern too (*la página catorce*). The answer to the second question is not so clearcut, though what we can say immediately is that productivity is certainly not total: direct Spanish equivalents for such English constructions as *the wine trade* (*el comercio vino) or *the population crisis* (**la crisis población*) are impossible. However, there are signs that Spanish is continuing to exploit noun + noun combinations in ways that are not merely calques of English, e.g. *hombre masa* 'average man', *hombre-anuncio* 'sandwich man'; and certain nouns seem to be particularly prone to this, such as *caso* (*el caso Gescartera*), *estilo* (*estilo mariposa*, *estilo Luis XV*, etc.) and *hora* (*hora cero*, *hora punta*).

Three construction which are not dependent on lexical borrowing are often cited as examples of English syntactic influence. I have already referred to the use of the *ser*-passive, especially in journalistic prose. Once again, although parallels with English may encourage use of this construction, it has existed in Spanish for many centuries, and it is probably only the prescriptive strictures of successive Academy grammars inveighing against its use (the *GRAE* of 1931 memorably declaring that 'la voz pasiva es muy poco usada en español') that have created sensitivity. It is of course unlike the English passive in the ways that we have mentioned in **5.5.1.4**, and is not at all frequent in spoken usage; but in neither of these respects does any major change seem to be taking place, and we may therefore predict that the influence of English in this area will be very circumscribed (Pountain 1999: 40–1).

Another target of opprobrium has been the gerund, which again is used in English in rather different ways from Spanish. The strict prescriptive rule in Spanish is that the gerund can only be used adverbially, never adjectivally, and that its subject must always be the same as that of the main verb of the sentence (see also **4.5.2.3**). Thus a sentence such as the following is deemed 'incorrect', or at least, undesirable, though, as can be seen from its English translation, a parallel construction using the *-ing* form in English is entirely possible.

> **(10.1)** *La policía detuvo un camión transportando café de contrabando*
> (*MEU*: 49)
> 'The police stopped a lorry carrying smuggled coffee'

Could such a development be due to English? The answer must be here again that while the example of English may encourage such structures, they are far from being innovations in Spanish. The use of a gerund in a qualifying adjectival clause (i.e. a substitute for a relative clause, see **4.5.2.3**) is already a feature of the admittedly very marked register of the *Boletín oficial del Estado*, where we regularly find such titles as *Decreto estableciendo nuevos impuestos*. The ease of giving the appropriate interpretation to a gerund, despite the lack of coreference between its subject and the subject of the main verb, is demonstrated by usages such as those of personal advertisements:

(10.2) *Necesito señorita sabiendo cocina*
'Needed: a girl who can cook'

where in fact there is no direct parallel to be drawn with English. The reason we readily interpret the subject of *transportando* in (10.1) as being *un camión* and not *la policía* and that of *sabiendo* in (10.2) as *señorita* and rather than *yo* is pragmatic likelihood: interpretations of (10.1) as 'The police stopped a lorry while they were carrying smuggled coffee' and of (10.2) as 'Since I know how to cook I need a girl' would be bizarre in the extreme. It is possible to construct examples that are less clearcut, e.g.:

(10.3) *Una señora halló al niño deambulando por el parque* (MEU: 49)
'A lady found the child wandering in the park'

but in such a case the meaning would be given by the discourse context in which the sentence occurs. Furthermore, there are prescriptively approved structures in Spanish which resemble those of (10.1), (10.2) and (10.3) very closely: the gerund is regularly used in the complements of verbs of perception instead of the infinitive (10.4a) and appears to be extending to the complements of other verbs too where it is often appropriate to express progressive aspect explicitly (10.4b–c):

(10.4) **a.** *Oímos a los niños gritando*
b. *Dejo el dedo indicando la línea*
c. *Encontré a mi amigo leyendo*

Even so, the use of the Spanish gerund is not unconstrained. It does not have the same syntactic properties as the English *-ing*: it can occur only as the equivalent of a relative construction and only when such a construction is not being used contrastively. Thus a construction such as (10.5) is unacceptable:

(10.5) **Me interesan sólo los camiones llevando cigarrillos*

It certainly shows no sign of being used as an adjective in the same way as English *-ing* forms; the only two such adjectivally used gerunds in Spanish, *hirviendo* and *ardiendo*, are heavily restricted in use and cannot be modified like other adjectives. In summary, it seems that prescriptive strictures against the gerund are against certain uses of the gerund which have been present all along in Spanish, rather than against significant innovatory usages in the modern language.

EXERCISES

1. What other potential changes do you think might take place in Spanish, on the basis of what you know of present-day variation?

2. A number of Spanish compound words consisting of verb + noun seem to be calques from English (e.g. *rascacielos* 'skyscraper', *limpiaparabrisas*, 'windscreen wiper', *matamoscas* 'fly killer'. However, there are also some words of this type which cannot be borrowings but must be original creations within Spanish (e.g. *matasuegros* 'party blower', *tragaperras* 'slot machine', *pasamontañas* 'balaclava'). Is it possible to distinguish the anglicisms? Are there patterns discernible in such word creation?

Notes to the exercises

Chapter 2

1. The *n* of *enfático* is a labiodental nasal [ɱ]; the *n* of *ente* is an alveolar-dental nasal, the IPA sign for which is simply [n], though you can distinguish it from the English alveolar [n] by indicating its dental nature with a subscript dental sign: [n̪]. Both [ɱ] and [n̪] show the effects of assimilation to the following consonant (see **2.3.1**).

   The *p* of English *pot* is an aspirated bilabial voiceless plosive, which can be symbolised in IPA by [pʰ]. Aspiration does not take place when the plosive is preceded by [s], so the *p* in *spot* can be symbolised by just [p]. The *p* of *shop* is essentially the same, though it is very often not released if followed by another consonant (e.g. in *shop-fitting*, *shoplifting*); the IPA has a special sign for this, though it is not usually used for most practical purposes: [p̚].

2. Here are some to start you off: *azar/asar, basar/bazar, casar/cazar, rebosar/rebozar, abrasar/abrazar, sierra/cierra, siervo/ciervo, sien/cien, siego/ciego, sueco/zueco*. Although it clearly is possible to find such homonyms, it is unlikely that most of these would ever be confused, since they belong to quite different semantic areas (but see **2.3.4**).

3. The syllable divisions are:

   Fres- | *co y* | *cla-* | *ro‿a-* | *rro-* | *yue-* | *lo*
   Por- | *que* | *de‿e-* | *sa* | *par-* | *te‿es-* | *tá*

The upright bar | marks the syllable divisions and the ligature ‿ shows *sinalefa*. Musically-inclined readers may like to see the impact of this on the underlaying of these words to music:

Fres - co‿y   cla - ro‿a - rro - yue - - - lo

Francisco Guerrero, 'Fresco y claro arroyuelo', from Christopher J. Pountain & Christine J. Whitbourn, *Songs from the Spanish Cancioneros* (Kilkenny: Boethius Press, 1988)

Por - que   de‿e - sa   par - te‿es - tá

Pedro de Escobar, 'Pásame, por Dios, barquero', *ibid.*

4. This calls for divergent thinking! One possibility (essentially the strategy adopted in Portuguese orthography) is to assume that sequences of two vowels are in hiatus rather than diphthongal, and to use the written accent accordingly: so the hiatus group /i/+/a/ is written *ía* in Spanish *María* but *ia* in Portuguese *Maria*, and the diphthong /ia/ ([ja]) is written *ia* in Spanish *historia* while Portuguese indicates the same phenomenon by the spelling *história*. Another possibility would be use a hyphen or a diaeresis to indicate hiatus: *Mari-a* or *Mariä*. The hyphen, as we have seen, is used in IPA to indicate syllable division. The diaeresis is sometimes used in modern editions of Spanish poetry to show hiatus which is crucial to scansion: the word *tenue* is spelt *tenuë* if it should be syllabified *te-nu-e*.

Chapter 3

1. What all these contexts have in common is that (a) the /i/ or /u/ occurs in an unstressed syllable, but that (b) the appearance of /i/ or /u/ is restricted to environments where this unstressed syllable is followed by a consonant and the semivowel [j] (so [sin'tjera] but [sen'timos], [dor'mi] but [dur'mjo]). Verbs like *sentir* and *dormir* thus have three root allomorphs: *sent- ~ sient- ~ sint-* and *dorm- ~ duerm- ~ durm-*, unlike radical-changing verbs of the *-ar* and *-er* conjugations which only have two (e.g. *cerr- ~ cierr-*).

Let us call the radical change of the *-ar* and *-er* conjugation verbs Type I and the radical change we are looking at in these *-ir* verbs Type II. We might say that *cerrar* undergoes only Type I radical change while *sentir* and *dormir* undergo both Type I and Type II. You may have noticed while thinking about this exercise that there are also verbs of the *-ir* conjugation which only undergo Type II radical change: *pedir*, for example, has the two root allomorphs *ped-* and *pid-* (but not **pied-*). (Verbs like *pedir*, however, also have the radical change in stressed syllables.)

2. The question of regularity is an extremely interesting one in this case. The largest group of such verb/nominalisation pairs is undoubtedly *-ar* verbs with nominalisations in *-ación* (like *imaginar*); but there is also a substantial number of pairs in which historically speaking a verb has been formed from the noun by adding *-ar* to the noun (*reaccion+ar*, *relacion+ar*, etc.). Many of the *-ación* nouns are learned borrowings (see **2.4.1**), but the formation of nouns ending in *-ación* continues to be a productive process in Spanish (see **3.2**). Some verbs in *-ar* yield 'reduced' forms in *-ión* (*opción*, not **optación*, *infección*, not **infectación*) which again is a consequence of learned borrowing, but they cannot be considered regular or productive in Modern Spanish. *Acepción* is a particular interesting case, since there is also the doublet form *aceptación*, which from both a semantic and morphological point of view is the more regular norminalisation of *aceptar*. *-er* and *-ir* verbs are much more problematic. There are no regular nouns in *-eción* formed from verbs in *-er* (for example, there is no verb **objecer* corresponding to *objeción*: the verb is *objetar*, and this pair is irregular), but a very few verbs in *-er* have nominalisations in *-ición*, such as *perder/perdición*; once again this reflects learned borrowing. There are relatively few nouns in *-ición* formed from verbs in *-ir* (you will find some others like *prohibición*, corresponding to *prohibir*; but most nouns in *-ición* relate irregularly to their corresponding verbs: *poner/posición*, *editar/edición*, etc. Although at first sight such pairs as *introducir/introducción*, *corregir/corrección*, *percibir/percepción* and *suspender/suspensión* look irregular, most of the verbs with similar endings in Spanish form their nominalisations in *-ión* in the same way, and so while such patterns are no longer productive (they are once again the result of learned borrowing), they are 'semi-regular' on statistical grounds.

3. Some of the features or parameters you might think of including in your account are: (a) for one person or several, (b) size, (c) purpose (*mecedora*, *sillín* and *trono* have very specific purposes), (d) having legs (this might discriminate *taburete* and *puf* which might otherwise be difficult to distinguish), (e) upholstered (this might discriminate *sofá* and *banco*), (f) having a back, (g) having arms. Even so, you will find *butaca* and *sillón*, *banqueta* and *taburete* difficult to specify uniquely. You will therefore have to consider contextual factors and connotative meaning (see **3.4**). The Internet is a powerful tool in giving a quick indication of the kinds of context in which a word is used. *Butaca* appears first and foremost in pages concerning the theatre because of its specialised meaning of 'theatre seat, stall', while *sillón* is most often used for a piece of luxury domestic furniture; *sillón* also appears in phrases such as *sillón alto*, *sillón de ruedas*, and has specialised meanings such as the seat occupied by a member of the RAE. *Banqueta* is often treated as a hyponym of *taburete*, and frequently implies a better-quality product.

You will also quickly find that the meanings of some of these words vary according to locality. *Banqueta*, for instance, is probably most frequently encountered in Latin America and the US in the meaning of 'pavement, sidewalk'. Again, featural comparisons can be made; the following table is taken from Ávila (1997) and is based on data from the VARILEX survey (see **6.2.4.2.4**):

Mueble con asiento

concepto	México	La Habana
1. con respaldo	*silla*	*silla*
1.1. con balancín	*mecedora*	*sillón*
1.2. con brazos		
1.2.1. móvil	*sillón*	*butaca*
1.2.2. fijo	*butaca*	
2. con tapicería		
2.1. para una persona	*taburete*	*banqueta*
2.2. para varias personas	*sofá*	*sofá*
3. sin tapicería		
3.1. para una persona	*banco*	*banco*
3.2. para varias personas	*banca*	

Chapter 4

1. Possible arguments in favour are that no other subject is possible (see example (4.5)) and that therefore *se* is the only candidate. Arguments against are (a) *se* is quite plainly an object pronoun in many of its other functions, (b) like other clitic object pronouns, it cannot receive stress, while subject pronouns such as *yo*, *tú*, etc., can be stressed. It is interesting to compare the properties of Spanish *se* with those of the 'dummy' subject *it* in English: *it* also has a clear subject use as a neuter anaphoric pronoun, though like *se*, it cannot receive stress in its 'dummy' function.

2. An open-ended exercise. The elliptical information is sometimes recoverable from the preceding discourse context, as in the example given, but sometimes it is only recoverable from general pragmatic expectations: in a sentence such as *Hay cerveza en la nevera, si tienes sed*, the invitation to take a beer from the fridge is not explicitly stated, but certainly implied; pragmatically, there would be no point in a speaker giving this information if it was not in connection with an invitation. Ellipsis is also a feature of some grammatical constructions, e.g. *A Sandra le gusta vino tinto, y a Miguel, vino blanco*, where *le gusta* (with *le* referring to *Miguel*) is 'understood'; or the comparative construction *Paco tiene notas más altas que Santi*, which implies *... más altas (que las notas que tiene) Santi*.

3. Some indications are given here for *cambiar* and *change*; you are left to work out *sonar* and *sound* for yourself.

You should consider at least these constructions:

(a) *Cambiamos el libro (por otro)*   *We changed the book (for another one)*
(b) *Cambiamos los euros (en dólares)*   *We changed the euros into dollars*
(c) *Cambié la lámpara de lugar*   *I changed the place of the lamp*
(d) *Cambié la pila a la linterna*   *I changed the battery in the torch*
(e) *Cambiemos de tema*   *Let's change the subject*
(f) *Se cambiaron (de ropa)*   *They changed (their clothes)*
(g) *Su voz cambió (de carácter)*   *His voice changed (in character)*

English *change* has an agentive subject and a patient object in (a–f), while in (g) the subject is the experiencer of change. Different prepositional phrases mark other kinds of argument: *for* in (a) and *into* in (b) indicates what might be called a SUBSTITUTE; the two functions are slightly different in that *into* is associated with a more literal conversion. *Of* in (c) indicates that the object, *place*, is an ATTRIBUTE of *lamp*, and *in* in (d) rather similarly signals that *torch* is the LOCATION of the object, *battery*. Spanish *cambiar* has the same arguments available, though their syntax is different: in (c), exactly the same functions attach to *lámpara* and *lugar* as to English *lamp* and *place* (the place is the thing changed, and is an attribute of the lamp), but Spanish makes *lámpara* the syntactic direct object and indicates its attribute (what is actually changed) by the preposition *de*; however, these relations could also be expressed in Spanish by the rather less usual *Cambié el lugar de la lámpara*, which is parallel to the English structure. *De* is used with essentially the same function in (g), which could be alternatively expressed as *El carácter de su voz cambió*, and in (f), where *ropa* is an attribute of the understood subject *ellos/as*, though here there is no ready equivalent alternative construction. The use of *de* in (e) reveals a covert difference in the nature of the relationship between the verb and its object. In Spanish, there is a difference in meaning between, for example, *Cambiamos el libro* and *cambiamos de libro*: the first sentence means that the book was exchanged for another, or for something else, while the second sentence means that an alternative book was used. In English this difference can be rendered by pluralising the object: *We changed the book / we changed books*.

The sentences of (f) reveal once again how an English verb that is apparently intransitive (see **4.3.5.1**) may in fact conceal a reflexive notion which is made overt in Spanish (however, unlike *wash*, *change* cannot be overtly reflexive: *I changed ('myself)*).

4. The constituent propositions in this sentence, presented in logical order, are:

(a) *(el caso es que) el marido se queda con todo*
(b) *a muchas (mujeres) les suele pasar (un caso así)*
(c) *eso está muy mal*
(d) *(por eso) tenían que arreglarlo*
(e) *(aunque) no creo que me pase un caso así*

The original sentence employs a number of fillers (*vamos, pero vamos, pues*). Subordinating conjunctions acting as logical connectors are generally lacking apart from *porque*; otherwise the coordinating conjunctions *y* and *pero* are used. The order of the propositions has the conclusion first, followed by the reasons, reflecting what is uppermost in the speaker's mind. Topicalising left-dislocation (see **4.4.3**) occurs in (d) (*eso tenían que arreglarlo*), and focus (see **2.7.2.1**) is achieved by the use of the emphatic subject pronoun *yo* in (e), by the cleft construction in (b) (see **4.4.3**, but here using the existential *haber* rather than *ser*) and by the juncture after *el marido* in (a) (see **2.7.2**).

Chapter 5

1. There is apparently no simple principle available, but *-do* and *-da* are associated with a range of meanings, some of which do seem to be discriminatory.

Both *-do* and *-da* can denote the result of an action:

> *moldeado* 'moulding', *decorado* 'decoration', *tecleado* 'keyboarding'
> *nevada* 'snowfall', *callada* 'silence', *herida* 'wound'

-da can also denote an action in itself:

> *llegada* 'arrival', *acogida* 'welcome'

-*do* expresses an office:

> *papado* 'papacy', *principado* 'principality'

-*da* has the meanings of 'blow' and 'load':

> *puñada* 'blow with the fist' (in this case, it is *puñado* 'handful' that expresses the meaning of 'load'), *martillada* 'blow with a hammer'
> *camionada* 'lorryload', *hornada* 'batch (of baking)'

The gender contrast has also been exploited to render a more subtle difference in meaning; in the following examples the masculine conveys the notion of an activity while the feminine indicates a single constituent action of that activity:

> *planchado* 'ironing (as task)' / *planchada* 'a single application of the iron'
> *peinado* 'hairstyle' / *peinada* 'quick combing'
> *pisado* 'treading (of grapes)' / *pisada* 'footstep, footprint'

The feminine sometimes renders a more concrete notion than the masculine:

> *picada* 'bite, sting' / *picado* 'act of grinding, mincing or chopping'
> *tostada* 'slice of toast' / *tostado* 'toasting'

It is difficult to see any regular pattern in the following, though the gender distinction is clearly exploited, since the meanings of these words are broadly related:

> *helado* 'ice-cream' / *helada* 'frost'
> *batido* 'milkshake' / *batida* 'beating, searching'
> *calzado* 'footwear' / *calzada* 'road'

2. This is an open-ended exercise. It is worth making a major distinction between those cases (like the use of *a* after *como*, with verbs of precedence (5.17) and in the syntactic contexts exemplified in (5.13–16)) where the use or non-use of *a* is crucial to determining the function of the following noun with respect to the verb, and those cases where the noun's function remains the same, the semantic difference lying in factors such as 'particularisation', 'kinesis', etc. Most difficult of all to discriminate is the use or non-use of *a* with the objects of verbs which are often said to have a 'preference' for *a* with their objects (see Butt & Benjamin 2000: 327): the verb *afectar* is regularly used both with and without the *a* with no appreciable difference in meaning (though you could test this on native speakers); examples from the Latin-American press are:

> *La disminución de turismo afectó la economía cubana*
> *La prolongada crisis afectó a la economía peruana*

3. It is an interesting question as to how far the 'nuance reflexive' actually changes the meaning of such verbs. Some 'nuance' reflexives have quite different lexical equivalents in English; you may also notice that it tends to be these that are also given separate entries in Spanish monolingual dictionaries, which suggests that native speakers perceive such a difference too. *Pasarse*, for example, has quite a wide range of such meanings, some of which seem to be much more than 'nuances' of the basic notion of 'pass':

> *Las manzanas se han pasado* 'the apples have gone bad'
> *Nos hemos pasado* 'we've gone too far'
> *Se pasó al bando enemigo* 'he went over to the enemy camp'

Some other verbs that you might like to investigate in this respect are *cambiar* (see above, Notes to Chapter 4 Exercise 3), *imaginar*, *ocurrir*, *salir* and *saltar*.

4. With a substantial number of verbs of 'communication' (saying, writing, etc.) the indicative and subjunctive express a declarative and an imperative meaning respectively; examples are *decir*, *convencer*, *escribir*, *establecer*, *insinuar*, *sugerir*. With verbs of 'thinking', the basis of the distinction is quite different, and is more difficult to appreciate and describe: the subjunctive seems to suggest a greater degree of diffidence or doubt, and is the 'marked' form (see **5.1**). Thus *Sospecho que el asunto no sea tan sencillo como usted cree* corresponds roughly to English 'I suspect the matter may not be quite as simple as you think' rather than the more neutral (and hence slightly less polite) *Sospecho que el asunto no es tan sencillo como usted cree* 'I suspect the matter is not as simple as you think', in which the speaker commits himself or herself much more definitely to the view expressed. The same kind of principle might account for the use of the subjunctive with *esperar* ('to hope', rather than 'to expect') and *comprender* ('to understand something as someone else's point of view' rather than 'to have understood for oneself').

5. Usage of *ser* and *estar* with prepositional complements does not seem to be inconsistent with the principles proposed for other contexts. *Ser* is used when the prepositional phrase denotes an inherent property (*de madera*, *de Costa Rica*, *de fiar*): in some of these cases, equivalent adjectives could be substituted (*costarricense*, *fiables*). *Estar* is used when the prepositional phrase denotes a state which is susceptible of change (*sin pintar*, *en proyecto*, *a dieta*, *de camarera*, *de vacaciones*). Notice that *estar de camarera* is not at all the same thing as *ser camarera*: the latter means that being a waitress is her (regular) job whereas the former implies quite the contrary, that this is not her normal profession. *Sin pintar* may be thought of as the negative of *pintado* ('unpainted' / 'painted'). *De broma* is similar to the gerund *bromeando*.

Chapter 6

1. This exercise should have shown you that it is difficult to say which development is most innovating, since, as is to be expected, none preserves the Latin form intact. For example, Castilian has sometimes been represented as being very innovating in the removal of the initial [j] of JANŬĀRĬU[S] [januˈaːɾiu], but in Portuguese and Catalan there is equally a change of [j] to the fricative [ʒ]. Catalan would appear to be most

'conservative' in its maintenance of the initial [pl] of PLĒNU[S] ['pleːnu], though the vocalic ending and [n] have been deleted. All three languages have reduced the geminate consonant [nn] of ANNU[S] ['annu], either by palatalisation (to [ɲ]) or by simplification (to [n]). Castilian seems to be most innovating in its treatment of the group [lt] in MULTU[M] ['multu] by palatalisation to [tʃ], but Portuguese also loses the [l] through a kind of palatalisation, perhaps originally to the offglide [i̯], though this has now become a full vowel, curiously enough nasalised, and Catalan again loses the final vocalic ending and consonant.

2. In areas where initial [h] from Latin [f] is preserved and [x] is weakened to [h], it is in theory possible that there is phonemic merger of /x/ and what might be taken as the Western Andalusian phoneme /h/. Thus, taking also into account the very widespread neutralisation of syllable-final /r/ and /l/, *huelga* and *juerga* might be homonymic as ['hwelɣa]. The number of homonyms so created would, however, not be great.

3. The text comes from Bacares in the province of Almería. You will notice that:

(a) the distinction between /s/ and /θ/ is maintained ([kaˈtorθe] *catorce*, [ˈsaka] *saca*).

(b) final /s/ is frequently lost and that this is compensated for by a distinction in vocalic opening; not only is the vowel originally preceding /s/ opened ([ˈombrɛ] *hombres*, [dɔ] *dos*, [ˈðia̜] *días*) but final [o] elsewhere is often perceived as being more close than in standard pronunciation ([ˈsanto̜ ˈkriʰto̜] *Santo Cristo*).

(c) there is thoroughgoing *yeísmo* ([kaʰˈtijo] *castillo*).

(d) Golden Age Castilian /h/ is not preserved ([aθen] *hacen*).

4. The text is by the Chilean author Óscar Castro (*El callejón de los gansos* in *Huellas en la tierra*, Santiago de Chile: Zig-Zag, 1940). It is immediately recognisable as coming from Chile because of the distinctive form of the *voseo* verb (see **6.2.4.2.3**): the *vosotros* form of the verb is used, but the final *-s* has been lost in the *-áis* ending, thus *estay* (though *creís*). The corresponding Argentine form of these verbs is *estás* and *creés*. Other linguistic features that are represented are:

(a) Initial /f/ is weakened, probably to [h], represented as *j* (*jundo* = *fundo*).

(b) In *sinalefa* involving a final /e/, the /e/ is lost (*qué'stay*, *qu'ir*).

(c) *Oyí* (standard *oí*) is probably formed analogically on the basis of *oyó*.

(d) The loss of intervocalic /d/ is very advanced (not only *entraor* = *entrador*, but also *fiera'e* = *fiera de*).

(e) The intensifying prefix *re-*, which is very widespread in the colloquial usage of Spain and Latin America.

(f) The word *entrador* 'daring', which is distinctively Latin American.

5. An open-ended exercise, in the process of which you will probably discover the linguistic features that are perceived as stereotypical of different regions.

Chapter 7

1. As in most languages, letters in Spanish follow set formulae according to social proto-col. There are tightly constrained salutations and valedictions (beginnings and end-ings) which depend on status of the addressee. Here the title *Excelentísimo Señor* is given, as convention demands, to the Prime Minister, and the valediction consists of respectful formulaic expressions (ll.44–5) followed by the simple but formal *atenta-mente*.

Apart from the use of such expected formulae, politeness is signalled explicitly in the first sentence (*saludo respetuoso*, l.6) and in the sentence (ll.36–7) *Apreciaremos, señor, se sirva considerar la posibilidad que sus asesores... tomen nota de esta misiva respetuosa*, where additionally the embedding of the request as the complement of *posibilidad*, which is in turn the object of the verb *considerar*, has the effect of making the demand less abrupt. Use of the explicit *apreciar*, in the future tense, the construction with *se sirva* and the use once again of the address form *señor* (cf. also ll.12 and 19) also contribute to the impres-sion of politeness. The use of *dignamente* in l.31 is another indication of politeness. A more general strategy is to put positive comments first: the first paragraph stresses the benefits to Peru from foreign investment, which is further underlined on ll.18–19. However, the substance of the letter is a fairly baldly stated series of complaints, with even the accusation of neo-colonialism (ll.40–3).

The register of the body of the letter is fairly 'neutral' with few marked features. Despite the formality of the mode and tenor, there are in fact some features which are more typical of the spoken language. Sentences are relatively short, and the sentence on ll.34–5 is introduced by a conjunction (*aparte que*), which is more usual in speech. *Que* rather than *de que* is used after *aparte* and after *la posibilidad* (l.36), which is more typical of the spoken language. More redolent of formal register is the circumlocution *tierra de Cervantes* for *España* (l.11) and the use of *misiva* in place of *carta* (l.37). The most for-mal paragraph is the one which begins on l.24. It contains some nominalisations (*com-pensación, manejo, resentimiento, identificación*), and there is a *ser*-passive (*son transgredidos*) on l.32.

2. As in **Text G**, the slang is almost exclusively lexical. There is a good deal of overlap with spoken Mexican slang, though one or two words are more specific to the Texas area. Here is a glossary:

raza = *raza (latina)*, *latinos*
bolillo = 'white' (i.e. 'Anglo-Saxon' rather than *latino*); this is a metaphorical extension of the literal meaning '(white) bread roll' in Mexico.
rinche = (Texas) ranger; a symbol of white authority and repression, and so a term of insult.
montonero = 'rogue'; originally 'guerrilla fighter' (general to Mexico)
tanate = lit. a large leather bag, but here the metaphorical meaning 'guts, courage' (gen-eral to Mexico)

huevos = widely used throughout the Spanish-speaking world in the meaning of 'testicles', and here, by extension, 'guts, courage'

de hueso colora(d)o = 'through and through' (general to Mexico; Pen. *hasta la médula*)

pedo = in colloquial Mexican Spanish, this word is widely used to mean 'fuss, difficulty', even in the expression *no hay pedo* 'it doesn't matter'. *Peda* has the meaning of 'booze-up', and *pedo* is also used as an adjective to mean 'drunk'. In Peninsular Spanish *pedo* means 'fart'.

cabronear = 'to annoy' (a Peninsular word based on the same fundamental root is *cabrear*)

cuña(d)o = 'mate, buddy', originally 'brother-in-law'

vieja = 'girlfriend'

chingar = 'to screw'. This word and its many derivatives are extremely common in colloquial Mexican Spanish. Although used with exactly this meaning on l.16, it is also used in the weaker sense of 'to annoy', and the past participle *chinga(d)o* (l.10) is an all-purpose expletive.

huerco = child (not general in Mexico, more typical of the north)

palomilla = group of friends; probably originally associated with *palomas* 'pigeons, because they hang around city streets. (Quite widely used in Mexico and other Latin-American countries.)

cañonear = to aim a gun at (general to Mexico).

Another feature of this register is the use of *uno* in the sense of *yo*.

Chapter 8

1. Sentence (b) gives the events in chronological, and hence logical, order (the resignation of the minister provokes the adverse effect on the economy and occasions media interest).

2. (a) See 4.5.2.1. The 'correct' relative is *cuyo*, representing the function of *de que* or *de quien*. However, the possessive notion is equally clearly represented here by the possessive adjective *su*, so the 'correct' version has little advantage over this colloquial equivalent from the point of view of the information being communicated.

(b) Prescriptively, an antecedent should not also be represented by a pronoun (here *lo*) in the relative clause. *Lo* is strictly speaking redundant.

(c) Only *que* is used for a direct object relative pronoun unless there is a risk of ambiguity, which here there is not.

(d) *Enterarse* has *de* + noun as one of its arguments, and so the 'correct' form of the relative pronoun is *del que*. The sentence is not incomprehensible as it stands (prescriptively it might be argued that the use of *que* implies that turns *accidente* into a subject or direct object of *enterarse*; but the syntactic result would not make sense; speakers would interpret it as if *del que* had been used).

(e) *Cuya historia* is prescriptively preferred, and is actually more economical.

(f) Prescriptively, *quien* cannot be used unless the antecedent is human, and *la que* is the 'correct' choice. Most Spanish speakers in fact follow the prescriptive rule, though the use of *quien* in this way is a relic of an older usage.

(g) This use of *cuyo* is associated with very formal register, and is proscribed in normal usage. Prescriptively *cuyo autor nació...* should be recast as *que nació....*

3. This is a very challenging text stylistically. The following features can be noted:

(a) It is rich in **intertextual reference** (see **7.2.1.1**) and allusion. In ll.1–3 there is reference to three *refranes* (popular sayings) which are each negated: *el que la hace la paga* (lit. 'he who makes it pays for it', i.e. 'as you make your bed so you must lie on it'), *el que a hierro muere a hierro mata* ('he who lives by the sword dies by the sword') and *el que da primero da dos veces* (lit. 'he who gives first gives twice', i.e. 'it is more blessed to give than to receive'). There is also Biblical reference: *ojo por ojo... diente por diente* ('an eye for an eye and a tooth for a tooth': Matthew 5: 38), *no siete sino setenta veces siete* ('not seven times but seventy times seven': Matthew 18: 22), and to the Book of Daniel (see below). Allusion is made to the legendary incident of the seduction of Cava (by Rodrigo, the last Visigothic king of Spain), which is supposed to have given rise to the invasion of the Peninsula and defeat of the Goths by the Moors in 711 with the help of Cava's father, Count Julián, who was bent on revenge; the River Tagus, on the banks of which the pair are supposed to have consorted, was represented in a poem by Fray Luis de León (c.1527–91) as having prophesied the demise of the monarch. Reference is then made to the moving finger which similarly wrote the doom of King Belshazzar in the cryptic Aramaic words *mene mene tekel upharsin*, interpreted by Daniel (Daniel 5: 26–28) as 'thou art weighed in the balance and found wanting; thy kingdom is divided and given to the Medes and Persians'. Lastly, there is a reference to Goethe's critical reworking of Euripides's play *Iphigenia in Tauris* the theme of which is how Iphigenia is to evade the order of King Thoas to sacrifice her brother Orestes.

(b) The intertextual references are reworked in various original ways. *Ojo por ojo* and *diente por diente* (ll.3–4) are changed to extended graphic images of a glass eye and a false tooth which draw on vocabulary from a medical register. In ll.10–11 *el que la hace* undergoes syntactic embedding (see **4.3.3**): *el que cree que la hizo* and *aquel de quien fue creído que la había hecho*. Following this, *el que la hace* is extended more thoroughly to *aquel que consiguió convencer...*

(c) There are several figures of speech:

   (i) **Asyndetic enumeration** in *pálida faz, amarilla mirada, sonrisa torva*; and the addition of these three noun phrases to the rest of the sentence is also asyndetic.

   (ii) **Anadiplosis** in the repetition of *no* (l.1).

   (iii) *La vida no es así, en la vida no ocurre así* (l.1) shows **anaphora** of *vida*.

   (iv) In *los envenenados dardos de su ira* (l.5) and *el negro manto del traidor* (ll.12–13) we see the conventional **epithets** *envenenados* and *negro*.

(d) The sentences are short and many do not contain verbs, consisting either of noun phrases (e.g. *La furia de los dioses vengadores*, ll.4–5) or a *refrán*.

(e) The connection between one sentence and the next is sometimes difficult to perceive, since there are no explicit logical connectors such as conjunctions, adverbial phrases or adverbial clauses.

Finally, you might like to think about how appropriate these stylistic features are to the artistic intention of the text, which represents the thoughts racing through the mind of a medical researcher who has, with basically good intentions, performed an illegal abortion and is having to leave Madrid.

Chapter 9

1. A number of views can be taken on what constitutes 'Spanish'. It is difficult to come up with any rigorous objective measure of 'distance' between varieties. A criterion which is sometimes entertained is that of mutual comprehensibility, and indeed the cultured variants of the various Spanish-speaking countries have maintained this to a considerable degree; however, it is doubtful whether it could be confidently claimed that there was mutual comprehensibility between some of the colloquial varieties of different areas, and certainly not between different *jergas* (see also **10.3.3**). The criterion of mutual comprehensibility would certainly exclude the creoles and contact vernaculars from the notion of 'Spanish'; arguably, there is more mutual comprehensibility between standard Spanish and standard Italian than between standard Spanish and Papiamentu, for example. The status of Judeo-Spanish in this regard is less clear, but it is probably more readily intelligible to a native speaker of Spanish than any foreign language, despite its individual development.

Another criterion is that of what speakers consider their language to be. We have already seen that names given to 'dialects' are unreliable guides to their nature (**6.2.2**) and the same might be said to be true of languages; moreover, different names are sometimes given to what is by most other criteria the 'same' language (e.g. Dutch / Flemish, Romanian / Moldavian). Spanish itself has two alternative names, *español* and *castellano*. On this criterion, Judeo-Spanish would be very firmly included within the notion of 'Spanish'.

2. It is doubtful whether it is really appropriate to call Chabacano 'español "aguado"', since (a) it has some grammatical features and many words which are quite different from Spanish and (b) it is not mutually intelligible with Spanish. It is doubtful, therefore, unless Chabacano is standardised rather artificially in the direction of Spanish, which would destroy its nature and effectively impose Spanish by the back door, that it could really come to qualify as a variety of Spanish. But Farolán is right in seeing no future for standard Spanish in the Philippines, and it may be that Chabacano speakers would preserve some sense of relationship to the Spanish-speaking world through the promotion of their language on an official basis.

3. All these words show evidence of integration into the structure of Spanish and considerable movement away from English, and so must be considered integrated borrowings rather than spontaneous borrowings or code-switches. There has been complete assimilation of these words into the sound pattern of Spanish through phonetic adaptation: English words ending in unusual or unacceptable final consonants in Spanish have an epenthetic [e] or [a] added (*cake* > *quequi*, *dump* > *dompe*, *truck* > *troca*, *knife* > *naifa*); English [ʃ] has been adapted to Spanish [tʃ] (*bunch* > *bonche*, *push* > *puchar*); the intervocalic [d] of American English *quarter* [ˈkwɑdəɹ], *sweater* [ˈswɛdəɹ] has been realised as [ɾ] (*cora*, *suera*), and the English vowels [ʌ] and [ʌː] have been adapted to [o] (*nurse* > *norsa*, *lunch* > *lonche*). English [h] is represented orthographically as *x* (phonetically realised as anything between [x] and [h]). Every noun has been assigned a gender, and it is worth noting that this gender is not invariably masculine (it is the feminines which add the epenthetic -*a*, in fact, which may be seen as a kind of hypercharacterisation of gender (**5.1**)). Sometimes the choice of feminine gender is determined by the reference to sex, as in *norsa*, and sometimes it is due to association with a corresponding Spanish word, as in *ganga*, which is presumably parallel to *pandilla* (or *palomilla*, see Chapter 7, Exercise 1), *naifa*, associated with *navaja*, or *baica*, associated with *bicicleta*. But in some other instances the basis for the assignation of gender is unclear: *la cora* but *el daime*, both *el troque* and *la troca*. But the apparent arbitrariness of gender in these cases reflects the properties of the majority of Spanish words. It is interesting how intransitive verbs have been treated as reflexive: *cherapearse*, *dropearse* and *liquearse*. We saw in **5.4.1** how there was a strong association between intransitivity and the reflexive; this tendency is in fact accentuated in Latin America, where verbs of motion and intransitives such as *desayunar* and *tardar* are often reflexive.

Generally speaking, few homonymic clashes (see **2.3.4** and above, Notes to Chapter 2, Exercise 2) have been produced. *Ganga* already exists in the meaning of 'bargain', and *gira* in the meaning of 'tour', but these are hardly likely to be confused with the new meanings. It will be more interesting to see whether these words displace existing words in Spanish (*norsa* for *enfermera*, *saine* for *letrero*, etc.) or whether new semantic distinctions result from their borrowing (*tíquete*, for example, is specifically a parking ticket, and *boleto* (Pen. *billete*) remains as the word for an entrance ticket).

Chapter 10

1. There are numerous candidates in the area of phonetic change, several of which were discussed in some detail in Chapter 6. *Seseo* is a majority pronunciation, though maintenance of the distinction between /θ/ and /s/ currently shows no sign of losing prestige in northern and central Spain, and hence in the Peninsular standard. The fall of intervocalic /d/ in the -*ado* ending is advanced enough for us to be fairly confident that it will soon be complete, though the fall of intervocalic /d/ in other environments is less general. The fall of final /d/ must be another strong candidate for future development. On the morphological level, the prevalence of the -*ra* form of the imperfect subjunctive over the -*se* form seems likely, as does the further extension of the use of the -*ra* form in hith-erto 'indicative' contexts. It is possible that there will be further movement towards the association of intransitive verbs with reflexive morphology. Another area of variation in both the Peninsula and Latin America lies in the phenomenon of *dequeísmo* (not other-wise discussed in this book): *de que* is increasingly used as a verbal complementiser in place of *que* (e.g. *pienso de que voy a ir*), and conversely *que* is sometimes used in place of *de que* as a noun complementiser (e.g. *la posibilidad que vaya* – see above, Notes to Chapter 7, Exercise 1). However, although there is a good deal of variation in this area, it is difficult to detect a consistent direction of movement. It also seems likely that ana-lytic verb forms (see **9.4.2.2.2**) will be increasingly used. It is not clear whether this will lead to a decline in the use of inflected verb forms, though it seems likely that the inflected future (*hablará*) will be more and more restricted: it already tends to be used in speech only in its modal senses: imperative (*¡Lo comerás!*), intention (*Sí, iré*) or suppos-ition (*Será medianoche*).

These suggestions have certainly not exhausted the list of possible future develop-ments.

2. The answer seems to be that true anglicisms are quite difficult to distinguish. *Rascacielos* is a clear example, because the first skyscrapers were built in North America and the image is a very striking one. But some verb + noun compounds may be coincidentally created in the two languages to label a new concept, e.g. *abrelatas* 'tin opener', *cuentar-revoluciones* 'rev counter, tachometer', *pasapurés* 'potato masher'; this is especially obvi-ous when the image is not quite the same, e.g. *matasellos* 'date stamp', *tirabuzón* 'corkscrew'. Sometimes the basis of the creation is quite different: *tragaluz* 'skylight, *saltamontes* 'grasshopper', *secarropa* 'clothes horse'. It is interesting that some verbs seem to be particularly productive (see **3.2**) in yielding such compounds: *mata-*, *saca-* and *traga-* are three examples. The overall conclusion must be therefore that while borrowing from English may have encouraged word creation in this area, the Spanish model was already firmly established, and that is why anglicisms are difficult to discern.

Glossary of basic grammatical terms

It is assumed that readers are familiar with the following traditional grammatical terms, and so they have not been defined in the text.

adjective   The part of speech which qualifies (describes, provides additional information about) a noun. In Spanish, adjectives can also function as nouns, e.g. *triste* 'sad', *un triste* 'a sad person'.

adverb   The part of speech which qualifies a verb: some important semantic classes of adverbs are manner, time, place. Adjectives are often said to be qualified by adverbs too: e.g. *muy bien*.

article   This is a somewhat arbitrary category with quite a wide range of functions. Spanish and English both have two kinds of article: the definite article which has a broadly identifying function (Sp. *el*, Eng. *the*), and the indefinite article which has the general meaning of 'one of a category' (Sp. *un*, Eng. *a*).

auxiliary   A verb used with another, non-finite, form of a verb. The underlined forms are auxiliaries: Sp. *quiero salir*, *estoy hablando*, *hemos visto*; Eng. *I would like*, *she has gone*, *we were seen*.

conjunction   A conjunction connects two grammatical elements. Conjunctions can be either coordinating (Sp. *y*, *o*; Eng. *and*, *but*) or subordinating, in which they typically introduce adverbial clauses (e.g. Sp. *porque*, *antes de que*; Eng. *because*, *when*).

demonstrative   An adjective or pronoun which expresses proximity to or remoteness from the speaker (e.g. Sp. *este*, *ese*, *aquel*).

determiner   A grammatical element qualifying a noun which expresses a very general notion of number, quantity, etc. Articles, numerals, demonstratives, quantifiers and possessives belong to this category.

finite   A finite verb is one which is inflected for person, tense and mood. In the verb-form *habló* we can see from the ending *-ó* that this is third person, preterite and indicative.

gerund   In Spanish, the non-finite form of the verb ending in *-ndo* is usually called the gerund (*gerundio*). The principal function of the gerund in Spanish is adverbial (see **4.5.2.3**).

infinitive	A non-finite form of the verb, which in Spanish is characterised by the ending *-ar*, *-er* or *-ir*. The infinitive often functions as a verbal noun, and as such can be the complement (see **4.3.3**) of another verb, e.g. *Me gusta <u>cantar</u>*.
interjection	An exclamation, e.g. *¡ay!*
mood	A verbal category broadly relating to modality. Modality is a category of meaning associated with the truth-value of a proposition, e.g. statement, possibility, command.
non-finite	A non-finite verb is not inflected for person, tense or mood. The non-finite forms of Spanish are the infinitive, the gerund and the past participle.
noun	Nouns typically denote things, people, animals or abstract concepts (e.g. *tío, Sarita, armario, belleza*)
participle	A non-finite form of the verb. Spanish has a past participle (e.g. *tenido*).
possessive	An adjective or pronoun which expresses possession (e.g. *mi, suyo*).
preposition	The part of speech that 'governs' nouns, pronouns and other elements used in a noun-like way, expressing notions such as direction, instrument, agent, etc.
pronoun	A form which is used in substitution for a noun, e.g. *él* for *Juan*. However, the term is also usually applied to first- and second-person pronouns (*yo, tú, nosotros, vosotros*) which do not really substitute full nouns; it is usual also in Spanish to call the 'neuter' forms *ello, lo,* etc. pronouns, even though they never substitute a noun but a full clause.
tense	A verbal category broadly relating to time-reference.
verb	A verb typically denotes an action, event or state.
voice	A verbal category which has to do with the relation of the subject and object to the verb. Active and passive are the two types of voice which are traditionally distinguished (see **4.3.4.1**); another type discussed in this book is middle (see **4.3.4.2**).

Bibliographical references

(The bibliography is restricted, as far as possible, to works written in Spanish or English.)

Agencia Efe, 1992. *Vademécum de español urgente* (Madrid: Fundación Efe).

Alarcos Llorach, Emilio, 1994. *Gramática de la lengua española* (Madrid: Real Academia Española/Espasa-Calpe).

Alonso, Amado, 1951 [1935]. 'Noción, emoción, acción y fantasía en los diminutivos', in *Estudios lingüísticos: temas españoles* (Madrid: Gredos), pp.195–229.

Alonso, Dámaso, 1964. 'Para evitar la diversificación de nuestra lengua, in *Presente y futuro*, pp.259–68.

Alonso, Martín, 1968. *Gramática del español contemporáneo* (Madrid: Ediciones Guadarrama).

ALEA – Atlas lingüístico y etnográfico de Andalucía, 1961–73, 6 vols (Granada: Universidad de Granada/CSIC).

Alvar, Manuel, 1960. *Textos hispánicos dialectales. Antología histórica.* 2 vols (Madrid: CSIC).

Alvar, Manuel, 1975–8. *Atlas lingüístico y etnográfico de las Islas Canarias* (3 vols) (Las Palmas de Gran Canaria: Excmo. Cabildo Insular de Gran Canaria).

Alvar, Manuel (ed), 1996. *Manual de dialectología hispánica: el español de España* (Barcelona: Ariel).

Alvar, Manuel, C. Alvar & J.A. Mayoral, 1995. *Atlas lingüístico y etnográfico de Cantabria*, 2 vols (Madrid: Arco).

Alvar, Manuel, A. Llorente, T. Buesa & Elena Alvar, 1979–83. *Atlas lingüístico y etnográfico de Aragón, Navarra y Rioja*, 12 vols (Zaragoza: Departamento de Geografía Lingüística, Institución Fernando el Católico de la Excma. Diputación Provincial de Zaragoza/ CSIC).

Alvar, Manuel, Antonio Llorente & Gregorio Salvador, 1961–73. *Atlas lingüístico y etnográfico de Andalucía*, 6 vols (Granada: Universidad de Granada/CSIC).

Alvar, Manuel, Antonio Llorente & Gregorio Salvador, 1995. *Textos andaluces en transcripción fonética* (Madrid: Gredos).

Alvar, Manuel & Antonio Quilis (eds), forthcoming. *Atlas lingüístico de Hispanoamérica*.

Alvar Ezquerra, Manuel, María Auxiliadora Castillo Carballo, Juan Manuel García Platero, Miguel Ángel Jiménez Cuenca & Antonia María Medina Guerra, 1999. *Manual de redacción y estilo* (Madrid: Istmo).

Álvarez Curiel, Francisco, 1991. *Vocabulario popular andaluz* (Málaga: Arguval).

Anon., 2001. *Qrs ablr? pqño lbro d msj txt* (Barcelona: Ediciones B).

Araya, Guillermo, 1973. *Atlas lingüístico-etnográfico del sur de Chile* (Valdivia: Instituto de Filología de la Universidad Austral de Chile).

Atlas lingüístico de la Península Ibérica, 1962. Vol. I, *Fonética, 1* (Madrid: CSIC).

Ávila, Raúl, 1997. 'Variación léxica: connotación, denotación, autorregulación', *Anuario de Letras*, 25, pp.77–102.

Badia Margarit, Antoni M., 1975 [1964]. *Llengua i cultura als països catalans*, 4th ed. (Barcelona: Edicions 62).

Batchelor, R.E. & Pountain, C.J., 1992. *Using Spanish: a Guide to Contemporary Usage* (Cambridge: University Press).

Bauer, Laurie & Peter Trudgill (eds), 1998. *Language Myths* (Harmondsworth: Penguin).

Bello, Andrés, 1981 [1847]. *Gramática de la lengua castellana destinada al uso de los americanos*, edición crítica de Ramón Trujillo (Santa Cruz de Tenerife: Instituto Universitario de Lingüística Andrés Bello/Cabildo Insular de Tenerife).

Bennett, Karen, 1982. 'Evaluative reactions towards regional varieties of Spanish', *Cambridge Papers in Phonetics and Experimental Linguistics*, 1, pp.1–15.

Bickerton, D. & A. Escalante, 1970. 'Palenquero: a Spanish-based creole of northern Colombia', *Lingua*, 24, pp.254–67.

Blake, Barry J., 1994. *Case* (Cambridge: University Press).

Bolinger, Dwight, 1974. 'One subjunctive or two?', *Hispania*, 57, pp.462–71.

Bosque, Ignacio & Violeta Demonte (eds), 1999. *Gramática descriptiva de la lengua española*, 3 vols (Madrid: Espasa-Calpe).

Bowen, J. Donald, 1956. *A comparison of the intonation patterns of English and Spanish*, *Hispania*, 39, pp.30–5.

Boyd-Bowman, Peter, 1972. 'La emigración española a América: 1540–1579', in *Studia hispanica in honorem R. Lapesa* (Madrid: Gredos), vol.2, pp.123–47.

Brown R. & A. Gilman, 1972 [1960]. 'The Pronouns of Power and Solidarity', in Pier Paolo Giglioli (ed), *Language and Social Context* (Harmondsworth: Penguin), pp.252–82.

Buesa Oliver, Tomás & Luis Flórez, 1956 [1954]. *El atlas lingüístico-etnográfico de Colombia (ALEC)* (Bogotá: Instituto Caro y Cuervo).

Butt, John W. & Carmen Benjamin, 2000. *A New Reference Grammar of Modern Spanish*, 3rd. ed. (London: Arnold).

Canellada, María Josefa & John Kuhlmann Madsden, 1987. *Pronunciación del español: lengua hablada y literaria* (Madrid: Castalia).

Canfield, D. Lincoln, 1981. *Spanish Pronunciation in the Americas* (Chicago/London: University of Chicago Press).

Carballo Calero, Ricardo, 1976 [1966]. *Gramática elemental del gallego común*, 6th ed. (Vigo: Galaxia).

Carricaburo, Norma, 1997. *Las fórmulas de tratamiento en el español actual* (Madrid: Arco).

Carrillo Herrera, Gastón, 1964. 'Tendencias a la unificación idiomática hispano-americana e hispánica. Factores externos', in *Presente y futuro ...*, pp.17–33.

Chandler-Burns, R. M. *et al.*, 1992. *ESPAÑOL-92: el primer análisis computacional del español contemporáneo* (Nuevo León: Universidad Autónoma de Nuevo León).

Chatman, Seymour (ed), 1971. *Literary Style: a Symposium* (London/New York: Oxford University Press).

Chomsky, Noam, 1957. *Syntactic Structures* (The Hague: Mouton).

Clave = 1999. *Clave. Diccionario de uso del español actual.* (Madrid: Ediciones SM).

Coles, Felice, 1999. *Isleño Spanish* (Munich: Lincom).

Coltharp, Lurline H., 1965. *The Tongue of the Tirilones* (Alabama: University of Alabama Press).

Contreras, Heles, 1976. *A Theory of Word Order with Special Reference to Spanish* (Amsterdam: North-Holland).

Corominas, Joan & José A. Pascual, 1980–91. *Diccionario crítico etimológico castellano e hispánico*, 6 vols (Madrid: Gredos).

Crews, Cynthia, 1935. *Recherches sur le judéo-espagnol dans les pays balkaniques* (Paris: Droz).

Dalbor, John B., 1997. *Spanish pronunciation: theory and practice*, 3rd ed. (Fort Worth: Harcourt Brace).

De Bruyne, Jacques, 1995. *A Comprehensive Spanish Grammar, adapted with additional material by Christopher J. Pountain* (Oxford: Blackwell).

DRAE = Real Academia Española, 2001. *Diccionario de la lengua española*, 22nd ed. (Madrid: Espasa).

El País, 1990. *Libro de estilo*, 7th. ed. (Madrid: Ediciones El País SA).

Elías-Olivares, Lucía, 1979. 'Language use in a Chicano community: a sociolinguistic approach', in J.B. Pride (ed), *Sociolinguistic aspects of language learning and teaching* (Oxford: OUP), pp.120–34.

Elizaincín, Adolfo, 1992. *Dialectos en contacto: español y portugués en España y América* (Montevideo: Arca).

England, John & José Luis Caramés Lage, 1978. 'El uso y abuso de anglicismos en la prensa española de hoy', *Arbor*, 390, pp.77–89.

Esbozo = Real Academia Española, 1973. *Esbozo de una nueva gramática de la lengua española* (Madrid: Espasa-Calpe).

Esgueva, M. & M. Cantarero, 1981. *El habla de la ciudad de Madrid* (Madrid: CSIC).

Espinosa, Aurelio, 1930. 'The use of the conditional for the subjunctive in Castilian popular speech', *Modern Philology*, 27, pp.445–9.

Ethnologue = *Ethnologue: Languages of the World*, 2002. 14th ed. (Summer Institute of Linguistics).

Ferguson, Charles A., 1959. 'Diglossia', *Word*, 15, pp.325–40.

Fernández-Ordóñez, Inés, 1994. 'Isoglosas internas del castellano. El sistema referencial del pronombre átono de tercera persona', *Revista de Filología Española*, 74, pp.71–125.

Fishman, Joshua, Eleanor Herasimchuk & Roxana Ma, 1971. *Bilingualism in the Barrio* (Bloomington: Indiana UP).

Flórez, Luis, 1981–3. *Atlas lingüístico-etnográfico de Colombia* (Bogotá: Instituto Caro y Cuervo).

Fontanella de Weinberg, Beatriz, 1979. *Dinámica social de un cambio lingüístico* (Mexico City: Universidad Nacional Autónoma de México).

Fontanella de Weinberg, María Beatriz, 1980. 'Three intonational systems of Argentinian Spanish', in Linda Waugh & C.H. van Schoonefeld (eds), *The melody of language* (Baltimore: University Park Press), pp.115–26.

Friedemann, Nina S. & Carlos Patiño Rosselli, 1983. *Lengua y sociedad en el Palenque de San Basilio* (Bogotá: Instituto Caro y Cuervo).

García Mouton, Pilar & Francisco Moreno Fernández, forthcoming. *Atlas lingüístico y etnográfico de Castilla-La Mancha.*

Gili Gaya, Samuel, 1955. *Curso superior de sintaxis española*, 5th ed. (Barcelona: SPES).

Gooch, Anthony, 1970. *Diminutive, Augmentative and Pejorative Suffixes in Modern Spanish (A Guide to their Use and Meaning).* (Oxford: Pergamon).

Graddol, D., 1997. *The Future of English?* (London: British Council).

Graddol, D., 1998. 'Will English be enough?', in Moys (ed.), pp.24–33.

GRAE = Real Academia Española, 1931. *Gramática de la lengua española* (Madrid: Espasa-Calpe).

Granda, Germán de, 1979. 'Calcos sintácticos del Guaraní en el español de Paraguay', *Nueva Revista de Filología Hispánica*, 28, pp.267–86.

Green, John N., 1975. 'On the frequency of passive constructions in Modern Spanish', *Bulletin of Hispanic Studies*, 52, pp.345–62.

Green, John N., 1977. 'How free is word order in Spanish?', in Martin Harris (ed.), *Romance Syntax: Synchronic and Diachronic Perspectives* (Salford: University of Salford). pp.7–32.

Green, John N., 1988. 'Spanish', in Martin Harris & Nigel Vincent (eds), *The Romance Languages* (London: Croom Helm), pp.79–130.

Green, John N., 1994. 'Language status and political aspirations: the case of northern Spain', in Parry *et al.* (eds), pp.155–72.

Grimes, B.F. (ed), 1999. *Ethnologue: Languages of the World* (Dallas: Summer Institute of Linguistics).

Gumperz, John J. & Eduardo Hernández Chávez, 1975. 'Cognitive aspects of bilingual communication', in Eduardo Hernández-Chávez, Andrew Cohen & Anthony Beltramo (eds), *El lenguaje de los chicanos* (Arlington: Center for Applied Linguistics).

Halliday, M.A.K., 1971. 'Linguistic Function and Literary Style: an Inquiry into the Language of William Golding's *The Inheritors*', in Chatman (ed), pp.330–68.

Halliday, M.A.K., 1978. *Language as Social Semiotic. The social interpretation of language and meaning.* (London: Arnold).

Harris, Martin, 1978. *The Evolution of French Syntax. A Comparative Approach* (London: Longman).

Harris, Tracy K., 1994. *Death of a Language. The History of Judeo-Spanish.* (Newark: University of Delaware).

Henríquez Ureña, Pedro, 1921. 'Observaciones sobre el español de América', *Revista de Filología Española*, 8, pp.357–90.

Hermerén, Ingrid, 1992. *El uso de la forma en* ra *con valor no-subjuntivo en el español moderno* (Lund: University Press).

Hernández Alonso, César, 1996. 'Castilla la Vieja', in Alvar (ed), pp. 197–212.

Hochberg, Judith O., 1986. 'Functional compensation for /s/ deletion in Puerto Rican Spanish', *Language*, 62, pp.609–21.

Hopper, Paul, & Thompson, Sandra A., 1980. 'Transitivity in grammar and discourse', *Language*, 56, pp.251–99.

Hudson, R.A., 1980. *Sociolinguistics* (Cambridge: UP).

Hymes, Dell, 1974. *Foundations in Sociolinguistics. An Ethnographic Approach.* (Philadelphia: University of Pennsylvania Press).

Jackson, Eugene, & Antonio Rubio, 1969 [1955]. *Spanish Made Simple* (London: W.H. Allen).

Jauralde Pou, Pablo, 1973. *Introducción al conocimiento de la lengua española* (León: Everest).

Juilland, Alphonse & Eugenio Chang-Rodríguez, 1964. *Frequency Dictionary of Spanish Words* (The Hague: Mouton).

Jungemann, Fredrick H., 1955. *La teoría del sustrato y los dialectos hispano-romances y gascones* (Madrid: Gredos).

Kany, Charles E., 1951. *American-Spanish Syntax*, 2nd ed. (Chicago: University of Chicago Press).

Kany, Charles E., 1960. *Latin-American Semantics* (Berkeley: University of California Press).

Keller, Gary D., 1975. 'Spanish *tú* and *usted*: patterns of interchange', in William G. Milan, John J. Staczek & Juan C. Zamora (eds), *1974 Colloquium on Spanish and Portuguese Linguistics* (Washington: Georgetown University Press), pp.84–96.

Klein, Flora, 1980. Pragmatic and sociolinguistic bias in semantic change', in Elizabeth Closs Traugott, Rebecca Labrum & Susan Shepherd (eds), *Papers from the 4th International Conference on Historical Linguistics*, pp.61–74.

Kliffer, Michael D., 1984. 'Personal "a", kinesis and individuation', in *Papers from the XIIth Linguistic Symposium on Romance Languages*, ed. Philip Baldi (Amsterdam:Benjamins), pp.195–216.

Kloss, Heinz, 1967. '*Abstand*-Languages and *Ausbau*-Languages', *Anthropological Linguistics*, 9, pp.29–41.

Kouwenberg, Silvia & Eric Murray, 1994. *Papiamentu* (Munich: Lincom Europ).

Lapesa, Rafael, 1980. *Historia de la lengua española*, 9th ed. (Madrid: Gredos).

Lass, Roger, 1980. *On explaining linguistic change* (Cambridge: University Press).

Lavandera, Beatriz, 1984. *Variación y significado* (Buenos Aires: Hachette).

Lázaro Carreter, Fernando, 1998. *El dardo en la palabra* (Barcelona: Galaxia Gutenberg).

Lehrer, Adrienne, 1974. *Semantic Universals and Lexical Structure* (Amsterdam: North-Holland).

Lipski, John M., 1985. *The Spanish of Equatorial Guinea: the dialect of Malabo and its implications for Spanish dialectology* (Tübingen: Niemeyer).

Lipski, John M., 1990. *The Language of the Isleños* (Baton Rouge & London: Louisiana State University Press).

Lipski, John M., 1991. 'In search of the Spanish personal infinitive', in Dieter Wanner & Douglas Kibbee (eds), *New Analyses in Romance Linguistics: Papers from the XVIII Linguistic Symposium on Romance Languages* (Amsterdam: Benjamins), pp.201–20.

Lipski, John M., 1994. *Latin American Spanish* (London: Longman).

Lipski, John M., 1998, 'Perspectivas sobre el español bozal', in Perl & Schwegler (eds), pp.293–327.

Lloyd, Paul M., 1987. *From Latin to Spanish* (Philadelphia: American Philosophical Society).

Lope Blanch, Juan M., 1965. 'Influencias de las lenguas indígenas en el léxico del español hablado en México', *Anuario de letras*, 5, 33–46.

Lope Blanch, Juan M., 1987. *Estudios sobre el español de Yucatán* (Mexico City: UNAM).

Lope Blanch, Juan M. (ed), 1990. *Atlas lingüístico de México* (Mexico City: Colegio de México).

Lorenzo, Emilio, 1980. *El español de hoy, lengua en ebullición*, 3rd. ed. (Madrid: Gredos).

Lorenzo, Emilio, 1996. *Anglicismos hispánicos* (Madrid: Gredos).

Lozano, Anthony G., 1975. 'In defence of two subjunctives', *Hispania*, 58, 277–83.

Luján, Marta, 1980. *Sintaxis y semántica del adjetivo* (Madrid: Cátedra).

Luján, Marta, 1981. 'The Spanish copulas as aspectual indicators', *Lingua*, 554, 165–209.

Luria, Max A., 1930. *A study of the Monastir dialect of Judeo-Spanish based on oral material collected in Monastir, Yugo-Slavia* (New York: Instituto de las Españas en los Estados Unidos).

Macpherson, I.R., 1975. *Spanish Phonology, Descriptive and Historical* (Manchester: University Press).

Mar-Molinero, Clare, 1997. *The Spanish-Speaking World. A Practical Introduction to Sociolinguistic Issues.* (London: Routledge).

Martín, Jacinto, Reyes Ruiz, Juan Santaella & José Escáñez, 1996. *Los lenguajes especiales* (Granada: Comares).

Martín Zorraquino, María Antonia, 1979. *Las construcciones pronominales en español. Paradigma y desviaciones.* (Madrid: Gredos).

Martos, Marco & Elsa Villanueva (1989). *Las palabras de* Trilce (Lima: Seglusa).

Matluck, J.M., 1965. 'Entonación hispánica', *Anuario de Letras*, 5, pp.5–32.

Matus Lazo, Róger, 1997. *El lenguaje del pandillero en Nicaragua (estudio léxico-semántico)* (Managua: Editorial CIRA).

Maurer, Philippe, 1998. *El papiamentu de Curazao*, in Matthias Perl & Armin Schwegler (eds), *América negra: panorámica actual de los estudios lingüísticos sobre variedades hispanas, portuguesas y criollas* (Frankfurt: Vervuert), pp.139–217.

McKaughan, Howard P., 1954. 'Notes on Chabacano grammar', *Journal of East Asiatic Studies*, 3, 2, pp.205–43.

MEU = Agencia Efe, *Manual de español urgente*, 4th ed. (Madrid: Cátedra).

Milroy, James & Lesley Milroy, 1991. *Authority in language: investigating language standardisation and prescription* (London, Routledge).

Milroy, Lesley, 1980. *Language and Social Networks* (Oxford: Blackwell).

Molina Redondo, J. A. de, 1987. *Usos de "ser" y "estar"* (Madrid: SGEL).

Moliner, María, 1966. *Diccionario del uso del español*, 1st ed. (Madrid: Gredos).

Moliner, María, 1998. *Diccionario del uso del español*, 2nd ed. (Madrid: Gredos).

Mondéjar, José, 1970. *El verbo andaluz: formas y estructuras* (Madrid: CSIC).

Moreira Rodríguez, Antonia & John Butt, 1996. *'Se de matización' and the Semantics of Spanish Pronominal Verbs* (London: King's College).

Moreno Fernández, Francisco, 1996. 'Castilla la Nueva', in Alvar (ed), pp.213–32.

Moys, A. (ed), 1998. *Where are we going with languages?* (London: Nuffield Foundation).

Navarro Tomás, Tomás, 1948. *El español de Puerto Rico, contribución a la geografía lingüística hispano-americana* (Río Pedras:Universidad de Puerto Rico).

Navarro Tomás, T., 1970. *Manual de pronunciación española*, 15th ed. (Madrid: CSIC).

Navarro Tomás, T., 1974. *Manual de entonación española* (Madrid: Labor).

Navas Ruiz, Ricardo & Victoria Jaén, 1989. *Ser y estar: la voz pasiva*, 2nd ed. (Salamanca: Publicaciones del Colegio de España).

Nehama, Joseph, 1977. *Dictionnaire du judéo-espagnol* (Madrid: CSIC).

Oftedal, Magne, 1985. *Lenition in Celtic and in Insular Spanish* (Oslo/Bergen/Stavanger/Tromsø: Universitatsforlaget).

Oroz, Rodolfo, 1966. *La lengua castellana en Chile* (Santiago de Chile: Facultad de Filosofía y Educación, Universidad de Chile).

Ortiz López, Luis A, 1998. *Huellas etno-sociolingüísticas bozales y afrocubanas* (Frankfurt: Vervuert).

Ortografía = Real Academia Española, 1999. *Ortografía de la lengua española* (Madrid: Real Academia Española/Espasa).

OSD = *The Oxford Spanish Dictionary*, 1998. 2nd ed. (Oxford: University Press).

Parry, M.M., W.V. Davies & R.A.M. Temple (eds.), 1994. *The Changing Voices of Europe* (Cardiff: University of Wales Press).

Penny, Ralph, 1986. 'Sandhi Phenomena in Castilian and Related Dialects', in Henning Andersen (ed), *Sandhi Phenomena in the Languages of Europe* (Berlin: Mouton de Gruyter), pp.489–503.

Penny, Ralph, 1992. 'Dialect Contact and Social Networks in Judeo-Spanish', *Romance Philology*, 46, pp.125–40.

Penny, Ralph, 2000. *Variation and Change in Spanish* (Cambridge: University Press).

Perl, Matthias, 1999. 'Problemas actuales de la estandarización del papiamentu', in Zimmermann (ed), pp.251–62.

Perl, Matthias & Armin Schwegler (eds), 1998. *América negra: panorámica actual de los estudios lingüísticos sobre variedades hispanas, portuguesas y criollas* (Frankfurt am Main: Vervuert).

Pfaff, Carol W., 1979. 'Constraints on language mixing: intrasentential code-switching and borrowing in Spanish/English', *Language* 55, pp.291–318.

Piñán, Berta, 1991. *Notes de sociolingüística asturiana* (Gijón: Pexe).

Poplack, Shana, 1980. 'Sometimes I'll start a sentence in English Y TERMINO EN ESPAÑOL: toward a typology of code-switching', *Linguistics* 18, pp.581–618.

Porroche Ballesteros, M., 1988, *Ser, estar y verbos de cambio* (Madrid: Arco).

Pountain, Christopher J., 1992. 'Aspect and Voice: Questions about Passivization in Spanish', *Journal of Hispanic Research*, 1, pp.167–81.

Pountain, Christopher J., 1993. '*De la construçion de los verbos después de sí*: la transitividad en la tradición gramatical española', in Ralph Penny (ed.) *Actas del Primer Congreso Anglo-Hispano*, Castalia, Madrid, pp.89–98.

Pountain, Christopher J., 1994. 'The Castilian reflexes of *abhorrere/abhorrescere*: a case-study in valency', in Coman Lupu & Glanville Price (eds), *Hommages offerts à Maria Manoliu-Manea* (Bucharest: Pluralia/Logos), pp.122–48.

Pountain, Christopher J., 1995. 'El difícil problema de la posición del adjetivo atributivo en español', *Donaire*, 4, pp.42–51.

Pountain, Christopher J., 1998. 'Gramática mítica del gerundio castellano', in Aengus M. Ward (ed), *Actas del XII Congreso de la Asociación Internacional de Hispanistas, Birmingham 1995*. I. *Medieval y Lingüística*, (Birmingham: University Press), pp.284–92.

Pountain, Christopher J., 1999. 'English and Spanish in the 21st Century', *Donaire*, 12, pp.33–42.

Pountain, Christopher J., 2000. 'Capitalization', in John Charles Smith & Delia Bentley (eds), Historical Linguistics 1995, Volume 1: General Issues and non-Germanic Languages (Amsterdam: Benjamins), pp.295–309.

Pountain, Christopher J., 2001. *A History of the Spanish Language through Texts* (London: Routledge).

Pratt, Chris, 1980. *El anglicismo en el español peninsular contemporáneo* (Madrid: Gredos).

Presente y futuro... – *Presente y futuro de la lengua española. Actas de la Asamblea de Filología del I Congreso de Instituciones Hispánicas*, 1964 (Madrid: OFINES).

Quilis, Antonio & Joseph A. Fernández, 1969. *Curso de fonética y fonología españolas para estudiantes angloamericanos*, 4th ed. (Madrid: CSIC).

Ranson, Diana L., 1991. 'Person marking in the wake of /s/ deletion in Andalusian Spanish', *Language Variation and Change*, 3, pp.133–52.

Revista de filología española (RFE), 1915, 2, pp.374–6.

Reyes, Graciela, 1999. *Cómo escribir bien en español. Manual de redacción.* 2nd ed. (Madrid: Arco).

Robins, R.H., 1964. *General Linguistics: an Introductory Survey* (London: Longmans).

Rona, José Pedro, 1963. 'El problema de la división del español americano en zonas dialectales', in *Presente y futuro*, pp.215–37.

Saavedra, Benjamin L., 1999. 'The Chabacano of Zamboanga (El Chabacano de Zamboanga)', paper read at the Symposium of the Chabacano of Cavite and Zamboanga, College of Arts and Letters, University of the Philippines, 29 September 1999.

Salvador, Gregorio, 1952. 'Fonética masculina y fonética femenina en el habla de Vertientes y Tarifa (Cádiz)', *Orbis*, 1, pp.19–24.

Salvador, Gregorio, 1964. 'La fonética andaluza y su propagación social y geográfica', in *Presente y futuro*, 2, pp.183–8.

Sankoff, D. & S. Poplack, 1981. 'A formal grammar of code-switching', *Papers in Linguistics*, 14, pp.3–46.

Sapir, Edward, 1921. *Language: an Introduction to the Study of Speech* (London: Hart-Davis).

Schwegler, Armin, 1998. 'El palenquero', in Perl & Schwegler (eds), pp.218–91.

Schwenter, Scott A., 1993. 'Diferencia dialectal por medio de pronombres: una comparación del uso de *tú* y *usted* en España y México', *Nueva Revista de Filología Hispánica*, 41, pp.127–49.

Seco, Manuel, 1998. *Diccionario de dudas y dificultades de la lengua española*, 10th ed. (Madrid: Espasa).

Sephiha, Haïm Vidal, 1986. *Le judéo-espagnol* (Paris: Editions Entente).

Silva-Corvalán, Carmen, 1984. 'Semantic and pragmatic factors in syntactic change', in Jacek Fisiak (ed.), *Historical Syntax* (Berlin/New York: Mouton), pp.547–72.

Silva-Corvalán, Carmen, 1987. 'Variación sociofonológica y cambio lingüístico', in Humberto López Morales & M. Vaquero (eds), *Actas del I congreso internacional sobre el español de América* (Madrid, Arco), pp.777–91.

Silva-Corvalán, Carmen, 1989. *Sociolingüística: teoría y análisis* (Alhambra, Madrid).

Smith, Colin, 1975. 'Anglicism or not?', *Vida Hispánica*, 23, pp.9–13.

Sperberg-McQueen, C. M. & Lou Burnard (eds), 1994. *Guidelines for Electronic Text Encoding and Interchange*, http://www.hcu.ox.ac.uk/TEI/Guidelines/index.htm.

Stahl, Fred A. & Gary E. A. Scavnicky, 1973. *A Reverse Dictionary of the Spanish Language* (Urbana: University of Illinois Press).

Stewart, Miranda, 1999. *The Spanish Language Today* (London: Routledge).

Tamarón, Marqués de (1995) 'El papel internacional del español', in Tamarón (ed.), pp.13–75.

Tamarón, Marqués de (ed.) (1995) *El peso de la lengua española en el mundo*. Valladolid: Universidad de Valladolid/Fundación Duques de Soria/INCIPE.

Thun, Harald & Adolfo Elizaincín, forthcoming. *Atlas diatópico y diastrático del Uruguay*.

Timm, Leonora, 1975. 'Spanish-English code-switching: el porque and how not to', *Romance Philology*, 28, pp.473–82.

Verhaar, John W.M., 1967–73. *The Verb 'be' and its Synonyms: Philosophical and Grammatical Studies*, 6 vols (Dordrecht: Reidel).

Vidal de Battini, Elena, 1963. 'El español de América', in *Presente y futuro*, 1, pp.183–92.

VOX = 1987. *Vox. Diccionario general ilustrado de la lengua española* (Barcelona: Bibliograf).

Wagner, Max Leopold, 1914. *Beiträge zir Kenntnis des Judeospanischen von Konstantinopel* (Vienna: Hölder).

Walsh, Donald D., 1944. 'Spanish diminutives', *Hispania*, 27, pp.11–20.

Weinreich, U., W. Labov & M. Herzog, 1968. 'Empirical foundations for a theory of language change', in W.P. Lehmann & Y. Malkiel (eds), *Directions for Historical Linguistics* (Austin: U of Texas Press), pp.95–189.

Weinreich, Uriel, 1954. 'Is a structural dialectology possible?', *Word*, 10, pp.388–400.

Wexler, Paul, 1977. 'Ascertaining the position of judezmo within Ibero-Romance', *Vox Romanica*, 36, pp.162–95.

Whinnom, Keith, 1956. *Spanish Contact Vernaculars in the Philippine Islands* (London: Hong Kong U.P. and Oxford U.P.).

Wierzbicka, Anna, 1996. *Semantic Primes and Universals* (Oxford: University Press).

Williams, Lynn, 1987. *Aspectos sociolingüísticos del habla de la ciudad de Valladolid* (Valladolid: Universidad de Valladolid).

Ybáñez Bueno, E., 1995. 'El idioma español en organizaciones internacionales', in Tamarón (ed.), pp.77–134.

Zamora Munne, J.C. and J. Guitart, 1982. *Dialectología hispanoamericana* (Salamanca: Almar).

Zamora Vicente, Alonso, 1960. *Dialectología española* (Madrid: Gredos).

Zentella, Ana Celia, 1982. 'Spanish and English in contact in the United States: the Puerto Rican experience', *Word*, 33, pp.41–57.

Zentella, Ana Celia, 1997. *Growing up bilingual: Puerto Rican Children in New York* (Oxford: Blackwell).

Zimmermann, Klaus (ed), 1999. *Lenguas criollas de base lexical española y portuguesa* (Frankfurt am Main/Madrid: Vervuert/Iberoamericana).

Index

(Words in **bold** are defined in the Glossary of basic grammatical terms on p.290. References in **bold** indicate that a definition or substantial coverage of a topic is given at this location.)